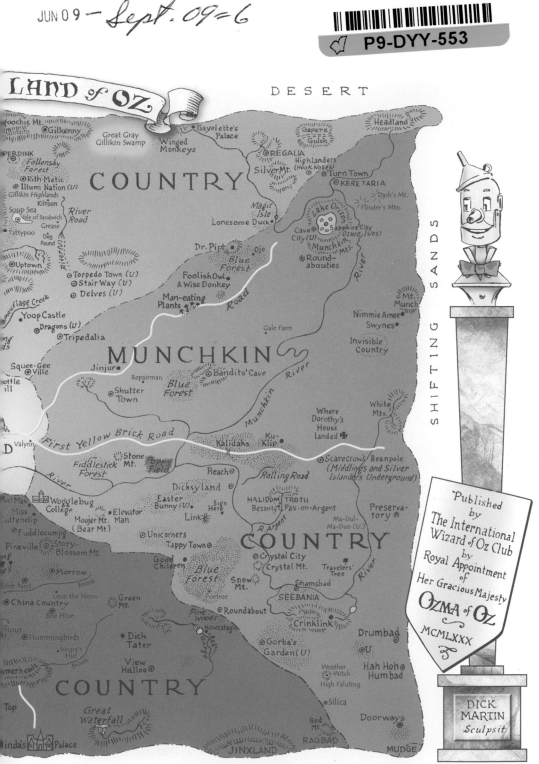

LAND of OZ

DESERT

COUNTRY

Goochie Mt.
Gilkenny
Great Gray Gillikin Swamp
Winged Monkeys
Gayelette's Palace
Gapers Gulch
Headland
PERDINK
Follensby Forest
REGALIA
Highlanders (Hook Noses)
Silver Mt.
Turn Town
Rith Metic
Illumi Nation (U)
KERETARIA
Gillikin Highlands
Kiltoon
Dash's Mt.
Flinder's Mtn.
Soup Sea
Vale of Sandwich
Grease
River Road
Magic Isle
Lake Orizon
Cave City (U)
Sapphire City
Azure Isles
Tattypoo
Dog Pound
Lonesome Duck
Munchkin Mts.
Round-aboutics
Uptown
Dr. Pipt
Ojo
Blue Forest
Torpedo Town (U)
Stair Way (U)
Delves (U)
Foolish Owl & Wise Donkey
Man-eating Plants
Road
Gale Farm
Mt. Munch
Camouflage Creek
Yoop Castle
Dragons (U)
Tripedalia
Nimmie Amee
Swynes
Invisible Country

MUNCHKIN

Jinjur
Repairman
Blue Forest
Bandits' Cave
Munchkin River
White Mts.
Squee-Gee Ville
Shutter Town
Bottle Hill
Where Dorothy's House landed
First Yellow Brick Road
Valynn
Kalidahs
Ku-Klip
Scarecrow's
Beanpole (Middlings and Silver Islanders Underground)
Stone Mt.
Poppy Field
Reach
Rolling Road
Fiddlestick Forest
River
Dicksyland
Easter Bunny (U)
Sign Here
Link
HALIDOM
Bezanty
TROTI
Pax-on-Argent
R. Argent
Ma-Dul-Ma-Dun (U)
Preservatory
Wogglebug College
Elevator Man (Bear Mt.)
Moojer Mt.
Unicorners
Tappy Town
Miss Cuttenclip
Fuddlecumjig
Pineville
Story-Blossom Mt.

COUNTRY

Good Children
Crystal City
Crystal Mt.
Travelers' Tree
Morrow
Blue Forest
Snow Mt.
Shamsbad
Leon the Neon
Green Mt.
Poetree
SEEBANIA
China Country
Bee Hive
Roundabout
Crinklink
Hummingbirds
Pine Woods
Drumbad
Singra's Hut
Howzatagin
Dick Tater
Gorba's Garden (U)
U.
Smerheads
View Halloo
Weather Witch
High Faluting
Hah Hoh Humbad
Silica

COUNTRY

Top
Great Waterfall
Doorways
Linda's Palace
Red Mt.
RAGBAD
MUDGE
JINXLAND

WASTE

SHIFTING SANDS

Published by The International Wizard of Oz Club by Royal Appointment of Her Gracious Majesty OZMA of OZ MCMLXXX

DICK MARTIN Sculpsit

FINDING OZ

Books by Evan I. Schwartz

THE LAST LONE INVENTOR:
*A Tale of Genius, Deceit,
and the Birth of Television*

JUICE:
*The Creative Fuel That
Drives World-Class Inventors*

FINDING OZ:
*How L. Frank Baum Discovered
the Great American Story*

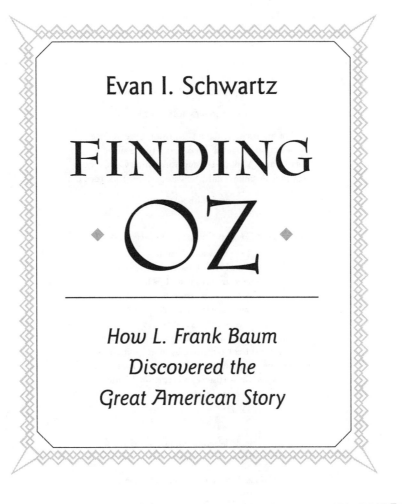

Evan I. Schwartz

FINDING ·OZ·

How L. Frank Baum
Discovered the
Great American Story

HOUGHTON MIFFLIN HARCOURT

BOSTON • NEW YORK

2009

www.hmhbooks.com

Library of Congress Cataloging-in-Publication Data
Schwartz, Evan I.
Finding Oz : how L. Frank Baum discovered the great
American story / Evan I. Schwartz.
p. cm.
Includes bibliographical references and index.
ISBN 978-0-547-05510-7
1. Baum, L. Frank (Lyman Frank), 1856–1919. Wizard of Oz.
2. Oz (Imaginary place) 3. Philosophy in literature. 4. Mythology
in literature. 5. Spirituality in literature. 6. Fantasy fiction,
American—History and criticism. I. Title.
PS3503.A923W5987 2009
813'.4—dc22   2008053296

Book design by Melissa Lotfy
Text is set in Goudy Old Style.

Printed in the United States of America

DOC 10 9 8 7 6 5 4 3 2 1

Photo credits appear on page 356.

To my daughters,
Lily and Michaela

CONTENTS

PROLOGUE

America's Adventure

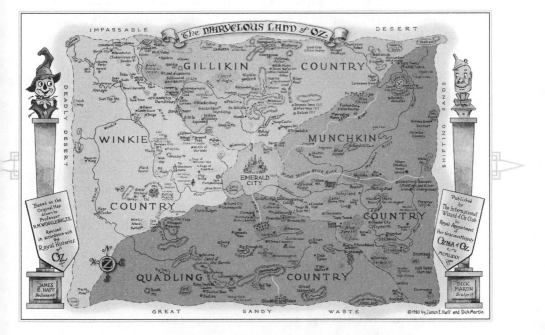

The world of Oz, as created by L. Frank Baum, has become
an adventureland of the heart and mind.

Then a strange thing happened.

— L. FRANK BAUM,
The Wonderful Wizard of Oz

O NE DAY IN 1898, an unusual sequence of images leaped from one man's mind: A gray Kansas prairie. A lively girl with a brave little dog. A terrifying twister. A mystical land ruled by both good and wicked witches. A colorful township of little people. A road of yellow bricks stretching through a dangerous frontier. A trio of comical characters — a scarecrow, a tin man, and a cowardly lion — who join the girl from Kansas on her quest, a journey to a magical city of emeralds controlled by a mysterious wizard. "The story really seemed to write itself," author L. Frank Baum told his publisher.

Baum relied on a favorite pencil as he put the tale to paper. By the fall of 1899 the pencil was just a stub, and he fastened it into a frame and surrounded it with a caption: "With this Pencil I wrote the ms. [manuscript] of *The Emerald City*." He sealed the frame and hung it on the wall above the desk in the den of his Chicago home. The final name of the novel would have to be changed, as Baum soon found out. "The publisher believes that books with jewel names in their titles do not sell well," he lamented.

Frank was forty-four by the time the book hit stores in the year 1900, and this business of being an author of children's stories was still new to him. By then he had failed at so many wildly different pursuits — as a breeder of chickens, as an actor in stage plays, as a purveyor of petroleum products, as an owner of a variety store, as a secretary for a baseball team, as a publisher of a newspaper, as a traveling salesman of fine china — that he might have simply given up on doing anything special with his life. If he had never experienced that one special moment that one day in 1898, he might even have gone on to succeed in his current full-time job — and gone down in history as the founder of the National Association of Window Trimmers of America. But the truth was, even that effort wasn't going so well.

Yet it wasn't in Frank Baum's nature to get down on himself, and he became newly energized by each of his schemes, determined to "*somehow* manage to provide for those dependent on me." He was a sunny man, tall and handsome with a graceful gait and a deep, resonant voice. Prone to flights of fancy, he was lucky to have a wife who kept him grounded. Her name was Maud, and as a young beauty she had dropped out of a good college to marry Frank, only to face years of struggle, constantly uprooting their home in search of a better situation. Together they raised four active sons, boys who demanded that their father tell them stories every evening, stories that seemed to give their lives a sense of constancy.

Rounding out the household was Maud's mother, who lived with the Baums for months at a time. Even by the high standards of the world's most menacing mothers-in-law, she set herself apart. Her name was Matilda Joslyn Gage, and she reigned as the most radical and principled leader of the women's rights movement in America. Mrs. Gage railed against religious leaders and politicians for a living and was so controversial and so scary to some that she was deemed "an infidel," her activities called "satanic." She had warned her daughter that she'd be a "damn fool" to give up her schooling to marry this man who showed little promise of holding a steady occupation — and for a long while she was right.

So Frank had to keep forging ahead, with the faith that something wonderful lurked beneath the surface of his failures, that something mystical swirled within the turbulence of his family, and something momentous stirred in America at large during this time of cyclonic change.

That *something* called him from his hometown in the East to an adventure out West, to the treeless Great Plains during the final days of the American frontier. Frank had tuned in enough to realize that he was traveling on his own journey of discovery, and he became fascinated with finding what spiritual sages had long called the True Self. But out there on the prairie, a land of killer tornadoes and deadly droughts, Frank came face-to-face with darkness and shadow, aspects of a mythic pattern of symbols and events that he encountered in his own life and times.

For too long he had suppressed his childhood dream of becoming a great writer, instead choosing to focus on the economic and social demands being placed on him. When such a choice is made, says mythologist Joseph Campbell, one's "vital powers disintegrate" and a would-be hero can become trapped by resentments and rationalizations "until he finds himself locked in the labyrinth of his own disoriented psyche." When this happened to Baum, when he found himself on the verge of losing everything, he gathered up his family and his last shreds of hope, hitting the road for Chicago, the host city of the glimmering Columbian Exposition, a majestic world's fair that would inspire his most fantastical fabrication, a place he would call the Emerald City of Oz.

It may have been the most incongruous instance of inspiration in history, an ordinary man struck by an extraordinary legend that would become America's most enduring tale of adventure. For no other story conceived on American soil would become as well known and as well loved as *The Wizard of Oz*. The stream of images that had built up over the years and that poured forth from Baum's mind that one day — every one of them would become a cultural icon, imprinted in the minds of billions. Heralded as America's first native fairy tale, the story is filled with references to the American spirit and its landscape. But even though it couldn't have been forged in any other country, the fable would go on to live as a universal touchstone, transcending national borders and language itself.

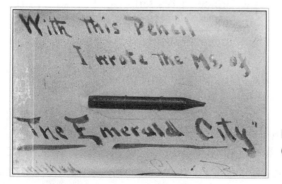

Framed pencil stub in Baum's Chicago home, 1899

One could, of course, attribute all this success to the 1939 film adapted from Baum's book, but the story had already been a classic for nearly four decades before MGM took on what it promoted as "the greatest bestseller in modern fiction." The movie deserves more than a little credit, though. Having been seen by more people than any other motion picture in history, the film that catapulted Judy Garland to fame is not only popular but enshrined. The oldest movie ranked among the American Film Institute's all-time top ten, the film features "Over the Rainbow," the AFI's number-one movie song. The Wicked Witch of the West endures as the most frightening female in filmdom, beaten out on the AFI's all-time villain list only by three men: Hannibal Lecter, Norman "Psycho" Bates, and Darth Vader. On the AFI's list of the top one hundred most memorable movie lines, *The Wizard of Oz* contributes three quotes—scoring with "Toto, I've a feeling we're not in Kansas anymore," "I'll get you, my pretty, and your little dog, too!" and "There's no place like home."

Though he could never have anticipated all his story would become, Frank Baum in his lifetime became an impresario of childhood epic, the J. K. Rowling of the age before talking pictures, radio, and television. Naturally, he was often asked just how it all came to be, how he discovered the Land of Oz. Like many authors of fiction, he was reluctant to say. Even if he wanted to, many of the tools for understanding how he transformed life into fantasy weren't yet devised, as the studies of psychology, creativity, and mythology were barely developed compared to today. So to appease newspaper reporters looking for an entertaining answer, Baum invented something whimsical but apocryphal: He held court in his Chicago home one day, telling a tale about a magical far-off place to his sons and some of their neighborhood friends, when one little girl asked what this land was called. Since Frank didn't yet have a name for it, he simply glanced around the room, until his eyes stopped on a filing cabinet. "The land is called . . . the land is called . . ." On the cabinet, underneath the drawers labeled A–G and H–N, sat one that said O–Z. "The land," said Frank, "is called the Land of Oz."

This episode probably never happened, but it always made good copy. And contrary to other fanciful beliefs of how the story came to be and what it means, there were no mind-altering drugs involved, and there's no hidden parable about Populist politics or Gilded Age monetary policy. Nor is *The Wizard of Oz* based around random nonsense. Instead, it is a story about the most meaningful of topics: the experience of being alive. It's a story that seems to fit into a spot in one's consciousness, a spot that was specially reserved just for it. This is why events in the Land of Oz seem to unfold over and over again so naturally in one's own mind and heart, as part of what Campbell calls your "private Pantheon of dreams."

But although this great American myth has become immortal, the mythmaker certainly wasn't. L. Frank Baum was like all of us, limited to living in his own here and now. And like all of us, he faced his own trials and errors with only a small window of time in which to search for truth and beauty. Yet all he needed was a flash, a single moment, to transform his own experiences into something bright enough and brilliant enough for everyone to know and love. This is the story of how one man managed to make myth from life.

L. Frank Baum at age forty-three in 1899

Great myths give us clues to the
spiritual potential of our lives.

— JOSEPH CAMPBELL,
The Power of Myth

It is a long journey, through a country
that is sometimes pleasant and
sometimes dark and terrible.

— L. FRANK BAUM,
The Wonderful Wizard of Oz

PART

I

1

No Place
Like Home

L. Frank Baum's childhood home, Rose Lawn

There were lovely patches of greensward all about, with stately trees bearing rich and luscious fruits. Banks of gorgeous flowers were on every hand, and birds with rare and brilliant plumage sang and fluttered in the trees and bushes. A little way off was a small brook, rushing and sparkling along between green banks.

— L. FRANK BAUM,
The Wonderful Wizard of Oz

I
N THE YEAR 1880, L. Frank Baum was twenty-four and still living with his parents at his childhood home. He held no steady occupation and he hadn't even quite settled on what people should call him. He loathed his first name, Lyman, from his father's side of the family, as it sounded like "lying man," and so he usually had people call him by his more "honest" middle name, Frank. Occasionally he'd insist on being called by a new first name, such as Louis. He had grown into a handsome man, tall and slim, with soft gray soulful eyes, thick dark hair parted slightly to the side, and a full handlebar mustache. Yet despite his good looks, Frank remained unmarried, an overripe bachelor in a time when the average male wasn't expected to live past sixty.

Judging by the size and beauty of the Baum family property, one couldn't blame Frank for growing all too comfortable there. The home had a name, Rose Lawn, and it rested on the northern outskirts of Syracuse, a city of fifty thousand tucked within the vast forests of central New York State. The New England–style farmhouse was enormous for its time, although hardly an architectural marvel. Essentially, the three-story, wood-shingled residence was a giant rectangular box, with a row of dormers jutting out from the pitched roof. Inside there were six bedrooms, each with a brass bed and a walnut washstand served by pitchers of water drawn from a well. Under each bed sat a ceramic pot for the times in the cold or dark when the occupant didn't yearn for a trip to the outhouse. Kerosene lanterns tossed sallow shafts of light about its large rooms, and stacks of firewood staved off the biting chill of winter.

The head of the household, Benjamin Ward Baum, was a rail-thin man with dark circles around his eyes and a bushy beard. A cooper by trade, he had been known locally as the proprietor of a factory that made wooden barrels. His wife, Cynthia Stanton Baum, was a devout Methodist turned Episcopalian with a face that was a road map of worry; understandably so, as the Baums had lost four children to early childhood diseases such as diphtheria. But those tragedies happened before the family purchased this nearly four-acre estate in 1866 for $5,000 and moved in with their five surviving children. Cynthia named it Rose Lawn, after the red roses that sprang open every year on the dozens of bushes arrayed about the lawn, but her son Frank turned it into a mythic palace of the mind. "This is the Rose Kingdom," he once wrote, "and it is devoted to the culture of the rarest and fairest roses grown."

In the distance a creek provided the sound of rushing water, and gravel pathways wound through the landscaping to clusters of apple, pear, and plum trees. The name Baum means "tree," in the old Germanic, so the family was at home living by the woods. Within a few years Mr. Baum greatly expanded the property with nearly three hundred acres of surrounding forest and farmland. The barn alone cost $25,000. "Few may be able to erect buildings with the handsomely painted exterior, the windows and blinds, slated French roof and ornamental tower seen in Mr. Baum's barn," one visitor marveled. The rooftop showcased four giant letters, so that no one passing by could mistake who owned it. The vast grounds also included a stable for purebred horses, pastures for cows, and coops for chickens so the family could have its own supply of eggs. Mrs. Baum hired a cook to keep the children well fed and a gardener to tend to the flowers and shrubs. To Frank and his siblings, there really was no place like Rose Lawn.

A general state of happiness pervaded the place when the children were young, but pretty soon they were all making their way into the world. The oldest child was Harriet, whom everyone called Hattie. She had married at age nineteen and now resided in town with her own family. Then came Mary, who was called Mattie. Her wedding was a joyous affair that took place at Rose Lawn itself. The eldest son, Benjamin Jr., sought an even more refined life and departed for his father's ancestral homeland of Germany, where he took a young Fräulein as his bride. The youngest son, Harry, also went away, to study medicine at the University of Michigan, becoming Dr. Harry Baum, a dermatologist.

Only the middle boy remained. Frank was the most imaginative of the bunch, inclined to lose himself in fictional worlds, but as a child he looked frail, having been stricken by a bout of rheumatic fever, which permanently weakened the four valves that directed the blood among the four chambers of his heart. This left him with shortness of breath and a susceptibility to fever. The condition had gone into remission, allowing him to live a mostly normal life, but doctors warned that eventually the valves would begin giving way, typically sometime around the age of forty. As a consequence, the boy spent long hours racing through books but rarely doing anything too physical, given the state of his heart. Along with Harry, he had been schooled at home, by an Oxford-educated tutor. When he wasn't in his lessons, he was usually found either reading in the living room, gazing out the win-

The magnificent barn at the Baum family farm

dow at the gardens, or reading outside on a wooden rocking chair on the broad porch that wrapped around the house. Books that passed through Frank's hands included satires by Dickens and Thackeray and the classics of Shakespeare. Frank got carried away by Swift's adventures, Grimm's fairy tales, Bunyan's allegories, Hawthorne's romances, the meditations of Thoreau and Emerson, Twain's humor, the fantasies of Lewis Carroll, and the American legends of James Fenimore Cooper. He confided in his sisters, telling Hattie and Mattie that he "longed to write a great novel that should win me fame."

But that was then, and by his early twenties Frank needed a way to make money, so he and his father decided to turn the estate's chicken coops into a full-fledged business, calling it Spring Farm. Every day, Frank would drive a wagon over to tend to his chickens, wearing tall boots and carting buckets of feed to the large square coops. "Kut-kut-kut, ka-daw-kut" is how Frank transcribed the sounds of the chickens, stored in his mind for use in his books. "Kut-kut-kut, ka-daw-w-w-kut!" His father often helped with the enterprise, but it was Frank's main responsibility to oversee the production and the sale of the eggs and poultry.

Frank grew so comfortable surrounded by hens and roosters that he imagined they were talking to him. "What's that?" he once wrote about a conversation with a "yellow hen squatting in the opposite corner of the coop."

"Why, I've just laid an egg, that's all," replied a small, but sharp and distinct voice.

"Tell me, how does it happen that you are able to talk? I thought hens could only cluck and cackle."

"Why, as for that," answered the yellow hen thoughtfully, "I've clucked and cackled all my life, and never spoken a word before this morning, that I can remember. But when you asked a question, a minute ago, it seemed the most natural thing in the world to answer you. So I spoke, and I seem to keep on speaking, just as you and other human beings do. Strange, isn't it?"

"Very."

"How is my grammar?" asked the yellow hen, anxiously. "Do I speak quite properly, in your judgment?"

"Yes, you do very well, for a beginner."

"I'm glad to know that," continued the yellow hen, in a confidential tone, "because, if one is going to talk, it's best to talk correctly."

Years later, references to chickens and eggs would appear somewhere in nearly every book written by Frank Baum. And the simple image of the chicken farm itself would live on forever, as Frank's single most famous book would be turned into an even more famous movie, and the very first sequence of that film would take place on a farm populated by dozens of chickens walking about, jutting their necks and fluttering their wings, while the main character complains about her life to an aunt and uncle who are busily attending to a broken incubator full of chirping little hatchlings. "Can't you see, we're busy?" scolds the aunt.

More than the Baum family's chicken farm or their vast land holdings, what made Rose Lawn so identifiable to the citizens of Syracuse was its precise location. The home featured a long, landscaped driveway that connected to a road known simply as Plank Road. A marvel of its time, it was the first passageway of its kind in the United States. No other thoroughfare nearly this long was fashioned purely of wood. Beams running parallel to the road's direction supported eight-foot crosspieces of hemlock boards, forming a uniform surface that made travel a breeze. It was a wonder that the sixteen-mile avenue of pale planks even existed in the first place. Completed in 1846, Plank Road allowed a way for farmers and merchants to quickly and safely transport barrels of salt, loads of livestock, and entire harvests of crops without getting stuck in the muck. From its beginnings in the northern farmlands, the road wound through thick woods, stretching past the famous salt mines by the shores of Onondaga Lake and ending in Central Square, the heart of Syracuse.

For the privilege of using the road, travelers had to pay a series of tolls along the way, amounting to a few cents per head of horse or ox. Rose Lawn happened to be situated right near the very first tollgate on Plank Road. From one of his perches, sitting under a favorite apple tree, Frank as a boy could spy horses of all different colors as he watched the toll taker tallying up charges for each. Most travelers, he knew, were on their way to the majestic Syracuse Weighlock Building, where the contents of carts and wagons would be unloaded onto flat, sturdy boats that were properly weighed, tagged, and taxed for the voyage along the Erie Canal. The man-made waterway had transformed Syracuse from a sleepy salt-mining settlement into one of the twenty largest cities in America, a thriving port with enough confidence to dub itself New York State's "Central City"—and the city owed much of its bustling canal traffic to the success of Plank Road.

The vision of this special path had to be imprinted in his mind, and to a boy enthralled by fictional journeys and adventures, the tollbooth by Rose Lawn must have seemed like a magical gateway between two worlds, a threshold between America's idyllic, rural past and its fantastical, man-made future. The contrast between the lush landscape surrounding Frank's childhood home and the wonders of the Central City in the distance would one day be reflected in Frank's own storytelling, as he would describe a "rich and pleasant" rural country that is connected by a conspicuous road to "a beautiful and wonderful place," and as one approached that central place "the green glow became brighter and brighter."

But to truly find that beautiful and wonderful place in the distance, and to transform it into story, Frank would have to leave his childhood home, just as everyone must. After all, the home of a child can be a cocoon of comfort, a perfect place to hatch one's hopes and dreams, yet it is not the place where one discovers the true nature of one's character. Rose Lawn was not where Frank could experience the world but rather where he took refuge from it. His parents, after all, were the ones who made the home, and he was different from them in many ways. Happiness, in Frank Baum's world, could come only from going away. "They had beautiful homes, splendid clothes, and ample food," Frank would one day write of a people who lived in the rural north country of Oz. But "something was wrong with their lives and they were not happy."

Frank Baum would discover that there's but one surefire way of finding one's inmost self—and that is to embark when the time comes on a journey. And the more arduous the adventure, the more perilous the path, the steeper the cliffs, the more dangerous the demons, the more choices one is forced to make—all the better for determining one's true character. Only if one is fortunate enough to return with new-found wisdom, compassion, and courage can one appreciate the higher meaning of home. The good witch Glinda would one day affirm this supreme life lesson: "That's all it is!" But she also said that it can be learned only through experience, that you "wouldn't have believed me" if she had simply tried to summarize the secret.

2

An Unexpected Journey

Frank, about thirteen, a cadet at the
Peekskill Military Academy

There were several roads near by, but it did not take her
long to find the one paved with yellow bricks.

— L. FRANK BAUM,
The Wonderful Wizard of Oz

T O FRANK, roads came to represent danger and difficulty as
well as hope and wonder. An unforgettable episode from his
childhood illustrates how a road can sometimes signal the start
of an arduous journey that one does not expect to take. This incident
goes a long way toward explaining why Frank as a young man seemed
so reluctant to leave Rose Lawn once and for all. Back when Frank was
twelve, his idyllic existence was interrupted for a time, and this distur-
bance came with cyclonic force. It happened when Frank's father decided to enroll his son in the Peekskill Military Academy, a boarding
school more than two hundred miles away.

Frank resisted. He wanted to stay right where he was, to continue
his homeschooling with his tutor. But Mr. Baum insisted that it would
be a good place for focusing Frank's meandering mind and building
up his frail body. Besides, all young men needed to learn how to fight.
New York had sent nearly half a million men to battle in the Civil
War — more than any other state — and the men who learned the discipline of war stood a better chance of returning in one piece. No matter that the war was over; there would always be a next one, against a
different enemy.

Frank's mother, Cynthia, knew that her sensitive son wasn't well
suited for life in a military academy, especially given his heart condition. But her only response to the predicament was to have faith
that the Lord would watch over her son and that God would see him
through this ordeal. Her empty religious piety profoundly disappointed
Frank. In his view, his mother failed to protect him. Next thing he

knew, he was packed up and whisked down Plank Road and put on a train. He would switch to a steamboat in Albany, traveling down the Hudson River en route to Peekskill, a hilltop town strategically perched near one of the river's choke points.

As the young Frank disembarked at the dock in Peekskill, carrying a suitcase or duffel bag, he stepped onto one of the many roads in town built from cheap but strong bricks known as "pavers." Since Peekskill had begun as a Dutch city, the town naturally favored Dutch brick for its pavers, which were bright yellow in color. Thousands of these bricks were carried as ballast on Dutch ships coming over from Holland and then used for roads. The Hudson River valley grew up as a center of manufacturing, and these paving bricks eventually became one of the region's many products. As a result, there were yellow brick roads all around town, especially near the waterfront, including a stretch by the old docks that still survives today. So if Frank had asked someone for directions from the docks to the academy up the hill, their answer would have been quite simple.

The incoming cadet must have set forth up the road of yellow bricks with trepidation, as he was about to enter a harsh new world. The Peekskill Military Academy was no place for daydreamers like him. Sitting atop Oak Hill overlooking the Hudson, the fifty-five-acre campus had served from 1776 to 1778 as the original military headquarters of the Continental Army under General George Washington. The command post was later transferred up the river to West Point. The academy that now stood in the same spot had since become known for building boys into modern military leaders, and so the atmosphere was steeped in duty and discipline.

Along with fifty other cadets in his class, Frank lived in the main dormitory, part of the set of three-story buildings that formed an L around the marching grounds. By the center staircase of the dorm was the giant gold-plated insignia of the academy, emblazoned with "1833," the year the school was founded, along with its proud motto, "Quit You Like Men," which referred to a line from an admonition by St. Paul to live and die with honor to God: "Watch ye, stand fast in the faith, quit you like men, be strong."

Frank's misery at Peekskill was immediate. As luck would have it, the school had just recently adopted a set of rigorous marching drills called Upton's Tactics. The drills were developed by Civil War hero General Emory Upton, who would soon be installed as the commander at West Point. At that time there was no foreign war on the horizon. Instead, the enemy that the young men would be training to face was the Native Americans. The "savages" and the "hostiles" out West were always blocking freedom and progress, the birthright of all good Americans. U.S. troops built large, well-equipped forts and hunted renegade groups that refused to settle on reservations.

This happened to be an ominous year for fighting the natives. Under the landmark Fort Laramie peace treaty of 1868, the warrior tribes of the Dakota Territory agreed to live in peace on the Great Sioux Reservation. In turn, the U.S. government agreed to provide them with sufficient food, clothing, and supplies. But the treaty provided barely a moment of quiet before it was violated by both sides, and war broke out once again. The Sioux chief who was most resistant to the terms of this treaty was the legendary medicine man who went by the name of Sitting Bull. He and his band of followers refused to live in captivity. For its part, the U.S. government rarely lived up to its word. "The government made treaties, gave presents, made promises, none of which were honestly fulfilled," acknowledged U.S. Army General Philip Sheridan, who led America's post–Civil War fight against the Native Americans. "We took away their country and their means of support, broke up their mode of living, their habits of life, introduced disease and decay among them, and it was for and against this they made war."

Every day at the Peekskill Military Academy, Frank was among the boys who were to report to the marching grounds, to train for eventual battle with the native tribes. Dressed in their blue woolen uniforms and their marching boots, clutching their rifles, the cadets resembled a troop of toy soldiers as they were ordered around by the drill sergeant. For hours, often under the blazing sun or in the driving rain, the cadets had to stay in line and obey commands such as "Halt!" "March!" and "Forward!" forming an axis that wheeled back and forth about the grass.

The daydreaming Frank would be among the least likely of these boys to stay in line and follow each order. In fact, Frank was punished all too often for letting his mind wander. "I complained to my father about the brutal treatment I felt I was receiving at the school," Frank wrote years later. The rigidity at Peekskill wasn't reserved for just the marching grounds but for the classroom as well. "The teachers were heartless, callous and continually indulging in petty nagging," Frank wrote. "They were about as human as a school of fish. They were quick to slap a boy in the face or forcibly use a cane or ruler to punish any student who violated in the slightest way any of the strict and often unreasonable rules."

One afternoon, in his second year at the school, one of Frank's teachers spotted him gazing out the classroom window at birds singing in a nearby tree. To punish Frank for such idle behavior, the teacher dragged him off to another room and began whipping him with a cane. Frank's tormenter must have been surprised when, in the middle of the punishment, Frank clutched his chest in agony and fainted to the floor. Frank Baum had suffered a heart attack at the tender age of fourteen—or he had faked one incredibly well. Either way, this spell would end Frank's time at Peekskill.

One could imagine the torment Frank must have received from his fellow cadets, not to mention the officers. The boys were being trained to fight with honor to the death. And now Frank was leaving, his tail between his legs, showing no sign of great courage, abandoning his classmates who were presumably going to grow up and become valiant Indian fighters, in the mold of the famous General George Custer. But not Frank. He simply packed his things, retreated back down the road of yellow bricks, hopped back onto the steamboat, and made his way back to Syracuse.

Frank was no doubt changed by his troubling time away. Indeed, this was the kind of episode that psychologists and mythologists alike call "shadow material," the deep, dark experience that can never be totally forgotten and indeed could serve as fuel for dreams and nightmares—or for fiction. Years later, of course, Frank would write about a child who is taken away from home and pitched into a place that is often unpleasant and sometimes terrible. Above all, the child simply wants to go back home again.

Perhaps Frank's father felt guilty about sending his son away, because not long after he returned from Peekskill, Frank received an extraordinary present, for his fifteenth birthday. Amateur journalism was a full-blown fad, and Frank was eager to join in, to take his first real stab at publishing his own stories. As a gift, Mr. Baum bought his son a small novelty printing press that was immediately put to good use. Built around a flat metal bed-plate and featuring a complete set of moveable type, the contraption was powered by a foot pedal.

Along with his brother Harry, Frank created a newspaper the boys named the *Rose Lawn Home Journal*. The Baum brothers distributed the paper of whimsical stories and cunning poems for free to friends, family, and neighbors. Issues were usually just four pages, but they showed Frank's early penchant for dark humor. One edition featured a "Wit and Wisdom" column, with this riddle: What do you call a pleasure grounds for murderers? The answer was "hanging gardens." Some of his puns were hopelessly clever:

> *A certain wit declared of late,*
> *That every act of magistrate*
> *Was water in a freezing state.*

The answer was *just-ice*. In another issue Frank began an epic poem based on a biblical retelling:

> *In ancient days as we are told,*
> *Noah marched the animals into the fold,*
> *Then closed the door of hickory bark,*
> *Of which material he'd made his ark.*
> *He shipped a man of monstrous size,*
> *Who was noted for his wond'rous lies.*

Frank had found where his joy was, in the telling of tales, especially humorous ones that rhymed. Years later, a few back issues of Rose Lawn's official newspaper could still be found around the house, serving as a reminder of the days when Frank was doing something he loved. The amateur printing press was not only something that influenced Frank's future; it was also emblematic of the happy part of his childhood, one that included many material indulgences.

Benjamin Baum was able to afford to give his family a life of relative luxury because he had literally found a fortune. Money was "the romance, the poetry of our age, the thing that chiefly strikes the imagination." That's what novelist William Dean Howells said about this era of schemers and dreamers and charlatans and wildcatters who set out to seek rumored riches and buried treasures. Haunted by the ghosts of the Civil War, men who had repressed their greed during the years of carnage were suddenly let loose on the land. Hordes of eastern city dwellers and former Union soldiers sporting derbies and bowlers and stovepipe hats boarded trains and wagons that bounded over hills and across bridges. Racing to exploit America's abundance of natural resources, the men of Benjamin Baum's generation invented new ways of amassing wealth at speeds that had been theretofore unimaginable. "It was such a period as seldom occurs," remarked banker Thomas Mellon, "in which it was easy to grow rich."

The times were marked by two signature events: the rush and the panic. A rush was the pandemonium that would happen when some valuable commodity or idea was discovered somewhere. There were land rushes, gold rushes, and rushes to build railroads and telegraph lines. When the opening signal of a rush was heard in the far-off distance, enterprising men dropped everything to try to beat the stampede and get in on the next big boom before everyone else did. This was the unsettling way America was settled. Plots of land would be seized and flipped at a higher price to those just joining the rush. New towns sprang up like cornfields, and these new points on the map were bursting with optimistic people on a buying binge, driving up the price of everything.

The panic that would inevitably follow the rush was also a stampede, but in the opposite direction. Anything could trigger a panic. A big bank in London could fail. Cries of "Sell, sell, sell" could be heard in the markets of New York City. The panic could be unleashed at any moment. When wilderness land or silver mines or railroad tracks or telegraph cables were deemed overvalued, there could be a rash of cashing out, and there was nothing in place to stop it. No central bank or government institution existed to stabilize things, to inject money into the system; there was nothing to halt the meltdown, to stop the sudden run on the banks. Deposits weren't insured, and when everyone wanted to withdraw all their cash and liquidate everything they owned at once, the economy would lapse into paralysis, limping along in a deathlike state for years.

L. Frank Baum saw his father embark on a journey into this mad-cap world. The rush that claimed Benjamin Baum actually began just before the war and continued during and after it. On August 28, 1859, word went out that a former train conductor known as Colonel Ed-ward Drake had struck oil in Titusville, Pennsylvania. No one cared that Drake wasn't a real colonel or that he knew nothing about oil or what it was good for. Men simply heard that oil meant money, and so the race was on to tap the ground for black gold. A mad gusher that spouted in a sleepy little place drillers called Pithole Creek drew twelve thousand men within months. Fifty new hotels cropped up along with at least that many saloons. A commodities broker from Cleveland named John D. Rockefeller didn't approve of all the drink-ing, but he saw in the new oil fields of Pennsylvania "vast stores of wealth . . . bountiful gifts of the great Creator."

At the time, Benjamin Baum's barrel factory in Syracuse had hit bottom, and the Baum family lived in a small home, struggling to get by. Within weeks of the Titusville cry, Benjamin set off on the rush, hightailing by wagon to the world's first oil region. "Baum has gone to PA," wrote his business partner at the barrel factory. "Has the oil fever. Hope he makes a *fortune*."

Benjamin Baum certainly did. He not only struck oil, at a deso-late spot called Cherry Tree Run, but he was smart about it. He didn't spend much time prospecting in the obvious places. Instead, he pur-chased patches of land more than a hundred miles northeast of Titus-ville, near the less frenetic fields of Bradford, Pennsylvania, by the bor-der of New York State, where he soon used his factory know-how to open a refinery, naming the new company after his wife: the Cynthia Oil Works. Refining crude oil and pouring the byproducts into barrels became the more reliable business. America suddenly craved the prod-ucts that could be extracted from crude, chiefly kerosene for lighting and lubricants for greasing the wheels of industry. By the time the war was over, Benjamin had prospered so greatly that he had also become the founder of the Second National Bank of Syracuse, lending money to other enterprising men. After the war he parlayed part of his oil for-tune into the stately home his wife called Rose Lawn.

But one day in the fall of 1873, a Philadelphia bank run by Jay Cooke, one of the corrupt tycoons of the Great Northern Railroad, shut its doors and refused to pay its depositors. The domino effect that followed, soon known as the Panic of 1873, forced a ten-day shutdown of the New York Stock Exchange. Everyone wanted to sell everything and no one was buying. Benjamin Baum's money was tied up in his own bank, now besieged by desperate men, and he lost almost all of his fortune at once. His oil refinery was idled for a time, as prices collapsed overnight.

Around this time Benjamin Baum had also become chronically ill. One doctor said it was because his "close application to business destroyed his health." His condition may also have been exacerbated by a sudden mental depression, as making and then losing such large sums in so short a time had to be hard on the man. No local doctor was able to supply a satisfying diagnosis. Mr. Baum made plans to travel to Germany for the best treatment and to visit his eldest son, who was living in Heidelberg. Before he boarded the steamship for Europe, the cash-strapped family put Rose Lawn up for sale. An announcement ran in the *Syracuse Journal*: "The elegant country residence of B. W. Baum, well known as Rose Lawn, is now offered for sale on very easy terms, or in exchange for property in the city. This place needs no description from us, as most of our citizens have passed it many times in the pleasant and popular drive on the Plank Road."

The estate stood unsold. The Baums weren't the only ones without money, as the Panic of 1873 had set off a brutal six-year economic depression. The Baums continued to run ads to sell their property, year after year. Eventually the family was forced to turn Rose Lawn over to the bank as collateral to secure a loan for living expenses. When that money ran out, and the bank was unable to collect on the mortgage, it moved to auction off Rose Lawn to the highest bidder. Apparently there was so little demand for the property that the highest bidder ended up being none other than L. Frank Baum himself, who paid $3,500 for it in 1880. He probably borrowed that money from his very own father, who wouldn't have been legally eligible to purchase his own house at auction.

It was around this time that the Baum family decided to turn Spring Farm into a business, with Frank serving as the prince of the chickens. Perhaps the farm could help save the house, and for a while the plan seemed promising. So now that Frank seemed to have something re-sembling an occupation, it was becoming more and more obvious that he should also pursue the opportunity to establish his own household, to have a family of his own. This was no simple task, as courtship in polite American society still clung to British custom. In the Victorian age there were certain rules to follow. If a young lady were to be intro-duced to a young man, a series of inquiries must first be made. Were there any common friends or family members who could vouch for the man's character? If so, the young lady's family would require in-formation concerning the bachelor's trade and whether his livelihood seemed capable of supporting a wife and family.

Making a case for L. Frank Baum as a prospective husband wouldn't be easy. True, he had no criminal record. He didn't smoke and was not known as a drunk. But the most pressing question about Frank was a straightforward one: Did he have a future as a chicken breeder? Judg-ing by the way he presented his business, he at least seemed to find great dignity in his work, as evidenced by a brochure that had made its way around the city. The title page spoke of chickens as an odd source of family pride: "B. W. Baum and Sons," it announced. "Cele-brated Strains of Thoroughbred Fowls." The brochure boasted that the Baums were "winners of the first prize for Houdan Fowls at the Eastern Poultry Association at Albany."

Fancy chickens—could that be a suitable livelihood for a man with thoughts of marriage? That wasn't clear, yet it did seem as if Frank had given a pursuit known for foul odor a certain air of respectability. L. Frank Baum, the brochure noted, was editor of the *Poultry Record,* a monthly journal put out by the Syracuse Fanciers' Club. He was also working on a monograph that he aimed to publish, to be titled *The Book of Hamburgs: A Brief Treatise on the Mating, Rearing and Man-agement of the Different Varieties of Hamburgs.* Yet the cloak of pres-tige that Frank had draped upon all the clucking and plucking that happened at Spring Farm couldn't change the fact that most people appreciated poultry for just one reason: food. The squawking, talk-ing chickens in which L. Frank took such an avid interest may have been magnificently stylish, but these breeds were generally too small to be of much commercial value. Frank's fowl may have possessed a rare beauty, but did they taste good? Were they laying enough eggs to earn much of a living?

Alas, they weren't. So it may have come as a relief for Frank to receive word one day in early 1881 that the bank had finally auctioned off the vast acres around Rose Lawn. The land that included Spring Farm fetched $13,864, acquired by a family acquaintance, George Crouse, who owned a successful grocery store in town. The amount, equivalent to about $300,000 in today's dollars, was only a small fraction of the property's value a decade earlier. But the sale brought much-needed cash to pay off family debts, and it meant that the Baums were out of the chicken business. The house at Rose Lawn, however, was still listed under the name L. Frank Baum, and it didn't seem that the newly unemployed son would be leaving anytime soon.

In deciding what to do next, Frank was susceptible to a bug that had been spreading through the family: the virus of the theater. Frank adored his aunt Kate, the youngest sibling of his father. Katherine Gray, as she was known professionally, taught elocution and established her own School of Oratory in downtown Syracuse, offering private lessons at a dollar or two per hour. From being around her, Frank gained his proper e-nun-ci-a-tion. The school also hosted a dramatics program, in which Aunt Kate organized a performance of *Mother Goose Entertainment* at the Unitarian church. The one-dollar price of admission included a family-style supper beforehand. Aunt Kate served as the narrator of the performance, and Mother Goose herself was portrayed by Cynthia Baum; L. Frank played her son, Jack. The cast of characters — filled in by family, friends, and students — included Old King Cole, the Pretty Maid, the Man in the Moon, Jack Sprat, and the Big Bad Wolf.

It didn't take much in the way of applause to infect Frank. He would never forget how the faces of the children lit up while watching these simple stories unfold. Pretty soon Aunt Kate and her favorite nephew organized a troupe of actors to stage more serious dramas. They took one of their shows to Chittenango, the nearby town where Frank had been born. A well-received performance there led to further engagements in area churches and union halls. Despite their popularity, the performances weren't earning much money, and Frank was in dire need of a livelihood. To really make a living in the theater, he must have thought, it would help greatly if one could actually own the theater.

Another member of the Baum family was in a position to help Frank. His "Uncle Doc," Dr. Adam Clarke Baum, had once served as an army surgeon in the Civil War, but he had abandoned medicine to join his older brother Benjamin in the Pennsylvania oil rush. Uncle Doc, like his sister Kate, also loved theater, and he already had thoughts of opening venues in the oil regions. Even before the economic depression ended, the oil business had been steadily picking up. Prices were stabilizing as cartels were gaining power. The Cynthia Oil Works was located in a border town called Bolivar, which had grown from a township of 150 to a bustling village of 4,500 in just a few short years, and other towns in the area were experiencing the same kind of surge. Like his Uncle Adam, Frank saw what these men and their families needed—entertainment, something to do at night other than drink at local watering holes. Benjamin Baum, always one to support his son's pursuits, agreed with the idea. And so the brothers decided to put up some money.

The first Baum Opera House opened in Richburg, New York, the next town over from Bolivar, and the second one opened just over the border, in Gilmore, Pennsylvania. The Baum brothers also purchased the Blake Opera House in Olean, New York, just ten miles west of Richburg. All three theaters were rather modest structures, holding no more than three hundred seats apiece. The management reins were turned over to Frank, who saw this as his golden opportunity to write his own plays. He apparently divided his time among the three towns and lived in small rooms above the stages of the three theaters, rooms where he could set up his typewriter and dream up stories and dialogue late into the night. Never before had Frank seemed as consumed in a task as he was while writing his plays. He worked ferociously, and by the fall of 1881, Frank had produced drafts of five scripts.

Under a new pen name, Louis F. Baum, he later registered three of these plays with the Copyright Office of the Library of Congress. *Matches* was a light romantic comedy that gently poked fun at the matchmaking customs of the time. *The Mackrummins* was also a comedy, in three acts, but it was never produced. The most elaborate was a production called *The Maid of Arran*, a melodrama set in Ireland that he adapted from *A Princess of Thule*, a William Black novel that was set in Scotland. In addition to changing the locale and altering some of the characters, the budding playwright also added his own music, composing six original songs. The other two plays by Louis F. Baum were not copyrighted. One was called *Kilmourne*; the other, *The Queen of Killarney*. These, too, were Irish dramas.

Frank focused on tales of the Irish because that was the predominant ethnic group in the region, and he apparently thought it would be wise to appeal to their cultural pride and the longing they had for their beloved homeland. In this regard Frank displayed one of his defining character traits: an acute sense of empathy, the ability to walk in another person's shoes. In his playwriting Frank proved adept at channeling the point of view of others, as a way to show audiences what they yearned to see. His empathy was his superpower, but like any talent it could be used for good or ill.

Back in the oil patch, the work that Frank carved out for himself was a bit more than one man could ordinarily handle. Not only did he book and promote three theaters, but he managed their upkeep, all while writing plays and conducting rehearsals. In some productions he even took on the lead role. Yet he didn't mind working hard, as he was finally doing something that made him happy. *The Maid of Arran* proved to be the most popular of the Louis F. Baum creations. The play premiered at the Baum Opera House in Gilmore in the late fall of 1881. As soon as the curtain came down and the clapping faded, Frank dreamed about where his new vehicle could take him. He envisioned performing in his home city of Syracuse and in the great metropolis of New York. This was just the start. The small chain of Baum theaters in the oil patch could serve as a springboard, as a way of gaining early acceptance and financial support for his work. His larger dream was to please audiences everywhere, to set the whole country on fire with his stories.

Yet as a profession, the business of acting and staging plays was not something that would win him much admiration in polite society, as theater was not then considered respectable. Theater on Broadway was a movable feast, relocating over the years from seedy downtown districts up to Herald Square. There had been various forms of theater in America going back to the 1750s, but the outcome of the Revolutionary War had given the Puritans the chance to rise up and start closing theaters. Church leaders saw theaters as competition with the kind of indoctrination they provided. Laws were passed in Massachusetts, Pennsylvania, and Rhode Island banning the performance of plays. Preachers spoke of theaters as "the Devil's Synagogues," places where fabricated human emotions were on display. The contempt continued into the nineteenth century, a time in which many religious leaders forbade dancing in public. Acting was considered an even viler form of expression, one step down from public drunkenness.

Most anti-theater ordinances were gradually relaxed, but events didn't help the cause. In 1849, during a performance of Shakespeare's *Macbeth* at the Astor Place Opera House in New York, a dispute between rival actors may have instigated tensions between different classes of people in the audience. Gunfire erupted and the militia was called in to quell what became known as the Astor Place Riot, pure bedlam that resulted in twenty-five deaths and injuries to more than a hundred other audience members. Worse, President Lincoln was shot in a theater, by an actor no less. The most popular forms of theater in the decades after the war were minstrel shows, burlesque, and vaudeville, all considered among the lowest forms of entertainment. Clergy continued to warn against "hotbeds of hedonism." In 1873 a theater in Brooklyn burned down, killing three hundred, prompting a preacher to proclaim that this was evidence of "God punishing them for being in an evil place." In the eyes of many churchgoers, actors were con men, and actresses were prostitutes.

In this light it isn't so surprising to learn that Frank Baum would have been deemed undesirable for marriage. He probably took on the pen name Louis F. Baum for this very reason. Sometimes he performed under the name George Brooks, to avoid bringing shame to the Baum family name. Perhaps in Syracuse his work would garner more respect. The city had an active theater life, and it was hosting performances that verged on respectability at its two magnificent venues, the Wieting Opera House and the Grand Opera House. Theater in Syracuse was so far ahead of theater in most other places that a young Samuel Shubert, while growing up in town, worked selling programs and tickets at both the Wieting and the Grand before leading his two younger brothers to New York, to become key players in establishing the modern theater district.

Fresh from his successful run in the oil fields, Frank Baum was now returning to Syracuse for the Christmas holiday of 1881, to stay at Rose Lawn with his parents. During this visit back home, Frank likely paid calls on the managers at both the Wieting and the Grand, to show off press clippings, photographs, and other evidence that his new play, *The Maid of Arran*, was quite a hit, for it was around this time that Frank secured a May engagement for the play at the Grand Opera House.

Among the relatives who were happiest for Frank's swift success was his elder sister, Hattie. She adored Frank, and she had not forgotten that her brother had always dreamed of becoming a famous writer. A thoroughly respectable member of Syracuse society, Hattie was a mother of two and the wife of the dry goods merchant William Henry Harrison Neal, proprietor of Neal, Baum & Company. As a teenager Frank had worked part-time at the store, which started with seed money from Benjamin Baum.

Yet Hattie would naturally be worried about her brother's welfare. Frank was still not married, and she probably couldn't bear to think of him rooming in cold, lonely theaters. She could vouch for her brother's character, despite what some might say about theater people. But what young lady would be in want of an introduction to this promising young playwright? As it so happened, Uncle Adam Clarke Baum and his wife, Josephine, may have been thinking the same things. They, too, would be delighted by his achievements but worried about his lack of a bride.

Aunt Josephine had in mind just the girl for Frank. Like everyone else in the family, she knew that Frank was unusual. But it turns out that her daughter Josie, Frank's first cousin, had a roommate at Cornell University who was also quite unusual. Josie had invited this girl, Miss Maud Gage, to the house and spoke of her often. Maud Gage came from one of the most progressive families in the area, so perhaps her parents wouldn't object to their daughter being introduced to a former chicken farmer who had just recently become an oil patch actor.

Aunt Josephine formulated the plan along with Frank's sister Hattie, who decided that the big introduction would take place at a small party for friends on Christmas Eve at Hattie's elegant colonial home on West Onondaga Street. Josephine would attend with her husband, Uncle Doc, and they'd bring their daughter Josie, who in turn would be accompanied by her college roommate, Maud.

And so Hattie extended an invitation to Frank, requesting his attendance on the twenty-fourth of December, 1881. "Show business doesn't leave me much time to run around with girls," he protested. "I haven't found one yet I could stay interested in." But she told him that this young lady was "different from the girls you've known around here." She was a student of English and American literature, someone who was "pretty but independent, with a mind and will of her own." He was told that he'd love her.

3

A Girl in a Man's World

The young college coed
Maud Gage

Portrait of Maud's mother,
Matilda Joslyn Gage, age fifty-four

"Won't you go with me?" pleaded the girl . . .

"No, I cannot do that," [the woman] replied, "but I will give you my kiss, and no one will dare injure a person who has been kissed by the Witch of the North."

— L. FRANK BAUM,
The Wonderful Wizard of Oz

MAUD GAGE HAD DARK HAIR, a shapely figure, and eyes as sharp as her mind. Nineteen years old, she had hardly spent a night away from her family's home, a finely kept Greek Revival residence on the main street of a charming Syracuse suburb called Fayetteville. Maud loved her gray-haired parents: the caring Henry Gage, a successful dry goods merchant, and the fiercely protective Matilda Joslyn Gage, a national leader of the women's rights movement. But one day in early September of 1880, it was finally time for Maud to leave. Wearing a fashionable hat, a long-sleeved, floor-length dress, her waist properly corseted, Maud couldn't move with much flexibility, and so she would need her parents' help loading her luggage aboard the train. With kisses and goodbyes, Mr. and Mrs. Gage sent their youngest child off into the world.

After about two hours' travel, Maud at the Ithaca train depot would have hired a carriage driver to take her and her bags to the campus of Cornell University, where she was to begin her freshman year. Despite her inexperience out in the world, Maud wasn't shy. She seemed ready to make her mark on the campus from the moment she arrived at her living quarters.

Sage College was perched on a plateau fashioned as a pedestal for a new kind of college dormitory: a place reserved for female students. Cornell was the first major university in the East to adopt coeducation, and this was only the sixth year in which young ladies were living on campus. An extravagant Gothic palace, Sage College was fashioned of bright red brick laced with ornamental bands of black and white stone. The pitched roof sported gray slate topped by a magnificent steeple that reached so far up to the sky that one could spot it for miles. The interior featured bathrooms on every floor, steam heating, the latest in modern ventilation, a botanical garden, a swimming pool, a gymnasium, a majestic dining room, a study, and a library with the finest of furnishings, plus its own classrooms and professorial offices. The dormitory rooms were on the second and third floors, with views of either Lake Cayuga, the town of Ithaca, or the central campus.

On the eastern end of the first floor was the parlor. Since the opening of Sage College, this room had become one of Cornell's social hot spots. Thick area rugs draped the wooden floors. Next to the plush sofas were wooden stands with vases of fresh flowers. Tall windows let in streams of sunlight. Round tables with plenty of chairs enabled groups to sit for conversation, and an upright piano sat against the wall. Above a fireplace mantel trimmed in decorative tile hung a stern portrait of the white-bearded Henry Williams Sage, the Cornell Board of Trustees member whose $250,000 gift to the university made everything here possible.

Maud was ready to become a leader like her mother. She had been taught to always assert herself, to make her presence known, to go after what she wanted with poise. Her older brother, Clarkson, had made it through Cornell as a member of the school's very first class, but her two older sisters never graduated a four-year college. She was to be the family's first female to earn a full degree. Her mother wished for Maud to become a doctor or a lawyer, practically unheard-of aspirations for a woman.

Maud arrived at Cornell determined not only to prove herself but also to have a good time. Down in the parlor someone was typically playing the piano. On the day of her arrival, Maud recognized a tune and took a few mock steps on the dance floor, proclaiming in front of a semicircle of girls she'd just met that "I dearly love dancing."

One of the girls in the parlor at the time was Jessie Mary Boulton, a proper Presbyterian from Oil City, Pennsylvania, who didn't partake in dancing. Now a sophomore, she was a shrewd observer and writer, having been elected class essayist the prior year. Jessie wrote detailed and witty letters home to her parents and younger sister. Her first letter of the school year contained only two pieces of news: that she had arrived safely on campus, and that there was an interesting new girl at Sage. "There is one that I think will make quite a stir," she wrote. "Her name is Gage and she is *lively*." *Lively* may have seemed like a compliment of sorts, but it was also a code word for trouble. "A girl scarcely dares look sideways here," wrote Jessie. A lively girl, it was understood, would not have an easy time on campus. Jessie expected this Gage girl to generate gossip.

Maud's father had given her money for her tuition, which was set at $25 per term, about equal to an average week's profits at his store in Fayetteville. As the academic year at Cornell was divided into three terms, annual tuition added up to $75. Books for the year would cost another $25. What caused the eyes of parents to pop was the price of "room, board, lighting and fuel." Living at Sage College cost $7.50 per week, or about $340 for the year. However, that was for a single room. If you shared a room with another girl, you'd save $40.

Maud decided that she would double up, and so she was assigned a room on the second floor with a roommate by the name of Miss Josie Baum. Josie was a year older, a sophomore, and she hailed from Syracuse, the city that bordered Maud's own hometown. Their room was bare, each girl having little more than a bed and a bureau. They had to bring their own towels, make their own beds, supply their own area rugs, and hang their own curtains and pictures. At first the two roommates addressed each other formally, as Miss Gage and Miss Baum. In discussing their families, Maud learned that Josie's father was in the oil business and spent much time away, prospecting in Pennsylvania. Josie worried deeply about her father, as she had heard just how cutthroat the oil business was, and if her father's business failed, it could spell the end of her time at Cornell.

The first order of business for the term was entrance examinations that lasted two days. Question number one was easy enough: "Write a short account of yourself," including "your purpose in entering." For geography, Maud was asked to look at a map of the United States with no borders and draw the outlines of Utah Territory, Kansas, and Minnesota. But one grammar question was "State the difference between

co-ordinating and subordinating conjunctives." And the math ex-
ams seemed so brain-splitting that Maud and the rest of the students
must have been exhausted after the two days were complete. Yet Maud
passed all the tests and was listed on September 16, 1880, as "Miss M.
Gage, Fayetteville" in the debut issue of a daily campus newspaper
called the *Cornell Sun*. She was one of just 19 women in a class of 131
incoming freshmen.

At first the girls could hardly tell one another apart. They were
all properly attired, in lovely long-sleeved dresses. On their heads
they wore jaunty, broad-brimmed hats, typically adorned with golden
threads and bird plumage. Most of the students had gone to single-sex
day schools, so they didn't know how to act in a coed setting. The boys
would simply gawk and follow the girls around. "Boys or young men
(as I guess they call themselves) abound," Jessie wrote in a letter. "We
have been surrounded everywhere we went. They stare at the girls so.
I supposed I will get used to it afterwhile." The boys would also tease
the girls at every opportunity. If a girl came more than a moment late
to class, the boys would start clapping their hands as she walked in and
took her seat. "The boys are quite rude here," wrote Jessie, "and they
seem very fond of applauding."

After a while they found common ground in a common language,
as detailed in Cornell's "Dictionary of Slang for the Uninitiated." To
"buzz" meant to entertain someone with interesting conversation, as
in "Josie put a buzz on that boy." Sage College, also known as the "Hen
House," was where "Roosters" would call on the "Hens." To "rag out"
was to put on fine clothes. A "lark" was an aimless walk, and a "toot"
was a walk so aimless you'd get lost. A "snoozer" was a harmless fellow.
Giving "magoo" was to pass off deceitful small talk, and "spooning"
was giving "magoo" to a Hen. And getting "gobbled" was to get caught
in the act. When something was "way up," it was excellent. Yet when
you wanted someone to stop doing something at once, the expression
was "Cheese it!" as in "Cheese it, Maud!"

As Maud learned the lingo and fell into the routine, going to literature and history classes every morning and studying for hours in the
late afternoons, meals became a focal point of social life. The food at
the dining hall was abundant; the typical meal featured chicken and
potatoes. For dessert there were usually two kinds of pie and a pudding.

In the mornings, breakfast ended at 9:00 a.m., which turned out to be a problem one day when three of the girls, Miss Gage, Miss Boulton, and Miss Yost, came down to eat seven minutes late only to find the dining room doors locked shut. The girls knocked on the door until Mr. Kinney, the master of the house, emerged with his pocket watch and a solemn air on his face. Despite their pleas, he would not let the girls into the dining hall. The hungry coeds then tracked down a professor on his way to the grocery store in town. They charmed him into bringing back crackers, dried beef, and cheese. Miss Gage and her friends deemed it the best breakfast yet. By early October the well-fed girls of the Hen House were starting to get so comfortable around one another that they usually went without their corsets.

Cornell University was actually having a tough time drawing and keeping female students, as there were only thirty women living at Sage, even though the dormitory could house at least a hundred. Because the Hen House was able to attract only a relative handful of Hens, each girl got plenty of attention by the boys of Cornell. Sage College was not designed to be a nunnery, and young men were welcome to visit. Almost every evening in the parlor there was a party, a dance, or a sing-along. The rule, set forth by Mrs. Kinney, the matron of the house, also known as "the Mother Hen," was that all Roosters were to be received in the parlor and were to leave before 10:00 p.m., and that the young ladies themselves were not to be out after the 10:00 p.m. curfew.

Boys were also welcome to join the ladies for dinner, and sometimes there were quite a few men in the Sage dining hall. Jessie Boulton, for instance, invited a family friend from back home in Oil City, a freshman named Charlie Thorp, to dine at her table. But that didn't last long. For some reason Charlie soon went back to eat with the boys. In Charlie's place Jessie invited Maud Gage to join the table, which already included Maud's roommate, Josie Baum. Jessie and Josie, sophomores, took the freshman Maud under their wings. They were both concerned that Maud's spirited personality would get her into trouble, as she would often display a temper whenever anyone teased her or crossed her in some way, especially if it was a boy. Since Jessie was so close to Charlie, she had a unique window into whom the boys were talking about. "I came to the conclusion long ago," wrote Jessie, "that Cornell was no place for lively girls. Charlie has gone farther. He thinks it is no place for girls at all. He has heard so much talk since he came. He says the boys talk terribly about the girls here."

In early October this loose talk reached a crisis point of sorts when it came time for the freshmen to elect class officers. There were a dozen different positions, from president and vice president, to treasurer and class essayist, to a marshal who would be in charge of planning class parties and social events. Most of these positions were strictly off-limits to girls. Yet there was a tradition every year that the boys would nominate the most precocious girl in the incoming class for the position of marshal and then gossip about her viciously. The prior year this honor had fallen to Miss Florence Yost, an attractive and vivacious girl who never asked for this kind of attention. For a couple of weeks the boys spooned all kinds of magoo about Miss Yost. She understandably got upset, but overall Miss Yost seemed to take it in stride.

This year the boys decided to submit the name of Miss Maud Gage for the position of class marshal, and she was in for a much bigger gust of gossip than usual. The rumors about Maud immediately grew out of hand, to the point where she stormed into her dorm room, locked the door, and cried for hours, as reported by Jessie:

> We have had a sensation here. I told you about a lively girl in the Freshman class. Monday, at the class of '84 election, her name was put on one of the tickets for marshal . . . She is a very sensitive girl and has been taking it very hard. She has tried to keep straight and her failure is what troubles her . . . She is quite young and has never been on her own responsibility before, which makes it doubly hard for her. Her mother is Mrs. Joslyn Gage. I think I told you about her.

This was the real crux of the issue. The young men of Cornell knew exactly who Maud's mother was and what her positions were. As the daughter of the notorious activist Matilda Joslyn Gage, Maud was open to a much larger set of strife than the other girls. Like most men of the time, the Cornell boys were split on the matter of women's rights: about half thought it was a joke, a grand opportunity for ridicule, and the other half thought it was a menace, a threat that needed to be stamped out. Maud wasn't prepared for this treatment and was deeply hurt by it. Tales from these troubled times seemed to shape the story that Maud would help bring about, as years later L. Frank Baum would re-create a scenario of a lively, capable girl who finds herself in an often hostile world. But he bestowed upon the girl a mythical form of protection. "No one will dare injure a person who has been kissed by the Witch of the North," he wrote.

At Cornell, Maud would be facing some determined young men, with no one to look out for her. And when the boys traded tales about girls on campus, it became a competition of sorts, a rivalry over who could turn the nastiest insults into poetry. As one fraternity drinking song went:

> I'm glad all the girls are not like Cornell women.
> They're ugly as sin and there's no good within 'em.
> The coed leads a wretched life,
> She eats potatoes with a knife.

Other songs suggested that the lively girls were the easy girls, that they were the ones who would invite you up to their room, or better yet, to one of the many empty rooms in Sage College, to have a go at it. One song was called "The Sage Maidens":

> I built me a house on the campus so high,
> and looked at the Co-eds as they did pass by . . .
> "Go way young man and leave me alone,
> For I am a Sage maiden a long way from home,
> Go away young man and come another day,
> When Pa Kinney's out and the Matron's away."

The talk about Maud Gage grew worse in a hurry. At the height of the ridicule, someone slipped a nasty limerick into the widely read humor column of the *Cornell Sun*, and it seemed to be a direct attack on Maud as a stand-in for her infamous mother:

> There is a gay maiden at Sage,
> Who flies into a terrible rage
> If one says in a crowd,
> In a tone a bit loud,
> "Matilda, may I ask your age?"

Maud's reaction to the hazing was severe. "I am alarmed for the future Freshman girls, if one out of every class has to suffer what Miss Gage has suffered in the last two days," remarked Jessie. "You never saw a girl change so; the boys must have noticed it. She cried almost all of the first night and Tuesday morning looked as if she had gotten up from a sick bed. She has partially gotten over it but it will be a long while before she is feeling herself again." The situation grew so out of hand that Jessie appealed to her friend Charlie Thorp. "You may think that this is a very little thing to feel badly over, but it is not," Jessie confided to her mother. "Charlie says the boys take it as a great joke. He thought it was terrible and has promised to do all he can. The boys try to make it as hard as they can for a girl here. A girl who is the least lively and can scarcely repress her life has no peace at all."

On an elite college campus in the middle of the most socially progressive area of the country, one might think that women's rights would get a fair hearing. Yet most of the time the obvious questions were conveniently skirted. On the eve of the 1880 U.S. presidential election between James Garfield and Winfield Hancock, the all-male editorial board of the *Cornell Sun* simply argued that the university should not hold classes that day: "A great many students will go home to vote, and in doing so, in exercising the highest right and duty of citizenship, they should have no obstacles placed in their path." That their female classmates couldn't vote at all remained unmentioned.

Still, it wasn't OK to be downright cruel to the coeds. The very same editors of the paper believed that it was mean for men to submit phony class election tickets just to poke fun at girls like Maud. "The excuse that the mock ticket was gotten up merely to create a laugh is of very little avail," a front-page editorial admonished, "for the authors of the ticket would doubtless resent any indignity if offered to one of their own kin. There is not the slightest reason . . . to hold the ladies up to ridicule. They have neither sought nor do they aspire to class politics, but have left politics to the more experienced sex. Let mock tickets be a thing of the past. They certainly do not show a very high order of wit."

For Maud, the entire class marshal episode was not easily forgotten, and there was little doubt that she was left with emotional scars that may have indeed changed her outlook on Cornell men in particular and what it would take to make her way in a man's world in general. Maud simply did not have the thick skin of her mother, and now that this was clear to her, how would she ever be able to knock down enough barriers to one day become what her mother expected her to be?

On Saturday evening, February 26, 1881, the girls of Sage College would be treated to a special lecture. Matilda Joslyn Gage herself was scheduled to arrive on campus to speak about equality. This was, of course, a recipe for trouble. Maud's mother had been causing a stir on campus even before the arrival of Maud, as she had personally petitioned Ezra Cornell, the university's founder, to open up the campus to females, following the example of Oberlin and a couple of other colleges out West. This was done over the vigorous objections of some students and faculty members, and at least one prominent professor resigned over the issue, declaring that Cornell "would sink at once from the rank of a University to that of an Oberlin or a high school." One campus publication called Mrs. Gage and her cohorts the "the Women's Rights monomaniacs."

But the fifty-four-year-old agitator had long grown accustomed to being called all sorts of wicked things. She took it in stride because she had studied history. Sometimes she wore the worst insults as badges of honor. "Those condemned as sorcerers and witches, as 'heretics,' were in reality the most advanced thinkers of their ages," she wrote. Mrs. Gage was now finishing up the first of a series of monumental books that she was coauthoring with Elizabeth Cady Stanton and Susan Brownell Anthony. A chronicle of women's struggle for basic human rights throughout the centuries, *History of Woman Suffrage*, volume 1, would be filled with reports on the progress of the movement to date.

The book paralleled Matilda's own life at the leading edge of what a female could be. She grew up in a quiet town north of Syracuse, as the only child of the town's only physician, Dr. Hezekiah Joslyn, and his wife, Helen Leslie, a lady of exceptional taste who decorated their home with fine furniture. They gave Matilda an unusual middle name, Electra. In Greek mythology Electra is the goddess of strength and power and the name means "bright one." This name appealed especially to Dr. Joslyn, who was a bona fide freethinker, in the tradition of the Buddha, who taught that wisdom can come only through one's own life experience, not from accepting the doctrine or dogma of others. "Do not go upon what has been acquired by repeated hearing," said the Buddha. In seventeenth-century Europe, freethinkers were the ones who stood in opposition not necessarily to religion but to Church power and authority—demanding the end of the notorious medieval witch-hunts. Many of the men who founded the United States and signed the Declaration of Independence also called themselves freethinkers.

Dr. Joslyn was a staunch abolitionist who turned his own home into one of the earliest outposts of the Underground Railroad. He home-schooled his daughter in Greek, mathematics, and physiology and wished that she would one day too become a doctor. Yet he didn't force his views upon her. Above all she was to think for herself but at the same time be aware of the danger of doing so. At age fifteen Matilda set off for the Clinton Liberal Institute, a small coed prep school that was producing an impressive array of thought leaders, including Clara Barton, who would establish the American Red Cross; Leland Stanford, who would found a great university; and Grover Cleveland, the only U.S. president to be elected to two nonconsecutive terms. Conceived by a branch of the Universalist Church, which believed in universal salvation and denied the existence of hell, the school sought to provide an education free of religious dogma. Matilda gained a well-rounded education in the liberal arts during her three years there.

Despite her education and background, Matilda took on a traditional life, getting married at the age of eighteen to Henry Hill Gage, a merchant eight years her senior who proved his commitment to social justice by building a hospital for unwelcome immigrants stricken with "ship fever"—and then rebuilt it after townsfolk burned it down in anger. Unfortunately Henry caught a strain of the disease, also known as typhus, which for him went in and out of remission. He and Matilda ended up settling in Fayetteville, where they would raise their four children. Henry's dry goods store prospered, in part because of its smart location by the docks of the feeder canal that led to the great Erie. Three of their children—one boy, Thomas Clarkson, and two girls, Helen Leslie and Julia Louise—were born in the 1840s, whereas

Maud didn't arrive until 1861, when Mrs. Gage was already thirty-five, as if she considered this last daughter to be her gift to the future.

Matilda's own freethinking only grew while she raised her children. Haunted by injustice, she was intolerant of an America that she believed was failing to live up to the ideals expressed in the Declaration of Independence, which stressed liberty for all. The way she saw it, universal freedom was just a matter of time and diligence, as history appeared to be a rational process in which progress toward liberty and justice was steadily achieved. "The true religion believes in . . . letting the oppressed go," Matilda wrote. As such, she saw the women's movement as part of the same arc of progress that began with the Renaissance and the Enlightenment. So long as women marched forward together and avoided becoming overly emotional damsels, they would soon win what was theirs.

All that had been standing in the way for centuries were the powers that be, the Church and the State. "Do not let the church or the state . . . govern your thought or dictate your judgment," she wrote. Driven by her rage at these institutions, Matilda decided early in life to get involved in a newly organizing movement. Unable to travel the sixty miles and leave her young children at home, she did not attend the inaugural National Women's Rights Convention in Seneca Falls of 1848. But by 1852, when the movement's third convention came to city hall in Syracuse, not only did she attend and meet future cohorts such as Susan B. Anthony, but she was now ready to speak her own mind. At age twenty-six she was the youngest woman on the platform and nervously trembling "with a palpitating heart" as she approached the podium to address a crowd of two thousand people. She spoke softly—some complained too softly to hear—but she seemed to carry a big stick. "There will be a long moral warfare before the citadel yields," she proclaimed. "In the meantime, let us take possession of the outposts. Fear not any attempt to frown down the revolution."

Her softly spoken fighting words caught the attention of the enemies of the movement, and she soon found herself locked in a war of words with religious leaders in various local newspapers. A local minister named Reverend Byron Sunderland called the convention "satanic." According to one of Sunderland's favorite proverbs, "a woman that feareth the Lord, she shall be praised." Another preacher called these women "infidels."

Curiously, the early leaders were not mocked so much for their ideas as for how they dressed. Special ridicule was reserved for the outfit of an activist named Amelia Bloomer, who sported a short tunic-like dress worn over trousers, a getup that became known as bloomers. "While the feminine propagandists of women's rights confined themselves to the exhibit of short petticoats," said the *Albany Register,* "the people were disposed to be amused by them, as they are by the wit of the clown at the circus. But the joke is becoming stale." Mrs. Gage, however, didn't wear bloomers. She was known for an appearance that was both feminine and stylish. "She is a medium-sized and lady-like looking woman," wrote a reporter, "dressed in tasty plaid silk, with two flounces," flared colorful ruffles worn around the waist.

Women's issues were still simmering when the other civil rights issue of the day turned into a great conflagration. Lincoln was forced to sell the war as an effort to preserve the Union, not abolish slavery, but the leaders of the women's movement saw right through his pitch. They recognized only one ideal: universal emancipation. Once the Civil War was won by the North and the Union was preserved, blacks would be enfranchised as voting citizens, and women would naturally gain the same rights. Such progress only made logical sense. To advance this ideal, Matilda joined the Women's Loyal National League, which was organized by Stanton and Anthony, and she worked to collect signatures for a petition pledging support of the war *only* if its aim was to abolish slavery. In 1862 Matilda was honored by a regiment of Fayetteville soldiers when she was asked to speak and present the American flag at their marching-off ceremony. "There can be no permanent peace," she declared, "until the cause of the war is destroyed. And what caused the war? Slavery! And nothing else."

After the bloodiest war in American history was over, after victory for the North was in hand, and after slavery was abolished, the leaders of the women's rights movement were promptly betrayed. Along with white men, the black men who pushed for changes in the Constitution conspired to cut off all funding for any efforts to win the vote for women. The Fourteenth Amendment, which protected the citizenship of black men, specifically defined *citizens* as "male," laying the groundwork for the Fifteenth Amendment, which guaranteed black men, as citizens, the right to vote. Women were now further behind than they had been when their movement started.

In response, a core of leaders banded together to form the National Woman Suffrage Association with Stanton as president, Anthony as the corresponding secretary, and Matilda Gage serving as chairman of the executive committee. Matilda wrote articles for the *Revolution*, the group's newsletter, showcasing her venomous logic. The flash point of the movement happened when Susan B. Anthony was arrested and thrown in jail for voting on Election Day of 1872, when President Grant sought a second term. Matilda came immediately to the aid of her friend and helped her get through the trial in U.S. Circuit Court in a town near Rochester. The judge, whom Matilda later described as "a small-brained, pale-faced, prim-looking man," refused to let the jury decide the case and convicted Miss Anthony all by himself. "With remarkable forethought," marveled Matilda, "he had penned his decision before hearing [the case]."

The showdown in court made Susan B. Anthony into a household name and brought enormous sympathy to the cause of passing a "Susan B. Anthony Amendment." Momentum for the cause was still building in 1876, when it was time for the Centennial Exhibition in Philadelphia, a spectacular celebration of the hundredth anniversary of the Declaration of Independence which brought together one out of every three Americans. Women's rights activists made a formal request to President Grant to present a document at the opening ceremony. But the request was denied. That, of course, wouldn't stop the ladies. During the ceremony Matilda Gage, along with Anthony and three other leaders of the movement, lurked just behind the press section, waiting for the right moment to strike. When a great-grandson of one of the original signers finished a reading from the Declaration and the program hit an emotional climax, Mrs. Gage clutched a three-foot-long scroll, stood up, and marched boldly behind Anthony toward the podium, through the cheering and confused crowd of 150,000 people.

What happened next would become an indelible scene in American history: Matilda passed the document to Susan, who then placed it with a flourish into the hands of the master of ceremonies, Vice President Thomas Ferry, as she announced, "We present to you this Declaration of Rights of the Women Citizens of the United States." Before the guards could catch them, the women scattered printed copies of their declaration about the crowd and dashed away as people began to read the words:

> The women of the United States, denied for one hundred years the only means of self-government—the ballot—are political slaves, with greater cause for discontent, rebellion and revolution, than the men of 1776 . . . We ask justice, we ask equality, we ask that all the civil and political rights that belong to citizens of the United States be guaranteed to us and our daughters forever.

After contriving this dramatic moment, the women decided that it was time to record their historic advancement in a book. Anthony, not much of a writer herself, believed the work could be done in a matter of months. But the process of recording the history of the women's movement was such a mammoth undertaking that it turned into a decade-long project. Most of the labor was split between Stanton and Gage, who together finished the first volume of *History of Woman Suffrage* in time for publication in 1881. Mrs. Gage was now visiting Cornell to give the coed audience a preview of what this important book would say.

It wasn't unusual for speakers of interest to appear in the parlor at Sage. A recent guest had been Amos Bronson Alcott, the eighty-year-old father of *Little Women* author Louisa May Alcott. "I have actually heard that at some of the co-educational colleges"—Mr. Alcott winked—". . . the girls are as bright as the boys." Sitting in an easy chair, distinguished by his long, bushy sideburns, he spoke of the inspiration received from his daughters as well as his Massachusetts friends—the wise Ralph Waldo Emerson, the reflective Henry David Thoreau, the reticent Nathaniel Hawthorne, as well as pioneering journalist Margaret Fuller—all of whom joined with him to establish a new school of thought known as transcendentalism, based around the belief that one's spirituality transcends the material world and can be found only through one's own experience, not through adherence to dogma. The *Cornell Sun* filled two issues of the paper with Alcott's talk.

This next event was a little different, as the speaker was so closely related to one of the girls. Maud naturally would be quite anxious about having her mother's brand of political fireworks on display in front of all her friends. A speech by Matilda Joslyn Gage had all the subtlety of being beat about the head and neck with a broomstick. The campus newspaper politely urged all to attend: "Mrs. Matilda Joslyn Gage is one of the most conspicuous advocates of the political emancipation of women." But at the same time the editorial writer slighted the subject of her talk, deeming it fanciful, not unlike the subject of travel by air. "The question [of women's rights] itself is one of very great importance; a political issue, if not of the present, certainly of the future."

For her appearance at Sage College, Mrs. Gage probably wore one of her dresses of black silk and velvet and a high angular hat. She had a striking appearance, "a grand looking woman, tall and queenly, with a silver crown of hair." When she was confronted by an idea she didn't like, her chin grew sharp and her gaze grew severe enough to cut anyone down to size. After she acknowledged what an unusual pleasure it was for her to speak before this group, she most likely lapsed into her standard lecture, and once Mrs. Gage got herself going, there was no stopping her soaring rhetoric. "No rebellion has been of like importance with that of Women against the tyranny of Church and State," she once proclaimed. "The progress of our movement will overthrow every existing form of these institutions; its end will be a regenerated world."

"Her discourse was well received," noted the *Cornell Sun*, but the campus newspaper ignored the content of the speech itself. In contrast to Mr. Alcott's talk, the newspaper didn't print a single world of it. What's more, her lecture very likely didn't change many minds, as the tone may have been too harsh for girls who were in the everyday trenches of sexual politics, trying to compromise and get along with young men who were feverishly courting and cajoling them during nearly all waking hours. The hard-to-accept truth was that these were society girls from traditional, religious families who were mostly neutral about women's rights. Sage College was perhaps the country's biggest beneficiary of the progress of the women's movement to date. Ironically, that seemed to make it a hotbed of social rest.

"Mrs. Gage, Maud's mother, lectured here on Women's rights last night," Jessie wrote home. "You remember that I told you she was a member of the Woman Suffrage Association." That Jessie didn't venture any opinion whatsoever on Mrs. Gage's talk is telling, especially since her letters were often filled with her detailed comments on the sermons of ministers and preachers who spoke at churches on or around campus. "Last Sunday, Rev. Bridgman (Baptist) preached and took the people by storm," she once wrote, telling her parents how listeners could barely contain themselves in their seats, as they "felt like rising and screaming 'Glory Hallelujah!'" There was no such reaction to Mrs. Gage and her radical idea that women deserved rights equal to those of men.

After the speech by her mother in her very own dormitory, life on campus seemed to grow lonelier for Maud. Soon, for instance, Miss Boulton and Miss Baum became deeply involved in the idea of starting a chapter of Kappa Alpha Theta, an all-female "secret society," thus becoming founding members of the first sorority on an Ivy League campus. Maud apparently was not invited to join, perhaps because one or more of the other girls objected to her. Either that, or she was invited but declined. Jessie and Josie also joined the newly formed Lawn Tennis Club for young ladies. Maud again sat out.

Maud did distinguish herself as the toastmaster at the annual banquet for the ladies of the freshman class. She induced a spell of hilarity when she proposed the official toast to "The Boys of '84," citing a quote: "Young men *think* old men fools. But old men *know* young men to be so." She also attended one of the year's biggest social events, the Bal Masque, wearing one of the most noticeable costumes, that of a tambourine girl. If her costume was anything like the smiling, dancing Tambourine Girl portrayed in the eighteenth-century John Hoppner painting, Maud wore sandals, a bright white blouse, and a skirt of flowing silk, with a broad cloth belt. She would have been waving and whacking a giant tambourine above her head.

By her sophomore year Maud was pretty much a loner. Many of the other girls were quite busy socially, especially the ones who joined

Kappa Alpha Theta and who proudly wore their gold pledge pins at all times. As part of their initiation, those girls learned special secrets that they swore they couldn't divulge. Of course, the boys who pledged fraternities had secrets of their own. Members of Alpha Delta Phi and Psi Upsilon would often come calling on the Theta girls just to talk about what they couldn't talk about. Few young men, if any, came calling on Maud. She was at least as smart and attractive as the other chicks of the Hen House, yet it was becoming clear that she had been deemed undesirable.

4

Heart of a Tin Man

The actor and playwright
at age twenty-six

◆

"I soon grew to love her with all my heart. She, on her part, promised to marry me as soon as I could earn enough money to build a better house for her . . . But the girl lived with an old woman who did not want her to marry anyone."

— THE TIN WOODMAN

FOR THE THANKSGIVING WEEKEND Maud Gage traveled home to her family in Fayetteville, and Josie Baum headed back to Syracuse. Cornell was too far away from Jessie Boulton's home in Pennsylvania to make the four-day stay there worth the trip, so she had accepted an invitation from Josie to spend the holiday with her. The three Cornell coeds likely rode the northbound train together, giving them the chance for an extended chat away from everyone else at school. But once their train arrived, Maud would go her separate way.

Josie's parents, Dr. Adam Clarke Baum and his wife, Josephine, loved to entertain and in fact had invited several guests to spend Thanksgiving with them in their elegant home at 163 West Onondaga Street. After a solemn prayer of thanks for the bountiful harvest, spirited conversation was in order. With such a large group around the table, the talk likely bounced around topics of interest to everyone. Dr. Baum was a jovial sort, and as a former surgeon he would have been inclined to bring up the outrageous quote being reported by the papers, the one uttered by Charles Guiteau, who was on trial for assassinating President Garfield a few months earlier. "The doctors killed Garfield," proclaimed Guiteau. "I just shot him."

As many in America by now knew, Guiteau was a deranged former member of the Oneida Community, the bizarre spiritual cult located about thirty miles east of Syracuse. Guiteau believed that a pamphlet he wrote helped elect Garfield. When Garfield failed to respond to his request for an ambassadorship, Guiteau decided that the Lord wanted "the ungrateful president" dead. Seeking his revenge, he stalked the president boarding a train in Washington, but the two bullets he fired from his gun only wounded Garfield, who was attended by doctors for the next eleven weeks before passing away. Many believed that the president indeed received shoddy medical care, giving Guiteau's absurdism a ring of truth.

The Oneida Community, with its belief in "group marriage," certainly had many strange followers, but it wasn't considered any stranger than any of a dozen other spiritual movements that sprouted in this part of New York State during the century. There were the Millerites of Low Hampton, who preached for years that the Second Coming would occur on October 22, 1844. Soon after it didn't, they sheepishly disbanded. There were the Fox sisters of Hydesville, who originated the practice of the spiritual séance. They invented a new way to communicate with the dead, by asking the spirits multiple-choice questions in a darkened room and waiting to hear raps and taps. There were the Mormons, a movement that began in Palmyra with a tale of Golden Plates buried in a hillside. Strong local opposition, however, drove the sect westward. Rochester hosted regular meetings of the Theosophical Society, which adhered to a new amalgam of Hinduism, Buddhism, and electromagnetism. There was the Niskayuna Community, a local offshoot of the nonprocreating Shakers. They soon died out. Upstate New York was also a prime recruiting ground for everyone from utopian visionaries to revivalist preachers who spoke of "the second great awakening," at least until it was time to start a "third great awakening." All this spiritual fervor concentrated in one area caused one historian to label it the "Burned-over District," joking that there was no more fuel, in terms of souls, left to consume, or convert.

The mere mention of spirituality and séances could have triggered a personal story for the Thanksgiving dinner table, a tale that Jessie Boulton called "dreadfully wicked" but "lots of fun." The episode happened at Sage College the previous Halloween. It was close to midnight on October 31 when nine of the girls crowded into a darkened dorm room to conduct their version of a séance. As most séances concerned communication from the Great Beyond, the intrepid girls of Sage wanted the spirits to give them information they could use, such as who among them would get married, to whom, and when.

As the séance began, the girls swore they felt the table tip, yet none of them was tipping it. That confirmed the presence of those from "the other side." The girls then asked the spirits different questions, which were answered by a series of raps on the table. The raps indicated that Jessie would be married in seven years to a man from the class of '82 whose name began with an M, and they were to have one child. Everyone there knew that Jessie was in love with Charlie Thorp, so this didn't seem to make sense. But Jessie revealed that Charlie's middle name was Monroe, so the spirits seemed quite prescient indeed.

The answers to Josie Baum's questions were the most curious. The spirits told her that she was to have two husbands and twelve children. Josie ventured to ask the initial letter of her first husband's name, and she repeated the alphabet until she came to T, when the girls heard a rap. There indeed was a man with the last name of Tracy in the class of '80 whom Josie had been dating. Josie then asked the date of her marriage. It was to be the thirty-first of May, 1885. But she would divorce him and marry again. The spirits spelled out the whole name this time—Farnaham. Josie then asked about her father, Dr. Baum. Would he face difficulty? Yes, said the spirits. Sickness? No, said the spirits. Difficulty in business? Yes, said the spirits.

Before Dr. Baum could jump in and regale everyone with tales from the oil patch, this may have been an opportune time for his wife, Josephine, to pick up on the subject of men and marriage. Josephine was a bit of a busybody, and this is probably when she learned about Josie's unusual roommate, Maud, and proceeded to hatch the plan to introduce this girl to her nephew Frank.

The matchmaking attempt took place on a white Christmas Eve. Syracuse has always held the distinction of being one of America's snowiest cities, averaging more than an inch of snowfall for every winter's day, and this season was looking like no exception. Nevertheless, there Frank was, all bundled up while driving his horse and buggy alone through the falling powder in the fading afternoon light.

For Frank, the most direct way from Rose Lawn to his sister Hattie's house would have been via the route of the old Plank Road. But nowadays Plank Road was in the process of being dismantled. Frank undoubtedly knew why. The planks would get wet, then rot and wear away, and the labor cost of replacing the wood was increasing at a time when revenue from tolls was decreasing. Not only had the local economy headed south in the mid-1870s, but railroads were becoming an ever-cheaper way to ship goods, replacing canal traffic, thus reducing the economic need for this special road to the canal's shipping docks. By this time much of the road was gone, and no longer was there much of a need for the skilled woodmen nearby who could fashion the precise planks.

If the Plank Road had still been intact, Frank's five-mile trip into town would have been a brisk fifteen minutes. Now it might take him triple the time, mainly on mud and gravel blanketed by a layer of white. Since he could still see the road in his mind's eye, its absence may have evoked a certain sadness, a longing for his childhood. Perhaps the road's disappearance turned his thoughts to the local woodmen who used to supply the planks — only to be replaced by the steam-powered woodchopper, a metallic machine. "I was born the son of a woodman who chopped down trees in the forest and sold the wood for a living," Frank later wrote about how one of his famous characters came to be. "When I grew up, I too became a woodchopper." Since he was about to meet a girl with whom he had been matched, Frank would naturally be focusing on courtship, too. "I made up my mind that instead of living alone I would marry, so that I might not become lonely," Frank would one day write of the character that became the Tin Woodman.

Despite the inconvenience of traveling in the snow along this uneven path, Frank had been told in no uncertain terms that it would be worth his while to forge his way to his sister's house on this holy night. Hattie's stately home was located in one of the city's finer neighborhoods. The Italianate-style house was all decked out for the holiday, with windows and banisters that would be roped in pine-scented garlands. Frank was greeted warmly by his sister, who was ten years his senior. He was also close to his brother-in-law, William Neal. Frank would have dusted the snow from his hat and topcoat before handing them off to Hattie.

Frank already knew the plan. While Hattie was hosting and ushering the guests into the living room, his cousin Josie would serve as the real matchmaker, and it would be Josie's mother, his Aunt Josephine, who would undertake the official task. Frank had heard only the sketchiest details about this twenty-year-old college girl, Maud Gage, and for starters he didn't think too highly of colleges in general. Only a tiny fraction of high school graduates attended college, and Frank was among the many who saw them as elitist and frivolous. "You see," Frank once wrote, "in this country are a number of youths who do not like to work, and the college is an excellent place for them."

As Hattie invited her guests inside, to partake of food and drink, a semicircle of guests may have joined Frank in conversation, probably inquiring about the plays he was writing and where they were to be performed. Coming from a family of German heritage, Hattie would have kept the traditions alive. Since the name Baum means "tree," the *Tannenbaum* had a little extra meaning in the family. Hattie's Christmas tree was likely trimmed with homemade cookies, sugarplums, and tin cutout dolls, all set aglow by white candles. She would have been preparing the traditional German meal for Christmas Eve, roasted goose.

Across the room were Frank's cousin Josie and her parents. Spotting Maud sitting in a chair, Frank's eyes widened. She had dark, flowing hair that framed a porcelain face and mysterious brown eyes. Maud was every bit as pretty as Josie had promised. Aunt Josephine came over, took Maud by the arm, and escorted her over to Frank. Their initial exchange was a memorable one.

"Frank Baum," said his aunt, "I want you to know Maud Gage. I'm sure you will love her."

"Consider yourself loved, Miss Gage," quipped Frank.

"Thank you, Mr. Baum," Maud retorted. "That's a promise. Please see that you live up to it."

Something special was happening on this luminous evening. Two very unusual young people had been brought together by people who knew them both. This man of budding talent tended to live in invented worlds that were somewhat more interesting than the real one. This lonesome college coed had studied literature and come from a family known for independent thought and a commitment to social justice.

And so these two unique people were given the chance to meet under exceptionally favorable circumstances. Perhaps some sort of magic was at work, and it would be a shame if this chance was squandered, as such an encounter might not happen again. Travel and communication in those times were easier than ever before, yet still difficult. Good fortune was shifting to different parts of the country. Opportunity tended to take people away from their homes, perhaps for the rest of their lives. Accidents happened frequently. People got sick and died with little warning. Women were expected to marry young, and men got old far too fast. There was no way of telling whether they'd meet again, if ever. What's more, neither had the burden of their parents present on this occasion. They had the freedom to speak their hearts and minds.

Frank and Maud were unlikely to be coy about themselves or their situations. They may have come close to pouring themselves out to each other, exchanging thoughts about their fears and hopes and dreams for the future. They knew they'd be able to continue their conversations by writing letters in the coming months, while Maud was away again at college and Frank was back in the oil patch with his theater troupe. But letters were much more formal and less private. Letters had the danger of being read by others and surviving for generations. If Frank and Maud detected a spark on this evening, the time to start fanning the flames was here and now.

Following tradition, Hattie may have initiated a sing-along around the glowing tree, and among the top selections would have been the German folk song "O Tannenbaum." That would have reminded Maud and Josie of "The Evening Song," from Cornell, as that song was sung to the very same tune. As class toastmaster, Maud would have known all the words, which had been penned by a member of the class of 1880. As Maud's roommate, Josie, too, would know the song.

When the sun fades far away,
In the crimson of the west,
And the voices of the day
Murmur low and sink to rest.
Music with the twilight falls

O'er the dreamy lake and dell;
'Tis an echo from the walls
Of our own, our fair Cornell.

As they sang and talked and got to know each other over dinner, their conversation and humor flowed freely and time got away from them. Frank was as impressed by Maud's confidence and intelligence as he was taken with her beauty, and Maud found Frank "very handsome and attractive," as she would write to a friend. Maud of course learned of Frank's ambitions as an actor and playwright—a clear warning to any young lady seeking to establish a proper home. Yet by the night's end Maud's interest was clear, as was Frank's. But according to the strict courtship etiquette of the day, he could not initiate the next encounter.

That task fell to the young lady's mother, who, at her discretion, could request a "call" to her home. She would typically send word by way of the party who introduced the two. The suitor would then pay a visit to the lady's home for refreshments and conversation, the entire encounter taking place under the mother's watchful eye. This protocol could be nerve-racking for any young man wishing to make a good impression, but it would be particularly grueling for the gentleman who wished to marry Maud Gage. Her mother, Matilda Joslyn Gage, was "argumentative" and known for her ability to "detect and register any masculine deficiencies with phenomenal accuracy." Whether deserved or not, people took her for an avid man hater.

In any case, Maud had to be back at college for the winter term, which was to begin January 3, 1882. That didn't give her time to arrange another meeting with Frank beforehand, and she wouldn't be returning home again until the break between terms, during the last week of March. Frank made it his business to be at Rose Lawn then, and when the request for his call arrived, as he hoped it would, Frank responded instantly.

This was his first chance to make the eight-mile ride to Maud's home. When he arrived at the Gage residence in his horse and buggy to try to take the courtship to the next stage, he must have been impressed by the pale yellow Greek Revival house at 210 East Genesee

Street looking out on the main thoroughfare of Fayetteville, with its four massive pillars and its emerald green shutters. The home was located kitty-cornered to the house where the twice-future president, Cleveland, had grown up. Frank may also have heard that it had been the first home in the county to feature indoor plumbing. He may also have heard that it was a secret nest for radical activities. In the years before the Civil War, this had been the local stop on the Underground Railroad. Escaped slaves on their way to freedom would often arrive for a hot meal. To elude the law, the fugitives would spend the night holed up in a crawlspace underneath the kitchen floorboards.

After Appomattox the Gage house was the site of dozens of meetings for those who believed in another outlaw cause: women's rights. This was where a radical newspaper called the *National Citizen and Ballot Box* was conceived and edited, a publication that proclaimed as its goal to "revolutionize the country, striving to make it live up to its fundamental principles." In the guest bedroom upstairs, Susan B. Anthony had carved her initials in a windowpane.

Frank must have been nervous and excited as he approached the front door and was greeted by Maud and welcomed inside. Both would have been dressed quite formally on this occasion, Frank in a jacket and tie and Maud in a favorite dress. They would be having tea in the front parlor, which was lit by oil lamp and featured windows with thick curtains. A floral pattern adorned the carpet, and the wallpaper was threaded with pale magenta, gold, and orange. There were plenty of comfortable seats, including a red velvet rocking chair and a peach-colored sofa. A bookshelf sat up against one of the walls, and the fireplace would provide enough warmth on chilly evenings such as this. Shawls draped on the arm of the sofa were there for backup. In the middle of the room was something quite unique: a small wooden knickknack table that held a great horned owl. Densely feathered and expertly stuffed, the owl dug its claws into a wooden perch, making the statement that this was a room reserved for wisdom.

Before inviting Frank to sit down, Maud would have called her mother from the back parlor. Mrs. Matilda Joslyn Gage spent much of her time on her own perch, as the back room was her special space, reserved for reading, writing, and painting watercolors of flowers and landscapes. When she emerged, Frank would have noticed that both mother and daughter had similar features, most notably their plentiful hair and penetrating eyes. Each projected an extraordinary intelligence, and each struggled with a tightly wound temperament. Mrs. Gage might have apologized to Frank that her husband couldn't come down to greet him. Maud's father, Henry Gage, was largely immobilized from typhus, so it was very likely he was upstairs resting. But for Frank, meeting Mrs. Gage was paramount. Matilda clearly held the power here. She was a "woman of force," as a relative later described her. "She ruled her mild, gentle husband and her four children with a rod of iron."

Mrs. Gage had known vaguely about the Baum family for years. The old Plank Road began near her own childhood home in Cicero, and she once wrote an article that referred to her passing by Rose Lawn, commenting on a beautiful "house and extensive barns belonging to one of those fortunate few who made money in oil when that mania prevailed." She took note of the owner's name on the barn's roof "which naturally falls from the lips of the passer-by." But by now she probably had heard that family had since fallen on hard times.

She also would likely have heard the news that Frank's new stage play was scheduled to open in May at the Grand Opera House. Frank extended an invitation for the entire Gage family to attend. In congratulating him and expressing interest in seeing the play, she would have wanted to know what was next for him. This was a touchy subject, as Frank intended to tour the play as widely as possible. Yet he very well realized that few mothers would want their daughters associated with a touring actor. So he would emphasize that he was a playwright as well, that this was where he saw his future. Matilda knew a thing or two about writing, as she was a prolific writer and a published author herself. Yet her earnings from her work were negligible. She knew from experience how impossible it was to make much of a living as a writer.

With that Mrs. Gage retreated to her perch. From the back parlor she would monitor the young couple's conversation over tea. The topic of books would have been most appropriate for an occasion like this, and commenting on the morality of famous fictional characters was the proper way to reveal glimpses of oneself. As a student of English literature at Cornell, Maud must have been impressed by Frank's knowledge of Dickens and Thackeray, not to mention the entire scenes from Shakespeare he could recite from memory. A thespian, he could have gladly performed a selection as light entertainment. Maud could share her enthusiasm for American fiction, discussing favorite writers such as Hawthorne and Alcott. She might even have mentioned that she had seen Louisa May's father speak at Cornell. Both agreed that Mark Twain was probably the best writer of the day.

All the while Matilda's presence in the back parlor was palpable to the young couple, and it must have loomed even larger when Maud showed Frank a copy of the newly published *History of Woman Suffrage*, volume 1, the book her mother had coauthored with Elizabeth Cady Stanton and Susan B. Anthony. The book began with a scintillating essay by Mrs. Gage called "Preceding Causes" and launched into her overarching thesis "how in all periods of human development, thinking has been punished as a crime."

All this was new to Frank. He certainly wasn't against women's rights and indeed held some sympathy for the cause, yet he had never before been forced to give so much thought to it. If it were up to him, he would want to change the subject. He wanted to get to know the views of Maud a little better, not the ones of her mother. As Maud opened up and told Frank about her mostly negative experiences at Cornell, Frank must have been reminded of his own traumatic episode of being sent away to the Peekskill Military Academy as a boy, and he may have relayed bits of the story to her. Or he may have wanted to be honest with Maud about his health, telling her how he had been stricken by a bout of rheumatic fever as a child, which permanently weakened his heart and potentially shortened his expected lifespan.

This information would not have pleased Mrs. Gage. The military academy episode may have seemed like an indication that Frank's father was a typical aggression-minded man, or that Frank's mother was a compliant, religious-minded woman, the kind who tolerated male oppression. Family patterns like these, Mrs. Gage knew, tended to repeat themselves. On top of all that, he was a traveling actor—one with a weak heart, no less. Mrs. Gage saw nothing but poverty, oppression, and heartache coming out of this relationship for her favorite daughter. The more she learned about this suitor, the more Maud's mother was determined to stop any union. She wanted Maud to finish college and establish her career.

To Frank, Mrs. Gage represented the one impediment to his goal of winning his true love, so much so that memories of this time may have influenced the backstory of how the simple woodman became the Tin Woodman. The young man had fallen for a beautiful Munchkin girl, but he came up against the girl's old mother, who arranged for the Wicked Witch of the East to cast a spell on him, causing him to lose his arms and legs — and eventually his heart — in ax-chopping accidents. He kept going to a tinsmith to have his limbs and chest replaced by hollow tin parts. "I thought I had beaten the Wicked Witch then, and I worked harder than ever," Frank would write, "but I little knew how cruel my enemy could be. She thought of a new way to kill my love for the beautiful Munchkin maiden."

Whether Maud married Frank or someone else was not even the main point. For Mrs. Gage, the main concern was that Maud have control of her relationships and her future family. Mrs. Gage was firm on that, for it cut to the heart of one of her staunchest beliefs: that matriarchy was the natural state for humanity, as mother-rule was the way of ancient civilizations until men began using religion and government as clubs to beat women into submission. But to Mrs. Gage and her cohorts in the women's suffrage movement, the act of facing down opposition from men was a lesson in frustration, as men favored the opposite argument, that patriarchy was the God-given order of authority, that the male domination of the female was "the way the Lord meant it to be." In all the European societies from which most Americans descended, this was indeed how it was, as males had ruled every realm of life for centuries, from the home to the church to the marketplace to the government to the courtroom to the battlefield.

In response, feminists would often go back further into history, citing ancient matriarchal civilizations from the Fertile Crescent and the Far East, in which men held femininity sacred, worshiped the power of the goddess, and associated the female spirit with Mother Earth, giver of all life. The mythology, art, and iconography from these long-lost societies taught men to revere women, not denigrate them. There was one supreme deity, the Mother God, and she was at one with the Earth. She was known as Inana by the Sumerians, Ishtar by the Babylonians, Isis by the Egyptians, Anat by the Canaanites, and Aphrodite by the Greeks. Each of these cultures created remarkably similar stories that placed the goddess at the center of their spiritual lives. What exactly became of the ancient matriarchy is difficult to determine, as the men who wrote history tended to forget that these goddesses ever existed.

Searching for more concrete examples of the matriarchy closer to home, Mrs. Gage hit upon one of the central insights that would come to define her life. The sacredness of the feminine was indeed all around her all the time, in the form of the matriarchal societies of Native Americans. This was especially true in central New York State, where so many towns, lakes, rivers, and roads were named after the Native American societies that white Americans were displacing. Indeed, the lower Great Lakes region remained home to the Six Nations of the Iroquois Confederation: the Cayuga, the Mohawk, the Oneida, the Onondaga, the Seneca, and the Tuscarora. Collectively these six tribal nations called themselves by their Iroquois name: the Haudenosaunee, "the people of the longhouse," as they lived in giant log cabins up to a hundred feet long and twenty feet wide, each of them home to a group of families headed by the eldest woman.

Matilda studied this Native American culture with great intensity and even went so far as to befriend a number of local Iroquois matriarchs. She learned of the culture's own creation myth, in which the Sky Woman descends from the heavens to create the world. These supposedly backward tribal women became in her eyes the prime examples of the modern, liberated female for which feminist leaders like her had been searching. The Iroquois women dressed comfortably, led lives beyond the confines of the home, and didn't become pieces of property or give up all their rights when they entered into marriage. Marriage empowered them with greater rights and responsibilities.

Matilda wrote a series of articles, first published in the *New York Evening Post*, that described the Iroquois system of "matriarchate," or mother-rule, in which "the division of power between the sexes in this Indian republic was nearly equal." Matilda spelled out a series of differences between the two societies. In Iroquois culture, she noted, violence against women was rare and strictly punished, women took responsibility for farming while the men hunted, women could vote and hold key tribal positions and even veto a war, and the tribe's spirituality was deeply connected to the worship of Mother Earth. "The women and Mother Earth are one—givers of life," went an Iroquois saying. "We are her color, her flesh and her roots. Now our minds are one."

In European and American cultures it was precisely the opposite: physical violence against women was widespread and permitted by common law as a proper way for men to discipline their wives, women could not hold important positions or vote, women were rarely given roles outside the home, and God commanded men to conquer and dominate nature, not sanctify it.

Matilda agreed that the Founding Fathers of the United States created a brilliant document in the Constitution, and it was even said that some of the Founding Fathers themselves had studied the Iroquois system of self-government. Yet somehow, in the final draft, the signers ignored the famous plea to John Adams from his wife, Abigail, to "remember the ladies." Instead, the white men who crafted the Constitution modeled their view of women's rights after English common law. "England protects its hunting dogs far better than it protects the women and children of its working classes," wrote a miffed Matilda.

Mrs. Gage was in a near-constant state of fury over such issues, and she seemed to view her younger daughter as her last best hope for restoring the ancient balance of power. This belief, the lost ideal of the matriarchy, is exactly what Matilda wanted to hand down and bestow upon Maud. But first Maud must go on to become a woman of true accomplishment and independence. Clearly, this professional pretender would not be able to help her reach these goals. This Frank fellow could only spoil the plan.

5

Roadblock

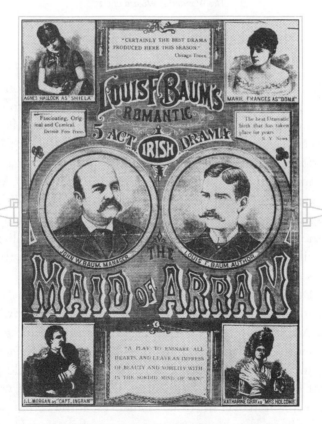

Advertisement for L. F. Baum's hit play, *The Maid of Arran*.
John W. Baum was his uncle and Katherine Gray his aunt.

They saw before them a great ditch that crossed the
road and divided the forest as far as they could see on
either side . . . The sides were so steep that none of
them could climb down, and for a moment it seemed
that their journey must end.

— L. FRANK BAUM,
The Wonderful Wizard of Oz

ANTICIPATION MOUNTED in the days leading up to the
hometown premiere of Frank's new production. At the
Grand Opera House of Syracuse, the play written by and
starring Louis F. Baum would be running for two nights, May 15 and
16, between engagements for a drama called *The Banker's Daughter*
and a performance of the San Francisco Minstrels. The *Syracuse Daily
Journal* announced "the sale of reserved seats for *The Maid of Arran* will
be opened at Zenner's Jewelry Store" for 75 cents each. With the arrival of spring, hope fluttered about the air. "The rain has laid the dust
finely," the newspaper noted. "The trees will soon be in foliage. Veg-
etation will fairly bloom." On the day of the premiere itself, the cherry
trees blossomed.

The Maid of Arran was trumpeted as a spectacle with "beautiful
stage settings, delightful music and an unsurpassed company," a show
featuring Mr. Baum opposite an attractive actress named Agnes Hal-
leck, who would play the title role of the Maid, short for *maiden*. The
cast also included Frank's aunt, Katherine Gray, who would play the
small part of the mother of his character. But Aunt Kate was really
there to keep watch over the troupe's finances, at the behest of Frank's
father, who knew that his son treated money like water. The production certainly did not skimp on advertising, and as a result the news-

paper was inclined to print many kind words about the playwright. "Mr. Baum has shown talent of no mean order," one article said. "Mr. Baum's many friends certainly wish him abundant success."

And so Frank could not have asked for a better set of circumstances. Ever since childhood he had wanted to be a writer, and that night he was performing his best material yet. Opening day in Syracuse also happened to be his birthday, his twenty-sixth. Frank, who had written the play as well as the score and all the songs in it, was hoping that this romantic melodrama would finally win him a career—as a playwright, as an actor, or as both. Success here would be the key to everything. If his future was going to change for the better, it would all begin that night.

On this fragrant spring evening, the crowd streamed through the triple doors of the stately six-story façade of the opera house. Located between East Genesee and East Fayette streets in the center of town, the Grand was designed as a replica of a European-style theater, with high ceilings, ornate balconies, and baroque trimmings—all illuminated by kerosene lamps and carbon arc lights. The audience was packed with miners and merchants, iron forgers and oil drillers, shopkeepers and their wives—in addition to Frank's friends and family. Given all the pressure, it would be understandable if Mr. Baum appeared to have a slight case of jitters backstage as he put the finishing touches on his costume—tight dark pants tucked into high boots, a matching jacket, a white shirt buttoned up to the collar, topped off by a light-colored fez.

Peering through the side curtain, Frank would have spotted the lovely Maud Gage, who made a special trip home from college to attend the opening. She was accompanied by her mother. Mrs. Gage brought with her a measure of skepticism, and the presence of the frightful feminist couldn't have calmed Frank's nerves, as she had a gaze so sharp it seemed to cut right through to one's soul. The very topic of the play was marriage and the relationship between husband and wife, a subject on which she had quite a number of her own opinions. Matilda Gage must have come to inspect the moral character of this Louis or Lyman or Frank or whatever his name was. What did her daughter see in this man?

As the curtain opened, the playwright took command of the stage, in the role of Hugh Holcomb, an artist from London who visits the island of Arran to paint a portrait of its romantic hilltop castle. It's there that he spots the lovely young Shiela, "a wild Irish rose," strolling by the shore. As Shiela sings the opening song, "The Legend of Castle Arran," Hugh is instantly smitten, and he asks her to pose for him.

"What?" says Shiela. "Put *me* in that beautiful picture?"

"Why not?" replies Hugh. "There is nothing in Arran more beautiful."

Later, after Shiela returns to the castle, Mr. Baum the actor makes Hugh's quest clear, in his baritone voice: "That girl has touched a chord in my heart, whose strain I have never heard before. She has the depth of the sea in her eyes, the music of the far off hills in her voice, and all the brightness and purity of the summer skies mirrored in her soul."

The people of Arran boast in their Irish brogues about being descended from a line of kings. Chief among these braggarts is Shiela's father, Con O'Mara, who sings about returning his family to the throne once again. So far, little about the plot would have appealed to Mrs. Gage, yet things got worse. During the play's signature song, "A Rollicking Irish Boy," one could imagine Matilda rolling her eyes during the lyric "There's just one lass, Who smiles when e're I pass, And makes my heart go bump'ty bump, A rollicking Irish lass." Mrs. Gage would not be amused by the cliché of the arrogant young male in hot pursuit of his object of desire. Neither would she be taken by the oversexed character of Oona, clad in a petticoat and sandals, who sings of lust and prances around the stage spouting lines such as "Ya can have a kiss, if ya can get it!" All this blarney simply didn't match Matilda's tastes.

As the play unfolds, Hugh wins over Shiela and soon takes her back with him to London. There he becomes embarrassed in proper company by Shiela's lack of manners, her thick brogue, and her unrefined outbursts. He insults, abuses, and offends his new wife to such a degree that she plots to leave him and return to Arran. Her departure is aided by a servant named Phadrig, a man who is sent by her father to check up on her. Once back in Arran, Shiela encounters Hugh's rival, Captain John Ingram, a ship commander who once courted her but lost out to Hugh.

Later, when Hugh runs into Ingram, the captain pretends to befriend the artist and convinces him to join an expedition at sea aboard his ship, the *Malabar*. But once he has Hugh on board under his command, the villain reveals his evil intentions: to frame Hugh on charges of mutiny and hang him from the *Malabar's* gallows. It's all part of Ingram's plan to return to Arran and claim Shiela for his own. The imprisoned Hugh holds out a sliver of hope, singing "Waiting for the Tide to Turn." It does, when Phadrig comes to the rescue, cutting Hugh loose from his shackles, all for the sake of Shiela. This sets Hugh free to journey back to Arran, wandering for three years while agonizing over the terrible way he treated Shiela and thinking of how he could win her back.

This plot twist may very well have appealed to Mrs. Gage, as it put the male lead in the unusual position of reflecting and repenting over the way he treated his wife. Perhaps it served as evidence that the playwright was sensitive to such matters. The play also put the wife in a position where she was calling the shots. After all, she was the one who broke off the relationship, and she was the one who would decide whether or not to take her husband back. This idea — that a woman could decide whether or not she wants to stay married — was an enlightened one. So perhaps Mrs. Gage was following with special attention whether Hugh could redeem himself in the eyes of Shiela. In the end, Shiela at the last possible second prevents her father from killing Hugh, and she takes her lost husband back in her arms as the curtain falls.

The Maid of Arran was enough of a hit to sell out its short Syracuse run and get signed up for an extensive tour. The *Syracuse Journal* gave the playwright a prophetic blessing: "Mr. Baum is a young man who has a decided taste for dramatic art, and it is probable that years and experience will clothe him with decided dramatic powers." However, the concept of objective, honest theater reviews was decades away. In those times, productions such as *Arran* that advertised in the newspaper got rave reviews and those that didn't advertise usually got poor reviews or none at all. Frank advertised.

Mrs. Gage wasn't one to be influenced by reviews anyway. She could form her own opinions just fine. In a letter to her son living in the Dakota Territory, she wrote that she "liked the Maid very much" and even went so far as to express pride that Mr. Baum's show would go on tour, including a stint in New York City. As a result, the performance seemed to remove at least one objection that Matilda Gage had to Frank's courtship of her daughter. She was no longer against Mr. Baum's entreaties simply because he was an actor or a playwright. Yet her main objection remained firmly in place. She did not want anything to disrupt Maud's studies in college. She still believed that marriage to a traveling man, especially now, would do her no good.

To his advantage, Frank was putting together a successful track record. After his show was well received in Syracuse, the company over the next five weeks toured the oil patch where the name Louis F. Baum was already known from prior productions. Reviews from around Pennsylvania and its border towns were spectacular, as newspaper ads were cheap there. "A more perfectly mounted and better enacted drama has not been placed on the boards for many a day," crowed the *Scranton Republican*. "At one moment the audience is in tears and at the very next they find themselves in uncontrollable laughter." The *Elmira Sunday Tidings* called it "a bright sparkling drama, abounding in catching musical numbers and original scenic effect. The ship scene, a full-rigged man-of-war, is . . . novel . . . attractive." The play simply "pleased every one."

Indeed, this would become Frank Baum's ultimate aim in life, to create a story that pleased all. He tended to think in universal terms: a story would appeal to either everyone or no one. And if it worked, the storyteller would be held in the highest regard, and that would be sheer bliss. But it's one thing to go over big in Scranton and Elmira, and quite another to make it in New York City, where audiences were far more discerning and advertising was far more expensive. And so it was seen as a major test when the *Maid of Arran* company rolled into the Windsor Theatre, which sat on the Bowery below Canal Street—for an entire week beginning June 24, including Wednesday and Saturday matinees. After the first night's performance, the *New York Mirror* gave perfunctory praise to Mr. Baum, whose acting was deemed "quiet and effective."

Then the critic proceeded to rip apart the rest of the cast. For instance, "Agnes Helleck [sic] is rather heavy for the part of Shiela," the paper noted. The part of "Captain Ingram was badly acted. C. W. Charles sang rather nervously. Frank Crane was the conventional Irish buffoon and poorly done at that. Mrs. Holcomb was overdone by Mrs. Katherine Gray." The reviewer also had some notes on the script. "The play can be much improved. The last act should have double the strength. The Irish agony over the whisky bottle in the first act should be cut out. That sort of stage business was long ago relegated to the variety halls." The good news was that theatergoers didn't seem to be bothered by any of this, as the very same newspaper critic had to admit: "*The Maid of Arran* was enthusiastically received by the large audience. Judging from the hearty reception Monday night, it will have a successful week at the Windsor."

This was not good enough for Frank Baum. He not only had to please the crowd, he had to please the reviewers as well, especially in New York. He enjoyed the energy of the city so much that he told Maud he someday might want to live there. He wanted his show to be worthy of New York. But in wanting this he had to make a trade-off. First of all, replacing cast members who were deemed subpar would undoubtedly cause bad blood. What's more, replacing them with more acclaimed New York actors would cost a lot more money. Worse, the one cast member who was almost always singled out by critics for overacting was his beloved aunt Katherine. How could he let her go, and if he did fire her, who would manage the books?

Riding high on all his accolades, Frank could not stop himself. The production would be going on summer break anyway, as it was too hot to travel by train then. This would be the best time to tell certain cast members that they wouldn't be returning for the next season, and that included Aunt Kate. Frank proceeded to hire a professional tour manager named John Moak, who would help find top performers and handle future bookings. Apparently, when Frank told his father about this, he was concerned enough to insist on installing another trusted family member to overlook the money. Benjamin Baum had plenty of siblings, and so he picked his younger brother, John Wesley Baum, age forty-seven, a former banker, to take over the finances.

New deals were reported: "Frank Aiken and Genevieve Rogers have concluded negotiations with John W. Baum, manager of the *Maid of Arran* company, and will this coming season appear as Capt. John Ingram and Oona in that drama. The parts have been greatly improved by Louis F. Baum, the author, and it is expected that these changes will insure the drama even greater success." With things looking so sunny career-wise, this would be the most opportune time for Frank to ask for Maud's hand. Soon after Maud returned home from her sophomore year at Cornell, the courtship picked up where it had left off. One evening that summer, Frank proposed right in the front parlor, and Maud accepted immediately and enthusiastically, though perhaps with some dread of her mother's reaction. Mrs. Gage, predictably, was vehemently against the union: "I will not have my daughter be a darned fool and marry an actor who is on the road most of the time, jumping from town to town on one night stands, and with an uncertain future." Frank may have stepped in to assure Mrs. Gage that he had ambitions beyond acting, that he would make a proper home.

But it would be Maud's words, not Frank's, that would carry the most weight. For Maud was educated in her mother's brand of feminism, and she was not about to accommodate her will to anyone, not even her mother. "All right Mother," Maud retorted, "if you feel that way about it . . . goodbye!" She and Frank would elope, she said, with or without her permission.

At this Mrs. Gage let out a piercing laugh. Maud caught it, too, joining in on the laughter. Mrs. Gage had signaled defeat, as Maud had put her in an impossible position. Matilda firmly believed that women should have freedom of choice in all matters. Indeed, she had fought for just that right for the past thirty years. She had been taught by her father to think and act for herself, and she had taught her daughter the same. But she also felt very strongly that Frank was the wrong man for Maud, and that staying in college was best. Torn between her conflicting sets of ideals, Mrs. Gage was forced to give in to her daughter's will and consent to the marriage.

Yet one obstacle to the union remained. Local churches wouldn't have any offspring of Matilda Gage getting married on their premises — especially not if Matilda herself were in attendance. Mrs. Gage had famously denounced the Church for its systematic persecution of women throughout the centuries, tracing this mistreatment back to the biblical story of Eve who commits the "original sin" in the Garden of Eden. In attacking the tale of Eve tasting the forbidden fruit again and again, Mrs. Gage alienated local clergy. "It is dogma that has wrecked true religion," Matilda declared, "it is dogma that has crushed humanity; it is dogma that has inculcated the doctrine of original sin; that has degraded womanhood; that has represented divinity as possessing every evil attribute."

In her view the ancient way of the matriarchy was wiped away by this tale in which Eve disobeys God and listens to a serpent who tempts her into taking a bite of the apple. Worse, Eve persuades Adam to taste it as well. In the classical biblical view, Eve alone is thus responsible for bringing evil into the world and for the downfall of humanity. Based on Eve's wickedness, God curses women with the anguish of pregnancy and declares thenceforth that the husband shall dominate the wife. Many interpreters of the Bible see this concept of original sin as the foundation of Christianity, for the resulting downfall of mankind in Eden created the need for the Savior. And by casting the serpent as an evil incarnation of Mother Nature, the story also rejects the Goddess, the principal divinity of the ancient world. "In other words, there is a historical rejection of the Mother Goddess implied in the story of the Garden of Eden," says mythologist Joseph Campbell. "Our fall in the Garden sees nature as corrupt, and that myth corrupts the whole world for us. Every spontaneous act is seen as sinful and must not be yielded to."

It would be Maud's father, Henry, a member of the Fayetteville Baptist Church, who would ultimately save the day for the newly engaged couple. In addition to being compliant to his wife's demands, Henry was hopelessly agreeable to everyone, including the local Baptist minister, W. H. Hawley. Henry managed to convince Pastor Hawley to come marry the couple at the Gage home.

Mrs. Gage could live with this arrangement, as long as Maud also agreed to stay in college. But that was not to be. Not only would Maud drop out of Cornell, but she was planning to join the national tour of Frank's play sometime after the wedding, which was set for November. In the meantime Maud would spend the next few months in Fayetteville, sending out invitations and making arrangements for the big day while Frank got his show back on the road. Over the summer Maud also worked on her embroidery, creating a much more elegant version of Frank's costume. A photograph shows "Louis F. Baum" sporting a new black coat trimmed at the lapels and cuffs with a bright pattern of embroidered thistle and clovers. Topping it off was a round hat sporting matching Irish flowers.

With its newly revamped cast, flashier threads, and a much higher payroll, the theater troupe kicked off the next season in style on August 21, with a successful stint of ten days in Toronto, at the Royal Opera House. The new management had new strategies for keeping the tour financially viable. John Moak's idea was to book more dates more closely together—playing every night if possible. Uncle John also aimed to better manage cash flow, which meant delaying outgoing payments as long as he could, and that sometimes included salaries to the cast. The troupe stormed into Grand Rapids, Michigan, for performances at Powers' Opera House on September 11 and 12, then set up for three nights at the Detroit Opera House, opening "to good-sized attendance," with the "performances well received." Next it was on to Coldwater, at the brand-new Tibbits Opera House, which was dedicated on September 21 by *The Maid of Arran*, then to Elkhart, Indiana, before the troupe returned to Coldwater for three more nights during a county fair.

Things may have first started to get dicey in Chicago, where the troupe was booked from October 9 through 15 at the Academy of Music. They were in town during a frenzied time, when cables for new electric streetcars were tangling with the city's newly installed telephone lines. Uncle John wanted to control expenses. Although bigshot actors like Frank Aiken and Genevieve Rogers could accept staying in divey digs in the smaller towns, in Chicago they'd want to live it up a little and enjoy the big city. This may also have been around the time that paychecks were drawn up late, to conserve cash.

Yet any resentment among the cast didn't seem to affect the performances immediately, as the *Maid* "did big business in Chicago," according to one newspaper, drawing "standing room only" crowds. "Certainly the best Irish drama produced here this season . . . with the finest mechanical scenic effects on the American stage," said the *Chicago Times*. "*The Maid of Arran* has become one of the popular successes of the day because it is a play that pleases the people." This was music to Frank's ears, and the reviews helped him fall in love with Chicago; he told Maud he was adding that city to the short list of places he'd like to live one day. From there, there were no breaks in the schedule—three nights in Indianapolis, a full week in St. Louis, then Greencastle and Lafayette in Indiana on October 30 and 31; Danville, Illinois, on November 1 and 2; then Champaign on the third and Peoria on the fourth before it was finally time for Frank to head home for his wedding five days later.

The wedding of L. Frank Baum and Maud Gage took place on November 9, 1882. The parlor at 210 East Genesee Street was jammed that day, so much so that the string quartet the family had hired was forced to play upstairs. In attendance were Frank's sisters, Hattie and Mattie, along with their families, as well as Frank's parents, Benjamin and Cynthia. On Maud's side, her three siblings were there. And although Susan B. Anthony couldn't make it, Matilda's colleague Elizabeth Cady Stanton was part of the crowd of well-wishers. The organizer of the seminal 1848 women's rights conference in Seneca Falls was accompanied by her husband, Henry Stanton, an early abolitionist and, as coincidence would have it, a distant cousin of Frank Baum's mother.

And, of course, their matchmaking cousin, Josie, came from Cornell to attend along with her parents, prompting Maud's old classmate Jessie to send home a spiteful letter. "Maud Gage is to be married tomorrow," she wrote. "It does not make me feel quite so badly as I would if it were myself, but I cannot help feeling a little sorry."

When the big moment came and the band struck up the wedding march, Maud emerged from one of the bedrooms wearing a flowing white dress and a tight pearl necklace. Her dark hair was now cut short in bangs that framed her glowing face, giving it a rounded, angelic shape. As the dozens of guests struggled to catch a glimpse of her, she descended the open staircase and walked across the parlor toward Frank, who was looking as sharp as any man ever looked in his silk top hat, black suit, and ascot with a white vest. The wedding vows were written by Maud and Frank, and they stressed equality, not the typical language of the wife promising to obey the man. "The promises of the bride were precisely the same as those required of the groom," noted a local newspaper announcement, in apparent surprise.

After the ceremony and reception, the couple took off by stagecoach to spend their honeymoon in Saratoga Springs. The November weather was awful, but the newlyweds didn't mind. They stayed at a fancy resort and consummated their union as the late autumn rain fell outside their window. Frank and Maud returned from their honeymoon to spend the Thanksgiving holiday with their families. Maud then joined her new husband on the tour. Their first train ride together took several days, as the next leg was to begin more than a thousand miles away, in Nebraska. Frank by now was wearing his fancier costume, created by his bride.

Maud therefore wasn't just the wife of the show's star. She was an artist just like the rest of the troupe, living this freestyle life on the road. She wrote a letter to her older brother, T. Clarkson Gage, who was now developing land out in the Dakota Territory, penned on stationery from their room at the Willard Hotel in Omaha. The new Mrs. L. Frank Baum seemed to be corresponding from a dream world. "I like the life very much and am *very, very* happy, but it seems so funny to think I am married," she exulted. "I can't believe it. At first I would forget to answer to the name. I am getting accustomed to it, but it does seem so funny. I always laugh when I think of it . . . Who would have believed a year ago that I would be so far away from home and married!!!!"

Maud had plenty of time on the road to reflect on her wedding. "Now as I look back on that day, my joy is perfect," she continued. "All that I love most in life were there, and such a happy wedding it was. I am very thankful dear that you were able to come home . . . Didn't I have a nice wedding?" And even though she had to make love with her husband in a sleeping compartment on a rumbling train, Maud took so much pleasure in spending time with Frank that she was practically bragging about it. "I would advise you to marry at once," she told her bachelor brother, "and then you will know what it is to enjoy life. Get some nice girl and try my advice."

That Frank and Maud were newlyweds only partially explained the thrill of the moment. Part of their happiness also came from Frank's joy in doing exactly what he wanted to be doing. He was actually getting paid to tell a story and see the reactions lighting up the bright faces in his audiences. In doing so he was tapping into a higher power that many people never get to experience, the universal power of creativity that now flowed within him and reflected back to everyone around him, especially his new wife. All he needed to do was continue along this path. "If one advances confidently in the direction of his dreams," wrote Henry David Thoreau, "and endeavors to live the life which he has imagined, he will meet with a success unexpected in common hours." Frank simply wanted to stay on this path.

The chugging of the train seemed constant, as the troupe had to pick up and head north for two performances in Sioux City, Iowa, then back south for the next night in Council Bluffs, Iowa, a riverboat town on the Mississippi. The distances out West were vast, and Maud soon grew tired of the idle hours. "I don't like the trains as they must stop at too many small stations and are very slow any way," she continued in the letter to her brother in Dakota. "Yesterday, at Council Bluffs, I thought of you very often when I saw the land office and the Northern Pacific Railroad . . . Was pretty near Dakota when I was at Sioux City, but a good many miles from you."

For Maud, the trip grew even more monotonous as the troupe entered the bleak, treeless plains of Kansas, for performances in Atchison, Topeka, and Ottawa. The gray landscape was parched, due to extremely low rainfall that season, yet the air was freezing, suddenly plunging to six degrees below zero in early December. For many members of the cast, Kansas was particularly austere and lifeless, as it just recently had become the first U.S. state to go dry, prohibiting all alcoholic beverages. Kansas was in many ways the birthplace of the Christian temperance movement that was about to sweep the country. Under its governor, John St. John, the state had become a laughingstock for passing what was widely referred to as a joke of a law. "The law is openly violated in a hundred towns in the state every hour of every day, and the whole prohibition scheme is the greatest farce ever enacted by an intelligent people anywhere on Earth," wrote one columnist. "The truth is that St. John aspires to be the President of the United States and seeks to ride into that important position on the prohibition lobby."

It was there in that hard, flat place that Maud's mood turned sour, as she continued the same letter to her brother, now switching to stationery from an inn in Ottawa, Kansas, called the Hamblin House, which was a hotel and opera house all in one. "Some of the hotels are dreadful," Maud wrote. "I don't think much of Kansas as a state. It's N.G. (No Good). I don't see how you could like the West. I couldn't be hired to live here."

Audiences for the play were getting harder to come by, yet the new tour manager insisted on booking a performance nearly every night. By now it was clear that they'd be on the road through Christmas and New Year's, and the cast must have been grumbling, especially since their paychecks were delayed more and more. With the wind howling and temperatures locked below zero, the terrain changed to gray ice. Even though these were among the happiest days of her life, Maud couldn't wait to get out of Kansas. Indeed, she would never return, and Frank would go back only through his fictional characters years later, when he would single out the gray Kansas prairie as the perfectly colorless setting to contrast with the magnificently colorful Land of Oz.

From Kansas it was back to St. Louis for yet another week, dates that took the tour through Christmas Eve, the first anniversary of Frank and Maud's introduction. By that time the morale of the cast had sunk so low and the conflict over the mounting back pay was growing so intense that it led to a big blowup. Tour manager John Moak quit and stayed on in St. Louis, taking a position as the manager of the Grand Pacific Hotel. A newspaper reported that "E. E. Brown, former manager of the Barlow & Wilson's Minstrels, has replaced John A. Moak as business manager of *The Maid of Arran*." On Christmas Day the troupe performed in Urbana, Illinois, then went on to Springfield. Things didn't stop as the calendar turned to 1883, beginning with New Year's Day in Columbus, where they put the show on for two nights, plus a matinee. Next was Toledo . . . followed by Detroit for three more nights . . . Iona . . . Greenville . . . Cadillac . . . Big Rapids . . . Muskegon . . . Grand Haven . . . back to Grand Rapids. The bitter cold and the big snows conspired to hold down audience sizes, which meant that many performances were failing to match expenses.

The road was relentless, but at least the company was heading in the right direction, east, on their way back home. They played the Royal Opera House once again in Toronto, for three nights in early February, skipping town just before a fire burned that theater to the ground. After a string of performances in Rochester and Buffalo, the company was finally returning to Syracuse, to play two nights at the Wieting Opera House, the city's very first site for incandescent lighting. The local newspapers switched into red carpet mode for "our popular young townsman." Mr. Louis F. Baum, "as everyone knows, is a Syracusean and he will undoubtedly receive a right royal welcome."

To return the goodwill, Frank printed up hundreds of copies of the sheet music for the songs he had composed for the play, and he had the Wieting box office hand them out free with every ticket purchased, an ingenious but expensive promotion. The reaction to Frank's return was overwhelming, as this was the tour's shining moment. *The Maid of Arran*, according to the local newspaper, was "a Great Success at Wieting Opera House . . . before a very large and fashionable audience." Mr. Louis F. Baum "played the hero of the drama with manly dignity and tenderness, and at times was forcibly dramatic to a remarkable degree," said the paper. "The performance was a capital one."

But it was all downhill from there, as the tour management kept up the bookings without keeping up with the payroll. During the next run, through Albany, Troy, New Haven, and Providence, star actor Frank Aiken quit the show and soon joined another troupe. The cast became divided; some peeled off and others pitched in to fill in the gaps, playing two or three parts. By the beginning of March it seemed to be all over, as one paper reported: "John W. Baum's *Maid of Arran* will close its season March 8 in consequence of some of the company refusing to play unless back salaries were paid to them." The company "is to be reorganized."

Maud discovered she was pregnant later that month. Frank was overjoyed, but the news also put him under tremendous pressure. After all, the couple literally had no home. Frank still resided with his parents at Rose Lawn, and Maud was still living with hers in Fayetteville. They had spent almost all of their married time together on the road, a situation that must have triggered no small amount of scorn from Frank's mother-in-law. But it wasn't just Matilda Gage who was worried about the future of the couple. Clearly, for Frank Baum, it seemed like it was finally time for him to grow up, settle down, and get a real job with reliable pay.

Yet Frank insisted on getting the show back on the road. After all, there were still more places to play, more people to please. Although the production had seemed to run its course, Frank decided to reorganize the company and have his Uncle John book more dates. But the momentum was gone, and John could manage only a few sporadic engagements. They all went badly. "The audience was not large" for a performance at the Brooklyn Academy of Music on March 26. Then, in the wee hours of April 10, after a performance in Astonia, Connecticut, the hotel where all thirteen members of the company were staying broke into flames. Everyone escaped without injury, but the ordeal seemed like a bad omen. The troupe made its way out to Indianapolis in early May and encountered driving rainstorms that kept audiences away, leaving the cast tired and broke by the bitter end. A year after it began, Frank's tour reached a dead end.

Frank returned to Syracuse only to face debts and obligations. His ego, which had been inflated by accolades, was now deflated by defeat. He had no place of his own to live with his pregnant wife and no job on which to fall back. With a child on the way and a disapproving mother-in-law, he was forced to make the painful decision to find a more conventional line of work. Frank's first instinct was to ask the people closest to him for advice on what to do next, and in his case that advice naturally came from his family, which was in the oil business.

Frank's older brother, Benjamin William Baum, had returned from his nearly decade-long stay in Germany, along with his attractive blond bride, Fräulein Augusta Maria Kruger. Ben, too, had been searching for a new opportunity when he began experimenting with some of the oil byproducts at his father's refinery, hitting upon a new mixture of castor oil and petroleum that worked especially well in all weather conditions, as a lubricant for buggy wheels and machinery. He was looking to start a new business to bottle and sell the stuff. In talking to his brother, one thing led to another, and Frank agreed to form a family partnership, Baum's Castorine Oil Company, with Frank acting as superintendent and sales manager.

He moved out of Rose Lawn, deeding the property to his mother for the price of $1, finally severing himself from his childhood home. He and Maud rented a small wood-frame house at 8 Shonnard Street near downtown Syracuse. Maud looked forward to keeping the household, managing its finances, organizing the kitchen, cooking, and practicing her favorite hobby, embroidery. Ever since she was a little girl, she had been impressed by the finely kept homes in her neighborhood. She felt secure in her belief that making a home and raising a family would be satisfaction enough for her. Besides, she knew that reaching the goals her mother set for her would involve a life of knocking down barriers, as there were virtually no female doctors or lawyers in America. Maud simply didn't fancy herself as a public agitator.

The Baum brothers set up shop on East Water Street. The first advertisements for Baum's Castorine Company appeared in newspapers and business directories in the days after the July 4 holiday. Their ad featured a rectangular, quart-size can with a spout on top. Emblazoned on the front was the name "Baum's Ever Ready Castorine." This was a new kind of "Axle Oil, for Buggies, Road Carts, Carriages and Wagons." What's more, the concoction "Never Gums" in the heat, and "Never Chills" in the cold. Selling axle grease was not what Frank Baum had in mind for his future. But he saw it as a temporary arrangement. He hoped to get his show back on the road on another tour.

It was around this time, however, that his decision seemed to become permanent. Frank's father and Uncle Adam were divesting their chain of theaters, not long after being set back by an accident during a performance in Richburg of one of Frank's less popular plays, the fatefully titled *Matches*. A flicker from a kerosene lantern sparked the rafters. The resulting flames burned the Baum Opera House down to the ground, perhaps giving rise to the greatest fear of one of Frank's characters. "There is only one thing in the world I am afraid of," says the Scarecrow. "A lighted match." The fire destroyed everything in the storage room, including all the sets, the props, and the costumes for *The Maid of Arran*. Any immediate hope of returning his show to the road had gone up in flames.

On December 4, 1883, Maud gave birth to a boy, Frank Joslyn Baum. The arrival of his first child was also the birth of a new level of responsibility for Lyman Frank Baum. He was a family man now, with a day job. His dream of becoming a great storyteller seemed to be over. Frank was now moving away from his calling in life, abandoning his childhood dream, defying his inner voice. He would spend his days doing work he didn't quite like, in order to make money.

The world's oldest forms of spirituality agree that the root of all our sorrow is the loss of contact with our true self. When this disconnect happens, "the world becomes governed by the seemingly un-ending rounds of birth and death, pain and pleasure, and happiness and suffering," according to one spiritual teacher, a swami from India named Vivekananda, who would arrive in America years later con-veying mystical inspiration. "Our recovery is possible only by reestab-lishing contact with our true, inmost self." Outwardly unaware of such wisdom, Frank embarked on modern life's most common course, trying new and different routes to contentment through material gain. The material, however, is the opposite of the spiritual. Cut off from the work that gave him bliss, Frank was destined for a string of disappoint-ments and dead ends, as each failure would force him to take a turn in a different direction, toward yet another way to achieve his material aims. He was about to get caught up in the great zigzag of life, the clas-sic Z-shaped pattern that never seems to cease.

Frank would later allude to those days by constantly placing road-blocks ahead of the companions along the Yellow Brick Road of his story. "What shall we do?" asks one of his characters in despair, when facing a deep ditch. "I haven't the faintest idea," says the Tin Wood-man. Offering little in the way of wisdom, the Scarecrow says, "We cannot fly, that is certain. Neither can we climb down into this great ditch. Therefore, if we cannot jump over it, we must stop where we are." And so it was for Frank. Blocked from doing what he truly loved, he set off in an entirely different direction.

Yet even with this detour, there was something deep inside Frank Baum that spoke of the larger journey, the eternal circle of life, that classic O shape, the path that takes one back home to one's true self. "The most powerful religious symbol is the circle," wrote psychologist Carl Jung. "The circle is one of the great primordial images of man-kind, and in considering the circle, we are analyzing the self." The wis-dom of the circle is common to every mythology and is especially cen-tral to the mythology of the Native Americans. "When we pitch camp, we pitch camp in a circle," said one wise old Indian chief. "When we look at the horizon, the horizon is in a circle. When the eagle builds a nest, the nest is in a circle." The sun follows a daily circle of rise and return, the moon follows a monthly circle, as does the planet Earth over the course of the seasons.

Mrs. Gage believed in the very same thing. "Anciently, motherhood was represented by a sphere or circle," she wrote. "It is eternity, it is feminine, it is the creative force, the creative spirit." The ancient Sanskrit speaks of the Mandala, the sacred circle of life. Plato said that the soul is a circle, representing totality, and in the center of the circle is the one thing that marks each true being, and that one thing is different for everyone.

As is the case for most people who veer off their chosen path, Frank Baum's life was now in pieces that he'd need to put back together. Traversing the zigzags, hitting roadblocks again and again, he would have to rediscover that center and somehow find a way to overcome whatever it was that was blocking him on his journey back to the childhood dreams that shaped him. He would need to realize that he had indeed left behind his true self, that he had moved outside his own sphere. His only hope of completing the journey—and thus ending back at the beginning—was to rediscover his own special O while traveling the treacherous path of life's unavoidable Z.

PART
· II ·

6

The Mythic Oilcan

Advertisements for the Baum
family's popular elixir

◆

"[My joints] are rusted so badly that I cannot move them
at all; if I am well oiled I shall soon be all right again. You
will find an oil-can on a shelf in my cottage."

— THE TIN WOODMAN

I N LATE-NINETEENTH-CENTURY AMERICA, progress became
the byword, and a cult of personality was rising up around the
men who achieved progress for the nation while amassing their
own personal fortunes. "Restlessness and discontent are the first ne-
cessities of progress," pronounced the man of invention, Thomas Edison. "While the old nations of the earth keep on at a snail's pace,
America thunders past with the rush of the express train," observed
the man of steel, Andrew Carnegie. Taking heed of these industrial
icons, men were building electric generators big enough to light Wall
Street, wielding steam shovels efficient enough to extract tons of iron
ore from the earth, and igniting dynamite powerful enough to blast
through any mountain that dared to stand in the way of the railroads.
"We live in an age of progress," a pompous professor named Woggle-
bug would one day declare in a novel by L. Frank Baum.

Back in 1883, Frank aimed forward along with everyone else, and
in a world of squeaky wheels, ill-fitting gears, and claptrap engines, he
believed he held the solution in his hands, in the form of a can of oil.
As the superintendent and chief salesman for Baum's Castorine Company, Frank now had a clear-cut mission in life: to grease the moving parts of progress. Wherever he went, Frank heard the noises — the
creak of a doorjamb, the whine of a wagon, the clatter of a carriage,
the groan of a locomotive, the clank of a tractor, the grind of a grain
mill, the wheeze of a wood saw, the swish of a sewing machine, the an-

guish of an axle. A few drops of Baum's magic oil, and America would be good to go.

Along with his older brother, Ben, Frank worked hard to make Baum's Castorine, their oil store on East Water Street in Syracuse, successful enough to support both of their households. Surrounded in their part of town by men who cobbled shoes or built stoves or made furniture, the Baum brothers were more intellectual than most, oddly out of place in this realm of tradesmen. Frank was, of course, a former actor and playwright. And Ben had just recently returned from Germany. He had been getting used to being called Professor von Baum, working in an academic setting, smoking a pipe, and wearing a jacket and tie. Now, dressed in a soiled white smock, his job was to find new mixtures of oil that could lubricate any sort of wheel or machine. With his receding widow's peak hairline, a thin mustache, and small ears, Ben could be found in the back room concocting his latest ointments, so that the Baum name would befit the family's preferred pronunciation: *balm*.

A visitor entering the smooth-swinging door at Baum's Castorine would have been instantly struck by the sweet and pungent odors wafting from the cans of oils, greases, and lubricants that began life in Ben's lab and made their way to Frank's neat rows of shelves behind the register. As for Frank, his role in the business was to cater to customers, finding new ways to gin up sales. At first, business seemed slow, which may have caused the brothers to blame the location. They soon moved to a new double storefront, at 28/30 James Street, where Frank used his talent for language to come up with new slogans for "the Great Lubricant." He advertised that Baum's Axle Oil was "so smooth it makes horses laugh." But the oil wasn't just for horse-drawn carts, buggies, and carriages. Frank constantly came up with new markets, packaging his brother's mixtures for different applications, including sewing machine oil and even cottonseed oil for cooking. Baum's oil was "The Only Perfect Oil for Farm Machinery," and according to an ad placed in the *Syracuse Standard,* Baum's Castorine carried "all grades of machine, engine, cylinder and paraffin oils." Baum's "makes the wheels spin," said one ad, "don't it?"

Business picked up as Ben's balms and Frank's phrases became well known. But Frank realized that he was tapping only a small portion of the regional market by selling from a single location. He needed to get on the road and convince general stores, lumberyards, carriage makers, and farming depots in different cities and towns to distribute the patented Baum solutions. When he loaded cases of Castorine onto trains to make sales calls, he must have noticed what a letdown this life seemed to be compared to when he traveled on the same trains as the talented Louis F. Baum, the acclaimed playwright and actor. People still remembered him when he arrived in his old haunts—Auburn, Elmira, Richburg, Olean, Bolivar, Bradford, Jamestown, Scranton, Troy, Albany, Rochester, Buffalo.

Yet Frank Baum wasn't one to get down on himself or dwell on the past. Though his humdrum job as an oil salesman stood in stark contrast to his love of acting and writing, he was a doer. He felt challenged by diving into a new endeavor, and so he found a way to apply his extraordinary powers of empathy and imagination to his new vocation. While on the road selling industrial lubricants to storeowners and other clients, he didn't focus so much on the products themselves as on the customers and their needs and desires. By putting himself in their shoes and imagining what they wanted in life, Baum didn't just sell oil and grease—he sold hopes and dreams.

He found himself telling tales once again, elevating the oilcan to mythic status, spinning stories of how this magical elixir could practically save your soul or shine your shoes. Make sure you tell all your customers to try it, he would say. Simply pour the liquid from its quart container into a hand-held oilcan with a tapered spout. A few squirts here and there on your wagon or plow or pulley or reaping machine, and it's as good as new. Don't be fooled by imitation; only Baum's Castorine can make horses laugh, so imagine what it could do for you. This oil displaces moisture. Rust will never be your worry again. No more squeaky wheels. Live a life free of friction.

"Oil my neck, first," pleaded one of Frank's immortal characters. Indeed, the Tin Woodman at first was so badly rusted that he couldn't move at all. "Now oil the joints in my arms," he said. "This is a great comfort . . . Now, if you will oil the joints of my legs, I shall be all right once more." The Tin Woodman couldn't have been more thankful to receive these dabs of grease. "I might have stood there always if you had not come along," concluded the polite, grateful creature, "so you have certainly saved my life."

Frank Baum was certainly an interesting fellow to meet, so the other storeowners he visited tended to listen to him, and they ordered his Castorine by the caseload. And why not? The markup was good, and the product actually worked. "We are using your Castorine on our road wagons and coaches," wrote the New York City stable manager for railroad tycoon William H. Vanderbilt, "and we have found it far superior than any oil we have ever used for our axles." Standing behind his product 100 percent, Frank collected and embellished stories of how his balm had changed people's lives. All he had to do was ask his customers what they'd always wanted. What's your heart's desire? If one could have taken the Castorine oil internally, Frank might have marketed it for all known human maladies, from skin rash to crankiness. Can it improve a marriage? Can it grow hair? Anything is possible in America, and customers will surely want to keep plenty of Baum's on hand, should any new situation call for it.

Pretty soon money streamed into Baum's Castorine from points north, south, east, and west. Frank's early success had him establishing what would become a tradition in his household. He was constantly searching for a better place in life. Come the first of May, when many apartment leases were up, Frank and Maud would try to move to a bigger house in a better neighborhood. On May 1, 1884, Frank and Maud and the five-month-old Frank Jr. did just that, relocating to 28 Slocum Avenue, still on the west side of Syracuse. It wasn't as fancy as where his sisters lived a couple of miles away, but still, life was getting better. In the summer Frank would usually be home from work in time to sit on the front porch with Maud and the baby, to drink lemonade and marvel as the blazing sunsets of the day gave way to the blue Krakatoa moon.

On the surface everything seemed OK, as Frank was doing what a man needed to do, plying a trade to support his family. Yet something was wrong. "There's something inside you that knows you are in the center, that knows when you are on the beam," says Joseph Campbell. That same intuition also "knows when you are off the beam, and if you get off the beam just to earn money, you've lost your life." The trade-off that Frank Baum made, dealing away his dream for duty, was all too common, but after a while it began to take its toll. He was trapped, because the money and the resources that Frank and Ben used to start this business came from their father.

Indeed, Frank had grown comfortable, perhaps too comfortable, working under his father's wing. Time and again Benjamin Ward Baum acted as his son's protector and benefactor, setting Frank up in business after business. It started small, with the purchase of the amateur printing press that the teenage Frank used to crank out his modest newspaper, the *Rose Lawn Home Journal*. This became the pattern, the father investing in a chicken farm, then a string of theaters for Frank to stage his plays, and now an oil enterprise. As a result, Frank had a great debt to pay. Although his heart wasn't in the oil business, he owed it to his father to turn Baum's Castorine into a success, as the name Baum beamed from the front door and from every can.

In the industry the name Baum meant something. Benjamin Baum was well known throughout the oil region as a man who had staged an impressive business comeback—so impressive, in fact, that it made Frank's predicament even worse. Frank had seen his father lose nearly everything in the Panic of 1873. When oil prices plunged, the refinery his father started was on the verge of collapse and the senior Mr. Baum was forced to liquidate the Second National Bank of Syracuse, the savings and loan he cofounded, emptying its vaults and closing its counters for good. The stocks he owned, in Nevada silver-mining companies, turned to scrap paper. To support his family he had to mortgage more and more of his Rose Lawn property at a time when his health was deteriorating.

To halt this downward spiral, to claw his way back, to gradually build up his petroleum enterprise over the next decade—this took real perseverance, a lesson that was not lost on Frank. There was so much of his father's sweat invested in the business that failure now would be unacceptable. Indeed, the resilient Benjamin Baum was one of the very few oil men who was able to remain standing on his own two feet during the years of John D. Rockefeller's rise, when the tycoon's cartel was tightening its hold on what would become one of the world's biggest industries. One of Mr. Rockefeller's key tactics was to squeeze out his rivals by arranging exclusive pricing with the railroad moguls, so that his oil was cheaper to ship than anyone else's. The *Petroleum Centre Record* reported the formation of a "gigantic combination among certain railroads and refiners to control the purchase and shipment of crude and refined oil from this region," Mr. Rockefeller being the mastermind behind the conspiracy.

The reaction against the double cartel was swift. A fiery, hard-drinking oil well owner named John Archbold agitated a series of angry protests, becoming the leader of the new Petroleum Producers' Union. Archbold held rallies in saloons and theaters, where he got others like him to refuse to sell oil to Rockefeller and his cohorts. During those early years, Benjamin's firm became associated with John Archbold in the oil business in Titusville, as one of a number of independent producers who "tried to break the grip of Standard Oil." Archbold's new union put pressure on the railroads to break their unfair deal with Rockefeller. Archbold won this first round with the backing of the Pennsylvania legislature, which called the Rockefeller contract with the railroads the "most gigantic and daring conspiracy ever to confront a free nation."

Although the union succeeded in thwarting Rockefeller for the time being, the tycoon used the years of economic depression to acquire dozens of rival refineries at rock-bottom prices. "The way to make money is to buy when blood is running in the streets," he said. Pretty soon Rockefeller approached Archbold himself with an offer that he could not refuse. If Archbold was willing to give up his hard drinking, Rockefeller was ready to acquire Archbold's oil wells at an attractive price and install his former enemy as one of the top executives of the emerging Standard Oil empire. After the deal was done, Archbold was transformed from an aficionado of whiskey to an advocate of sobriety, from a rabble-rouser to a loyalist, from Rockefeller's chief critic to his chief negotiator.

At one point Archbold must have come knocking on Benjamin Baum's door to make him an offer. Typically the deal was very simple: we will give you Standard Oil stock or cash for the appraised value of your refinery. "I advise you to take the stock," Archbold would say. "It will be for your good."

Yet Benjamin Baum refused to do business with a cartel that soon controlled more than 90 percent of American oil refineries and pipeline capacity. It is not clear whether Benjamin's resistance was based on principle or whether the elder Baum just didn't like the price, but either way it meant that he would go it alone against one of the great forces in business history. "Rockefeller and other industrial captains aimed to kill competitive capitalism in favor of a new monopoly capitalism," writes biographer Ron Chernow. The industrial titan himself put it this way: "The day of combination is here to stay. Individualism has gone, never to return."

Frank saw how his father tried to avoid being trampled in the unstoppable march of Rockefeller, who rose to power through cunning and a single-minded vision, but also through extortion, collusion, bribery, leaking lies to the press, tax evasion, and getting away with polluting Cleveland's Cuyahoga River with a waste product called gasoline for which there was no known market. "Thousands and hundreds of thousands of barrels of it floated down the creeks and rivers," Rockefeller confessed, "and the ground was saturated with it, in the constant effort to get rid of it." *Cuyahoga* originally meant "crooked river" in the Iroquois tongue, but it became known to the local Native Americans as "river that catches fire." In 1883 Rockefeller uprooted his family and company from Cleveland, leaving the mess behind, and moved Standard Oil into an imposing stone fortress of a headquarters in lower Manhattan.

As Rockefeller's wealth and power grew, he mushroomed into a national villain, a popular target of hatred. "It seemed as if half the country wanted to lynch John D. Rockefeller," while the other half wanted a loan or a handout. One newspaper article estimated that he earned more money every hour than the average man earned in a year. Cries for help arrived at Standard Oil's offices in New York by the sack full each day. "People wrote to Rockefeller the way small children pray to God for presents."

Frank would one day model one of the many faces of his shapeshifting character, the Wizard of Oz, on his father's nemesis in the oil patch. Before the companions on the Yellow Brick Road actually encounter the Wizard, he is nothing but wonderful, not unlike Thomas Edison, the Wizard of Menlo Park, who was the single most admired American of the age. But once they arrive in the Emerald City and make their way inside the Wizard's Throne Room, he appears as a giant hairless head. "I am Oz, the Great and Terrible," he bellows. "Who are you, and why do you seek me?"

By portraying the Wizard as a tyrannical, hairless head, Frank seemed to be referring to the most notable symptom of a mysterious illness that struck John D. Rockefeller later in life: alopecia, or the total loss of hair on his head and body. Suddenly it was all gone. Even his mustache fell out. Rockefeller was only fifty-four when this happened, but all of a sudden his appearance aged what seemed like thirty years, from youthful to that of a "bald, wizened man, a desiccated fossil." The transformation was stunning. "He suddenly looked old, puffy, stooped—all but unrecognizable. He seemed to age a generation. Without hair, his facial imperfections grew more pronounced." At one point Rockefeller attended a dinner hosted by J. P. Morgan and took a seat next to his old colleague, Charles Schwab, the president of U.S. Steel. When Schwab failed to recognize him, Rockefeller was mortified. "Charlie," he muttered, "I see you don't know me. I am Mr. Rockefeller."

Not surprisingly, people were terrified to approach him. "Rockefeller's alopecia had a devastating effect on his image. It made him look like a hairless ogre, stripped of all youth, warmth, and attractiveness, and this played powerfully on people's imaginations." One of the many people whose imagination was sparked by this very image was L. Frank Baum, who would one day write of a mean and terrible figure lurking behind a partition, "a little old man, with a bald head and a wrinkled face."

Despite all the competition, Frank seemed to have little choice but to help keep his father's business alive and well. Financial security was important to his wife, as Maud had grown up accustomed to living in a comfortable home. Yet despite being fully agreeable to living this conventional life, Maud seemed to harbor a tinge of regret, in her case the regret of giving up her college and career aspirations, a resentment that was undoubtedly fed by her activist, career-minded mother. Whether intentional or not, Maud naturally took out her frustrations on Frank. The home was the one realm that she could control, and she exercised that control with absolute authority. The undisputed boss of the house, she always told Frank what should be done, and he always listened to her, never arguing. "It's nonsense for a man to complain that his wife's temper will not allow him to enjoy a happy home," he once wrote.

Frank had a real reason for being easygoing: fear of damaging his fragile heart. This fear governed not only his work life but also his home life with Maud. So whatever happened, Frank would take it all in stride, always avoiding undue stress. "You can judge a man by watching him at the breakfast table," Frank wrote of his even-keeled, happy-go-lucky attitude. "A man who is genial over his cup of coffee will be agreeable throughout the day." In a sense their relationship mirrored Maud's own parents; Maud took her mother as a role model and Frank followed in the tradition of Henry Gage, readily acceding to all of his wife's demands.

One day this dynamic escalated to an absurd level, in an incident that has gone down in family lore as "the affair of the Bismarcks." Walking home from the store in the evening, Frank smelled and spied something delectable in the window of a bakery. Calling out to him from behind the glass were Bismarck doughnuts, named after the famous chancellor who unified Germany, as if delicious pastries were part of Otto von Bismarck's strategy for bringing the Prussians and Bavarians together. Filled with sweet jam and topped with confectioners' sugar or cinnamon, they're also sometimes known as Berliners. Frank found himself entering the store and ordering a dozen Bismarcks to go.

When he arrived home and opened the box to show the treats to his wife, Maud scowled and scolded her husband in her refined, high-pitched voice. "You are not to bring food into this house," she said. "I am the one who plans the meals."

When Frank argued that the doughnuts would be delightful as a breakfast dish, Maud continued her lecture. "But I also cannot accept wasting food." And so Maud let Frank have two doughnuts for breakfast the next morning. He loved them and got sugar all over his mustache.

But Frank's custom of being genial during his morning coffee was put to the test when Maud insisted that he had to eat his Bismarcks every day until they were gone—this in the era before preservatives. By the third day the doughnuts were growing so stale that Frank wrapped them in newspaper and put them away in the cupboard.

Maud retrieved them and told Frank that if he bought them, he must keep eating them, and so he did. By the fourth day mold was growing, and Frank decided to bury the remaining Bismarcks in the backyard, according to the family legend. Maud witnessed the deed through the window, dutifully dug them back up, dusted them off, and served one more doughnut to her husband.

"For Heaven's sake, Maud, let's stop this nonsense," Frank declared. "Those things are not fit to eat and you know it."

"You bought them without consulting me so you will have to eat them," she replied. "I am not going to have food wasted. But I'll let you off this time if you promise never again to buy any food unless I ask you to." Frank nodded, at which point Maud finally threw the rest of the doughnuts into the trash.

Amazingly, the doughnuts would reappear briefly years later, forever captured in celluloid as a plate of fresh-baked crullers that Aunt Em serves to her farm hands and her niece, as if Uncle Henry had brought them home as a special treat for everyone and she needed to get rid of them before they went bad and moldy. Maud would one day serve as a "technical consultant" to MGM for the movie, which explains the subtle biographical references to her life with Frank that were embedded into the script.

Maud's domestic dominance was not limited to her relationship with her husband. Her "unpredictable temper" also governed her interactions with her children, as another family legend from a few years later illustrates. One day their young son thought it would be amusing to throw the family's cat out a second-story window. The cat landed on its feet and survived, but Maud was determined to teach her son a lesson. She took the boy over to the same window, lifted him up, and dangled him outside, clutching him by the ankles until the boy apologized and promised never to mistreat an animal again.

Later, when Frank came home, he was the one who comforted the traumatized little boy. Frank was generally the one who cuddled their children, telling them bedtime stories every night or singing them to sleep. Story time was an essential outlet for Frank. Supporting a family with a job that clearly didn't suit him, Frank must have taken much comfort in telling tales to his son. As he repressed his own dreams and desires, as his heart began to harden, the myths that he could make up about mere cans of oil sustained his interest less and less. "If the person doesn't listen to the demands of his own spiritual and heart life and if that person insists on a certain program, you're going to have a schizophrenic crack-up," warns Joseph Campbell. "The person has put himself off-center. He has aligned himself with a programmatic life, and it's not the one that the body's interested in at all."

Frank found another tiny outlet for his humor and creativity during the summer of 1884, when the condition of Maud's father became dire. His typhus flared up again and was getting a firmer grip on his body. To bring a little joy and levity into the Gage household in Fayetteville during this difficult time, Frank and Maud decided to help Matilda throw a festive family dinner party for a small group of relatives.

The dinner was set for Sunday, July 20, and Frank made a special effort to design the menu himself. Written in a mock French style, the menu was filled with inside jokes. For starters, Frank took a jab at the fact that the dinner was being held at the famous feminist gathering spot of Matilda Joslyn Gage. At the top of the menu he called the place "HOTEL LA FEMME, Residence de Gages." The headings of the menu were formally printed on card stock, and then Frank penned the entries in his most elegant script handwriting. He listed "La Contents de la Soupdish" as tomato and announced that "La Piece de Resistance" would be roast rib of lamb. For "La Dish de Side" there would be string beans, "with strings," as well as "Chopped Cabbage, a la Knife." For "La Deserta," they would be serving a choice of "Boston Crystal Ice Cream," "Peaches in Jelly," "Fruit Cake," "Cocoanut Cake," or all of the above.

Despite the enjoyment of sitting around the table and partaking of such delectable dishes, Frank may have caught a glimpse of his future that evening while dining with his in-laws. He admired Henry Gage and hoped to become as successful in business. Like Mr. Gage, he knew he could become a reliable provider for his family. But in the end, what would he have created and who would really care? One day he'd be too sick to work. He'd close the shop and he'd have one last great meal as he prepared himself for his descent into death. Would that be a life well lived? For some, perhaps. But given his talents, Frank must have asked himself, Isn't there something special I should be doing with my life?

7

Witch-hunting

The first meeting of the International Council of Women, Washington, D.C., 1888. Seated are Susan B. Anthony, second from left; Matilda Joslyn Gage, second from right; Elizabeth Cady Stanton, third from right.

◆

"In the civilized countries I believe there are no witches left, nor wizards, nor sorceresses, nor magicians. But, you see, the Land of Oz has never been civilized, for we are cut off from all the rest of the world. Therefore we still have witches and wizards amongst us."

— THE WITCH OF THE NORTH

L OSING HIS LONG BOUT with typhus, Henry Gage passed away on the sixteenth of September, 1884, at the age of sixty-five. The Indian summer leaves still held their green as dozens of friends and relatives gathered to send the old shopkeeper off at the small cemetery a few blocks away from the Gage home in Fayetteville. Frank and Maud arrived with their nine-month-old son, grieving over their loss along with Maud's brother and two sisters. As Henry had wished, a proper Baptist burial was performed by Pastor Hawley, the same clergyman who had joined Frank and Maud in matrimony just two years earlier.

What could the pastor have said about Henry? Few men of his time were so overshadowed by a wife as Henry Gage was almost totally eclipsed by Matilda. He seemed to make few decisions on his own and seldom disagreed with her. That he was widely respected by his fellow townsmen made him an anomaly. He was successful in business for decades, treating everyone fairly, and he wore his success well, yet those who knew him must have wondered just how he was able to put up with the shocking behavior of his wife and still retain any sort of pride. This was not the way a modern man was supposed to live, yet he had lived quite well.

Years later, in the literary afterlife, Henry Gage would be reincarnated by his son-in-law as Uncle Henry of Kansas, a passive but hard-working man who "looked stern and solemn, and rarely spoke."

For Matilda, her husband's death was not unexpected, so it was no surprise that even before her period of mourning she had already been thinking deeply about how losing her companion of forty years would change her life. No one would have believed that Matilda was holding back any of her opinions, but her behavior following the death of her husband seemed to speak otherwise. Without Henry to care for, Matilda was a river after a season of heavy rains. At age fifty-eight she raged forth, possessed with a new reason for wearing black.

As Matilda found herself growing more and more frustrated with the timidity of her old colleagues, she also grew more and more empowered to speak her full mind, for she felt she had little left to lose. For sixteen years in a row she had watched as Susan B. Anthony optimistically presented her case to the U.S. Congress, hoping that the men of Washington would approve an effort to garner support for a "Susan B. Anthony Amendment," and for sixteen years in a row the idea had been shot down with little ceremony. It was high time, Matilda believed, to start doing things her way.

In her public speeches Matilda's high-pitched voice grew more forceful as she launched into a full-throated telling of what she saw as history's most suppressed story: how governments and churches have persecuted innocent women throughout the centuries by accusing them of heresy, obscenity, and witchcraft. She began by telling of the dark times between 1400 and 1700—known as the Burning Years—when countless human beings, mostly women, were accused of witchcraft and put to death by fire, hanging, torture, drowning, or pressing by heavy stone. (Current research consensus puts the witch murders somewhere between forty thousand and one hundred thousand.) At gatherings of women's rights activists from around the state of New York, Matilda spoke of an unmistakable link between the teachings of the Church and the accusations of witchery:

> As soon as a system of religion was adopted which taught the greater sinfulness of women, the saying arose, "One wizard for every 10,000 witches," and the persecution for witchcraft be-

came chiefly directed at women. The church degraded women by teaching her to feel conscious of guilt in the very fact of her existence. The extreme wickedness of women, taught as a cardinal doctrine of the church, created the belief that she was desirous of destroying all religion, witchcraft being regarded as her strongest weapon, therefore no punishment for it was thought too severe.

A witch, Matilda would note in her speeches, was defined in the Dark Ages as "a woman who had deliberately sold herself to the evil one." In practice, anything could be, and was, used as evidence of witchcraft—possessing rare knowledge, having an unusual "witch mark" on one's body, not looking others in the eye, suffering from mental illness, owning black cats, performing "black magic," or having an ability to float or swim.

The accused were often the wise women of the community, practiced in the art of homeopathy, the medicinal use of herbs to relieve pain and disease. Herb healers would mix up brews of knapweed, tansy, wild chamomile, mullein, plantain, and dandelions. The old widows would often be penniless, living alone, with nothing but soiled clothes, teeth falling out of their mouths, half out of their wits from the diseases they tried to cure. Their magic herbs were often seized by church leaders and presented to judges as evidence of their wicked sorcery.

Several passages from the Hebrew Bible condemn witches and wizards. "Thou shalt not suffer a witch to live," says Exodus 22:18. "A man also or woman that hath a familiar spirit, or that is a wizard, shall surely be put to death: they shall stone them with stones: their blood shall be upon them," says Leviticus 20:27. But Matilda concentrated the blame on that one seminal story from the book of Genesis, the aforementioned episode of the Garden of Eden, in which Eve commits the "original sin" by listening to the serpent, tasting the forbidden fruit, and then coaxing Adam to take a bite, too. "Women must think for themselves," Matilda scolded, "and realize the story with the pair in the garden and the speaking serpent standing on his tail was a *myth*."

Over the years Frank Baum would be forced to listen countless times as his mother-in-law fleshed out and interpreted the original sin story. Whether he agreed with her or not, it would gradually dawn on him just how powerful this parable was. The story evoked easy-to-visualize symbols—the innocent man and woman, the evil snake, the forbidden fruit of nature representing forbidden knowledge. With these symbols a major idea was put forth: that you shall obey God, not nature, or you shall suffer great consequences.

This simple but vivid tale was repeated so many times, especially to children, that it actually shaped how billions of people saw the world and their role in it. It was a lesson that few people spared much time to ponder: myth could transform humanity. Nothing was as useful for propagating an idea as an easy-to-remember parable that carefully presented an idea. Whether the message contained in the parable was true or false was the choice of the mythmaker.

Matilda was in the process of cataloguing the atrocities committed under the guise of the greater wickedness of women. In 1577 the French Parliament of Toulouse, she reported, "burned four hundred women in one hour on the public square, the women dying the horrid death of fire for a crime which never existed save in the imagination of those persecutors, based on a false theory as to original sin."

Similar events took place across Europe, most often in Germany, Austria, Switzerland, Spain, France, England, Italy, and Scotland. Sometimes churches showcased witch burnings as holiday spectacles, and these events, although free to the public, were big moneymakers. "Trials for witchcraft filled the coffers of the church, as whenever a conviction took place, the property of the witch and her family was confiscated to that body," Matilda wrote. "The church always claimed one-half, it divided the remainder of the accused's possessions between the judge and the prosecutor." She cited passages from law books that were created to justify the barbarism. "To deny the possibility, nay the actual existence of witchcraft and sorcery, is at once to contradict the revealed word of God," said Blackstone's *Commentaries on the Laws of England*.

These witch beliefs were carried across the ocean from Europe by the early settlers of the New World. Matilda spoke of an especially moving event that had taken place the previous year in Salem, Massachusetts. On July 18, 1883, two hundred descendants of Mrs. Rebecca Nurse—one of the most famous women put to death in the Salem Witch Trials of 1692—had gathered to understand the past. "Rebecca was a woman seventy years of age," wrote Matilda, "the mother of eight children, a church member of unsullied reputation and devout habit; but all these considerations did not prevent her accusation, trial and conviction. She was hung by the neck till she was dead."

Haunted by his mother-in-law's vivid descriptions of witch-hunting, Frank Baum's storyland would be darkened by a fearful shadow cast by wicked witches. Indeed, the entire adventure in the Land of Oz would be marked by two major events, when each of the two mythical women would be killed in metaphorical ways. The first time it's a flying house that does the honors, freeing the Munchkins from the bondage of the Wicked Witch of the East.

"I have not killed anything," protests Dorothy.

"Your house did, anyway," replies the Good Witch of the North, with a laugh, "and that is the same thing. See!" she continues, pointing to the corner of the house. "There are her two feet, still sticking out from under a block of wood."

The story builds to the point where Dorothy is challenged by the Great Oz to finish off the dead witch's sister, that famous symbol of fear, the Wicked Witch of the West.

"But I cannot!" exclaims Dorothy, greatly surprised.

The Wizard will not tolerate her protests, and he commands all the companions to get the job done, to hunt down the terrible enemy. "There is now but one Wicked Witch left in all this land, and when you can tell me she is dead I will send you back to Kansas—but not before."

Matilda Joslyn Gage, of course, knew that wicked witches never existed, that they were only created in the minds of twisted men who wielded this myth to instill fear in people as a pretext for seizing power. This was part of an age-old con, and Matilda aimed to put a stop to it. Since 1884 was an election year, Matilda believed that the best time to end the male monopoly on power in America would be right now.

Both major parties had held their nominating conventions in Chicago that summer, and Matilda's son-in-law was following these developments closely. Frank was a great lover not of politics but of newspapers. In this golden age of big-city broadsheets, Frank had ink in his veins. Sitting in his living room easy chair, he seemed most comfortable when the newsprint was staining his fingers. His attitude toward politics was opposite that of his mother-in-law. Whereas Matilda was an activist, Frank simply watched politics more for amusement than anything else. As Mark Twain noted, "The political and commercial morals of the United States are not merely food for laughter, they are an entire banquet."

The biggest issue in the campaign of 1884 was corruption. New York City's Tammany Hall, an extension of the Democratic Party, had become the premier political crime ring of the day. But it was the Republicans of Washington who nationalized the practice of patronage. This was a form of bribery in which capitalists paid officials for the privilege of ravaging natural resources, obtaining land grants, and monopolizing shipping, communication, and railroad networks. "One might search the whole lot of the Congress, Judiciary, and Executive during the twenty-five years between 1870 and 1895, and find little but damaged reputation," lamented social critic Henry Adams. "The period was poor in purpose and barren in results."

In the 1884 campaign the divided Republicans nominated Secretary of State James Blaine of Maine, shunning the sitting president, Chester A. Arthur, a gentlemanly sort who was deemed uninspiring and unelectable. The Democrats selected New York Governor Grover Cleveland, a rotund bachelor with a bloated face. Known for his honesty, Cleveland was running on a platform of anticorruption. He was immediately attacked not so much on his record but with allegations that he had fathered an illegitimate child. Wherever he went, hecklers chanted, "Ma, Ma, where's my Pa?"

Both parties refused to add a women's suffrage plank to their platforms. As the campaign heated up, Matilda Gage found herself at odds with her closest colleagues in the women's movement. Susan B. Anthony and Elizabeth Cady Stanton were deciding which of the two parties was the less offensive, but Matilda wanted no part of either, as neither seemed to care a whit about women. Instead, Matilda urged women to play hardball. "When men begin to fear the power of women, their voice and their influence, then we shall secure justice, but not before," Mrs. Gage declared. "When we demonstrate our ability to kill off, or seriously injure a candidate, or hurt a party, then we shall receive respectful consideration. We must be recognized as aggressive."

Susan B. Anthony, however, had a different approach. She favored a softer and broader appeal. She attended a meeting of the Women's Christian Temperance Union. Although Catholics, blacks, Jews, and immigrants could not join the WCTU, Anthony was sympathetic to its signature cause, the prohibition of alcohol, and now she became "quite attached" to the union's charismatic leader, Mrs. Frances Willard, a mousy woman with a pointy nose, small spectacles, and hair pulled back into a short, tight bun. On her epic speaking tours Willard would describe her vision to take down the wall between Church and State and embed Christianity into the U.S. Constitution. We have "one absorbing purpose," said Willard. "It is that Christ shall be this world's King. King of its courts, its camps, and its commerce; King of its colleges and its cloisters; King of its customs and its constitutions."

For now, the favored tactic of Willard's women was entering saloons to pray and sing songs of Jesus until the patrons and bartenders couldn't take it anymore. Anthony succeeded in winning an endorsement from Willard and proclaimed that "the Christian craft of that great organization has set sail on the wide sea of women's enfranchisement." The WCTU, meanwhile, was receiving major funding from none other than John D. Rockefeller and formed its own party, the Prohibition Party. Matilda was adamantly against this alliance with what she called "the religious right," and she deemed Willard "the most dangerous person upon the American continent today."

Mrs. Willard first used Miss Anthony to help recruit money and members into her own organization. But once, when talking behind Anthony's back, Mrs. Willard revealed her true intentions. "When the time comes in which it will be political expediency for the Prohibition Party to throw women's suffrage overboard altogether, over it will go," Willard remarked to a close colleague.

The way Susan B. Anthony saw it, the best hope for women lay with the Republicans. Mrs. Stanton went along with her. Together they created a pamphlet entitled "Stand by the Republican Party" that urged all good men who believed in the cause of women's rights to vote for Blaine. Matilda was outraged by the endorsement. Breaking with her compatriots, she threw her support behind the tiny, under-funded Equal Rights Party, which stood for the enfranchisement not just of women but also of blacks and Native Americans and immigrants. Most of the people in the party couldn't vote in the election, but that wasn't the point. The purpose was to build a new coalition among those who believed that civil rights was the centerpiece of the American ideal. If even a small fraction of white men could be moved by this ideal, the new party would succeed in achieving Matilda's immediate goal, to hurt one of the major parties.

The candidate chosen by the Equal Rights Party was a fifty-four-year-old former schoolteacher named Belva Lockwood. Matilda attended meetings and held some gatherings at her home. The name Matilda Joslyn Gage was even chosen to be placed on the Equal Rights Party ticket as one of two electors at-large. Together with a small band of activists, she fought to get the party's nominees added to state ballots.

In November, Cleveland narrowly edged Blaine, winning twenty out of the thirty-eight states. The refrain of "Ma, Ma, where's my Pa?" was now answered with "Gone to the White House, Ha, Ha, Ha!" As for the popular vote, when all of the nearly 10 million ballots were tallied, Cleveland had won by the slimmest of margins, by only about 25,000 votes. The Prohibition Party served as the spoiler. Its candidate was the former Kansas governor, John St. John, who had succeeded in making Kansas the first dry state. St. John received almost 150,000 votes, meaning the religious right effectively held sway over presidential politics for the very first time. Meanwhile, the Equal Rights Party received 4,711 votes, double what it had received its first time around, in 1872, thus growing from having the support of virtually nobody to having the support of nearly nobody.

Frank Baum was not among that tiny minority, as he resisted getting swept up by his mother-in-law's brand of radical politics. As usual, Frank voted Republican, which he still viewed as the party of Lincoln even though those days had now faded. "I've always been a Republican when I've dabbled in politics, which is not often," Frank once wrote. Now that the Prohibitionists had effectively removed his favored party from the White House, Frank Baum had a fresh new reason to scorn Kansas.

The election turned out to be disastrous for the women's movement, as Miss Anthony's pamphlet had the effect of alienating the Democrats who were now suddenly in power. Although it was true that Grover Cleveland's childhood home sat across the street from the Gage home in Fayetteville, there was no personal connection, as Cleveland's family had moved out around the time the Gages moved in. Cleveland himself carried no sympathy for the cause of women. Thus far not a single U.S. president had even uttered the words *woman* or *women* in his inaugural address, and Cleveland was not about to start a new trend.

Among those the new president turned to was Reverend Byron Sunderland. He was the Syracuse preacher who had lashed out at Matilda Gage in the newspapers years before, calling the women's suffrage convention of 1852 "satanic." Sunderland had since become an expert on how women should behave in public, and he even authored a book called *Discourse to Young Ladies*, a series of sermons that expounded on his favorite proverb, "A woman that feareth the Lord, she shall be praised." His writings helped land him the position of chaplain of the United States Senate.

Soon, when the forty-nine-year-old Cleveland became the only president in history to get married in the White House, he would tap Sunderland to perform the ceremony. The marriage was a controversial one, as the bride, Frances Folsom, was only twenty-one years old at the time. The youngest First Lady in history was the daughter of Cleveland's former law partner, and as executor of his late partner's estate, the president was in charge of supervising the daughter's education. The new president had thus demonstrated the way men should treat women, as possessions.

Matilda felt she had no choice but to soldier on with the relentless work of keeping the women's movement true to itself. In mid-February of 1885 she traveled to New York City to attend the annual convention of the New York State Woman's Suffrage Association. "There were a great many gentlemen present," reported the *New York Times*, in apparent surprise. The chief order of business was the election of six officers for the coming year. Matilda Joslyn Gage and Susan B. Anthony were each voted in as vice presidents. Mrs. Gage stepped up to the podium as the convention's first speaker. Of all the things she uttered, the reporter for the *Times* selected only one comment, Matilda's remark that in the world of insects, the female is the ruler. "In the case of bees," she joked, "the males are so helpless that they are unable to feed themselves." The newly elected president of the association, Lillie Devereux Blake, picked up on this stab at humor and dug it in even deeper. "Mrs. Blake cruelly remarked that men were always in that condition." The *Times* featured these quotes under the headline "Mrs. Blake Alleges That Man Is a Helpless Animal." Such was the current state of public relations for the women's movement.

After the convention the most immediate task at hand was completing *History of Woman Suffrage*. What began a decade earlier as a simple book project had now grown into an epic trilogy, each volume topping a thousand pages. Volume 2 was completed in 1882, and the third volume would take the history almost to the present, so that all three books could be sold as a complete set and make money for its principal authors: Anthony, Stanton, and Gage. The triumvirate had signed a contract in which they agreed to split the profits equally.

Problems began to arise when it became clear that they would not be dividing the work equally. "Susan B. Anthony does not write," Matilda noted. "Her forte is letters—nothing otherwise, but she is a good suggestor, critic, etc., looks over letters, reads proofs, attends to the publishers, is general factotum, while Mrs. Stanton and myself do the writing." Susan did not dispute this. "It is the one drawback at every turn that I have not the faculty to frame easy, polished sentences," she admitted, proving her point with her writing. On another occasion her lamenting grew worse. "This is the biggest swamp I ever tried to wriggle through. Oh, to get out of this *History* prison. I am too tired to write—I mean too lazy. I love to make history but I hate to write it."

This forced Susan to rely on Matilda to an even greater extent, despite the fact that they quarreled over how to portray the role of the Church in oppressing women, Susan usually getting her way to omit harsh criticism. In the frenzy to complete the trilogy, Susan found herself visiting and staying at the Gage home more and more often. "Every few weeks she was obliged to rush over to Fayetteville to confer with Mrs. Gage, who was industriously preparing her part of the work," wrote Anthony's official biographer. "Mrs. Gage has a wonderful file of facts and data," Anthony once noted.

On top of their rift over religion, Susan and Matilda argued about money, as their endeavor had thus far failed to pay out anything but paltry sums. During the time her husband was ill and unable to work, Matilda was forced to take out a mortgage on their home for living expenses. She had planned to pay back the loan when profits from the *History* books materialized. The situation must have been deeply unnerving to her. Since she knew her Latin and therefore the meaning of her own surname, Matilda must have realized that the term *mortgage* means "death pledge." Matilda needed a source of income to avoid having her beloved home that she *pledged* to the bank become *dead* to her, in effect, if she would be unable to make the payments.

Under the terms of their contract, the three women agreed that Anthony would be in charge of the joint account, and that it was her obligation to issue a monthly statement of income and expenses. Yet over the past decade Anthony had issued only one such statement. Stanton and Gage, growing more and more exasperated, finally accused Anthony of charging some of her lavish travel expenses against book sales while failing to account for them. But proving this wouldn't be easy, and the three women did not want their private spat made public. As a solution to this ugly matter, Susan proposed to purchase all rights to the books for a one-time sum paid to each of her partners.

Matilda was especially susceptible to this devious offer, as she needed money immediately to retain control of her home. By mid-1885 all copyrights to these seminal works were transferred to the sole possession of Susan B. Anthony. So when *History of Woman Suffrage*, volume 3, was finally ready for the printer by the end of the year, it would be Anthony who would have the final edit and Anthony who would stand to gain all income from future sales, even though she had hardly written a single sentence. The entire episode created a widening chasm between Matilda and the other leaders of the suffrage fight.

Driving Matilda even farther from the mainstream were her antics at the October 28, 1886, dedication of a new statue in New York City's harbor which was given as a gift from France to America. At the ceremony President Cleveland declared, "We will not forget that liberty has made her home here." Matilda and some of her more radical colleagues were so outraged at the idea of using a female figure to sym-

bolize freedom that they chartered a boat and circled around what became known as Liberty Island, waving signs and placards: "The Statue
of Liberty is a gigantic lie!" "A travesty!" "A mockery!" How could it
be possible that a woman could represent liberty when females were
so enslaved by men worldwide? Lady Liberty was, in Matilda's eyes, an
oxymoron and "the greatest sarcasm of the nineteenth century." Such
harsh words about the popular new symbol of the American dream
didn't win Matilda many new friends—and alienated her old ones.

At the same time she was growing more and more isolated, Matilda
was also trying to fill her own spiritual void. Even though she was skeptical of organized religion, she was still seeking answers to life's mysteries. A faith called Theosophy attracted her with a force so great that it
was as if Matilda had willed this mixed bag of beliefs into being. Meaning "god-wisdom," Theosophy had been founded by Helena Petrovna
Blavatsky, the Ukrainian-born occultist said to be endowed with keen
psychic powers. An amalgam of Western science and Eastern mysticism, Theosophy was defined as a search for the center of one's self using all the knowledge of "modern magic," including the knowledge of
electricity and magnetism. Blavatsky created Theosophy as a threefold
quest—for the establishment of a universal fellowship of humanity,
for the forging of an understanding of all religions and sciences, and for
the finding of the keys to the unexplained and the mysterious.

Matilda Gage was one of a growing number of followers who were
making Madame Blavatsky into a great sage of spirituality. The Madame certainly looked the part. Her giant moon-shaped face sat atop
broad shoulders and a thick body draped in richly layered dresses of
velvet. But she was best known for her liquid eyes that seemed to func-
tion as portals to higher levels of consciousness. Called the "Mother
of the New Age," she possessed a boisterous and rollicking laugh that
once caused the poet Yeats to dub her "the most living person alive."

She had the travel itinerary of a ship captain. Born in Ukraine, she
was forced at the age of seventeen to marry a man old enough to be
her grandfather, her face flashing anger when the priest told her she
must obey her husband. "I shall not," she whispered. She held off the
consummation of the marriage for months, then finally escaped one
night on horseback, finding her way to a sailing ship bound for Con-

stantinople. Then it was on to Greece, Egypt, and France before en-
countering a mysterious man in London during the time of the great
Crystal Palace exhibition of 1851. He was "a tall Hindu in the street
with some Indian princes" and she "immediately recognized him" even
though they had never physically met. He approached her and said he
was bound for an important mission in Tibet and that she must come
along. Soon she found out his name: Mahatma Moyra. She simply
called him Master M.

Helena promised her new lifelong mentor that she would join him
as soon as possible, but she said that she must first go to America,
as she wrote that "it is in America that the transformation will take
place, and has already silently commenced." She believed that Americans were in the process of becoming a new people "whose mission and
karma it is to sow the seeds for a forthcoming, grander, and far more
glorious Race than any of those we know at the present." She spoke
about the formation in America of a higher level of consciousness in
which "cycles of matter will be succeeded by cycles of spirituality and
a fully developed mind."

Blavatsky spent the next quarter century on the path to enlightenment—traveling throughout America, India, Japan, Burma, the
Middle East, the Balkans, and Europe, studying with swamis, yogis,
and rabbis of the mystical Jewish Kabbalah. In her eyes they were all
mahatmas, or "great souls" who bestowed wisdom and compassion.
She studied Buddha, Krishna, Zoroaster, Moses, Abraham, and Jesus,
whom she greatly admired as "one of the grandest figures" of human
history. With her mysterious Hindu master she entered Tibet, to learn
the teachings of the Dalai Lama and to take on the painstaking work
of translating sutras penned in Tibetan calligraphy. Each sutra was a
sacred prescriptive teaching that could take months or years or a lifetime to understand, and then only if a person was open to receiving
the wisdom.

Endlessly questioning the ideas of others, Blavatsky found deficiencies in Darwinism, feeling that Darwin's theory was "not big enough"
because it failed to address the evolution of human consciousness. She
was wounded in a Russian war, shipwrecked on an island near Egypt,
and experienced the highest revelations and the most crushing set-
backs—before hearing a voice one day telling her she must return to

America at once. She immediately boarded a steamship for New York City, where she launched the Theosophical Society in 1875. "America is the only land of *true* freedom in the world," she declared.

Blavatsky soon became a U.S. citizen and published a two-volume opus, *Isis Unveiled*, that became a smashing worldwide bestseller, selling out its initial printing in just ten days. "The demand for it is quite remarkable," noted the *American Bookseller*. The book revealed the eternal secrets of the infinite mind through an investigation of the Egyptian goddess Isis, the archetype of the sacred and divine feminine, a prime symbol of the ancient matriarchy. The "Mother of the Gods" and "the Great Lady of Magic," Isis was also the mythic model for Christianity's Madonna.

Books on Theosophy were required reading in the home of Matilda Joslyn Gage, who studied the writings of Blavatsky to such an extent that Theosophy eventually become integrated into her own worldview. In March of 1885 Matilda attended a conference of the Theosophical Society in Rochester. It was there that she accepted fellowship in the society. Theosophy had a natural appeal for Matilda, as there was no concept of original sin — no forbidden fruit, no evil serpent, no dominance of one gender over the other, no conflict between God and nature, and no conflict between God and humanity. In Theosophy, as in Eastern religions and Native American tradition, there was no such "duality" at all. All was one. God and nature were the same. Divine consciousness could be reached by elevating one's own human consciousness. Just as a leaf turns toward the sun, so the mind turns toward the spiritual energy of the universe.

In Theosophy, Matilda had found a home. She decided to embrace this nascent movement wholeheartedly, hoping to gain a rational basis for her own spirituality. Matilda called Theosophy the "crown blessing" of her life and was particularly attracted to the concepts of the divine feminine and the reincarnation of karma, once telling her young grandchildren that "what is called 'death' by people is not death. You are more alive than ever you were after what is called death. Death is only a journey, like going to another country. After people have been gone for awhile, they come back and live in another body, in another family and have another name."

This unusual new belief system had received a giant boost when

Thomas Edison himself read a copy of *Isis Unveiled* that Madame Blavatsky had personally sent to him. Edison filled out a membership form, accepting fellowship and paying his dues in 1878, the year after he unveiled his phonograph and not long before he publicly displayed his electric light. During that same year the cofounder of the Theosophical Society, Henry Steel Olcott, reported that "Edison and I got to talking about occult forces, and he interested me greatly by the remark that he had done some experimenting in that direction. His aim was to see whether a pendulum, suspended on the wall of his private laboratory could be made to move by will-force."

Had Edison been living two centuries earlier, he might have been branded a wizard and burned at the stake for such an experiment. It was stories such as these that caused many people to consider Theosophy bizarre, heretical, pagan. Blavatsky was called "a spiritualistic charlatan" and "a consummate imposter"; one newspaper wrote that Theosophy was "imposed upon the credulous by ingenious trickery." Scattered reports around the country attributed all sort of bizarre behavior to this new cult. "Massachusetts Woman Driven Insane by Theosophy" was one such headline picked up by newspapers nationwide. Yet Theosophy was founded on American soil and it was taking root, growing bigger and more popular year by year, which only enraged those who felt threatened by its teachings.

For critics, perhaps the most lunatic aspect of Theosophy was a belief in a place called the Astral, a sphere somewhere not far from this world where anything was possible. The Astral was a realm of emotion and illusion, a place of intense meditation where one could have an out-of-body experience and work through one's fears and struggles. For L. Frank Baum, who started out with a skeptical view of his mother-in-law's newfound beliefs, it was the fantastical possibilities held by the hidden world of Astral Light that would influence him most deeply later in life, when he would create his own plane of spirituality, an otherworldly land not very far away, a place that would offer a visitor a newfound path to her true self.

To adherents of Theosophy, the Astral Plane was not an imaginary dream world but real terrain that could be investigated scientifically. An esteemed medical doctor and scientist with the Smithsonian Institution named Dr. Elliott Coues (pronounced "cows") caused a stir when he transformed himself from a clean-cut, well-dressed pillar of the establishment into the next president of the Theosophical Society of America. "Today his dress is careless, his trim beard has grown to almost patriarchal length, and his clear blue eyes now have a dreamy look of mysticism, the gaze of an opium eater," wrote one reporter. Dr. Coues claimed he could "project his spirit from his body" and "that he could appear to people at a distant place while his real body was in another."

One can find many subtle references to the views of Madame Blavatsky throughout the works of L. Frank Baum and the movie based on his book, yet there's one grand overriding Theosophical allusion: the Land of Oz itself. To get to the Land of Oz, one projects a phantom of oneself, magically flying to a spectacular place, just as Dorothy does. In Theosophy, one's physical body and one's Astral body are connected through a "silver cord," a mythical link inspired by a passage in the Bible that speaks of a return from a spiritual quest. "Or ever the silver cord be loosed," says the book of Ecclesiastes. "Then shall the dust return to the earth as it was: and the spirit shall return unto God who gave it."

In Frank Baum's own writing, the silver cord of Astral travel would inspire the silver shoes that bestow special powers upon the one who wears them. "The silver shoes are yours," says the Good Witch of the North, "and you shall have them to wear." She reaches down and picks up the shoes, "and after shaking the dust out of them," she hands them to Dorothy. In the film the color of these silver shoes was altered in a late draft of the script, becoming the ruby slippers. It turned out that the glittering red contrasted much more brilliantly with the glow of the Yellow Brick Road.

Several years after Mrs. Gage joined the Theosophical Society, a leading Theosophist named Dr. W. P. Phelon would oversee the indoctrination of Frank and Maud into the movement. "Man has received his ideas on the throne of the Infinite," Dr. Phelon would write. In the film these kinds of beliefs are at first mocked by the character of Professor Marvel, who spouts nothing but new-age mumbo jumbo. After Dorothy runs away from home, just before the tornado, she encounters this sideshow con man and amateur balloonist. Professor Marvel sits Dorothy down in his caravan to perform a mind-reading trick on her. "This is the same genuine, magic, authentic crystal used by the Priests of Isis and Osiris in the days of the Pharaoh of Egypt . . . and so on and so on," says the professor. "Now you better close your eyes, my child, for a moment in order to be better in tune with the infinite. We can't do these things without reaching out into the infinite."

8

Frontier of Hope and Fear

The first known photograph of a tornado or cyclone, taken
August 28, 1884, in Howard, Dakota Territory

The north and south winds met where the house stood,
and made it the exact center of the cyclone . . . The great
pressure of the wind on every side of the house raised it
up higher and higher, until it was . . . carried miles and
miles away as easily as you could carry a feather.

— L. FRANK BAUM,
The Wonderful Wizard of Oz

FRANK'S FATHER, Benjamin Baum, was riding his carriage
from home into the city on a crisp autumn morning when,
suddenly, at the corner of Park and Turtle streets, his horse
became frightened and bolted. The horse darted so quickly that Mr.
Baum couldn't control the reins, and the wagon careened to one side
of the street and collided with a hitching post, smashing apart. Benjamin's legs became entangled in the reins, and he was dragged by the
rampaging horse for about fifty yards, his upper torso bouncing again
and again on the unpaved road, rocks tearing at his scalp, before being released.

A newspaper headline on October 19, 1885, told how "A Startled
Horse Dashes Away with His Master and Flings Him Bleeding into
the Street." The terrible accident was a common one, but the vic-
tim wasn't common at all. "The Proprietor of Rose Lawn Farm Badly
Hurt," announced the *Syracuse Herald*. "Benjamin W. Baum, a well-
known resident of Onondaga County, was seriously injured this morning by a runaway horse." An ambulance arrived at the scene to treat
his wounds and to carry his bruised, broken body home. A day later
the *New York Times* came close to printing his obituary. "Benjamin W.
Baum, . . . a member of the firm Baum, Richardson Co., . . . was thrown

from his carriage here to-day and probably fatally injured," the paper reported. "He is well known throughout the oil country and was one of the original projectors of the Cherry Tree Run," one of the earliest oil wells near Titusville, Pennsylvania.

Frank must have rushed to Rose Lawn to find his mother, Cynthia, praying at her husband's bedside. Frank's siblings, Harriet, Mary, and Benjamin Jr., must have also hurried over as soon as they could. The youngest son, Dr. Harry Baum, would have arrived with his medical bag. As a dermatologist, his skills would be invaluable at this time. The elder Baum's brother, Uncle Doc, may also have come to assist the patient. The injuries that the sixty-four-year-old family patriarch suffered were indeed serious, leaving him immobilized and bedridden, but as the days turned into weeks, it appeared that Mr. Baum would survive.

What a shock it must have been to the family to learn just a few months later, on February 18, 1886, that Benjamin W. Baum was dead. The deceased was not the father but the thirty-six-year-old son, Frank's partner at Baum's Castorine. Sometime over the bitter winter, Benjamin Jr. caught pneumonia and never recovered. Frank's older brother left behind his wife of six years and a group of family businesses that were already in turmoil due to his father's misfortune. After the funeral, Benjamin Sr. made a request from his sickbed that his own younger brother, Adam Clarke Baum, join the business as Frank's partner, to keep the oil company running—an apparent sign that the father lacked confidence in his son as a businessman.

Frank had lost interest in the enterprise anyway and could hardly keep up his false enthusiasm. "I see no future in it to warrant my wasting any more years of my life in trying to boom it," he wrote. He would persist in his quest for success, but not the way his father did. It was around this time that Frank wrote that he wanted "an opportunity to be somebody," to be his own man, not to follow his father, but to find his own path, and he was becoming increasingly sure that the place he was seeking was not in or around Syracuse, but somewhere else, someplace that wasn't overrun with too much competition for too little business. "In this struggling mass of humanity," Frank wrote of life in the East, "a man like myself is lost."

He would seek his place in the world, but if it wasn't where he happened to be looking, he would search somewhere else. With the near
death of his father and the tragic loss of his brother, this search took
on a new urgency, as Frank's thoughts must have turned to his own
mortality and the fact that his damaged heart would not last forever.
He might die young like his brother or grow old like his father, but the
greater tragedy was not to live life in full. Weighed down by his past,
financially attached to his family, Frank yearned to break free as soon
as possible, to launch his true quest in earnest. He imagined the call
of wide-open spaces, someplace where he could discover who he really
was. Frank now got that faraway look in his eyes.

But any thoughts of questing had to be put on hold for now, as Maud
on February 1 had given birth to their second son. They named him
Robert Stanton, honoring the family name of Frank's mother. This delivery had been far more difficult than the first one. The complications
of childbirth nearly killed Maud, as she was diagnosed with a serious
case of peritonitis, a potentially fatal inflammation of the membrane
lining the abdomen that causes severe pain at the slightest touch and
would nowadays require emergency surgery. Kept on bed rest not just
for days and weeks but for months, she was well attended to—by a
nurse, by Frank, and by her mother, Matilda. With his brother dead
and his father and his wife both suffering through terrible pain, the
demands being placed on Frank, both at home and in business, were
nothing like he'd ever felt before. It would have been understandable
for Frank to get swallowed whole by all the pressure and responsibility,
and for him to respond accordingly, struggling through the trials of his
all-too-ordinary life, attending to his family's physical and economic
needs, yet never seeking what he was looking for, never making much
of a mark on America.

The arrival of spring that year seemed to renew Frank's spirits. He
had moved his slightly larger family to a slightly larger home, at 43
Holland Street, where Frank sat down on May 4 to pen a note filled
with thankfulness. Written in his elegant, backward-leaning script,
on Baum's Castorine letterhead, the letter was addressed to Maud's
brother, Thomas Clarkson Gage, in the Dakota Territory township of
Aberdeen. Named after a famous English abolitionist, Clark would be

a key ally along this crucial next stretch of Frank's journey. The previous summer Clark had finally given up his bachelorhood at the age of thirty-seven, when he wedded Sophie Taylor Jewell. The thirty-year-old bride had given birth on April 22, and the couple named the girl Matilda Jewell Gage, after her grandma. Now Frank was sending his brother-in-law some words of wisdom on raising a child. "I have been intending for a long time to write you a congratulatory letter but I have so much on hand," he wrote, "with Maud's sickness, business and moving combined—that it is only now that I see my way clear to tell you how lucky you are, and how happy you ought to be—and probably are."

The heart of the letter had Frank cracking his wit and lashing his brother-in-law for having a girl instead of a boy, as if he had had a choice in the matter. "A man's duty is to rear *Statesmen*—not patrons of millinery shops," those places where women try on fanciful hats. Even though Frank's mother-in-law probably wouldn't appreciate these jabs, Frank roared on. "Can a girl of tender years cuss, chew terbacker, smoke corn-silk, run away to swim in treacherous waters, and follow a band innumerable miles? NO!" He was making a comical case for having sons. "A boy can split kindling, run for Kerosene, carry bundles, get trusted at your grocery for candy and raisins, throw stones . . . what can a girl do? Nix."

Frank concluded by switching to a more tender tone, perhaps catching his brother-in-law off guard.

> You can now awaken a dozen or two times each night and sooth[e] your daughter . . . You can walk the floor with her over you shoulder, and have a friend point out when you reach the store [that] streak of milky substance down the back of your best coat. You can—but why harrow our mutual feelings this way? We are both in boats similar built . . . Let us shake hands gently . . . and forgetting the ills of life, cling only to thoughts of the sweet, innocent child faces that will brighten our lives for years to come, and make us thank God heartily that they have arrived at all.

This was Frank Baum, the proud father and gracious uncle. But the letter also signaled an emerging man, a humorist, an observer of life, someone all stirred up by the stories of Samuel Clemens, a ne'er-do-well drifter with a gift for language who headed far out west and reinvented himself as Mark Twain, a newspaper reporter in a Nevada silver-mining town. Baum must have recently read Twain's 1884 masterwork, *The Adventures of Huckleberry Finn,* as the exploits of Huck and the escaped slave Jim, rafting down the Mississippi—a story dismissed by critics for being written in American vernacular rather than proper English—clearly inspired the imagery, language, and attitude in Frank's letter. These were Huck's kind of activities—cussing, chewing "terbacker" (Twain spelled it *tobacker*), smoking corn silks, running away, swimming in treacherous waters, journeying for miles. Images of adventure had gotten into Frank's head. "The accusation of my friends that I have the 'Western Fever' is not wholly unfounded," Frank mused.

Yet another famed American figure was riding out West at this very time as well, to stoke more brave images in the minds of easterners. Theodore Roosevelt was just two years younger than Frank Baum, and the two men had much in common—sickly childhoods, successful fathers, and family tragedy. The youngest elected representative in the New York State legislature, T.R. was already fed up with politics and growing restless. On the verge of abandoning his career, T.R. rediscovered himself out West, investing in twenty thousand desolate acres during the great cattle boom in the Dakota Badlands, with a plan to make a fortune selling beef to be shipped in newfangled refrigerated railroad cars. The hard work and the "vigorous open air existence" transformed his feeble body into that of a Rough Rider.

On horseback on the wide-open range that he called "the Real West," T.R. cut a dashing figure for photographers, posing in a wide-brimmed hat, a fringed buckskin shirt, alligator boots, and all the accouterments of a horseman: the leather belt, the ivory-handled Colt revolver, the Winchester rifle, the bowie knife, the silver spurs, and a belt buckle that shone like justice. Not bad for a New York City slicker. T.R. romanticized his glorious times in a monograph entitled *Hunting Trips of a Ranchman,* in which he recounted his kill ("I was very proud of my first bear") and extolled the high life on the plains ("leaning back on my rocking chair . . . on the broad ranch veranda . . . gazing to the plateaus"). Baum greatly admired T.R. and later inserted specific references to his heroism into the stage version of *The Wizard of Oz.*

Such fables from out West, the land of big skies bursting with blue hope, tugged at a Frank Baum who turned thirty years old on May 15, 1886. He was a man itching to escape the shadows of his past and to reinvent himself just like Twain and T.R. Perhaps without even knowing it, he was being lassoed by the central myth that drove the westward expansion. Ever since a newspaper columnist in the 1820s wrote that it was our "Manifest Destiny" to "overspread and possess the whole continent . . . in order to advance the great experiment of liberty," this rallying cry grew decade by decade into America's core ideology. The fantasy of starting over, of finding fortune in the new place "out there," had already laid claim to the minds of three million easterners.

Yet the danger of saddling up and beginning life anew in a strange land of loose laws and murderous climate was enough to keep even greater millions from ever daring such an adventure. If a man failed at whatever endeavor he tried out West, there was no safety net to catch him, no government assistance, nothing to keep a family with no money fed and sheltered through a harsh winter or a scorching summer. No one was immune to failure, not even Teddy Roosevelt, who soon learned a crushing lesson: that the Dakota Badlands were no place for cattle. During the relentless blizzards of 1886–87, the snow got so deep and the air so polar that entire herds of cattle were buried alive and frozen to death. Unlike buffalo, cattle simply weren't big enough, strong enough, or well insulated enough to withstand a Dakota winter's ambush.

Nevertheless, Frank was eyeing the harsh Dakota Territory as his next destination. Not only had Maud's brother, Clark Gage, moved out to Aberdeen in 1881, but Maud's two sisters had followed. Julia Louise Gage had married a man named James D. Carpenter, and since 1884 the couple had been homesteading about seventy miles north of Aberdeen, near a settlement called Edgeley. Under the preemption rules of the Homestead Act, the territory was carved into rectangles measuring 160 acres. A man simply had to build a house on an unclaimed plot and live there for six months. After that, the government or the railroad company would sell the claimant the land for as little as $1.25 per acre.

Julia Gage Carpenter painted a bleak picture of life on the prairie, a place where temperatures could plunge from thirty degrees above zero to thirty below in a matter of hours. Julia called the winters "deathly cold" and described her life as "franticly lonely," with no neighbors for twenty miles in any direction and nothing but scorched prairie grass to break the mind-numbing flatness. Her Dakota home was a two-room shack, just twelve by twelve feet, built with lumber carted by wagon over the treeless plains.

Nearly every spring was good for at least one tornado, often ripping from the horizon at speeds above 250 miles per hour, destroying entire farms. The world's very first photograph of a live black twister, captured in Howard, Dakota Territory, in 1884, helped generate heightened popular interest in what these beasts were and how they formed. The monsters could strike Dakota at any time during the spring and summer. In early April of 1887, a ferocious one hit Watertown during the same time as a prairie fire, setting off piercing alarm bells throughout the town. The twister-whipped flames consumed the eastern part of the village while the swirling winds became a dust devil that emptied a lumberyard, filling the skies with soaring splinters. Railroad freight cars were blasted from a depot and lifted aloft. Miles of land were transformed into blinding clouds of gray specks.

A deadly demon had formed in June a few years earlier, whirling into Grand Forks from the west, killing five people instantly, then injuring at least twelve more while overturning a church, pulverizing a fledgling university, and uprooting dozens of houses. In late July, also in 1887, a homicidal horror show came from the east, racing into Dell Rapids. Blackish blue in appearance, this one featured rapid-fire hailstones that became aimless bullets, assassinating cattle and cutting visibility down to the length of one's arm. "Some farmers reported their horses and cattle blown away and not a vestige of their houses or barns left," according to newswires. "The occupants were saved by fleeing to their cellars."

Julia's home was never leveled by one of these whirlwinds, but in her worst moments she might have wished it had been, because she hated life on the harsh prairie. "This is awful country," Julia once wrote from the depths of her Dakota despair. Her sister Helen Leslie Gage, meanwhile, must have witnessed a cyclone firsthand, because she wrote an evocative article about a certain house where an old man was climbing down into his cellar to seek shelter from a cyclone—when all of a sudden "the house went off its foundation, knocking him along with it." The house itself "was carried a little above the ground to the southeast, where it struck the earth and then was lifted over two or three feet north and set down at an angle of forty-five degrees." Helen's article was published in a Syracuse newspaper, where Frank undoubtedly read it and remembered it for a long time.

Neither Julia nor Helen could have imagined that the shacks they described on the tornado-plagued plains would one day become prototypes for a remarkably similar one that would be reset in a fictional Kansas—a house fitted with a cyclone cellar "in case one of those great whirlwinds arose" in the distance. "From the far north they heard a low wail of the wind," Frank would write of that fateful day in Dorothy's life. "There now came a sharp whistling in the air from the south, and as they turned their eyes that way they saw ripples in the grass coming from that direction also." In the film one of the farm hands cries out, "It's a twister! It's a twister!"

Life wasn't as isolating in Aberdeen, a bona fide southern Dakota boomtown where Clark's early success had encouraged Maud's other sister, Helen, to move as well. Helen had married a far distant cousin, Charles Gage, who liked the idea of joining his new brother-in-law in the speculation of real estate. They relocated to the middle of the village, which was now flooding with settlers and investors from Syracuse, Fayetteville, and scores of other points back East. Soon after Helen and Charles arrived in Aberdeen on the Chicago, Milwaukee & St. Paul Railroad, Maud wrote about how she already missed her sister. "I have thought of you all so much, and I am so lonely, I shall miss you so much," Maud wailed. "I feel dreadfully. I said very little to you before you went about how much I hated to have you go, and how much I would miss you, because it seemed best for you to go and you felt so badly about it. We will never live near each other again and [will] only see each other once in a while."

But the death of Benjamin Ward Baum on February 14, 1887, seemed to release Maud's husband from his business obligations in Syracuse. The passing of Frank's father at age sixty-six was in many ways a relief, as he had never recovered from his accident fourteen months earlier. Cynthia Baum, his wife of forty-five years, had already closed down Rose Lawn, as she was unable to run the place on her own, and she had relocated her fading husband to a rental house in central Syracuse. Then, sometime after the funeral, she finally sold off the grand Rose Lawn estate for a sum of $6,000, just $1,000 more than the purchase price twenty years earlier. For a time Cynthia lived with her son Dr. Harry Baum, and later with her daughter Hattie. Frank knew his mother would be well cared for, supported by his Syracuse siblings, and so he allowed his thoughts to keep drifting. In his father's will Frank received $2,500, enough money to start a new enterprise and keep his family fed for about a year of uncertain times.

Now that he had some money in his hands, Frank resumed his westward gaze, dreaming about parlaying his inheritance into a fortune on the frontier. He wasn't the only one. Even his mother-in-law, Matilda, was taken in by stories of how plots of land in a good location could multiply a small stash of cash tenfold within a few short months or years. "I must find some way to make money," Matilda wrote to her Dakota son. "Let me know at once just where you think I had better invest."

During the summer of 1887, Frank, Maud, and their two boys spent several weeks living full-time with Matilda in Fayetteville. Still ill, Maud needed the care her mother lavished on her. Frank took up a new hobby, amateur photography, buying one of the hot-selling inventions of George Eastman and using his new black-box Kodak to capture and develop dozens of images of Fayetteville roads and of Matilda's Greek Revival house on East Genesee Street. This may have been the first time that Frank witnessed his mother-in-law meditating. Matilda would spend time every day sitting silently in the back parlor, by her painting easel and her tray of watercolors, channeling her thoughts to a place somewhere in the sky, a place where anything was possible, a place where women were in charge, a place of emotion and illusion not too far away from this world.

Her stillness in these moments contrasted with her action in others. Matilda corresponded vigorously during this time with her Dakota children, beseeching Clark for information on real estate opportunities, to the point where Clark sent his mother a detailed map of Aberdeen that showed the dimensions and locations of each lot on the town grid. Both she and Frank read articles sent by Clark that publicized Aberdeen as "the next Chicago," perhaps unaware how many other boomvilles were boasting the very same thing. At least Aberdeen had something special going for it, as the town was the meeting point for seven lines of three great railroads, a distinction that had it touting itself as "the Hub City." Aberdeen claimed to be nearly established, boasting of a telephone system, electric lights, an ample water supply, and a growing population of six thousand. "Invest in Aberdeen before prices double again," wrote a self-interested local real estate developer named Hagerty. "Her future is certain and her growth is substantial." Matilda pored over the maps, plucking choice lots for Clark to buy with $300 she had set aside.

Clark didn't carry out his mother's urgent plans, possibly because these lots had been snapped up by the time he got her letter. The correspondence continued, and at one point Clark told his mother that he was starting a new firm, a general store, under the name Beard, Gage & Beard on a corner lot, at least taking heed of his mother's faith in corner locations. The Beard brothers were old family friends who grew up just down the street from the Gages in Fayetteville. Matilda liked the idea of the business just fine but was outraged by the sequence of the names. "The firm should be Gage, Beard & Beard," she wrote. "By all means follow my advice. To have your name first will be of great advantage to you."

But Clark didn't or couldn't carry out this wish, for whatever reason, and Matilda's intuition proved to be dead-on. Because of the new store's corner location, the entire street became known as "the Beard Block," and the name Beard became known throughout Aberdeen when the store prospered because of its smart merchandising at a strategic location. Clark and the Beard brothers soon plowed some of their profits into additional real estate, investing in sizable acreage on a higher elevation just west of Aberdeen. They promoted the area as West Hill, a quiet place for families who wanted a larger home away from the bustle of downtown.

Back in Syracuse, Maud was finally on her feet, feeling well enough by the end of the summer to resume housekeeping on Holland Street. On November 9 she and Frank hosted a small dinner party with friends and family, to celebrate their five-year wedding anniversary. They were grateful to be getting their lives together again after this two-year string of misfortunes. Frank still hadn't made any definitive decision to relocate the family out West—after all, he had little idea how he would support the family there. It would be a dangerous move, a life-transforming choice, and as the father of two little boys, ages four and eighteen months, Frank had become a careful man.

The catalyst that triggered Frank's decision came in the spring of 1888. Uncle Adam's health was deteriorating, to the point where he wasn't able to come to the store. To pick up the slack, Frank had hired a young clerk to help keep the place running. This was during a time when Baum's Castorine Company was faltering. Frank was making hardly any sales calls, and fewer and fewer customers were buying the products. Worse, the clerk whom Frank put in charge of manning the register was tempted into skimming cash and gambling it away. Frank was notoriously bad at keeping tabs on the flow of money and didn't notice.

Then, one day in April, Frank arrived at the store to find the clerk dead on the floor. His remorse over committing a crime that drove the Baum family business to the brink of ruin apparently caused him to take his own life. According to a company history, the clerk shot himself in the head. When Frank arrived at the store that day to discover the dead man in a pool of blood, the hot gun still in his hand, he became terrified and almost had a heart attack right then and there. There are no documents from outside the company or family descendants to confirm this incident, or even what the clerk's name was, but suicides were considered so shameful that editors often kept them out of the newspapers. Within weeks Frank was in negotiations to dispose of the business for a modest sum of money to a pair of brothers named Stoddard who were in the scouring powder business and were looking to diversify. The enterprise would go on to do fine without Frank, operating continuously under the Baum brand name to this very day—more than 120 years later.

By early June of 1888, Frank was off on an exploratory mission, a trip he was trying to keep secret from everyone except his immediate family, so as not to raise expectations. Dressed in his best business suit and his Syracuse-manufactured Nettleton shoes, the same shoes that T.R. wore when he was in the East, no one would have mistaken Frank Baum for a western cowboy. With his hair and mustache neatly trimmed, Frank boarded a train that fed into the Northern Pacific Railway. Leaving the thick canopy of trees behind for the endless horizon, he sat for hours in a vibrating seat, reading newspapers and gazing out the window at the June skies, watching the sunlight dance on distant mountains, perhaps striking up conversations with other businessmen.

He was now heading into the land of contrasts and contradictions, the Northern Pacific itself serving as a perfect example. Few people questioned how the most fiercely capitalist enterprise in the country was formed in a most extreme act of government largess, via the largest land grant in U.S. history. A fifty-million-acre corridor stretching from Buffalo clear across to Oregon—an area about the size of England and Scotland combined—was placed for free into private hands. To help fund the laying of the transcontinental track, the executives of the company sold off the "cheap" but "valuable" land that surrounded the railroad. The contradictions compounded as the train pushed farther west, into the homeland of the Great Plains Native Americans, as this land of "freedom" and "opportunity" also held the continent's largest zone of captivity and despair, the Great Sioux Reservation.

Frank Baum was struggling with contradictions of his own, filled with the hope of a better life in these wide-open spaces yet not untouched by the fear of failure and physical danger in the untamed territory. Eager to discover what he could see and do along this frontier, he was journeying to the center of himself at the same time he was headed into the geographical center of North America. On his research mission Frank was not only scouting Aberdeen as a place for his family to live, but also looking for a new livelihood, a new business to start. His logic went something like this: If Aberdeen was to become the next Chicago, there must be certain kinds of businesses that it would need along the way. So it would make sense to spend a couple of weeks visiting midsize cities to see what enterprises those places had in common with Chicago yet were lacking in Aberdeen.

The eighth of June had Frank Baum staying at one such midsize city, La Crosse, Wisconsin, at an inn called the Cameron House. It was from there that Frank first sent word to Clark that he was about to visit, emphasizing in his letter to "*Keep it mum.*" He was not yet letting on that he was planning to move his family out to Aberdeen, as he wanted to make this decision objectively, based on information, not on impulse. "I am on a business trip," Frank wrote to his brother-in-law, "and as I shall go to St. Paul & Minneapolis have decided to call on you all in Aberdeen and pay my respects. I don't want Helen or Julia to know I am coming, as I'd like to surprise them, but as I did not know whether or not Helen was at home, I thought I'd write and ask you, and see if the coast was clear. Please write and let me know."

On the train to St. Paul, Frank picked up the trail of the Sioux, a people central to the history of America. Minnesota, meaning "sky-tinted water," was the ancestral homeland of those who spoke the Siouan language. For centuries these stocky, red-skinned people had lived in the region's forests and farmed maize along its rivers. The introduction of the horse transformed their civilization, turning the men into bison hunters and proud, face-painted warriors. By 1700 the Sioux had crossed the Red River into the land they called Dakota, meaning "friend," and by 1750 they had traversed the Missouri River toward the mountains that they called the Paha Sapa, the Black Hills. The majesty of this land gave rise to great myths, and tribal storytellers told tales of how their ancestors once lived in the underworld until they passed through the Wind Cave deep in the hills to emerge as the First People of the Great Plains. This was a whole lot more interesting than saying you came from Minnesota.

Growing larger than all the other tribes in the region combined, the Western Sioux became known as the Lakota, for "alliance of friends." Chief among their rituals was the hunt itself, which the Sioux saw not as a slaughter but as a sacred sacrifice in which the animal gives its spirit to the warrior in order to sustain a fellow life. The Sioux didn't just subsist on the buffalo's meat but made use of every body part—fur for clothing, skins for tepees, bones and horns for tools and ornaments, dung for cooking fuel.

But then came the rallying cry of Manifest Destiny, the divine mandate that told the white men that the whole continent was theirs to conquer. By the 1830s settlers were stampeding, and in eastern Dakota one Sioux tribe was pressured to sell its land to the U.S. government and live on reservations. The holdouts were either shot, sent to prison, or otherwise dispersed, and the land was opened to homesteading. Resentment boiled over, and some Native Americans retaliated against the encroaching white wagon trains, staging deadly ambushes and posting scalped heads on poles along trails as warning signs. By these acts the Sioux and other Plains tribes became known as the terrorists of the nineteenth century.

Fear of the natives gathered into a unifying force, resulting in a war banner under which much could be accomplished. Perhaps the greatest fear of all was the image of a marauding band of warriors riding into a white settlement, shooting the men, stealing livestock, and capturing women and children, then turning them into their slaves. The Navajo were notorious for this practice, provoking settlers throughout the West to raise money for new forts to guard new white population centers. Of the Navajo, Charles Bent, the governor of the New Mexico Territory, wrote in a letter to Washington that "a large portion of the [Navajo] stock has been acquired by marauding expeditions against the settlements. They have in their possession many prisoners, men, women and children, taken from settlements of this Territory, who they hold and treat as slaves." Of course, the Navajo who were forced to live on the reservations were actually confined in greater numbers. Nevertheless, such stories had the cumulative effect of tapping into primal fears. Tales of terror traveled by telegraph from the West to Washington and back again—the nation's East-West axis of anxiety.

In his fiction L. Frank Baum would one day create his own East-West federation of fear controlled by the Wicked Witches of Oz. But with the demise of the eastern witch in the blue country, the Munchkins were liberated. Only one zone of terror remained: the land of the West, a yellow country inhabited by a people known as the Winkies who were enslaved by the one remaining Wicked Witch. In this context yellow signals both danger and cowardice. Yellow was the color of gold, well known to be buried in the hills of Lakota country, as well as the color in that most famous western name, the region known as Yellowstone.

"And that country, where the Winkies live, is ruled by the Wicked Witch of the West, who would make you her slave if you passed her way," Frank would write. "The yellow Winkies [are] too afraid of her not to do as she told them." But by the end of the story the Winkies, too, would be liberated. To express respect, they bestow gifts, not unlike Native Americans during a friendly trade mission. One of the Winkies is a goldsmith, who crafts a special gold handle for the Tin Woodman's ax as a gift of thanks for his extraordinary compassion. They also present him with a jeweled oilcan.

In real life the Lakota Sioux were not always a captive people living under the rule of the U.S. military. But then came the Battle of Little Bighorn. In the aftermath of that 1876 confrontation—in which the legendary Chief Sitting Bull led the slaughter of General Custer and more than two hundred men of the Seventh Cavalry—the recriminations were merciless. U.S. soldiers began attacking Sioux villages more frequently, and hunters began shooting hundreds of buffalo at a time with repeater rifles. The Northern Pacific Railway bisected Sioux land and divided the bison into northern and southern herds. After removing a few tongues, tails, and hides, the riflemen would leave the giant carcasses to rot. In some places one could walk a quarter mile on dead buffalo and see no earth, only flesh and blood.

To the Native Americans of the Great Plains, the buffalo were more than the source of their food, clothing, and shelter. The buffalo were central to tribal mythology. The Great Spirit told them bison were sacred, that killing must be done with respect, that the recycling of the animal's spirit was part of the circle of life. At one time more than fifty million bison were said to roam the country, outnumbering the people of the United States. But in the decade after Little Bighorn, the beasts were slaughtered to the verge of extinction, destroying the religion and the history of an entire people, the ultimate sacramental violation. "Can you imagine," asks Joseph Campbell, "what it would be like, in just ten years, for a people to lose their environment, their food supply, and the central object of their ritual life?"

And so as L. Frank Baum arrived in Aberdeen, located about a hundred miles east of the Standing Rock Reservation, about a day's ride on horseback, the stage was set for a final clash of cultures. The Euro-Americans, who believed in their glorious Manifest Destiny, would pit their ideology against the Native Americans, who believed in their sacred bond with the land and the last remaining buffalo. The transfer of the continent was nearly complete—only the renegades of Sitting Bull's Lakota stood in the way—and those who chose to make their home in Dakota at this time would be confronted with near daily newspaper reports about these dangerous developments.

Like most other frontier Americans, Frank Baum would be forced to grapple with chronic fear. Calling Sitting Bull "the greatest Medicine Man of his time," Frank became fully aware of the pent-up anger harbored by the Lion of the Lakota. "What wonder that a fiery rage still burned within his breast," Frank wrote of Sitting Bull, "and that he should seek every opportunity of obtaining vengeance upon his natural enemies." For someone like Frank Baum who had the ability to spot symbols and transform life into story, the Dakota Territory would become a frontier of the mind. "There was the sense of a stirring of the mythic imagination," says Joseph Campbell about this time in Dakota. "All the evidence you need was there, the full evidence of the mythic imagination."

9

The Story Store

L. Frank Baum's photo of the storefront that became Baum's
Bazaar. Sister-in-law Helen Leslie and husband, Charles,
in windows; nieces Leslie and Matilda Jewell sitting on stairs.

The American people love to be humbugged.

— P. T. BARNUM

"Exactly so!" declared the little man, rubbing his hands together as if it pleased him. "I am a humbug."

— THE GREAT OZ

ON JUNE 15, 1888, Frank arrived by train in Aberdeen. After nearly two weeks of travel amid strangers, Frank was pleased to see his brother-in-law, T. Clarkson Gage, whose face was weathered from his years raising new homes and storefronts under the prairie sun. Clark was part of a small group of men who had arrived in 1881 with piles of lumber when the Milwaukee Road first stopped there. The buffalo in this part of the James River valley had already been slaughtered, leaving only scattered bones as a reminder that this was once a land of thunderous stampedes. To the naked eye of the white man, it was simply another patch of nowhere, part of the vast void labeled the Great American Desert. But the town's founders were blessed with the gift of imagination, naming the town after a verdant city in Scotland. Novelist Hamlin Garland was one of many who came to homestead nearby, and he couldn't help but romanticize the mood: "Free land was receding at railroad speed . . . and every man was in haste to arrive . . . All around me . . . the talk was land, land! Every man I met was bound for the Jim River Valley, and each voice was aquiver with hope, each eye alight with anticipation of certain success . . . Aberdeen was the end of the line."

All that Frank saw had been accomplished in just seven short years, a feat that made Aberdeen shine with pride. The township was laid out in a well-planned grid, not unlike New York City. Plenty of people milled about, but there were fewer western cowboy types with six-shooters and stovepipe hats and far more transplanted eastern men like himself, dressed in jackets and bowlers. In the center of town sat a large U.S. land office and a number of stately banks and fine hotels, including the newly built Kennard Hotel, which boasted a steam-powered elevator and a cream-colored brick exterior that climbed three stories into the sky. The streets were unpaved, but many sported wood-plank sidewalks so pedestrians could keep their shoes clean. For a frontier town the numbers were notable. Aberdeen was home to four restaurants, five music teachers, six saloons, seven of its own newspapers, eight doctors, and thirty-five lawyers.

Aberdeen used to have a problem with flooding during heavy rains —rival villages called it "the town in the frog pond"—but the men fixed that by digging a network of artesian wells to round up the water and reserve it for drinking and washing. The town was only partially rigged for electricity, but just two years earlier a man named Zietlow, the founder of the Dakota Central Telephone Company, planted himself there. He sank dozens of wooden poles into the ground and then strung up ten miles of telephone line, selling more than a hundred phones and counting. His wife served as the local switchboard operator, and their children signed up new subscribers. The Zietlows were so successful in creating one of the first western phone networks that Alexander Graham Bell himself threatened to sue them for patent infringement.

Frank was greatly impressed. "Aberdeen is destined to be a good city," he predicted, "and it *may* be a metropolis."

The town's economy tied itself to the fate of the surrounding farms. The seat of Brown County, Aberdeen encompassed more than 1,700 square miles, about the size of Delaware. Farmland was said to support thirty-eight bushels of wheat per acre, as long as the rain cooperated, and this land could be developed at a tenth of the cost of back East, as there were absolutely no trees to clear. The golden fields of wheat stretched far and wide, melting into the horizon. This alone made Dakota seem like a different country to Frank, as the big skies came down to meet the land in a way he'd never witnessed living by the forests back home. Frank could also see that this was a deeply religious community, as Aberdeen supported a dozen handsome churches, and the denominations included everything from Lutheran to Catholic to Episcopalian to Baptist to Congregationalist to Methodist to Evangelical to Presbyterian, many led by pastors and ministers from Syracuse and other points back East. People out here wanted to start over fresh, and they couldn't do it without God on their side.

At the corner of Main Street and Third Avenue sat Beard, Gage & Beard, the busy dry goods store co-owned by Clark. Inside, the wall behind the front counters was crammed with small items held in boxes arranged in neat rows, offering everything from hardware to coffee beans to spices. Canned goods weighed down rows of shelving. Rolls of area rugs, wallpaper, and drapery were off to one side. The clothing section showcased shoes and boots, shawls and satin dresses, underwear and hosiery, as well as jackets, gloves, and scarves. Clark's partners, Henry and Frank Beard, came from Fayetteville but were now true Aberdonians. They were not only working hard running the store and managing their real estate holdings but were also active in the statehood movement. Real estate prices had already multiplied many times over the past five years, and official statehood could only accelerate the land grab.

Staying at his brother-in-law's new house in the West Hill section, Frank finally met Clark's wife, Sophie, a lovely young lady with upswept brown hair. He also had the pleasure of saying hello to their two-year-old daughter, Matilda, whom Frank came to call Tillie, in part to distinguish his little niece from her namesake grandmother. Uncle Frank happened to have a son, Robert, just about the same age as Tillie, and he couldn't help but think how nice it would be for the cousins to grow up together.

If Frank was pretty much sold on Aberdeen by now, there was still one big remaining question: What kind of work would he be able to take up once he moved the family there? If Frank wanted to resume his acting and playwriting, Aberdeen had a small opera house, but he had learned the hard way how little money that line of work held. If Frank wanted to sell Castorine oil, there certainly was demand for such a product. If Frank wanted to take up chicken farming once again, land and livestock were available at cheap prices.

Frank, however, was looking to try something new, most likely capitalizing on his retail and sales experience. He paid a visit to his sister-in-law Helen, her husband, Charles, and their small daughter, Leslie. They owned a two-story building, constructed just three years earlier, that was located at 406 Main Street, near the corner of Fourth Avenue. The family lived on the second floor, above a retail setup that had just been vacated by a land office. Helen told her brother-in-law that the lease happened to be available at this prime location. Frank had brought his Kodak camera on the trip, and he asked the family if they'd be willing to be in a picture of this building, so he could show Maud what it looked like. Captured in a photograph, the storefront featured large display windows on either side of the front entrance, and in the picture one can spot Charles and Helen sitting in the upper-floor windows. Right next to the building, sitting on the steps in the alleyway, are the tiny images of Frank's two nieces, Tillie and Leslie, in summer dresses.

All in all, Frank took a strong liking to this western town and its pioneer spirit. "In your country," Frank wrote back to his brother-in-law, after arriving back in Syracuse, "there is an opportunity to be somebody, to take a good position, and opportunities are constantly arising where an intelligent man may profit." And so Frank had made his decision, after discussing it with Maud, of course. "It seems as though it [is] not too late to throw my fortunes in with the town, which appears to be only in its infancy." Frank's remaining question was quite specific: What kind of store would go best in that location?

Frank Baum brainstormed his business idea, outlining the basic concept in a letter to Clark written on Baum's Castorine letterhead and marked "confidential." The letter, dated July 3, reveals his thinking in a way that opens a fascinating window into his mind. "I've got an idea into my head," he wrote, "and before I return to let it influence my actions I want your advice on the matter." It was imperative that he get approval from Clark on this idea because he didn't want to be seen as competing with Beard, Gage & Beard in any way. This would be a difficult issue to skirt, as Clark's store was expressly designed to sell nearly everything that the households of Aberdeen needed.

Recognizing that fact was the brilliance of Frank's idea. If Clark is selling everything people *need*, Frank thought, I will sell everything people *don't* need.

What seems to be missing from Aberdeen is a "Bazaar" that would sell fancy goods . . . sporting goods, out-door games, baseball supplies, bicycles, amateur photograph goods, fancy willowware, cheap books & good literature, stationery, toys, and crockery specialties . . . Not a 5¢ store, but a Bazaar on the same style as the "Fair" in Chicago (on a much smaller scale).

Frank didn't directly ask the touchy question of whether Clark would view this as competition. As long as Clark understood what the idea was and didn't object, Frank would take that as tacit permission. Instead, Frank's main question for Clark was whether Aberdeen was ready for such a store, as Frank had seen such operations in larger cities. "Is the town big enough," he asked, "to enable me to sell these kind of goods and to make money?" Specifically, did Clark think that such a store could be started with $2,000 capital, and could it sell $1,000 worth of goods per year?

The challenge of convincing the people of Aberdeen to buy what they didn't need not only didn't bother Frank; he relished it. The knack for creating belief was one of his talents, honed in his playwriting and salesmanship. In this respect Frank was ahead of his time. The ability to drive demand for stuff people didn't know they wanted would one day become a defining characteristic of the American economy. The way Frank put it, he "would make an effort to render such goods popular." Frank had a natural sense of the magic trick. He knew that objects alone don't sell. What sells is the *story* that attaches to the object, and so Frank would stock his store with the best stories from around the world, alongside his own homegrown tales.

And so Frank's plan was set in motion. He would relocate his family and hold a grand opening of Baum's Bazaar by the first of October, well in time for the holiday retail season. During the summer Frank went about ordering his first stock of goods, to be delivered just prior to opening day. September had the family packing up their home, saying goodbye to their friends, and getting ready for the big move west. Frank and Maud, along with Frank Jr. and Robert, arrived at the depot in Aberdeen on September 20 and stayed with Clark and Sophie until they could find a suitable place of their own. Within a couple of weeks they moved into a simple house at 211 Ninth Avenue, in the south-east section of town.

To grab the attention of customers and introduce the idea that his store would be like no other, Frank ran an advertisement in the *Aberdeen Daily News*, the largest of the town's seven newspapers. Above all, Baum's Bazaar had to be a fun place to shop, and so Frank decided to create a whimsical poem for the occasion, making up a story about how the poem was actually generated by some newfangled machine:

> We have just received from the patentee a new Poetry Grinder and having set it up in the midst of our beautiful stock, we turned the crank with the following result:

> *At Baum's Bazaar you find by far,*
> *The finest goods in town;*
> *The cheapest, too, as you'll find true*
> *If you'll just step around.*

> *There's glassware neat and new and sweet,*
> *Their crockery is a wonder:*
> *There are sets for water, cups and saucer*
> *At twenty cents and under!*

> *And then their line is extra fine*
> *In goods real Japanese;*
> *The albums plush go with a rush,*
> *The lamps can't fail to please.*

> *You're sure to find just what you mind,*
> *The bric-a-brac so rare.*
> *The baskets light, the jewels bright,*
> *The flowers so fresh and fair,*

> *And then the toys for girls and boys*
> *Are surely . . .*

> (Here the machine got stuck, and on taking it apart it was found so full of enthusiasm that we were obliged to send it to one of the old-fashioned up-town stores to enable it to ooze out.)

Frank also advertised that "every lady attending on opening day will be presented with a box of Gunther's Candies," an assortment of chocolate bonbons crammed with delectable fillings that were shipped directly from Chicago. And so Baum's Bazaar opened as scheduled with great fanfare. About a thousand customers lined up and passed through the door that first day, an incredible turnout given the size of the town, and the newspapers gave their newest advertiser rave reviews, as if Frank once again were premiering a new musical. Mr. Baum "has the push and enterprise necessary to the western businessman," said one reviewer. The store offers "the finest stock of this line that has ever been in this city."

Frank's unusual humor didn't seem to get in the way of sales. First month's revenues were $531, a tidy sum considering his goal for the first year was $1,000. With a successful wheat harvest that fall, times were good, encouraging Frank to make more expansive plans. He would

Advertisement for the opening of Baum's Bazaar

start new clubs for amateur photography, for lawn tennis, for bicycle riding, for stamp collecting, for scrapbooking—and then sell the necessary accoutrements. He also wanted to see the town launch its own baseball team, so that he could supply bats, balls, and uniforms, and to establish a better opera house, where he could maybe stage plays and provide costumes for the cast. Baum's Bazaar wasn't just a place to buy toys, gifts, home wares, knickknacks, and reading material; it would be the town's official connection for the entire leisure side of life.

In November, Frank ran an ad under the headline "Peruse, Ponder, Purchase" that listed an astounding array of merchandise, more than three hundred kinds of items, ranging from tea sets to molasses jugs to lunch baskets to knife rests to foot warmers to feather dusters to piano lamps to picture frames. The store sold bamboo screens, silk shades, gold toothpicks, oxidized hairpins, music boxes, manicure sets, perfumery, umbrella stands, parasols, magic lanterns, candlesticks, buffalo horns, and silver gongs. Kids could find dressed dolls, wax dolls, crying dolls, and talking dolls as well as picture books, building blocks, tricycles, hobbyhorses, popguns, swords, swing sets, harmonicas, jackstraws, tin trains, steam engines, soldiers, trumpets, drums, toy monkeys, talking parrots, nodding donkeys, paper animals, snow sleds, and play villages.

Each and every item seemed to have a story attached to it. Frank named the toy village Phunnyland, a whimsical place where candy grew on trees. The Chinese lanterns and the Japanese lanterns came from different places, represented different magical legends, and were used in different ways. When Frank held a tin soldier or a toy monkey in his hands, these items could march or fly or hold conversations.

Although no one in Aberdeen needed any of the stuff sold there, people loved to visit the store, especially children, who flocked to hear "Uncle Frank" tell amazing stories during hours when the register wasn't busy. After school the kids would come to buy penny candy, an ice cream cone, or a bottle of pop and gather 'round. He actually wasn't particularly good at making up stories from whole cloth, but rather would more often draw on his real-life experiences. To entertain small children, Frank would tell simple tales of talking animals, sometimes based on his memories of the farm at Rose Lawn. But for older kids he recounted more involved tales, including one of his all-time favorites, the incredible saga of the Cardiff Giant, a story that he once spoofed in the *Rose Lawn Home Journal*.

The true story of this remarkable untruth happened around the time the young Frank was away at the Peekskill Military Academy. In October of 1869 an unusual bit of news came out of Cardiff, a town near Syracuse. Two workmen were digging a well at a farm there when their shovels struck something large and hard. After a little more digging and dusting, they discovered nothing other than a giant petrified man. Local newspapers printed photographs of the twelve-foot-tall "Cardiff Giant" being hoisted out of the ground by ropes. Theories about the giant's origins were suddenly on everyone's lips. Was it a statue from an ancient civilization? Was it a relic of an Indian tribe? Was it really a petrified man? Was it confirmation that giants once roamed the Earth, as the book of Genesis says? Frank's poem picked up on this very theory:

> [Noah] shipped a man of monstrous size,
> Who was noted for his wond'rous lies
> There was but one of his race to be found,
> And he was so wicked Noah had him bound.
>
> After three days amid the flood,
> Noah called the man of Giant Head,
> And brought him on the deck of his ship,
> As he wished to talk to his Giantship.

Within days of the discovery of this fabled giant, William Newell, the owner of the farm in Cardiff, erected an enormous tent over the finding and began charging a quarter to come inside for a viewing. When he couldn't control the crowds, Newell doubled the price. Before long the Cardiff Giant became a tourist attraction, drawing crowds every day, including religious groups who saw in the stone beast something of biblical significance. "The interest in the Stone Giant found at Cardiff increases," wrote the *Syracuse Standard*. "Go where you will in this city, it is the topic." When the deluge continued unabated, Mr. Newell agreed to sell the giant to a group of Syracuse businessmen for $37,500, an outrageous amount that could purchase an entire city block. The new owners put it on display in a leased storefront downtown. The admission price was raised again, and the local economy was boosted by the traffic.

Archaeologists, meanwhile, examined the statue and proclaimed that it was a fraud, that the "ancient relic" was in fact quite new. Soon after this report a Binghamton factory owner named George Hull admitted that he had commissioned its creation—just to prove how easy it was to fool Americans, especially religious-minded ones. It all grew out of an argument Hull, an avowed atheist, had waged with a fundamentalist preacher who said he literally believed the Genesis passage about how giants once roamed the Earth. Hull had sculptors craft the statue from gypsum before shipping it to the farm of his cousin William Newell, who buried it and kept the secret until they hired workmen to "dig a well." These were the workmen who "found" the giant.

For many people the story ended there, but Frank found the final twist the most compelling part of the tale. Even after the hoax was widely reported, the crowds kept coming, until the famous showman and museum curator P. T. Barnum offered to buy the giant for $60,000. After all, Barnum specialized in locating and displaying fake mermaids and mummies and other dubious artifacts. He made a fortune charging admission to see these and other curiosities at his American Museum in New York City. But that structure had just recently burned to the ground after a quarter century of brisk business, and now Barnum was desperate for spectacular new attractions for a new venue.

When his offer was rejected, an angry Barnum commissioned a replica. In ads Barnum claimed that his Cardiff Giant was the *real* one and the original was the *fake*. This outraged the Syracuse businessman who was the majority owner of the "real" one, causing him to proclaim, "Well, I guess there's a sucker born every minute." The entire matter ended up in court—until an exasperated judge threw the whole case out. Later, the famous "sucker born every minute" line was erroneously attributed to Barnum himself. To Barnum, however, the true insight ran even deeper, and it was this bit of wisdom that made him one of the wealthiest men of his time: "The American people love to be humbugged," he observed.

It was this very insight that later inspired Frank Baum to turn the Wizard of Oz into a fraud. Before meeting the Great Oz, the companions expect him to be nothing but a wonderful wizard. But then they find him to be a giant head who bellows mean and terrible things. When they next encounter him, however, Toto pulls away the partition to reveal a little old man who breaks down and admits that "I am a humbug," confessing that he created illusions with ceiling wires and ventriloquism.

"Really," says the Scarecrow, "you ought to be ashamed of yourself for being such a humbug."

"I am—I certainly am," answers the little man sorrowfully, "but it was the only thing I could do." The people there were eager to be deluded and were willing "to do anything I wished them to."

In telling the story of the *real* fake and the *fake* fake, Frank Baum would never forget this powerful lesson: Americans not only don't *mind* being fooled, or humbugged, but they desperately *want* to be taken for a ride—and the greater the number of people who are strung along by a great humbug, the more others want to be in on it, too.

As perhaps the greatest hoax of the nineteenth century, the tale of the Cardiff Giant was so rich and so multilayered that Frank didn't need to embellish it. But with some stories embellishment was very much in order. Another experience that Frank recalled from his childhood involved an episode from 1871, when Frank was fifteen. A great man of letters named Professor Coe arrived one day in Clinton Square, a gathering spot in the very center of Syracuse. But it was the means by which this mysterious professor arrived that caused thousands of men, women, and children to turn out to greet him, for the professor descended from the sky riding in a hot-air balloon. A photograph of the event survives, showing an enormous crowd forming around the giant balloon. Frank Baum and his family were among the spectators that day. But this wouldn't make much of a story unless Frank concocted an interesting ending that may have had Professor Coe taking off, waving goodbye, and floating away to a faraway land, where he was welcomed by a credulous people who worshiped him as some sort of wizard.

"Well, one day I went up in a balloon and the ropes got twisted," Frank wrote years later, in the voice of the Wizard, "so that I couldn't come down again. It went way up above the clouds, so far that a current of air struck it and carried it many, many miles away. For a day and a night I traveled through the air, and on the morning of the second day I awoke and found the balloon floating over a strange and beautiful country."

As Frank was finding early success at his story store and Maud was making their new home as comfortable as could be, the Baums were finally settling into their surroundings in Aberdeen when Matilda Joslyn Gage blew in from the East for a visit. Despite the fact that she was now in her early sixties, her hair completely white, Matilda was not about to slow down. She was still full of fury, in the prime of her notoriety, speaking out for women and railing against male-dominated religion. Earlier in the year she had helped convene a meeting of the International Council of Women in Washington, DC, a historic conference that celebrated the fortieth anniversary of Seneca Falls, a dubious milestone given that women had little to show for their four decades of struggle. The meeting not only brought Mrs. Gage together for a famous photo with her colleagues, sitting next to Mrs. Stanton and Miss Anthony, but it also brought her scowl-to-scowl with her archenemy, Frances Willard of the Christian Temperance movement, who gave a speech on "social purity." Mrs. Gage didn't miss her chance to confront. "It is especially surprising," she told the delegates, "that the advocates of social purity fail to recognize the femininity of the divine—of God."

As a widow getting on in years, Matilda didn't feel comfortable spending the winters alone anymore. It made sense for her to come out to Dakota, not only to spend time with Maud but also to see Clark, Helen, and Julia and her growing gaggle of grandchildren. She arrived in Aberdeen in time for Thanksgiving and would stay through Christmas and the rest of the winter as well. This way she'd be in town for a string of birthday parties, with Frank Jr. turning five and Robert turning three, and she would preside over the holiday gatherings like the grand matriarch she was. This visit would start a new family tradition, in which Matilda would close up her home in Fayetteville every November and come to stay with the Baums every winter for the rest of her life.

Of course, Matilda couldn't help but stir up some trouble on such visits. When Mrs. Gage stopped by Baum's Bazaar, she would have noticed Frank's section of books and other reading material, and she saw to it that books about women's rights and Theosophy were added to the store's stock, no matter what her son-in-law thought of such matters. She was especially eager to get others to absorb the wisdom inside the covers of Blavatsky's *Isis Unveiled*, as well as issues of the *Path*, the Theosophical Society's official magazine. The monthly publication was named after one of the Tibetan sutras that Blavatsky had translated years earlier, one that expresses a mystical, eternal truth:

> *All beings desire liberation from misery.*
> *Seek, therefore, the causes of misery and expunge them.*
> *By entering on the path, liberation from misery is attained.*
> *Exhort, then, all beings to enter the path.*

Madame Blavatsky had just published her second major book in the late fall of 1888, and this opus, *The Secret Doctrine*, was written during a four-year period in which she was under relentless attack. Critics charged that the Madame was a fake and a fraud. The assault was based around Blavatsky's claims that she could produce "phenomena," paranormal acts in which she could summon the spirits to move furniture, make spontaneous noises, and send her messages from the Great Beyond. She was mostly interested in talking about spirituality and working toward "the day when humanity shall awake in a mass from its spiritual lethargy and open its blind eyes to the dazzling light of TRUTH." But she knew that the market for pure spirituality was not nearly as big as the one for psychic phenomena, so she appeased her public, to the point where people came from hundreds of miles around to witness her paranormal powers. "Whatever I do," she lamented, "they're never satisfied."

Emotionally wrecked by the constant accusations, the Madame's health at one point went into free fall until she was so gravely ill that she lapsed into a coma. For two days she lay in bed motionless, as the deathwatch grew around her. Then, the next morning, she opened her eyes and asked for breakfast. She told her colleagues that she had seen her Mahatma M materialize clearly in the Astral light. Her master gave her a choice, either "to die and pass on in peace, or to live on a few more years and write a book about 'the secret doctrine.'" Blavatsky chose to live and to write. In the meantime the controversies surrounding her amplified her fame. Before the accusations there were chapters of the Theosophical Society in a hundred cities, but by 1888 branches could be found in two hundred cities. Blavatsky had become a household name around the world.

This, of course, meant that the Madame and her views were more polarizing than ever before. To many mainstream, religious-minded Americans, Theosophy represented a poisonous viewpoint antithetical to Christianity. Frank and Maud didn't see the harm in it. They enjoyed reading Theosophical material and they even hosted séances in their house, not unlike the ones Maud had attended at Cornell, where she and her friends would try to channel the spirits of dead loved ones.

Frank saw it all as an opportunity to have his store supply goods to a new kind of club, as he could sell its members Ouija boards, crystal balls, books, magazines, and more things that people didn't need. But many of the townspeople in Aberdeen were repulsed by pagan rituals, Theosophy, and Blavatsky's nonsense about how the lost goddess Isis was the redeemer of mankind. The people of the Dakota Territory were just as devoutly religious as the people back East, perhaps more so. Once customers saw that Baum's Bazaar sold books and magazines filled with "heresy," they tended to stay away. In towns such as Aberdeen, the founder of Theosophy became known as Madame *Blasphemy*. The swelling backlash soon took its toll on Frank's business.

Matilda, of course, was used to kicking up dust wherever she went and didn't much care whether Frank lost a few customers because of her influence. She simply enjoyed spending time at the store, especially when it was filled with the town's children, as she loved to watch them gather around Uncle Frank at the cash register to listen to his stories. Mrs. Gage, recognizing her son-in-law's gift for storytelling, encouraged Frank to type up his tales. "Frank," she once said, "you'd be a damn fool if you didn't write those stories down!" But Frank resisted, saying they were only children's stories, nothing of great importance. Besides, he was preoccupied with running the store, always brainstorming ideas to increase sales. Writing? Who has the time anymore? But the suggestion must have planted a seed. In Frank's mind Mrs. Gage was slowly changing, from a scornful mother-in-law into more of an intellectual mentor.

Frank held his hopes high for his first Christmas selling season, as there was no better time of year to convince people to desire things they didn't need. His newspaper ads promised that all kinds of new surprises were in store: "Mr. Baum . . . requests the honor of your presence . . . to examine and criticize his magnificent collection of articles." Each lady would be treated to a complimentary gift. As a result, the opening of the holiday season at Baum's Bazaar on the first of December drew an incredible crowd of twelve hundred patrons. Many ladies walked away from the festivities with a free Christmas tree ornament or some such gift—but without actually buying anything—and sales didn't pan out as well as expected.

Yet by the first signs of spring, Frank's spirits were renewed as usual, and he began planning for a major Easter Day promotion. Aberdeen was nurtured on boosterism, but in a full-page ad in the *Aberdeen Daily* on April 19, Frank took blind optimism to a whole new level. The ad featured a drawing of two bees happily buzzing. "A glorious Easter is about to dawn upon us," Frank wrote. "Aberdeen stands upon the threshold of the grandest era in her history. About her are millions of acres covered with tender, ambitious shoots of infant grain . . . now thrusting their delicate heads above the generous soil to bring our city wealth and prosperity." Spreading more of his gleeful prognostications about the future, he was now laying it on extra-thick: "The sun of Aberdeen is rising; its powerful and all-reaching beams shall shed glory all over the length and breadth of the continent and draw wondering eyes of all nations to our beautiful land."

Frank's wondrous vision for the coming of spring was of course part of a strategy to sell more stuff by telling the people of his fair city exactly what he thought they wanted to hear. If they in turn believed in this common fantasy, they would buy the things to celebrate the life to which they aspired. He yearned for his store to please everyone, and he wanted everyone to love him in return. "To show a feeling of good will at this joyous season [and] to supply a sort of safety valve to the exuberance of our spirits — we shall present each of our customers on Saturday with a beautiful potted plant." Was this a tongue-in-cheek jab at local boosterism, or was Frank just projecting the world the way he wanted it to be? It seemed as though his optimism was genuine, as it was right around the time Maud became pregnant with their third child.

Now that he was in such a fertile frame of mind, Frank thought it was high time to realize one of his grandest aspirations, to launch a baseball club. Frank had always loved "base ball," then spelled as two words. As a teenager at Rose Lawn, he had played as often as he could, sometimes even on Sundays, against the wishes of his mother, who thought it was a sin to slide around in the dirt on the Lord's day. People who played baseball on Sunday were often called sinners, and sinners went to hell. Since Frank professed all his life not to believe in the concept of hell, it could be that this doubt of the devil developed along with his love of baseball on Sundays. It was such a beautiful game to him, a pastoral sport that always started at the loveliest time of year. How could men go to hell simply because they chose to play this glorious game on a Sunday?

Along with Harvey Jewett, who owned a large grocery store next to Baum's Bazaar, Frank formed a new organization, with Jewett heading the board of directors, bank president Henry Marple named the team manager, and L. Frank Baum as club secretary, in charge of recruiting players and setting up the schedule. To build a new stadium, citizens contributed $3,000 for stock in the Aberdeen Base Ball Association, sold at $10 per share. A site was selected on the outskirts of town near one of the railroad depots, and within just a few weeks a new field and a grandstand were built. To cover costs, the club sold advertising space on the outfield fence.

The South Dakota League adopted National League rules, recently changed to quicken the game. A strikeout was now just three strikes, down from five, and a walk was now four balls, also reduced from five. Profanity and gambling were prohibited, and there would be no games on Sundays. Frank placed ads and wrote letters to local men of known ability, offering $50 and game-day meals for the season to join the Hub City Nine. He quickly had plenty of takers, young men with names such as Jud Smith, Bud Jones, Mike Cody, Pat Ward, and a shortstop named Frank Hough. Secretary Baum put up a box of fine cigars as a bonus for the first player to hit a home run. On May 30 an exhibition game against a team from Redfield brought in $300 in ticket sales from nearly a thousand spectators, and the home team won the game 18 to 16. "The crowd enjoyed it and howled itself hoarse," noted the *Aberdeen Daily News*.

A few days later the uniforms that Frank had ordered arrived at his store. The lettering and trim were emblazoned in maroon over dark gray flannel, complemented by matching caps. Each player was fitted with a thin leather hand glove that resembled a winter mitten. Baum's Bazaar would front the team the full $93.61 cost of the uniforms, with a promise to be paid back from profits by the end of the season. Frank ran ads every day touting Baum's Bazaar as the official supplier of Spalding's Sporting Goods, with the expectation that he would cash in if baseball caught on among kids.

During exhibition games the quality of play arose as the league's major problem, as many games were riddled by wild pitches, dropped popups, and fights over calls. In one early game it became clear that one of the umpires had no idea what the game's rules were, and the ump had to be ejected after two innings. "Aberdeen Forgets How to Play Ball," said one headline. In one game against Groton, the fans "were treated to some of the rottenest ball playing ever seen in Dakota." Secretary Baum took it upon himself to feed the newspapers with quips and quotes, in an effort to keep the interest in the team growing. "No one feels an error more keenly than the one who makes it," he empathized.

By the time the official season was set to open, Frank had tied his own success and self-worth to whether or not a sports team over which he had little control would live up to his immense hopes. For Independence Day, Frank promised that he himself would present for the families of Aberdeen "a grand display of fireworks" on the evening of a double-header.

Frank was now fully caught up in the circumstances around him, doing absolutely everything he could to raise a well-fed family, to build his store into a success, to make a name for himself, to field a winning team, to avoid letting down the fans and the stockholders, to assure the future greatness of his city. Somewhere lost in the middle of all this activity around his public aspirations was his true self, his private myth, the person he really wanted to be. Whether or not the people of Aberdeen would help Frank become that person was another matter. "If your private myth, your dream, happens to coincide with that of the society, you are in good accord with your group," says Joseph Campbell. "If it isn't, you've got an adventure in the dark forest ahead of you."

The summer of 1889 brought a sweltering heat to Dakota, with temperatures hitting 109 degrees by late June. Living with the fear of losing their crops to the dry heat, the farmers in the fields seemed to catch a break when Mother Nature intervened with the summer's first drenching downpour, on July 2. Unfortunately for L. Frank Baum, this was to be the opening day of official play for the Hub City Nine. To rebound from the rainout, the pressure was on for a successful Fourth of July double-header against Watertown, but that team had to cancel when it had trouble finding enough players to take the trip, leading to the league's first crisis. "Watertown never showed up," said the *Redfield Observer*, "and the base ball league which started with so much gusto has most likely gone up the flume."

Frank reassured the press. "Just contradict the rumor in regard to Watertown not coming into the league," club secretary Baum said. "I am in position to know that city will have a first class team." Frank got a club from nearby Wahpeton as a substitute. "The games on the Fourth will be decidedly interesting," Frank promised. The games were indeed played, but interesting they were not; the home team ran up scores of 24 to 8 and 35 to 2. The visitors gave the "rankest display of chump playing ever seen on the Aberdeen grounds," said the *Daily News*.

The season finally perked up with a close game against the team from Claremont played under an unbearable sun, with no breeze to provide relief and no clouds to give at least temporary cover. The heat edged off a bit the next day, and Aberdeen shut out Claremont, in an errorless 3–0 victory that had the newspapers calling it "a daisy" and "the best game ever played in a Dakota city." Secretary Baum followed the successful series against Claremont with his biggest catch of the summer, attracting a real big-city team, the St. Paul Indians, to Aberdeen during the Republican political convention. Every hotel room in the city was booked, and so ballpark admission was doubled, to 50¢. The club spent $450 on advertising and transportation for the July 26 game, and most local businesses, including banks and stores such as Baum's Bazaar and Beard, Gage & Beard, closed for the afternoon, so that employees could attend.

The games "gave the public an opportunity to see what good ball playing is, and replenished the association's treasury" with more than $1,000 in ticket sales. Both manager Marple and secretary Baum "are enthusiastic admirers of the national game, and it is due entirely to their efforts that the club has proven such a success." Aberdeen finished in first place, setting up a highly anticipated playoff with one of the top teams of the North Dakota League, from Jamestown. Manager Marple couldn't go on the trip, so Frank stepped into the field marshal role, probably leaving Baum's Bazaar in the care of his sister-in-law Helen, who still lived upstairs with her husband, Charlie. The *Daily News* commented that "it will be a cold day if the [home team] fails to return with the base ball scalps of the northern cities dangling from their belts."

Sporting a manager's uniform rather than his customary street clothes, the temporary skipper led his team to a convincing 18 to 8 victory over Jamestown to set up a crowning best-of-three-game series against Bismarck. "The battle for the championship of Dakota will be the most interesting sporting event of the year," said the *Bismarck Tribune*. Frank's boys wrestled home a 14–2 win in the first game and another commanding 18–9 win in the second to emerge as the kings of Dakota baseball.

The squad celebrated by eating watermelon and playing cards, and during the party Frank presented each player with a broom labeled "From Aberdeen to North Dakota—a clean sweep—1889." A rival town's newspaper conceded that the Hub City players "are good fellows and deserve to be champions," and the hometown paper said that "not only is the club the strongest ever organized in Dakota . . . but has demonstrated that good baseball can thrive in Aberdeen." On August 16 the fabled Hub City Nine were welcomed home by a cheering crowd at the train depot, and the team paraded down Main Street brandishing their brooms. Waving to friends and family, Frank Baum was happier than he'd been in a long time, for he had found a new way to please the people.

The brief baseball season of 1889 held a tidy summary of everything characteristic of L. Frank Baum, showing off his unflagging optimism and his consistent diligence in working to make his wishes come true. No one had ever done a better job under such trying circumstances of getting a new ball club off the ground. But Frank was once again done in by his poor business sense. He had little wisdom of how to pace himself, of how to invest time and money not for short-term success but for the long haul.

As with his *Maid of Arran* tour seven years earlier, Frank spared no expense in creating a success in the here and now. He rarely skimped on equipment, advertising, or travel. He couldn't do anything halfway. Worst of all, he made the mistake of signing talent for a full season, even though he didn't have firm commitments for enough dates to make it profitable. Like *The Maid of Arran*, the Hub City Nine baseball team turned into a big hit for a short time. But with payroll due through October 5, Frank now had nearly six weeks left to schedule exhibition games—or the team would lose money for the year.

Most teams were breaking up as the dry weather had turned into a full-fledged drought. The Hub City pitcher left to work for an elevator company. Others went back to jobs with railroads and manufacturers. Frank was able to stage a double-header on August 27, but overall he couldn't retain any profits for the season. By October, when the newspapers reported that the ball club had lost $1,000 for the year, the financial failure finally hit Frank with full force. When a reporter asked him whether there would be a team the next year, secretary Baum expressed an uncharacteristic bitterness. "No," he snapped, "I don't want any more to do with base ball. I expended no little time, and worked hard for the success of the organization, but I am out both money and time. If we have a team next year, I am of the opinion that someone else will have to do the work."

Although Frank Baum wasn't personally liable for the loss, Baum's Bazaar was out at least $93.61, the sum due for the team uniforms it supplied but for which it was never reimbursed. Within a few weeks Aberdeen's baseball grandstand was leveled and the lumber hauled away. What had seemed like an incredible, unlikely success story had suddenly turned into another sour failure. Worse, the collapse of the Hub City Nine franchise had unfortunate ramifications for Baum's Bazaar. Instead of baseball becoming a moneymaker for the store, it had become a time sink. Down the drain were scores of hours that would have been better spent attending to a store that was in deep trouble. The harsh weather did even more damage. The lack of rain left fields of wheat susceptible to a brutal sun that literally burned stalks of grain into dust. The drought led to massive crop failure during harvest time, and the townspeople were left with no money to spend on extravagances such as knickknacks, Japanese parasols, and boxes of chocolates.

The deep dive in the local economy could not have come at a worse time for the Baum family. In anticipation of their new baby, the Baums had recently moved into a larger house, at 512 South Kline Street, just a short walk to Main Street. Prior to Christmas, on December 17, 1889, Maud delivered their third son at the house. They named him Harry Neal Baum, honoring Frank's brother Harry as well as Hattie and William Neal, his dear sister and her husband. For her winter visit Mrs. Gage had come in time for the baby's arrival, to help Maud through the delivery and to assist her daughter with running the household over the next few months. Frank now had his hands full at home, dividing his attention among a six-year-old, a three-year-old, a new baby, an exhausted wife, and a demanding mother-in-law—all while his livelihood hung by a thread.

Everything was now riding on whether the Christmas shopping season would stage a late surge, and to make it a success, Frank had once again spared no expense. To attract people who normally didn't come into the store, Frank had printed up a lavish catalog showing off all that the store offered, listing more than six hundred items. He distributed it as far and wide as he could, to capture not only walk-in traffic but also those inclined to order by mail. But as Christmas came and went, it became clear that Baum's mix of merchandise was ill suited to the needs of the populace, especially in those bleak times. "The store was too impractical for a frontier town," said sister-in-law Helen. "Frank had let his tastes run riot."

The aftermath of Christmas was devastating for Frank, as Baum's

Bazaar was still stocked to the gills with wicker baskets, art pottery, stuffed animals, and toy soldiers. All that Frank had done for his city, all his boosterism, all his civic pride, all his enthusiasm for the leisure side of life, all the time he volunteered for the baseball club, all he had spent on advertising—none of his goodwill and leadership had been repaid or recognized in any tangible way by the people of Aberdeen. They let him down by failing to buy his merchandise, even if they did buy his stories.

Frank's credit was now maxed out, so Maud stepped in and struck a deal with Henry Marple, the banker who had managed the ball club. On December 28 she entered into a "Satisfaction of Chattel Mortgage" agreement with Mr. Marple, borrowing $550 for ninety days at 12 percent interest per annum, using the store's stock of goods, furniture, and fixtures as collateral. Yet Frank refused to admit publicly that this was the end. "The matter is simply a temporary embarrassment," Frank told the newspaper.

Baum's Bazaar closed for good on the first day of the new decade, just fifteen months after it had opened with such great fanfare. By January 18 Maud finalized a deal to sell the entire inventory to her sister Helen, the bill of sale showing that the price was $772.54. In turn Maud was able to pay back the original loan of $550 plus a few dollars in interest, keeping the rest of the money in the family. In one transaction Maud enhanced cash flow by $200, equivalent to two months of good profit at the store. Within a few days the store reopened as Gage's Bazaar. Over the coming months Helen did her best to sell off her brother-in-law's frivolous items at a deep discount while refocusing the business on food, clothing, school supplies, and other more practical items. She didn't get much help from her husband, Charlie, who was now terribly ill, so she alone deserved the credit. Helen's sensible approach to merchandising was decidedly more successful, and Gage's Bazaar would remain in business for years to come.

10

The Brainless
and the Heartless

Frank Baum was editor and publisher of Aberdeen's weekly newspaper.

◆

"I don't know anything. You see, I am stuffed,
so I have no brains at all."

— THE SCARECROW

"The greatest loss I had known was the loss of my heart."

— THE TIN WOODMAN

THE U.S. CENSUS would tally sixty-three million people in 1890, a remarkable leap of 25 percent since the census of a decade earlier. In deciding what to do next, Frank Baum also took a broad survey. He was exasperated by the retail business, having spent the past seven years in it with absolutely nothing to show for his efforts. He looked around at all the different kinds of enterprises in Aberdeen and soon settled on the best kind of opportunity for him. A man of ideas, Frank found himself yearning to return to his childhood passion of being a writer and publisher. In Aberdeen, a town with seven newspapers, one could buy the weakest paper for cheap, then try to convert it into the strongest. Frank knew the competition would be fierce, but inspired by Mark Twain, who began his writing career as a journalist in the West, Frank decided to go for it.

In this way Frank seemed to be taking a giant step in the right direction on life's path, back toward his true self. As a man who seemed to have ink running through his veins and as one who loved newsprint on his fingers, newspapers had appealed to him since he was a teenager. He knew how to set type, and he now had plenty of experience with the local papers — as an advertiser, as a source, and as an occasional contributor.

Frank used the store liquidation money to purchase the *Dakota Pi-*

oneer, a weekly broadsheet averaging eight pages, taking it over from John H. Drake, a former army colonel who also had relocated to Aberdeen from the Syracuse area. A Republican stalwart, Drake had been appointed by President Benjamin Harrison to a diplomatic position in Germany, and so he agreed to sell the paper to Baum for a series of low monthly payments. By the end of January, Frank rechristened it the *Aberdeen Saturday Pioneer* and sold copies for $1.50. The paper became a virtual one-man show, operating from a handsome three-story brick building on the Excelsior Block that housed not only editorial offices but also its own press machines that Frank could make available for job printing to supplement his income. Frank personally delivered copies of the first edition of January 25, 1890, to local advertisers so he could collect the money and buy himself a ham sandwich and a cup of coffee for lunch.

Writing under the name L. F. Baum, Frank began his tenure as editor and publisher with his usual burst of idealism, promising in his debut issue to work "zealously and energetically for the wellfare [sic] and advancement of our beautiful city." Since it was a weekly, the *Pioneer* couldn't compete with the daily papers for news scoops. Instead, the paper was filled with features and human interest stories—much of it purchased from national and regional syndication services. Frank's first page 1 featured an ode to Robert Burns, the poet of Scotland, as well as an article about renovations at Madison Square Garden. Page 3 contained short items from around the country: a train robbery, a man divorcing his wife of thirty-eight years because she started making him do the washing and housecleaning, and an item about how Mark Twain had invested his life savings in a newfangled printing machine.

Frank happened to be taking over the editorship at a politically ominous time, as South Dakota along with North Dakota had just been admitted into the Union as states that past November. As a result there was a mad scramble to clarify the state constitution and establish laws determining what kind of states the Dakotas would be. Frank thus found himself in a position to voice his views on a number of key issues, including Prohibition, which he opposed. Another key debate was raging over where to locate the state's new capital. The leading

choices were Huron and Pierre. Frank penned a poem urging citizens
to choose Huron, the first letter of each line spelling out the none-too-
cryptic message:

> **H**ow can any living man,
> **U**nless his brain is cracked,
> **R**esolve to put the capital
> **O**n any town side-tracked?
> **N**o one can fail to understand—
>
> **F**ew men should fail to teach it—
> **O**ur future capital should be
> **R**ight where we all can reach it.
>
> **C**onsider what while Huron has
> **A** road to every section,
> **P**ierre is with difficulty reached.
> **I**t lies in such direction
> **T**hat we must all to Huron go
> **A**nd then to Pierre—that's bad—and so
> **L**et's vote for Huron's election!

Readers responded to the editor's wit and humor, boosting circulation. Suddenly Frank had a platform from which to address the biggest
statewide issue of all. That issue was equality, as 1890 was shaping up
to be a year in which South Dakota would become the epicenter in
the struggle for women's voting rights. Just a week after statehood was
made official, Susan B. Anthony had arrived and submitted a statewide women's suffrage amendment to be voted upon a year later, on
election day of 1890. The campaign kicked off in January with Miss
Anthony's speech at the Aberdeen courthouse, in which she joined
forces once again with her old colleague Matilda Joslyn Gage against
their common foes. As a gesture of solidarity, Anthony prepaid lifetime dues to the national suffrage organization for the movement's six
longest-standing leaders, a short list that included herself, Stanton,
and Gage.

It was about time Susan came around to recognizing Matilda's contribution, since by now Anthony had finally realized that she had been
betrayed by Frances Willard, the leader of the Women's Christian Tem-

perance Union. "The WCTU woman who introduced me last night publicly proclaimed she had not yet reached women suffrage," Susan sulked.

> Isn't it discouraging? When I get to Washington, I shall see all of the South Dakota congressman and senators and learn what they intend to do. I want to help our friends throughout this State to hold the canvass for woman suffrage entirely outside all political, religious or reform questions—that is, absolutely keep it by itself. I advise every man and woman who wishes this amendment carried at the ballot box next November to wear only the badge of yellow ribbon—that and none other. This morning I cut and tied a whole bolt of ribbon, and every woman went out of the court house adorned with a little sunflower colored knot.

Frank, Maud, and Matilda began wearing their yellow ribbons just about everywhere. The political winds of change seemed to be at their backs when two of the state's most powerful voting blocs came out in favor of the suffrage amendment. First the Farmers' Alliance adopted a resolution in support of "giving our wives and sisters the ballot." Then the Knights of Labor, a group of industrial workers, did the same, vowing to "support with all our strength the amendment to be voted on at the next general election giving women the ballot . . . believing this to be the first step toward securing those reforms for which all true Knights of Labor are striving."

If these two groups could put the measure over the top, South Dakota would set a national precedent, becoming the very first state to recognize women as full Americans. Women could already vote in Wyoming, but it was still just a territory. A victory in this new state could thus break the whole issue wide open across the country.

Anthony toured twelve towns, and she donated a full set of *History of Woman Suffrage* to the public libraries in each. To those who objected that she, at age seventy, was putting her health at risk by embarking on such a vigorous campaign in the harsh Dakota climate, she retorted, "Better to lose me than to lose the state!" Friends and fans now called her "Saint Susan." Standing side by side with Matilda, she urged supporters to visit every farmhouse and school, to circulate pamphlets, and to organize committees in every district and village. "With

this done, the entire State will be in splendid trim," she said. "I am securing the subscriptions lists of every single newspaper. If reading matter in every home and lectures in every school house of the State will
convert the men, we shall carry South Dakota next November with
a whoop!" She was also rallying support nationwide, to "galvanize all
our friends in every state to concentrate all their money and forces
upon South Dakota." Not only did cash contributions pour in, but several women sent in their jewelry and several men mailed in land deeds,
all to be liquidated for the great cause.

The all-out campaign would keep Matilda Gage staying with the
Baums in Aberdeen not just for the winter but for almost the entire
year of 1890. Mrs. Gage would make a long series of fiery speeches, and
she would set aside her bitter differences with Miss Anthony to work
together to win. For her part Maud enlisted her friends and neighbors to join the effort, sitting for hours at the kitchen table stuffing
envelopes with literature and making campaign signs. "No Person
Shall Be Disenfranchised," read some signs. Other signs took the state
motto "Under God the People Rule" and added under it the rejoinder
"Women Are People!"

Taking cues from Miss Anthony and his mother-in-law, Frank became secretary of Aberdeen's Equal Suffrage Club, and he wrote an
editorial extolling "our brave, helpful western girls" and supporting
passage of the referendum. "We are engaged in an equal struggle for
competence," Baum wrote in his regular "Editor's Musings" column.
Matters of universal equality and freedom moved to the center of his
opinion pieces. "The key to the success of our country is tolerance,"
Frank wrote. "The 'live and let live' policy of the Americans has excited the admiration of the world. Bigotry, if not wholly unknown, is
so intolerable, as to be nearly entirely suppressed. Still, we have one
more lesson in tolerance to learn. We must do away with sex prejudice
and render equal distinction and reward to brains and ability, no matter whether found in man or woman."

Pretty soon Frank was going even further, echoing his mother-in-
law by urging his readers "to stop the attempt to place God in the
Constitution, an encroachment on the sacred liberty of thought, a departure from the intentions of the founders of the government." In another editorial he went on the attack, giving a name to the men who

believed in separating women "from the rights which justice and humanity would accord them." He called such men "bears in the household."

To get his points across in a different way, Frank created a comical alter ego. His "Our Landlady" column was based around an ingenious character named Sairy Ann Bilkins, an older woman who mispronounced and misunderstood everything yet was never afraid of giving her commonsense opinions on the issues of the day. All the while she was constantly dropping her false teeth in her soup, losing hairpins in the mashed potatoes, and popping buttons from her housecoat into the cake batter. A widow, she supported herself with the rent paid by her three boarders, a cigar-smoking colonel, a store clerk named Tom, and a kindhearted doctor. Imaginary conversations among these four fictional people formed the basis of each weekly column.

Using the cover of Mrs. Bilkins, Frank was able to say things in print he couldn't get away with otherwise. The newspapers were generally looked on for boosterism, to encourage more people to move to town, not to print the truth about how difficult frontier life was during the drought and the economic downturn.

> "It beats all," said our landlady, as she threw down the plate of pancakes and wiped the turner on her apron, "it beats all how hard the times really is. There's no end to the sufferin,' right here in our own neighborhood . . . Why, only yesterday a poor woman from the country was beggin' the grocery man to trust her for a pint o' kerosene, and he wouldn't let her have it. It made my heart bleed, that's what it did, and if any o' you boarders had a paid up lately I'd have gin it to her myself."

Mrs. Bilkins took special aim at the way women were treated. She was appalled by a tradition at St. Mark's Episcopal Church, in which single women in their late teens and early twenties attended a special supper party that was passed off as a fundraiser to buy the church a new pipe organ. Before the supper each young lady was weighed on a scale, and her weight determined her price. The men would then choose which of the girls they wanted to buy as a dinner date that evening, and their dollars would go into the church coffers. Since such arrangements would often lead to further social occasions and sometimes marriage, one could imagine what Matilda Gage thought of this demeaning practice. Yet since everyone seemed to go along with it, any serious criticism might fall upon deaf ears.

Only Mrs. Bilkins could get away with raising a stink. "Why to these goin's on about buyin' gals at auction," she said, "as if they was so many slaves at the market! It's outrageous, that's what it is, and oughten ter be allowed in a christian country! . . . Who'd marry a girl as was weighed 'afore the whole world? And at a church sociable, too! What can the ministers be thinkin' of?"

In the middle of March the state legislature caved in to the religious lobby and passed a law putting Prohibition into effect starting May 1, a prospect that prompted much commentary from Mrs. Bilkins. She made reference to a provision of the law under which drugstores could continue selling alcohol-based medicine only if they took out a $100 permit. All nine drugstores in Aberdeen refused to pay up.

> "This is terrible times!" sighed our landlady . . . "All the town is riled up as if you'd stirred 'em with a stick like you would a hasty puddin'."
>
> "Anything wrong?" queried the colonel . . .
>
> "Everything!" declared our landlady. ". . . all them hard measures to prevent . . . feller-citizens from gettin' drunk."

Mrs. Bilkins then went about telling how she visited the druggist only to hear complaints. "Why ma'am, they'll arrest a feller fer smilin' after the fust o' May, because it's agin' the law to be in good spirits!". . . "Them prohibish fellers is pretty hard on our perfeshin, but so long as they lets us sell Soda water with a wink in it I guess we'll pull through."

She continued, telling her story while dropping a hairpin in her soup, accidentally biting it and breaking a tooth. "'They've decided as vinegar is intoxicatin', an' can't be sold without a license,' the druggist said. "'Try reducin' the molasses with it,' sez I sourcastically."

Sometimes Mrs. Bilkins would foreshadow Frank's famous fiction. Asked for her suggestions on how townsfolk could feed their animals on "Dakota dust," Mrs. Bilkins told a story about how her cousin Jake was asked if he had any feed for his six horses. "'No,' says Jake, 'I put green goggles on my hosses and feed 'em shavin's an' they think it's grass.'"

In a similar way, those who would enter the Emerald City had to wear green eyeglasses in order to make everything there appear green. "Even with eyes protected by the green spectacles," Frank would write, "Dorothy and her friends were at first dazzled by the brilliancy of the wonderful City."

Frank was now fully enjoying himself while running his newspaper, and by the time spring rolled around, his seasonal optimism returned in full bloom. When rains seemed to signal the end of the drought, Mrs. Bilkins called the weather "croptious" and editor Baum conjured another poem:

> Oh, the wet, the elegant wet!
> Continue to arrive, my pet.
> All of our troubles we'll now forget,
> Over the crops we'll cease to fret.
> Who cares now if we are in debt?
> We'll get out again in the fall, you bet!

The wet weather included the late May arrival of a mild cyclone, which destroyed a number of barns in Aberdeen, including one just a few blocks from the Baum residence that was "completely demolished," as Frank reported. Inside the barn a pig was hiding in a buggy. The cyclone blew the top off the buggy with the farmer's pig inside it, launching it a full three hundred yards into the air, until it landed in someone else's yard. "The pig was quite uninjured." The fact that a live being could be carried so far by a cyclone seemed to fascinate Frank.

Out in South Dakota campaigning for suffrage, Susan B. Anthony encountered a cyclone around this time as well. But she refused to seek shelter when a twister approached. "A little thing like a cyclone doesn't frighten me," she said.

Feeling ambitious, Baum expanded his newspaper to twelve pages and proclaimed it the largest weekly in South Dakota, with a circulation of more than fifteen hundred households. In his eyes, every glass right now was half full. In an editorial he quoted a prediction that the suffrage cause would win by twenty-five thousand votes and stated that "there is practically no important opposition to the cause . . . which is gaining converts every day." Politically, Frank made his position clear: he was a staunch Republican and the *Pioneer* would back Republican causes. In a citywide election for mayor that spring, Frank expressed jubilation that the Republican candidate was elected, defeating not only a Democratic candidate but also an independent fellow running on the People's Party ticket.

Even the enactment of Prohibition didn't seem to get Frank down. "Well, the first of May has come and gone," Frank mused, "and the saloons are all closed and prohibition reigns supreme throughout the infant state." Editor Baum took the position that citizens should abide by the law even if they didn't agree with it. This way everyone would know what a failure the law was sooner rather than later. "If driving out the liquor interests will kill all business in South Dakota and make our state as stagnant as a mud hole, we want to know that." In the meantime, the U.S. Supreme Court had deemed it perfectly legal to order liquor through the mail, and so those who wanted to drink were rarely denied, and this was already making a mockery of the law. "Unrestricted liquor packages are coming in state and sold to drunks and minors and women," Frank wrote.

At home Maud's life fell into a busy routine. After all, she was the practical one in the household. "Mother was father's exact opposite," recalled their son Harry years later. "She was serious, unimaginative and realistic, and it was a good thing too." Whereas Frank saw the patterns of life, Maud saw problems. Whereas Frank saw symbols, she saw surfaces. She would cook breakfast in the morning, send her husband off to work, pack Frank Jr. off to school, attend to little Robert and baby Harry, wash the clothes, hang them to dry, do some ironing, perhaps write a letter or catch up on her embroidery, and prepare dinner. Sometimes she'd be helped by her mother, but more often than not Matilda was meditating, writing pamphlets, or going off to a suffrage campaign event somewhere in the state. Like Frank, Matilda was an idea person. At night the whole family would spend time together, and then it was Frank's job to put the children to bed with a story.

One of the stories that Frank told from his days at the newspaper would be retold by his sons years later. The story involved a misprint of a local wedding announcement. Instead of setting type that said the bride had a "roguish smile," meaning mischievous, the article said that the bride had a "roughish smile," meaning ugly. When the new husband read this, he immediately took offense and rushed down to the newspaper office to confront editor Baum. Someone persuaded the two quarreling men to fight a duel, as this would be the only honorable way to settle the insult. An assistant was dispatched to retrieve a set of dueling pistols. The guns were loaded and given to each man. The instructions were simple. The men had to stand back to back at the front door to the newspaper office, walk around the block, and come face-to-face on the back street. Each man could fire just one shot at the other.

As soon as he rounded the corner, Frank ran off in the opposite direction. He heard someone chasing him, and so he ran faster. Then he heard a voice: "Stop, Frank, stop." It was the assistant who had arranged the duel. It turned out the rival man had scrambled away, too. "You damn fool," he said. "The other fellow's running."

Frank then turned around and ran back toward the site of the duel and shouted, "Where is he? Where is he?"

The madcap tale, ending with Frank's comical showing of false courage, was funny but fictional. Although Frank had made up it, his sons generally treated the episode as one of their fondest memories of when their father was a frontier newspaper editor.

As the town's big Fourth of July celebration approached, Frank was able to fuse his optimism and his desire to make money, as he was paid to create and print the official program for the festivities, which listed events such as an exhibition baseball game, pony races, and dancing by Native Americans. "A Great Day," his poster proclaimed. "Aberdeen is preparing to celebrate July 4 in Grand Fashion! A Great Procession, Sports Contests and Fireworks Display are on the Programme. All Are Invited." The printed program was supported, in part, with ads placed by Beard, Gage & Beard as well as Gage's Bazaar, which planned to sell frozen sherbet in a rainbow of flavors throughout the day. "There is nothing so delicious on these warm days and the people know it," Frank wrote.

Editor Baum also served as a judge in a cutest baby contest, which prompted Mrs. Bilkins to comment that "the fool judges guv the prize to the homliest babies an' the prettiest mothers." He also judged the contest for the best decorated theme wagon in the parade. This being an election year, many of the issues up for the vote were represented in the procession. A "Goddess of Liberty" wagon promoted women's suffrage, and brass marching bands were sponsored by the cities of Pierre and Huron. The winning wagon was the "Chariot of State," which featured forty-two "wee misses," each dressed in white with a sash emblazoned with the name of a U.S. state.

A group of Native Americans dressed in full ritual costume was invited to dance that day, as a gesture to assure local settlers that the natives weren't hostile. This event was staged to contradict the fearmongering in the newspapers that kept many people from locating to Dakota. Although there were an estimated twenty-five thousand Lakota Sioux living on the giant reservations to the west of Aberdeen, the townspeople had invited only members of a tiny tribe of Sisseton Sioux, who lived closer, to the east, as they were deemed friendly. Their nighttime dance routine was "barbaric . . . weird . . . ludicrous," according to Helen Leslie Gage.

Picking up on rumors that the visiting natives stole food and clothing from the locals, Frank made light of the situation in his "Our Landlady" column. "Them injines spiled all o' my enjyment, said Mrs. Bilkins. "Jest when the bands were playin' the beautifulest, I'd think o' them custard pies in the back kitchen and wonder if some injine warn't pryin' up the winder an' stealing 'em for his squaws, an' that brought my heart up inter my throat."

Despite Frank declaring earlier in the year that bigotry was "intolerable," his alter ego didn't stop there.

> "I'd a got along fust rate if I hadn't took it inter my head ter see the injine's war dance. I paid my money to a greasy lookin' injun an' walked in an' stood up. At one end of the hall was a big chief named Cowjumps, an' back o' him were some sleepy-lookin' squaws . . . an' in the circle were the villainest lookin' lot o' red devils as I ever seed, pushin' each other round the ring and yellin'.

"'Hi-yah! hip-yah! Hi-yah! hip-yah!' an' drummin' on a big kittle an' shakin' some tommyhawks and knives over their heads . . .

"'What's got 'em riled?' says I.

"'Nothin',' says [a policeman], 'they're dancin'.'

"'Oh!' says I; . . .

"An' just then I catched sight o' my red bed-spread . . . on one o' the dancin' injins' shoulders. I didn't wait for nothin', but I jest busted inter that ring o' war dancers an' clubbed my umbreller in my fist an' belted him a good whack over the shoulders."

Frank seemed to be using Mrs. Bilkins to play into the general state of ignorance and prejudice. Frank knew that it was popular to spread mistrust and ill will about the Native Americans, and doing so became for him an all-too-easy way to unify his readers around a noncontroversial issue.

All in all, Frank clearly loved when everyone could rally around common beliefs and rituals—whatever they were. "All 6,000 of us celebrated in a right royal manner," Frank concluded. "We had our sweethearts, wives, children, friends and relatives all together, and we enjoyed ourselves hugely the entire day."

Frank kept projecting a sense of harmony onto his fellow Aberdonians as the summer wore on. But behind the ideal picture that Frank was painting in his newspaper writings was a real image of discontent and division. The relentless drought was now in the process of ruining another year's wheat crop, and the farmers were fuming, not just at the weather but at the fact that they couldn't get crop insurance or credit, and the U.S. dollar's ties to the gold standard was making money increasingly scarce for working people.

The Farmers' Alliance found common cause with the Knights of Labor, and the two groups agreed to merge and form the Independent Party, fielding its own slate of candidates for the fall election. The leader of the revolt was the new Independent candidate for governor of South Dakota, a farmer turned political activist named Henry Langford Loucks. The long-bearded rabble-rouser was best known as the editor of the *Dakota Ruralist*, a newspaper that was based right next door to Gage's Bazaar and was founded to rage against industrial robber barons and eastern money powers. The nomination of Loucks was the very beginning of a new Populist movement that would soon sweep across all of America's farm states.

Pathetically, the merger of the two groups that had ardently endorsed women's voting rights just months earlier resulted in a new political party that no longer considered it worth the risk. Loucks's new Independent Party simply refused to add suffrage as a plank in its platform, instead choosing to focus only on the issues that united farmers and other working men. Susan B. Anthony and Matilda Joslyn Gage were apoplectic over this turn of events. They'd seen political betrayals before, but nothing like this. After all, the pledge of support from the Farmers' Alliance was the very reason that Anthony made South Dakota her top political battleground, her main cause for fundraising. Addressing the Independent Party convention later that summer, Anthony begged the men not to leave their wives and daughters behind, calling such a move a "death blow" to women's rights. She lost her appeal, and now the women faced three hostile political parties.

Frank Baum was not a Populist, nor would he ever become one, nor would he ever write a "Parable of Populism," despite revisionist theories purporting that he did. It was Frank's view that most Independents were good people, but that they were misguided. "The Independents are not wholly degenerate," Frank wrote in his "Editor's Musings" column. "But we are members of one great family, Republicans, the family which saved the union. Republicanism is the emblem of prosperity. We must deal gently with our erring brothers." In reviewing a high-profile political speech, Frank wrote that Henry Loucks "made a fool of himself before all intelligent men — and a hero of himself to his firmest adherents." Frank dismissed the Populist farmers as complainers. In an October editorial entitled "Hard Times Bemoaned," Frank ranted: "Did you ever hear a man declare that times were good? Emphatically, no! This fall, people are saying we need to leave this cursed country behind. Some are going. It's this class of people who are leaving every state, bemoaning hard times."

Despite the now overwhelming obstacles to achieving women's voting rights, the leaders of the cause marched on. "All of us must strain every nerve to move the hearts of men as they never before were moved," Anthony insisted. "I shall push ahead and do my level best to carry this State, come weal or woe to me personally." There certainly was plenty of woe to go around. At the state's Democratic political convention that summer, one politician named E. W. Miller stood up, turned to Anthony and her supporters, and declared that "the women who ask for the ballot are a disgrace to their homes." If women were allowed to go out and vote, Miller continued, men would have to stay home and "suckle the babies." His words were met with prolonged and vigorous cheers. The Republican convention was even worse, as women weren't even allowed to take seats inside the hall. The grueling campaign was summed up in the next volume of *History of Woman Suffrage*: "It would be difficult to put into words the hardships of this campaign of 1890 in a new State through the hottest and driest summer on record. Frequently the speakers would have to drive twenty miles between the afternoon and evening meetings and the audiences would come thirty miles. All of the political State conventions declined to endorse the amendment."

Yet by the end of the campaign, the list of women's events that had taken place was astounding: nearly sixteen hundred total speeches and rallies for the cause, including about eight hundred by national speakers and more than seven hundred by state speakers. Local suffrage clubs were organized in nearly every city and town, and literature was sent to the homes of every voter in South Dakota.

The *Aberdeen Saturday Pioneer* was one of the few newspapers in the state that was advocating the passage of the amendment, causing Mrs. Bilkins to nickname the rival papers "the Daily Nuthin'" and "the Daily Anythin'," saying that "no brains is necessary" for those papers to print what they were printing. Even though he was largely alone, editor Baum believed that giving women the vote was such an article of common sense that the amendment would carry the day. His faith in his fellow man is what filled him with confidence.

Despite cries of hard times, Frank boosted the circulation of his newspaper to twenty-five hundred, extending many new subscriptions to households on credit during the South Dakota State Fair, a massive event held in Aberdeen in mid-September. Ten thousand people came in from out of town, and as the official printer of the state fair's program guide, Frank was able to get his paper's name before the public as never before. He also used his platform to promote Anthony's speech at the fair, helping to turn out one of her biggest audiences ever. But all the political speeches about alcohol, gambling, voting rights, and state capitals left people confused, according to Mrs. Bilkins. "Things was so mixed up that I didn't know when I got home whether I was a woman-suffrage-anti-Pierre-prohibition-jack-pot woman, or a anti-rights-anti-Huron-anti-up-anti-prohibition-anti-boodle-all-wool-an'-a-yard-wide politician; but judgin' from my conglomerated feelin's I guess I was."

Now that he boasted a higher profile as well as a wider readership, Frank raised advertising rates by 50 percent, even though price hikes could be dangerous in tough times. "Never before has the paper been more prosperous," he concluded. He also put an entirely new publication on the drawing boards, calling it the *Western Investor,* a newspaper full of boosterism that would be circulated in the East to attract money and people to places like Aberdeen. Frank was optimistic that capital could be raised to build an irrigation system so as to prevent future droughts from destroying the crops. "Two years will find the Jim River Valley under thorough irrigation," Baum predicted, "and producing crops which will be the wonder and admiration of the world."

He couldn't have picked a worse time for his rosy outlook. New population figures showed that Aberdeen was now the fourth-largest city in the state, down from number two a few years earlier. And shortly after the fair closed, the bleak numbers started coming in. The South Dakota wheat fields were widely promoted as being able to produce fifteen bushels per acre in a bad year and forty bushels in a good year. But this year they produced only *eight to ten* bushels per acre, and the crop was so inferior that a bushel was lucky to fetch 25¢ instead of the usual dollar. Thousands were considering leaving the area, and cash became so scarce that stores such as Beard, Gage & Beard stopped accepting credit and put everything on drastic "cash only" markdown. Yet Baum continued to ridicule those who espoused pessimism, grouping all complainers into what he called the Hard Times Club. It's "one of the nonsensicalist things I've heard of," said our landlady. "What'll it amount to?" There was nothing wrong with this land, she said. "Why here we are in the very flower garden o' the yearth . . . If only every man would say 'I will do suthin'' instead o' sayin' 'why don't somebody else do suthin'' times would change mighty quick."

Stepping up his wishful thinking, Frank Baum made his endorsements and his predictions crystal clear just before Election Day, in the November 1 issue of his newspaper. First, he predicted Huron would beat Pierre in the battle for state capital. Second, he predicted that the Republicans would sweep all statewide offices. "Our nation has prospered greatly under Republican rule," he wrote. "Abandon all myths —cling only to realities. A practical salvation of all our ills can be found in supporting only the party of justice and progression."

Finally, Frank was expecting a victory for women's rights. "The great question, involving the future of our wives, mothers, sisters and daughters will be decided for South Dakota next Tuesday," he wrote. "Remember that the enfranchisement of one-half of the citizens of this great state is in your hands." He concluded by echoing the language of his mother-in-law. "A person without a vote is a political slave. Help [women] to freedom on Tuesday by voting for Woman Suffrage."

When Election Day dawned on November 4, nearly seventy thousand men across South Dakota went to the polls. As the votes were tabulated over the next few days, it became clear that everything Frank Baum advocated had been shot down. Pierre became the new state capital over Huron, despite Frank's insistence that supporters of Pierre had cracked brains. Although the Republicans retained the governor's office, it was by only the slimmest of margins, as Independent Henry Loucks garnered an impressive 40 percent of the vote. In Brown County, where Aberdeen was the county seat, a remarkable trouncing of the Republicans took place. Both state senators were now Independent and all eight state representatives were also now Independent. Frank was gracious in congratulating the new party, writing that they "may well be proud of what successes they have gained," but he was also convinced the Populists were still wrong in "seeking to rectify some evils which have never existed."

Then there was women's suffrage, the big issue of the day. In the end it wasn't even close. When all votes were counted, the men of South Dakota had voted overwhelmingly against the right of women to vote, with 45,862 voting "no" to 22,072 choosing "yes"—a two-to-one trouncing.

It was clear to Frank Baum that the men of the Farmers' Alliance and the Knights of Labor made brainless and heartless choices in the election of 1890. Mrs. Bilkins simply threw up her hands. "I've had enough of politics to last me a life-time," she harrumphed. Real people had similar reactions. Miss Anthony was greatly saddened by the loss, as were Matilda and Maud. For his part, Frank couldn't comprehend how his logical arguments had failed to sway people. Maybe his sensible reasoning simply didn't penetrate people's brains, or maybe most men in the state lacked any sense of compassion. "The defeat of Equal Suffrage will stand as a lasting reproach to the state of South Dakota," editor Baum wrote. "What a reproach upon our civilization, and upon the people of a state who have made a pretense of being liberal and just!"

Somehow, years later, he was able to turn this bitter experience into fodder for satire, as he would one day invent a Scarecrow with no brains who reflected the Dakota farmers as well as a Tin Woodman who lacked a heart, reflecting the industrial workers. "You may come with me, if you like," Dorothy tells the Scarecrow that she finds stuck on a pole in a cornfield. "If Oz will not give you any brains you will be no worse off than you are now."

Farther down the road, the two companions encounter the rusted Tin Woodman. "Do you suppose Oz could give me a heart?" he says after being properly oiled. "Why, I guess so," answers Dorothy. "It would be as easy as to give the Scarecrow brains."

Despite the crushing disappointment, Frank would conclude that change was indeed possible. Maybe someone who seems deficient in brains could learn how to think properly, and maybe someone who seems to lack a heart could grow emotionally. Perhaps people could begin to change just by listening to themselves instead of blindly following a group. "All the same," says the Scarecrow to the Tin Woodman, "I shall ask for brains instead of a heart, for a fool would not know what to do with a heart if he had one."

"I shall take the heart," returns the Tin Woodman, "for brains do not make one happy, and happiness is the best thing in the world."

But it's one thing to use the power of myth to transform other people, and quite another to go through such a transformation yourself. For L. Frank Baum, the election of 1890 wasn't just another temporary setback. This defeat was the newest end to a lifelong line of failures, everything from the chicken farm to the production of his plays to his oil enterprise to his variety store to his baseball club. Compounding the bad news, his newspaper suddenly stood on shaky ground, too. Frank had thought himself to be a great student of human nature. He professed to know what motivated people, what values Americans cherished, what made his neighbors angry or happy or riled them up. Yet in reality he seemed nearly blind to what people really believed and how they really behaved. This much was made clear by the election results. Either Frank Baum was losing faith in his fellow man, or he was losing faith in himself. Something fundamental to his very outlook on life was now giving way.

11

Field of Blood

Baum's image of a field of brilliant scarlet poppies is rife with symbolic meaning.
This poster promotes the 1902 stage play of *The Wizard of Oz*.

Soon they found themselves in the midst of a great meadow of poppies . . . When there are many of these flowers together their odor is so powerful that anyone who breathes it falls asleep, and if the sleeper is not carried away from the scent of the flowers, he sleeps on and on forever.

— L. FRANK BAUM,
The Wonderful Wizard of Oz

THE CHILLS OF NOVEMBER brought a sense of dread to the prairie. For the second year in a row the wheat harvest had been an utter disaster, and farmers without enough money to last the winter couldn't afford to wait and see whether the rains would return the following year. Many Dakotans were now abandoning their farms. Droves of wagons were rolling away from Aberdeen, either hightailing back east or forging farther west for the next land rush. The spokes of the Hub City were now overloading, as train compartments jammed with belongings and equipment were packed off in every direction. When farmers suffer like this, everyone else in the economy feels it, from the merchants to the industrial workers to the newspaper publishers who rely on revenue from advertisers and subscribers to stay afloat. Frank Baum, ever the optimist, was forced to predict that the Thanksgiving celebration that year would be "the hollowest and most insincere of all the mockeries."

The editor of the *Aberdeen Saturday Pioneer* wanted to save the prairie in order to save his city in order to save his business in order to save his family. Frank had to acknowledge reality now, yet it was his view that this place was home and nowhere else was any better. "Hundreds of settlers have felt that this was the last straw and have gone to other states that are in worse condition than this," Frank editorialized. "The partial crop failures we couldn't help. They were the result of two successive dry seasons, and the same combination is not likely to occur again in many years—if ever."

To be sure, the Baum family wasn't budging. Frank couldn't bear the thought of yet another business in ruins, and with Maud in her second trimester of pregnancy, this was a time to burrow in for the long months of winter. But to stick it out he'd need to replace the considerable number of subscribers he'd already lost, and so Frank announced in his paper a special promotion. He'd pay $100 cash to any church society that "appointed a dozen or so ladies" to obtain two hundred annual subscriptions at $1 each. This scheme was doomed, as people could see that Frank was trying to get them to become sales agents with no assurance of ever getting paid.

For the task of banishing the bleakness from Thanksgiving with humor, he enlisted Mrs. Sairy Ann Bilkins, the fictional dispenser of common sense in his "Our Landlady" column. Said the colonel:

> "I was thinking," . . . as he took a tooth out of the mince pie and laid it on the side of his plate, "that I ought to be thankful because when I bought my last suit of clothes I got two pair of pants instead of one—otherwise I should have to parade the streets this winter in my natural-wool underware."
>
> "There!" cried our landlady, triumphantly, "ye see we've all got suthin' to be thankful for if we only stop to think it out . . . People in the effet yeast thinks us Dakota sufferers won't give no thanks today, but that's where they're off their belt. This thanskgivin' is a glorious instertution, an' I for one am glad as I live in a state where there's still suthin' to be thankful for."

As for herself, Mrs. Bilkins said she was thankful that "turkeys is cheaper nor beefsteak!"

Perhaps such perspective may have helped soothe some people, but it was unlikely, as the crop failure wasn't even the most immediate problem facing the stalwarts of Dakota right then. The farm crisis was exacerbated by what everyone was calling the "Indian scare." The lack of wheat, corn, and grazing grass in the region hit the local Sioux tribes the hardest, and so when agency officials at the Standing Rock and Pine Ridge reservations announced that the already insufficient rations of food would be cut by 20 percent, the Sioux knew they faced a winter of starvation that could kill off a large swath of their people. This naturally set off alarms at Fort Yates, the U.S. military outpost on the Missouri River constructed to control the Native Americans. "Discontent has been growing for six months," General Nelson Miles wrote in an urgent bulletin to Washington. "A good many Indians have been on the verge of starvation. They have seen the whites suffering, too, and in many cases abandoning their farms."

To retaliate, the men of the reservation seemed to be preparing for an uprising. Rather than watch their wives and children die a slow and painful death, it would be better to go on the attack before the frozen white desolation arrived. It was widely reported that Sioux warriors were getting ready to raid agency strongholds as well as nearby ranches, cities, and towns—massacring the whites and stealing what they needed to survive. The scare reached a series of flash points in mid-November when a pack of Sioux chiefs arrived at agency headquarters for their rations. Appalled by the meager amounts being doled out, they brandished their knives and nearly set fire to the building. Chief Thunder Bear was taken into custody, and three companies of cavalry and five companies of infantry were called in to set up camp at the edges of the reservations. The specter of marauding bands of wild Indians, the primal fear of every American in the West, was now in play.

Around Thanksgiving there was a report that a rancher who lived by the reservation was threatened by a Lakota warrior who vowed that "there will be an uprising soon." The newspapers now printed the most savage language. The Indians are "surly and defiant in manner," said one newswire report. "One Indian said that he had seen the time when he used to beat out the brains of white children and drink the women's blood, and the time was coming when they would do it again." Accounts flooded the daily newspapers, telling of raids on more than a dozen white ranches near the reservations, of Indians breaking open front doors, smashing every piece of furniture and china, gathering all the food they could carry, setting fire to barns, and then rounding up all horses and cattle and driving them away.

Such tales had a name: ranch stories. They were almost always fictional, yet there they were, printed in black and white, stoking the most widespread terrors. "The leaders of the Indian war party said they would sweep the country," said one article.

At first Frank Baum tried remaining sensible, aiming to keep his readers cool concerning "this false and senseless scare." He even ran a disclaimer that "it is well known" that the wire reports he was printing were often "not literally true" and that readers should "exercise their own judgment" in whether to believe them. "According to the popular rumor, the Indians were expected to drop in on us any day the last week," Frank quipped in an editorial. "But as our scalps are still in healthy condition it is needless for us to remark that we are yet alive and undisturbed." He lashed out at his colleagues and rivals in the press for their sensationalism. "Probably papers who have so injured the state by their flashy headlines of Indian uprisings did not think of the results of such actions beyond the extra sale of a few copies of their sheets."

Frank, for one, could readily identify with the plight of the Native Americans. He lived in the same rain-forsaken region, and he himself had little money at a time when food prices were soaring. With a fourth child on the way, he dreaded the same horror that they did, of not being able to feed his children, and he knew things were unspeakably worse on the reservations. Denying the fear at this point would be futile, as the foreboding grew deeper and darker with each and every day.

Soon even Frank found himself catering to the rampant fears of his readers. "The Indian scare has accomplished one thing, at least," he acknowledged.

It has shown us how very poorly equipped we are for protection of any kind in case the Indians *should* rise. Many of the settlers nearest the reservation do not possess even a revolver, and had the Indians come upon them they would have been entirely at their mercy. In Aberdeen there are but fifty rifles and some of those are not fit for use. So that fifty Indians bent on murder and destruction and armed, as they are reported to be with Winchester rifles, could undoubtedly have our city completely at their mercy should they surprise it.

Once he became convinced that an attack on Aberdeen was at least possible, he felt an impulse to take a position on the situation. In doing so he was succumbing to an "us versus them" stance on the crisis rather than speaking out for sending emergency food aid to the reservations. He was choosing conflict over compassion. The potential threat by the natives "should be remedied in some manner," he wrote. "The least the government can do is to give our settlers, who have paid good money for their lands, full protection from the Indian neighbors in case the latter choose to revolt." Once again Frank Baum was telling people what they wanted to hear, turning on his superpower, only this time what they wanted to hear wasn't pretty.

What spread across the Great Plains at this time could not simply be described as a scare, as the events of December of 1890 would go down in American history as much more than a series of momentary flash points. What happened on the cold, hard Dakota prairie was more of a great reckoning, a clash of civilizations not just between two different races of people but also between their opposing mythologies, the myths of both cultures being acted out through a series of instinctive rituals that seemed destined to spin out of control.

The Battle of Little Bighorn was now fourteen years in the past, but the legend of that day had only grown taller with each telling. In death General Custer had become the martyr for Manifest Destiny, resurrected as an even greater national hero; towns and parks were named for him and monuments erected in his honor. Chief Sitting Bull remained alive, but he had gone through a more complex series of transformations. Soon after the battle, the Lakota medicine man talked down the rumor that he thirsted for more war. "I have never made war on the United States government," Sitting Bull protested. "The white man made me fight for my hunting grounds. The white man made me kill him or he would kill my friends, my women, and my children."

Sitting Bull refused to live on the reservation, proudly asserting that he was no agency Indian. "I don't want a white man over me," he declared. This posed a special problem for the U.S. government, which could not tolerate the number-one enemy of the American people roaming free on the plains, setting up camp with his roving band of armed men and their families. If he chose to remain where he was, he would almost surely be hunted down and killed. Rather than keep fighting to defend his way of life in the United States, Sitting Bull took flight, leading his followers over the northern border into Canada, where Major James Walsh of the Royal Canadian Mounted Police allowed the "noble savage" to live in peace.

A reporter for the *New York Herald* praised Major Walsh "as one who alone had tamed the Lion of the West." Those who accompanied Major Walsh while he was keeping a watch on Sitting Bull also referred to him as the lion of his people. "I have followed Sitting Bull around long enough," wrote a reporter from a Chicago newspaper, "and now I shall behold 'the lion in his den' in earnest."

But during the next five years in exile, Sitting Bull and his followers suffered from near starvation on the barren Canadian land. It had come time, he declared, to make his return to Dakota. "God made me to live on the flesh of the buffalo," he said, perhaps not realizing the extent to which the buffalo had vanished. When he arrived at Standing Rock along with his tattered band, however, he found that he had lost his authority. He tried winning it back through his oratory and his medicine man magic, but his people would no longer listen to him. Pretty soon U.S. troops arrived to place Sitting Bull under arrest. He said he would go peacefully. More than three thousand fellow Lakota came to witness a surrender that Sitting Bull treated like a ceremony. He laid down his knife and his tomahawk and presented them to the captain of the transfer expedition. Then, acting out the hero's part, he threw himself on the ground and asked the captain to take his life right then — but to spare his people and treat them kindly forever.

What Sitting Bull had hoped would be perceived as the ultimate act of sacrifice and bravery was seen by his fellow Sioux as a pathetic stunt. Most of the Lakota there laughed at him. The captain didn't have any intention of killing Sitting Bull and making him a martyr for freedom. He helped the old medicine man to his feet and then watched as the other Sioux chiefs ridiculed their former leader, literally pushing him off the reservation. The Lakota lion was now seen as cowardly, and this is how he was viewed for most of the 1880s, as a living oxymoron.

Frank Baum would one day create a character who at first seems fierce and brave. "There came from the forest a terrible roar," he would write, "and the next moment a great Lion bounded into the road. With one blow of his paw he sent the Scarecrow spinning." But when confronted, the Lion withers. Aghast at seeing the beast open his jaws to take a bite of Toto, Dorothy steps forward and whacks him on the nose.

"Don't you dare to bite Toto! You ought to be ashamed of yourself, a big beast like you, to bite a poor little dog!"

"I didn't bite him," says the Lion, as he rubs his nose with his paw.

"No, but you tried to," she retorts. "You are nothing but a big coward."

"I know it," says the Lion, hanging his head in shame. "I've always known it. But how can I help it?"

In real life the prized prisoner was taken in shackles to a U.S. Army fort, where he promised that if he was simply permitted to return to the place of his birth, on the Grand River, he would live in peace and persuade his followers to do the same. By 1885 Sitting Bull was so timid and tamed that he received an unusual invitation. Buffalo Bill Cody, the famous rodeo impresario, requested that the chief join his Wild West Show, set to tour New York, Philadelphia, and Washington that summer. Under the guise of earning money for his people, Sitting Bull accepted. The tour came to the Wieting Opera House in Syracuse for a full week while Frank Baum was still living there. Decked out in a full Sioux headdress of eagle feathers, the medicine man spoke the wisdom of his people, but his meaning was often lost on white audiences, who would chant out, "Hang him, hang him!" and then line up to spend $1.50 for an autographed photo. The chief quit the tour after one season and headed home.

Then came the years of drought and hunger and a string of broken promises by agency officials. The year 1890 saw life on the reservation reach crisis proportions, and by November more than twenty thousand Sioux of the region were on the verge of mass starvation. They complained loudly to the corrupt agency officials who had been busy skimming the provisions and lining their own pockets, but their cries were predictably ignored. When some chiefs argued for taking desperate measures, a series of exaggerated threats, misinformation, and ranch stories began flying through the newswires. "We will have a big eat before starving time comes," Chief Two Strike was quoted as saying. "After that we shall fight our last fight and the white man shall see more blood, more dead by us from our guns than ever before."

Sitting Bull and many of the elder leaders knew that if they fought, they were likely to lose many men, leaving their women and children alone to face starvation. It was at this dire moment, when all hope seemed to be lost, that a powerful idea was born out of wretched desperation: the Messiah was coming. According to folklore, the great savior would arrive just when he was needed the most. Along with him would come all the medicine men and warriors of the past as well as their wives and children. They'd all return to life, and the resurrected chiefs would lead their people to great victory over their white oppressors. Also returning to roam the prairie would be the lost herds of buffalo, turning the Great Plains into the happy hunting grounds they once were. The central mountains would erupt and spew forth lava and ash that would bury white cities and villages, leaving the First People to live in harmony in the kingdom of the Great Spirit.

No one knows who started the Messiah rumor—some say it originated with the Arapaho or the Paiute of Nevada—but once it began it spread like an epidemic among nearly every tribe. The four winds carried the news not only to the Sioux, but also to the Cherokee, to the Navajo, to the Apache, to the Iroquois, to the Blackfeet, to the Chippewa, to the Ogalallah, and the virus took hold in every region, from Arizona to Alaska, from New Mexico to New York, from Oklahoma to Dakota, from Nevada to California, from Minnesota to Wyoming. Indeed, the Messiah craze erupted with such speed that it seemed as if the message had broken forth spontaneously in each location.

The Sioux had a special myth for how such communication happened: the news might have been carried along with the weather by a flock of *wakinyan,* a Lakota word derived from *wakan,* meaning "god," and *kinyan,* meaning "winged one." The *wakinyan* is a mysterious gargoyle-like creature with multijointed wings that was created to serve Inyan, the god of all things. Some *wakinyan* have beaks and some do not, and they come in many colors—yellow, green, blue, and red. Each *wakinyan* has *ton,* the power to perform supernatural acts, and they live on a high mountain in the West. From there they travel with the west wind. Able to swoop from the clouds at any moment, these fabled birds have the voice of thunder and the eyes of lightning.

The supernatural "winged ones" of Lakota legend may have inspired a similar flock of creatures that lived in the Winkie country in the west of Oz and performed difficult tasks as commanded. Frank Baum would one day name these fierce flying beasts "the Winged Monkeys," writing that they "would obey any order they were given. But no person could command these strange creatures more than three times."

Back in 1890 the Messiah message triggered a series of tribal gatherings known as the Ghost Dance. This religious ritual was said to prepare the Native Americans for the savior's arrival. The dancing had actually begun in August and had now caught on in dozens of locations. In a typical Ghost Dance ceremony, a tall tree trunk would be placed in the middle of a field, and four elder chiefs or medicine men would sit on four different sides of the pole as scores of Indians danced wildly, moving in a constant circle around the pole, all wearing painted faces. Women and children danced equally. Dancing for days at a time, the natives would became so ravished by hunger and so giddy with exhaustion that they'd fall to the ground talking with the spirits. Then the dancers would tell the medicine men their visions about what the Messiah would bring. The ceremony would end with a big feast of raw meat from freshly slaughtered cattle.

Sitting Bull saw the Messiah craze as his golden chance to regain his old standing within the Sioux Nation, and so the Ghost Dancing he staged at his camp became more vigorous than anywhere else. His followers erected a tall pole with flags flying on it, and Sitting Bull set up a special tepee near the pole. All men, women, and children who took part in the dancing and the chanting lined up to step inside the tepee to be painted by the old medicine man.

To agency officials and military leaders, the Ghost Dance was perceived as a war dance, as a signal of imminent attack. "The dancing Indians have the agency and the surrounding country in a state of terror," one report alerted. "There are 600 of the painted redskins dancing . . . their guns strapped to their backs as they dance." One Saturday night James McLaughlin, the head agent at Standing Rock, snuck up to observe the dancing in its full glory. "I learned that such a dance was in progress in Sitting Bull's camp on the Grand River," McLaughlin wrote to the commissioner of Indian Affairs. "We got upon them unexpectedly and found a ghost dance at its height. There were about 45 men,

25 women, 25 boys and 10 girls participating," plus about two hundred others just watching. "There seems to be something about this craze that invests the women with greater importance, and it is supposed that in case of hostilities the women would fight as the men. I did not attempt to stop the dance then going on, as in their crazed condition under the excitement it would have been useless to attempt it."

After this report the U.S. government issued orders that all Ghost Dancing everywhere must be stopped, but a special focus was directed to Sitting Bull's camp, as "evidence was gathering" that he was marshalling his forces. McLaughlin arranged to visit Sitting Bull in his lodge the next morning to convey the order, but when that proved fruitless, he ordered Sitting Bull's arrest. It was at this point that Sitting Bull was reinvigorated with bravery, summoning the lost courage within himself. "God Almighty did not make me an agency Indian," Sitting Bull roared, "and I'll fight and I'll die fighting before any white man can make me an agency Indian."

Based on a rumor that Sitting Bull was preparing a rush into the Badlands to take up a fighting position, a plan to capture the chief was put in motion by the tenth of December. "There was a quiet understanding between officers of Indian and military departments that it would be impossible to bring in Sitting Bull alive to Standing Rock, and even if they did, they wouldn't know what to do with him," reported the Chicago Tribune. "Under arrest he'd still be an annoyance, and his followers would continue dancing. There was a complete understanding between the Indian police . . . and government authorities, from President Harrison to General Nelson Miles on down, that they preferred the death of the famous old savage to his capture."

At the offices of Frank Baum's Aberdeen Saturday Pioneer, a confusing array of alarming reports were pulsing over the wires, and yet it wasn't clear to Frank how seriously to take the situation. It seemed comical to him that each side was just as scared as the other. Ridiculously, the government initially sent in Buffalo Bill Cody—a showbiz soldier—to negotiate with Sitting Bull, but then quickly retracted him. In the "Our Landlady" column of December 6, Mrs. Sairy Ann Bilkins reported that she had personally gone in herself—on a dangerous expedition into heart of Sioux territory. "Oh yes," she said, "I've been to the reservation all right enough—bearded the lion in his whiskers so to speak, an' I'm alive yit to tell the tale."

Frank Baum was using an expression—"bearded the lion in his whiskers"—that meant his fictional alter ego was confronting the powerful Sitting Bull in his own den. "Ye see, arter the president wouldn't let Buffalo Bill run this campaign . . . I made up my mind I'd take the thing inter my own hands and find out what the red demons intended to do."

And so an elderly woman in a housedress, armed with nothing more than knitting needles and supplied only with cheese and crackers, "tuk the President's Message" and "started fer the seat o' war" on horseback. When she came upon a "large body of Injins jest ahead o' me," she yelled, "Hol' up!" But they gave a "whoop o' terrer" and ran "fer their lives." Finally, she came upon the great chief, "the bravest Sioux outside o' Sioux Falls." Our landlady then discovered that he was more afraid of her than she was of him. "Don't hurt us, Miss' Bilkins," said he, quivering.

In Frank Baum's remarkable homespun fantasy, he foreshadowed the very creation of the Cowardly Lion himself. "What makes you a coward?" Dorothy would ask one day, looking at the great beast in wonder.

"It's a mystery," replies the Lion. "Whenever I've met a man I've been awfully scared; but I just roared at him, and he has always run away as fast as he could go."

In real life the madness continued throughout the coming week. In his issue of December 13 Frank ran a long series of stories on the Ghost Dance and the Sitting Bull situation. One wire dispatch estimated that about two thousand armed, war-painted fighting Indian men were fortifying their camp; another report disputed the danger, and yet another relayed a separate set of troubles with twelve hundred starving Sisseton and Wahpeton east of Aberdeen. "One day's dispatches would indicate that the Indians were on the eve of a bloody outbreak, and on the next that no attack was anticipated," Frank wrote.

Yet on balance Frank was leaning toward fear, becoming more and more convinced that conflict was indeed at hand. "A man in the East can read the papers and light a cigar and say there is no danger," he mused, "but put that man and his family on the east bank of the Missouri, opposite Sitting Bull's camp, at night, where he can see 150 to 200 redskins dancing the ghost dance, he will draw a different picture." There was news that the U.S. Interior Department had authorized an expenditure of $2,000 in emergency relief for the starving natives, but the amount worked out to less than one cent per day for each person—way too little and way too late to make any difference.

The expedition to arrest Sitting Bull for illegal Ghost Dancing set out on the morning of December 14. The wagon train from Standing Rock was headed by twenty Indian police working under the supervision of Agent McLaughlin. Backing them up was a troop of U.S. Cavalry, riding with rifles, as well as a troop of U.S. Army Infantry, armed with heavier artillery. In contrast with Sitting Bull's exhausted, half-starved compatriots, the Indian police were well rested, well fed, and dressed sharply in blue uniforms provided by Uncle Sam. They were led by Bull Head, who arrived to spot Sitting Bull's camp of shacks and tepees by the banks of the Grand River in the early morning of December 15.

There were at least two different accounts of what happened next. According to the Lakota version, the Indian police swooped into the camp, razed Sitting Bull's tepee, pulled him from bed, handcuffed him, and hoisted him up on a horse. Even though a dozen Winchester rifles were pointed at his head, Sitting Bull shouted orders directing his rescue. Several compatriots were already on the scene with guns. There was a sharp crack of a rifle, and one of the Indian police reeled in his saddle, toppled over, and was trampled by rampaging horses in a mad helter-skelter. The police answered with a volley of shots and several tribesmen went down. "Sitting Bull was still shouting, directing the fight, when suddenly his body straightened up and dropped limp on the hard prairie." Thinking it was a trick, the police called in the cavalry for support, and machine-gun fire opened on men who were bolting for the river to take cover. Sitting Bull was finally slaughtered, and among those joining him in death was his twenty-year-old son, Crow Foot.

But according to the report filed by Agent McLaughlin, Bull Head and his men arrived at Sitting Bull's lodge with an arrest warrant. Sitting Bull's wife gave out a piercing yell, which the police took as a battle cry, and then two Sioux men enveloped in blankets stormed the cabin and opened fire on the police. Without hesitation, one of Bull Head's men fired at Sitting Bull, the bullet piercing his chest. Reeling, Sitting Bull drew a revolver and shot a bullet into Bull Head's thigh, the great chief's last action before dying. Crossfire broke out, resulting in the death of Crow Foot and at least ten other followers. Bull Head died from his wounds, as did seven other Indian police.

However it happened, the news that Sitting Bull had been killed went out far and wide. The first reaction among the white population was one of good riddance, that the world was relieved of a trouble-maker, under the popular theory that the only good Indian is a dead Indian. But the deeper reaction was more complex. "There were those who raised a cry of exultation at the death of Sitting Bull," wrote historian W. Fletcher Johnson. "But the real mind and heart of the American people felt sad and ashamed, with a sadness and a shame too deep for words." Since Sitting Bull had not harmed anyone for years, the circumstance of his death was a national tragedy accompanied by deeper and darker foreboding.

The people of Aberdeen immediately anticipated the worst, some imagining that a bloodbath would follow. "Expect an Attack at Any Moment," screamed a wire report headline in Frank Baum's newspaper. "Sitting Bull's Death to Be Avenged by a Massacre of Whites in the Near Future." That the Sioux continued Ghost Dancing only heightened tensions. A wire went out to Washington calling for more troops: "Indians are dancing in the snow and are wild and crazy . . . We need protection and we need it now." In the primal battle of hope versus fear, fear had crowded out everything else.

L. Frank Baum could no longer resort to humor. Desperate to save his dwindling newspaper business and protect his family from economic ruin, he told his readers exactly what they already believed, that fear must consume us all. In a scathing editorial the man who had hardly said an unkind word about anyone in his life argued for a final solution to the "Indian problem." About the death of Sitting Bull he wrote:

> With his fall, the nobility of the Redskin is extinguished, and what few are left are a pack of whining curs who lick the hand that smites them. The Whites, by law of conquest, by justice of

civilization, are masters of the American continent, and the best safety of the frontier settlers will be secured by the total annihilation of the few remaining Indians. Why not annihilation? Their glory has fled, their spirit broken, their manhood effaced; better they should die than live the miserable wretches that they are. History would forget these latter despicable beings, and speak, in latter ages of the glory of these grand Kings of forest and plain that [James Fenimore] Cooper loved to heroize.

L. Frank Baum had succumbed to the potent narcotic of racism. In dehumanizing the Native Americans, by calling them "whining curs" and "miserable wretches," he was inhaling and exhaling a message that had seduced just about everyone around him in Aberdeen. At the time of Frank Baum's bitter editorial, there were no protests or angry letters to the editor. His genocidal message was met with near complete acceptance in the community. To most townsfolk the editor of the *Aberdeen Saturday Pioneer* was merely putting his stamp of approval on what thousands of fellow Dakotans were already thinking and saying. The harsh fact was that frontier settlers had been eviscerating Native American cultures since Columbus had arrived on the continent four centuries earlier. Baum's editorial propounded the very fulfillment of Manifest Destiny, the nation's core ideology. In putting such thoughts on paper, he was merely repeating a great American myth, that the conquering of the continent had been fated. He even reflected the phrase "the pale-faces are masters of the earth" from the final paragraph of Cooper's classic, *The Last of the Mohicans*. And with the expression "King of the Forest" he foreshadowed what would become the Cowardly Lion's signature song in the movie: "If I were King of the For-r-r-e-s-s-s-t."

When a good person like Frank Baum performs a deed this bad, he is often overtaken by shadow forces, personal demons mixed with archetypal emotions, the set of primal impulses and instincts that one inherits as a part of being human. In this case the archetypal fear of being attacked gave rise to intense group loyalty, which led to the dehumanization of the perceived enemy of the group. The dark demon that made Frank susceptible to this emotion could have been his long-repressed shame over quitting the Peekskill Military Academy, the dishonor of not being courageous enough to become a soldier fight-ing on the frontier. After all, it was his former classmates—or people like them—who were now readying their rifles and cannons, massing around the camps of the Lakota reservations. Frank's showing of false bravery may have been triggered by lingering guilt over abandoning his fellow cadets.

With cruel hypocrisy, Frank's editorial appeared in the issue right before Christmas. In that very same edition he wrote that "it is a pleas-ant duty to wish all our readers a Merry Christmas. And so with 'peace and good will to all,' we joyously welcome the coming holiday, and from the bottom of a heart overflowing with gratitude we cry, 'A merry Christmas to all!'" There could be no greater evidence that Frank's mind was infected with a classic case of us-versus-them–ism.

Indeed, Frank Baum's writings at this time were laced with many false beliefs and self-deceptions. "The success of the *Pioneer* during the past year has been due to the kindliness of our patrons," he wrote, even though he knew that many of his readers and advertisers had deserted him and that his newspaper was on the brink of failure. "And to you, brother journalists . . . a joyous Christmas . . . well have you plied your arts to the advancement of home and country," Frank re-marked, even though he knew very well that many of his newspaper colleagues were printing intentionally destructive fiction masquerad-ing as news. Despite his insistence that it was so, Frank clearly could not be wishing "peace and good will to all" in one column while wish-ing destruction and ill will to others in another column.

Christmas of 1890 was a tense day of worship, with snow blanketing all of the Dakotas. The Sioux continued their Ghost Dances through-out the holiday, and this continued to alarm the U.S. troops stationed there. One report was particularly ominous. During a wild Ghost Dance in the snow, one dancer directed everyone's attention to the top of a bluff. There in the whiteness stood a stark figure—or a fig-ment—that stood perfectly motionless.

Suddenly, one of the dancers cried out: "It's Sitting Bull!"

"Then did the marrow in the bones of these Indians grow cold, and their teeth chattered like beans in a barrel," according to one account of the apparition. "The phantom commenced waving an arm as if motioning them to follow." With this ghostly vision, Sitting Bull had been resurrected, returning to Earth as the Messiah, and he was beckoning his people to join with him to deal with the enemy in the name of his spirit. The new Christ had indeed arrived at long last, or so it seemed at the moment.

This was just one of a dozen or so Messiah sightings around this time, and it was so absurd that it should have been taken as harmless, yet it was this kind of report that further stirred the wrath of the U.S. soldiers sent in to subdue the Sioux. On December 28 the Seventh Cavalry, the very same regiment once led by General Custer, rode into the Pine Ridge Reservation to pursue a band of Sioux men led by Chief Big Foot who were misperceived to be on the warpath. These troops were known as "Custer's Avengers," as they were soldiers who had a long-standing grudge to repay. They chased nearly three hundred Sioux men, women, and children into a dead end in the landscape, until their backs hit up against a gulch, home to a frozen creek called Wounded Knee.

The troops formed a cordon around the natives and sent for reinforcements. Among those cornered were most of Sitting Bull's former followers. The troops told the Sioux to lay down their arms, but they didn't trust that they wouldn't be shot immediately after complying. A standoff ensued, and both sides set up camp for a night of nerves. By eight o'clock the next morning, after four rapid-fire Hotchkiss cannons were rolled in and five hundred troops arrived as reinforcement, Seventh Cavalry commander Samuel Whitside ordered the Sioux to lay down their guns, twenty at a time. But when only two guns were produced, Whitside became irritated and ordered his men closer, within ten yards of the camp. Whitside then told his men to search the tepees, and within moments the braves let out a death dirge that morphed into a war chant.

A single shot escaped a rifle, and in a burst of chaos the whole field erupted in gunfire and smoke. Greatly outnumbered and short of guns, some Sioux rushed the soldiers with tomahawks and scalping knives. The artillery was called in and sheets of bullets rained down on a battlefield broiling with hand-to-hand combat. A battle cry rang out: "Remember Custer!" Dozens of women and children raced toward the gulch, some getting gunned down and others escaping into the landscape. The battle had turned into a massacre, the meadow of whiteness transformed into a field of blood.

After a half hour of fighting and shooting at Wounded Knee, not a single live Sioux was in sight. Big Foot lay in the snow, his body riddled with bullets. Twenty-five U.S. soldiers were killed, and nearly three hundred Sioux were either shot dead or would soon die from their wounds and hypothermia. Included among those slaughtered was a group of more than sixty Sioux women and children who broke for the creek. A young Sioux named Black Elk witnessed the massacre's aftermath and spoke about it years later: "When I look back now from this high hill of my old age, I can still see the butchered women and children . . . as plain as when I saw them with eyes still young. And I can see that something else died there in that bloody mud . . . A people's dream died there. It was a beautiful dream."

Wounded Knee would mark history's last major confrontation between U.S. forces and Native Americans. Clear across to California, the whites controlled all the land they wanted, and the remaining Native Americans were corralled onto reservations as if they were specimens in a nature preserve. The West was won, Manifest Destiny fulfilled. The long campaign exacted an ungodly price, as a report around this time estimated that the U.S. government had spent a billion dollars fighting, pacifying, and civilizing the Native Americans over the past hundred years, more than the combined cost of all the country's foreign wars to date.

Yet this turning point went unrecognized at the time, and as the new year arrived the newspapers were still buzzing with fears of reprisals and counterattacks. Among those newspaper writers whose capacity for compassion was still blocked by his own fear was L. Frank Baum, who penned yet another unfortunate editorial, published on January 3, 1891: "The *Pioneer* has before declared that our only safety depends upon the total extermination of the Indians. Having wronged them for centuries we had better, in order to protect our civilization, follow it up by one more wrong and wipe these untamed and untamable creatures from the face of the earth."

One of the only places that this twisted rationalization would be unwelcome was Frank Baum's own household, as his wife, Maud, and his mother-in-law, Matilda, were firm believers in universal equality and justice for all. Frank would never again in his life express views like this. Yet in the here and now, he'd have to account for himself, especially when he walked in the door at 512 South Kline Street. Just as she did every winter, Matilda Joslyn Gage was staying with her daughter and son-in-law, and one can only imagine her reaction, as there survives little about what happened inside those walls during those terrible days. But the disappointment and hurt that must have permeated the Baum household in the aftermath of Frank's bitter editorials can be inferred from the fact that Mrs. Gage credited Native Americans with inspiring much of her core identity and beliefs. "The women of the nation might take hint from the Indians," she once wrote after studying the dynamics of tribal life. "Never was justice more perfect, never civilization higher."

Over the years she had come to expect bigotry from others, but not from Frank. How could a decent man like him, an ardent crusader for women's rights just weeks earlier, advocate the annihilation of an entire people? For Mrs. Gage, this dark episode may have confirmed that her bright and talented daughter had indeed chosen the wrong man and the wrong life for herself, as she had suspected years before. Perhaps it came as no shock to Matilda that this man had fallen from grace, as she had seen him fail over and over again at nearly everything he attempted. Her daughter Maud would thus be caught in the middle of the two most important people in her life, feeling confused and alone. Matilda knew that her daughter loved her husband dearly, that Maud believed Frank was good and she would not forsake him.

Frank, meanwhile, had some tough decisions to make. His newspaper enterprise was collapsing because of dire drops in circulation and advertising. In his very next issue the debate that was tearing at him —whether he should stay or go—exploded into the center of his "Our Landlady" column. "To think of the idjuts leavin' Aberdeen just at the time when her troubles is about over, nearly makes me sick," said Mrs. Bilkins.

> "Why should one stay?" demanded Tom; "with the same amount of energy it requires to earn a crust here, I could get a full loaf anywhere else. Why should I stay? Do I owe anything to Aberdeen?"

"Prap's not," replied our landlady, putting the dinner upon the table, and sharpening the carver upon her instep, "but you owe suthin' to yourself, certain . . . We are as sure o' gittin' a crop next year as we are o' livin' til the time comes . . . Before you can hardly git settled in some other locality, you'll be startled by the news o' the crops in South Dakoty, by reports o' the thousands flockin' in to the most fertile country on the yearth . . . Gentlemen, there's goin' ter be the biggest excitement in these parts the west has ever knowd."

It was now high time that Frank stopped deluding himself. Just days after he wrote this column, one of the biggest banks in the city, Hagerty's Savings and Loan, went belly-up. Hagerty was known as the town's richest man and its earliest real estate speculator. That he could no longer pay his creditors and depositors spoke volumes about how grim things really were. If Hagerty had no money, things were about to get pretty depressed around Aberdeen.

Frank Baum knew he had to dispose of his newspaper, as it now cost him money to run it. He decided to drop the next few editions down to eight pages and run mostly boilerplate copy. What Frank Baum would do next was anyone's guess. Now nearing the age of thirty-five, he had no job, no career, and no prospects. He no longer even knew who he really was, as he was now lost among the great zigzags of life's journey, well off the path to his true self.

Indeed, L. Frank Baum was trapped by the greatest obstacle he had ever faced—the seductive power of a dark myth—and the only way to escape it would be to atone for his small role in the great American tragedy that had just transpired, to somehow commemorate those whom he had wronged with his bitter pen. To fight a myth of darkness one is best served by wielding a myth of light. Mrs. Bilkins herself put it best. "We ain't lookin' fer truth," she proclaimed. "Can get all we want fer a cent a line, but a good lie is wuth a dollar a word to us any minnit."

And so Frank Baum would reach for a way to refocus his superpower of empathy. Of the many obstacles that the traveling companions of Oz must overcome, by far the most difficult one is the field of beautiful scarlet poppies whose "odor is so powerful that anyone who breathes it falls asleep . . . forever." In Frank Baum's fiction, that which has the power to seduce also has the power to kill. Although many readers take the symbol of the deadly poppy field only at face value—the deadly seduction of opium—that is a characteristic of the oriental strain of the poppy plant. The corn poppy, however, is known for its beauty. This brilliant red flower was mythologized during the Napoleonic Wars, after this mysterious plant was seen blooming around the fresh graves of fallen soldiers. The red color was said to come from the blood of the slain, serving as an emblem of commemoration.

Seen in this light, the deadly poppy field can be read as a powerful symbol of Frank's—and America's—sadness over the destruction of native cultures and the bloody slaughter of the Native Americans and their sacred buffalo. That Dorothy can't help but fall asleep among the red flowers is rife with symbolic meaning. Only those of flesh and blood are affected. The Scarecrow and the Tin Woodman try to devise a rescue plan as Dorothy and the Lion are in danger of sleeping forever in this mythical field of blood. As she slumbers, Dorothy becomes metaphorically at one with the dead spirits. To be "at one" is to "atone"—something Frank Baum needed to do at this moment in his life.

He was in desperate need of something spiritual to grasp. Matilda had told Frank many times about her beliefs in Theosophy. Frank had even written about Theosophy from an intellectual point of view in his newspaper columns. He knew that the word means "divine wisdom." "Theosophy is not a religion," Frank wrote. "Its followers are simply 'searchers after Truth.'" Frank knew the critical difference between truth with a small *t* and Truth with a big *T*. Theosophists "accept the teachings of Christ, Buddha, and Mohammed, acknowledging them Masters, or Mahatmas, true prophets well versed in the secrets of nature . . . The Theosophists, in fact, are the dissatisfied of the world, the dissenters from all creeds. They owe their origin to the wise men of India. They admit to the existence of a God—not necessarily a personal God. To them God is nature and nature God."

Now that Frank sensed a deep need for a new way of coming into contact with the center of his personal sphere, he turned to the underlying principles of this ancient mysticism on a deeper level. By now he could see that his old way of being was no longer working, leading only to cycles of ups and downs, zigs and zags that would repeat as endlessly as the seasons. In a house filled with literature of ancient wisdom, Matilda had the tools to persuade her son-in-law to begin his transformation in earnest. With these books Matilda would be able to show Frank the particular disease of the soul from which he was suffering, for it was an exceedingly common disease. According to Mrs. Gage, almost everyone in America had it, as it was at the root of all racism and materialism.

The book she would have given to Frank at this time was *The Key to Theosophy*—published just months earlier—Blavatsky's most accessible book for the beginner. The passage that applied to Frank the most was based on wisdom that showed how the soul was composed of two parts, what both Aristotle and Plato called the animal soul and the reasoning soul: "The future state and the Karmic destiny of man depends on whether Manas (the soul in general) gravitates more downward to Kama rupa, the seat of the animal passions, or upwards to Buddhi, the Spiritual Ego."

But for Frank, reading this would only be the start of the rediscovery process, just as studying a map isn't the same as going somewhere new. His search for a meaningful spirituality that could help subdue what had corrupted him led him to a primary source: the Vedas, the scriptures of ancient wisdom that formed the basis of Hinduism and influenced all Eastern religions as well as Theosophy. In the January 17, 1891, edition of the *Pioneer*, there appeared a highly unusual letter to the editor that was signed simply "XYZ" and seemed to be written by Frank Baum himself to clue his readers in to something in an indirect way. "I believe you yourself are accused of studying the Vedas," the letter said. The editor replied back that he "has been accused of many things" and "claims religious freedom."

Continuing his reply, editor Baum went on to reveal something truly significant about his new intention. "I am looking forward to a time when both Christians and Spiritualists will stand awed before the unfolding of great truths of nature," he wrote. "Spiritualism is a stepping stone to something higher which shall yet be revealed to mankind." Here was evidence that Frank was ready to embark on a new road, a spiritual adventure complete with many steppingstones and leading to a higher level of consciousness. This is exactly what all Eastern religions and Theosophy have in common, the concept of using mindful concentration to journey through dark and treacherous territory along what is sometimes called the Golden Path to enlightenment.

Yet spiritual awareness could only inform his journey. Frank also needed a new way to support his growing family. There was little choice now except to sell the *Pioneer* back to its original owner, John H. Drake, and accept whatever pittance he could get for it. The deal would be completed within weeks, and Drake would simply shut it down, write off what was left of the goodwill, and resell the printing press and the other hard assets.

Racking his brain to figure out how and where he should begin life anew, Frank couldn't help but notice in the final weeks of running his newspaper that more and more wire stories were focusing on a certain subject: that the city of Chicago had won the right to host a world's fair like no other. It would be called the World's Columbian Exposition — in honor of the four hundredth anniversary of Columbus's discovery of America — and this city within a city was now being constructed at breakneck speed. Chicago, Frank read, would be at the center of everything. The exposition would be the largest single event in the history of the United States, and it would feature all the new and wondrous technologies that were rushing into the mainstream of society — electric lighting, the telephone, the horseless carriage, the phonograph.

Showcasing his newest inventions, the Wizard of Menlo Park himself would be in attendance, as would nearly every luminary in the world. It was as if dozens of tiny inner voices were summoning Frank to go to this so-called White City in order to seek what he needed most. The exposition would be the brightest of spectacles, with more electric lights on the fairgrounds themselves than in all of the rest of Chicago. To L. Frank Baum, it seemed that the only way to triumph over his own inner shadow was to gather his family and follow the road toward the glimmering in the distance. "Hold onto your breath, hold onto your heart, hold onto your hope," the Optimistic Voices would sing one day in the MGM film. "March up to the gate and let it open."

PART
· III ·

12

The Golden Path

On Baum's first day writing for the *Chicago Evening Post*, a front-page story observed that "there is no place like home." One illustration shows a "soul" taking wing while another shows a girl, a dog, and her three companions heading down a road with trepidation.

◆

"If this road goes in, it must come out, and as the Emerald City is at the other end of the road, we must go wherever it leads us."

— THE SCARECROW

NEVER ONE TO WASTE any time getting on to the next thing, L. Frank Baum was bound for Chicago just as the January 17, 1891, issue of his dying newspaper reached the hands of his dwindling number of readers. From the window of the train, the Great Plains looked flat and nearly lifeless for hundreds of miles, and then out of nowhere arose this spectacle, a metropolis in the distance that appeared to be a civilization from another planet. Frank arrived at Chicago's newly built Grand Central Station, with its soaring ceilings, castlelike tower, stained-glass windows, and marble floors. It was among the many recent additions to a city that had been undergoing transformations every few months.

Only twenty years earlier, in the aftermath of the Great Fire that consumed four square miles, Chicago was in cinders, a pit of ash. The frenzy of rebuilding that followed was unprecedented because it coincided with so many technological jolts—from the advent of steel for scaffolding to the sprouting of electric lights to the spread of streetcars—enabling Chicago to leapfrog into a position as the world's most modern destination. That it had also become a magnet for people full of hopes and dreams was confirmed by the 1890 census: the town at the crossroads of the continent now hosted more than a million souls, narrowly surpassing Philadelphia to take its place as America's Second City.

Arriving along with the freezing winds, Frank checked into a modest boarding house on Western Avenue, where he received a telegram from Maud saying that there had been a death in the family. Maud's sister Helen Leslie Gage had just lost her husband, Charles, who had been ill for two years. The letter that Frank immediately penned to his sister-in-law speaks volumes about his newly developing mindset, reflecting basic tenets of Theosophy. "The news of Charlie's death came to us today," Frank wrote to Helen. "It is with you that I sympathize for he, I believe, will rejoice in his release from what must have been a trying and unsatisfactory life. We are all prone to cling to life, but when the pain of parting is over, for those who like Charlie lived his life well, there must come a great peace and contentment. For myself, I regret the great suffering of Charlie's later years more than his death."

Embedded in this very short passage are nothing less than the Four Noble Truths, the foundation of Buddhist mindfulness, which like Theosophy is a practice aimed at purifying the soul. To live is to suffer. That is the first truth. Frank's letter was an expression of this understanding. Suffering is caused by clinging, by attachments to certain things or ideas. Frank invoked this second truth in a universal way, saying we are all prone to attachments. But there exists a possibility to end one's suffering. This is the third truth, although you don't have to die in order to release yourself from clinging and suffering. The possibility exists in the here and now, at any time in this life.

Finally, there is a path leading to liberation and bliss. This fourth truth is fleshed out in great detail by Buddhist teachings about how to journey down Buddha's Golden Road, often called the Eightfold Path. This road to self-awareness and enlightenment is also central to Hinduism and Theosophy. Madame Blavatsky had written that "there is a Road, steep and thorny, beset with perils of every kind, but yet a Road, and it leads to the very heart of the universe." Indeed, nothing from the ancient wisdom literature is more profound than the metaphor of the dark and difficult path leading to Nirvana, the state of transcendence, the epiphany that the entire universe exists in microcosm within our own minds, the understanding that divinity lies within ourselves.

But now that he was in Chicago, Frank had to attend to more practical matters. In desperate need of a job, he had to make a quick study of the two lines of work he knew most about: newspapers and retail. After all, this wasn't the time to try something entirely new. He had to rely on his experience. When it came to journalism, Frank had arrived at the right place at the right time, for Chicago was the battleground for a dozen or so boisterous papers—foremost among them the *Times*, the *Herald*, the *Globe*, the *Daily Journal*, the *Daily News*, and the *Tribune*. Frank took a portfolio of his *Pioneer* clippings around to most of them in an area of town known as Newspaper Row.

Headlining all the papers was the news about the coming Columbian Exposition. Chicago had already beaten out New York City in the rough-and-tumble battle to host the fair; Chicago's politicians and businessmen had spewed so much hot air about their city's ascendancy that a writer from the *New York Sun* dubbed that town in Illinois "the Windy City." Just days before Frank Baum's arrival, an elite group of America's most esteemed architects had converged on Chicago to begin drawing up plans for the world's fair in earnest. Anchoring the group was landscape maestro Frederick Law Olmsted, the famed designer of New York's Central Park, as well as Chicago's own leading urban planner, John Wellborn Root, and his partner of nearly two decades, Daniel Burnham. But when the architects bundled up for a carriage ride on a cold, damp day to survey Jackson Park, the lakeside site chosen for the fairgrounds, a sense of "discouragement" and "hopelessness" set in when it fully struck them that they were dealing with low-grade swamplands. As Olmsted himself put it, "If a search had been made for the least park-like ground within miles of the city, nothing better meeting the requirement could have been found."

The U.S. Congress had mandated that the exposition was to open on May 1, 1893, in just twenty-seven months, and the architects literally had no designs or plans for how they were going to move heaven and Earth to get this monumental job done. Doom set in when John Root, "the guiding force of the fair," literally dropped dead of pneumonia just days after the carriage ride, at the age of forty. A funeral was being held for the late Mr. Root just as Frank Baum was arriving in town, and so the newspapers reported the dread, about how Root's untimely departure probably meant the death of the fair itself. But the forty-four-year-old Daniel Burnham rose to the occasion, vowing to fulfill the vision of his late partner. "Gentlemen," he declared at a special planning dinner, "1893 will be the third great date in our country's history. On the two others, 1776 and 1861, all true Americans served, and so now I ask you to serve again."

As Frank Baum made the rounds of the various newspaper offices, he found out exactly what he'd been told: that jobs at the major dailies were indeed hard to get. Frank, however, did luck into a possibility at a smaller paper, the year-old *Chicago Evening Post*. A visit to the office proved to be fortuitous, as the paper was still hiring, and so Frank found himself with the promise of a job. At just $20 per week the pay was dreadful, but Frank had no doubt that he could prove himself and earn a raise or skip to a different paper in no time, so he ended up reserving for himself a spot as a general assignment reporter, committing to come back to start in the springtime.

On his visit Frank also found himself fascinated with the sophistication of Chicago's retail economy, especially Marshall Field's department store, which he'd seen on prior trips but which had now grown into the largest store of its kind in the world. The window displays were true works of commercial art, and the sheer variety of fine goods inside could make any American salivate. Finally, he needed to find a place for his family to live, and that was not easy, given the size of the Baum household and his new salary. Riding a streetcar down Harrison Street to the city's West Side, he was able to locate an area with affordable monthly rents. On a thoroughfare with lots of trees and a broad, grassy divider, he spotted a cottage at 34 Campbell Park sporting a For Rent sign.

This was the part of Chicago that hadn't burned down, populated by old rows of Dickensian slums. Many places had no gas lines for lighting, and it was a luxury there to have running water. Yet this was only a start, and that's all Frank really needed — the promise of a new beginning, the chance to live in this remarkable city at this auspicious time, to see what had never been seen. He signed a lease to start May 1.

The hectic trip to Chicago and all its uncertainty took their toll on Frank. As soon as he was on the train back home, his hope for a better life began to be overtaken by his fear of failing once again. By the time he returned to Aberdeen, his excitement about the journey ahead seemed to have worn off, replaced with a case of second thoughts. His predicament triggered despair and then anger over the fact that he had been working so hard for all those years yet had nothing to show for it. He started using his newspaper as a platform to lash out at those whom he blamed for the lousy state of affairs in South Dakota.

His list of rogues and rascals included local preachers, politicians, and business proprietors whom he saw as being in cahoots with one another. He reserved special ire for Hagerty, the banker who happened to be part owner of the *Aberdeen Daily News*, the town's most powerful newspaper. He suggested that Hagerty was a felon for accepting deposits and selling stock in his bank even though he knew it was bound to collapse. Frank condemned the patronage system, in which politicians parceled out government contracts to those who supported them in the elections. Officials favored the owners of the *News* with custom printing jobs while passing over his newspaper. He took a swipe at one of the state's U.S. senators, Gideon Moody, "with his massive brain," for not being able to solve the state's problems. He blamed pastors for not speaking up. "What good are your churches, preacher?" Frank raged in his issue of January 24. "What good are the Christian teachings . . . when such a state of affairs is permitted to exist?" Corruption was rampant, ruining everything, and religious leaders were part of the racket. "Alas," Frank concluded, "mammon rules the world and not morality. Where will the end be?"

And so there he was, fighting his way out of the last ditch. Perhaps he really could save his newspaper if he just took this more provocative approach. The transfer of the business back to its original owner was not yet finalized, and maybe he could just tear up the lease he had signed. His social antennae told him that people were angry and yearned for an honest expression of that anger. The *Pioneer* could be that voice. Frank announced he was converting the paper into a Sunday publication and moving back up to twelve pages.

But then came the counterattacks. An enraged Hagerty led the charge, calling Baum's tirades "the acme of meanness" in an editorial. "Were it possible to dissect a soul like Mr. Baum's, I opine that it would be found smaller than the historic mustard seed."

Frank may have been able to withstand abuse from a crook like

Hagerty, but he soon pushed the debate way out of bounds when he started a spat with the superintendent of schools. That man's salary of $1,600 exceeded that of superintendents in neighboring towns, and Frank suggested that the padding in his pay was a form of patronage. "Why pay $1,600 for a $600 article?" Frank wondered in print. Even if he was right, it didn't matter. At this moment Frank once again seemed to completely lose himself, as even his trademark humor was missing. In addition, he was wholly unprepared for the level of animosity that his ranting unleashed. Within days the *News* began printing letters supporting the school official, including testimonials from kids. "Editor Baum Gets a Fine Dose from the Pupils of the High School," read one headline. The public is "radically opposed to Mr. Baum's editorial screed" and "the actions of the *Pioneer* and others are unwarranted, ungentlemanly and beneath the dignity of the public press." Then came the final blow. "Baum conspires against the welfare of the Aberdeen schools and is therefore a traitor to the best interest of the city and its children."

This knocked Frank out completely, to the point where he became physically ill. By the third week in February he was so humiliated, so exhausted, and so frightened about his family's survival that he collapsed. For a week he lay sick in bed, lying next to Maud, who was eight months' pregnant. Maud's mother was on hand to take care of both of them, bringing hot tea to their bedroom and helping to look after Frank Jr., Robert, and Harry. She could see that the bitter backlash, the trashing of his reputation, the prospect of immense change—all of it was simply too much for Frank. His heart ached, and the chest pains grew severe. The doctor diagnosed him with a case of angina pectoris, which meant that his heart was receiving too little oxygen, his valves weakening earlier in life than expected. He also had something else wrong with him, a tumor beneath his tongue, ironically enough, to be removed in a minor surgical procedure.

Plenty of bed rest was in order, so Mrs. Gage offered to pitch in and help publish the remaining issues of the *Pioneer* before the transfer back to its original owner was complete. "Mr. Baum has not been out[side] since last Saturday, having been very ill the present week," the issue of February 28 noted. "We apologize for any imperfections."

By now it was all over for L. Frank Baum in South Dakota. He was ruined—financially, physically, emotionally. With no other option available, the Baum family would be forced to pack up and go.

March 24, 1891, was the sixty-fifth birthday of Matilda Joslyn Gage, and on that very same day Maud gave birth to a fourth son, Kenneth Gage Baum. The Baum family would forever believe that Kenny's birthday was no coincidence, that he embodied the spirit of Matilda and the Joslyn Gages. Just as Matilda considered her youngest daughter her gift to the future, so would they look upon Kenneth. The span of time was breathtaking, as Matilda's mind touched both the distant past and the far future. Matilda knew her grandfather, who served as a minuteman in the battles of Lexington and Concord; and her grandson Kenneth and his three older brothers would all live well past the Second World War.

Frank's spirits lifted with the birth of his new son and the arrival of spring. His tongue was back in working order, his heart was back to pumping as it normally should, and he must have started preparing his boys for the adventure ahead, telling tales of Chicago, energizing them with stories about how great builders were creating a majestic city of the future by the shimmering water, and about how Edison, the world's most wonderful wizard, would be there. If Frank's writings from his final weeks in Aberdeen are any indication of the kinds of tales he was telling to his boys at home, those stories would have focused on the future. Once again he relied on his alter ego, Mrs. Bilkins, to shift the mood.

She spoke of a man who demonstrated what was known as an "air ship." It remained aloft for only a few seconds, but think of the possibilities. If it ever works, said her boarder Tom, "the railroads will be ruined." Mrs. Bilkins also spoofed *Looking Backwards*, the hot-selling novel by Edward Bellamy that follows a contemporary man who falls asleep in his basement only to have his house burn down, and when he awakens he finds himself alive in the year 2000 and reports on moving sidewalks, space travel, and other science fictions. Our landlady's version of the story glimpsed only five years into the future, predicting airships that could take people on instant shopping sprees, as well as a publication called *Baum's Hourly Newspaper*. "Everything progresses an' evolutes an' merges an' bubbles an' emanates an' convalutes inter suthin' else," concluded Mrs. Bilkins. "Everything changes."

Matilda, meanwhile, also began looking to the future. She was through with Susan B. Anthony and the mainstream women's movement, which she believed had sold out to the religious right. She had already formed her own action group, the Women's National Liberal Union, and she was determined to spread her message about how the Church and the State had been oppressing women for centuries and how America needed to live up to its original promise, to finally create a "regenerated world." Matilda would stay on with the Baums until the move to Chicago was complete. Then she would return to her home in Fayetteville to focus on penning what she saw as her life's magnum opus, a book to be entitled *Woman, Church and State*.

The plan was already in motion. Matilda would help the family pack up clothing and other personal items, but they would be selling or giving away their furniture because of the high cost of shipping. Frank headed to Chicago at the end of April to begin his new job at the *Chicago Evening Post*. He'd buy some beds, dressers, and tables for the new apartment. Once he arrived, the prospect of a new beginning became so energizing for Frank that he began working on his first newspaper piece even before he showed up for work. The *Post* was published in the late afternoon, which meant that feature stories and analysis were just as important as the covering of daily events that would have mostly been reported in the morning papers. Most households got both kinds of papers.

Frank's first piece was indeed a feature story, and it turned out to be one of the most amazing things he'd ever written. The editors apparently agreed, as they published it right on the front page, in the middle column, on Frank's very first day at his new job. The subject of the story was moving day, and it drew from Frank's immediate personal experience. "This Is the First of May," read the subheadline, "Time for the Annual Exodus." The *Post* offered its writers no bylines, but this piece and several others to follow were unmistakably Baumian, as they were peppered with trademark phrases that would reappear in his famous fictions and live on forever.

Many a proud man will sleep on the floor tonight . . . For this is moving day. This is the day when man lives as it is written he shall, by the perspiration of his brow. Also is it the day when the wife . . . whispers in your ear the beauty of the poet's tip that there is no place like home.

Frank's use of this sentiment — there's no place like home — seems intended as a joke. After all, he wrote it on the day he moved into a slum, the worst place he would ever live, and his family wasn't even there with him. Yet it was part of a beautifully written story that was accompanied by custom illustrations that would foretell the future. One of the drawings pictured a family of four, traveling companions who were carrying their possessions down a road — and they were accompanied by a little dog. The new L. Frank Baum had indeed arrived in Chicago, determined to give up his delusions and self-deceptions, resigned to hanging his hat and placing his heart in a new place called home. "Byron has said that it is a fearful thing to see the human soul take wing," he continued. "Moving breaks the spirit of a man." But as the story also suggests, moving into a new place also gives a man a new lease on life.

Frank's next opportunity for a major front-page story came a week later. The morning papers carried the news: "Mme. Blavatsky Dead," trumpeted the Chicago Tribune. "The Grip Triumphs over the Supernatural Gifts of Theosophy." Helena Petrovna Blavatsky was sixty years old and died at the society's European complex at Regent's Park in London, where she had been living for the past six years. Curiously, her death had occurred three weeks earlier, the wire reports noted, and she had already been cremated, but "the fact has only now become publicly known." The official cause was influenza, also known as the grippe, aggravated by her chronic kidney trouble. Within a few days this minor scandal over the alleged concealment of Blavatsky's death would be corrected by the Madame's private secretary, who said that the death indeed occurred on May 8, the very day that the announcement had been cabled around the world.

But at the time Frank Baum wrote his story for the afternoon edition, he assumed that the three-week delay was true. He decided to make some hay of it. Instead of penning a serious piece about the Theosophy movement or of Blavatsky's accomplishments, Frank took a humorous slant. "An Astral Vacation," read the headline for Frank's outrageous article. "Mme. Blavatsky Is Not Dead, but Taking a Rest." Quoting "local Theosophists," he informed readers that the Madame "has been reported dead before and will reappear again." Frank quoted a religious journal editor named Colonel Bundy, who was laying odds that the reports of her death had been greatly exaggerated and "you will see that Blavatsky will rise . . . in good shape" for "if she had really died it would have been impossible to conceal the fact or suppress it."

This Bundy character rambled on, stating, "This isn't the first time [she] has died." Years before, she died in Egypt and witnesses saw her body buried in Cairo, and then weeks later she was spotted walking the streets of New York City. One local follower known simply as "the Chohan" served as Frank's second source. "Mme. Blavatsky is just taking a much needed vacation in the astral and will come around all right at the proper time," Frank quoted the Chohan as saying. "You see we are just now on the very crest of the Kali Yuga," the dark, materialistic age described in the Vedas, "and the Madame couldn't stand the press of the bad magnetism." He was referring to a Blavatsky prediction in *The Secret Doctrine* that the final years of Kali Yuga would bring shocking scientific discoveries that would rock the foundations of religious faith. "No, sir, she is not dead. She is simply in Samadhi." This is the name in the Vedas for the realm of "god consciousness," a spiritual ecstasy induced by means of mystic concentration.

"Where is Samadhi on the map?" asked the reporter.

"What! Samadhi is not a blooming country. It is a psychic state."

With that, the Chohan blew a cloud of smoke through his ears. When asked how he managed to work these little phenomena, he replied: "O, it's a trick that me and the Madame learned from our Guru in Darjeeling."

The fact that Frank's quizzical story ran on the front page of a big-city newspaper that was supposed to be printing nonfiction was incredible enough, especially since the humor was prompted by the death of a major world figure. But between the lines of his writing one could see something even more astonishing, with telltale themes starting to emerge. Not least among these concepts is the idea of astral travel, the notion that someone could be transported to an alternate state of consciousness and then return to this world transformed. Also hidden between the lines of the story is the fact that Frank didn't think Blavatsky's ideas were ridiculous at all. He certainly didn't want to be perceived as taking Theosophy seriously, not during his first week of work at a new job in a new city. But he did end his piece on an appropriately somber note, writing that "Mme. Blavatsky's death will be mourned by every theosophist in the world."

A few days later Frank met Maud and the boys, including the eight-week-old baby, at the Chicago train station and took them and their luggage directly to their new home at Campbell Park. Maud probably traveled with either her mother or someone else who could help with everything. Maud could not have been thrilled by their shabby new home. After all, she had grown up with the luxury of indoor plumbing yet now would have to rely on neighborhood pumps for their family's water. This wasn't just inconvenient; it was downright scary. Keeping their children safe from rampant diseases was the major concern of parents in the city, as typhoid was spreading through sections of the city's water supply drawn from Lake Michigan. Raw sewage was being pumped into the lake and proper filters weren't in place. An average of 375 people in Chicago, mainly children, perished from typhoid every year. Yet the city's health commissioner declared that this was no epidemic. Talk of such "is done to hurt Chicago," he said. "This [rumor] is started to frighten people from coming to the World's Fair."

Somehow Maud managed to make the best of it. All they needed was a little faith. To help compensate for their lack of material status in this alien setting, both Frank and Maud looked to develop their sense of spirituality. They began attending meetings of Chicago's Theosophical Society, which burgeoned into one of the world's largest branches, from just sixty members in 1890 to hundreds of people just two years later. Located in a plain building at 66 Adams Street, the branch held regular meetings in which followers read and discussed passages from The Key to Theosophy and practiced regular meditation.

The death of Blavatsky had drawn unprecedented attention to her writings along with the surge of new members, and the daily newspapers were now covering Theosophy as part of their regular beats. This newfangled faith was rushing into the mainstream of life, especially in Chicago, which was already steeped in every variety of spirituality. "In America," the *Tribune* noted just a few weeks later, "the theosophic 'boom' is on. The eternal laws of the theosophists remain the same, and a large number of people in this country seem to be accepting them as good. They appertain to *mighty mysteries* . . . and they allow for reincarnation." Blavatsky was constantly vilified and ridiculed while alive, but within a few months of her death, the *Tribune* called her "that wonderful queen of theosophy" in a story that covered the power struggle to succeed her, a contest being waged between two of her closest colleagues, the dour American lawyer William Q. Judge and the charismatic British occultist Annie Besant.

Frank and Maud wanted to join the society, to finally embrace this belief system along with Mrs. Gage, who had been a member of the Theosophical Society for seven years. But gaining membership was no simple matter, as applicants had to study, become proficient in the society's wisdom, and win the respect of a mentor who recommended their admittance. Over several months Frank and Maud submitted to these tests and won the support of a Dr. William P. Phelon, a prominent local leader in the society for the past five years. Records of the society show that Mr. Lyman F. Baum and Mrs. Maud G. Baum of Chicago, Illinois, were admitted to the society on September 4, 1892, upon the recommendation of Dr. Phelon and issued permanent diplomas by the global parent organization in India on December 5 of that year.

Theosophy challenged Frank to change, as members had to abandon religious dogma that justifies the killing of fellow human beings. "The differences in religious dogma were not created by the saints, but by all-sinful mortals," wrote Blavatsky. Those who twist these religions for their own purposes often prompt people "to kill each other . . . and to create a hell for each other." To become a member of the society, one must renounce such violence not only in deed but in thought. Frank's genocidal editorials certainly qualified as an action that went directly against the teaching of Theosophy, and so he had to renounce and atone for his behavior, either out loud or in his own private meditations. "This is a difficult undertaking," says *The Key to Theosophy*. "A pledged member has to become a thorough altruist, never to think of himself, and to forget his own vanity and pride in the thought of the good of his fellow creatures."

When it comes to respecting life, Theosophy goes even further, deploring the mistreatment and abuse of animals, too. This doesn't mean that Theosophists must become vegetarians, only that they must not indiscriminately kill or hurt animals. The Astral Sphere is said to be filled with the terrified bodies of abused animals, which cannot distinguish between the physical world and the world of the Astral. Animals serve as a key clue toward helping humans realize that the physical world and the Astral world are not separate but are indeed part of one another, as one must come to view "the Eternity of the Universe *in toto* as a boundless plane." The italics are Blavatsky's.

When it would come time years later for Frank Baum to name Dorothy's canine companion, he chose the unusual name Toto. In mythology, animal companions are attuned to the supernatural realm, and they guide the character into a special passage or to places of safety. This brave little dog helps Dorothy again and again along her quest, finding ways over rough patches in the Yellow Brick Road, biting the Wicked Witch, revealing the little man behind the partition. Toto unites both worlds of the story just as the Eastern philosophy of *totality* speaks to the unity of matter and energy, of both the real and the imagined. "Toto did not really care whether he was in Kansas or the Land of Oz," Frank would write, "so long as Dorothy was with him."

Apparently following the belief in respecting animals, the Baum family all during their time in Chicago kept dogs and the occasional cat. Little is known about these pets, except that Maud once wrote that "Mr. Baum was good to animals but I am the one that loves them, especially dogs. We always had dogs, both good and bad."

And so both Frank and Maud, along with their children and their dog, were now companions on "the path," that difficult inner journey to enlightened self-awareness, the mystic way to the very heart of the universe where one is to find the center of the circle of one's consciousness. Visually this road might look different to each adherent, but Helena Petrovna Blavatsky herself noted that in the sacred places of this world, one can see parts of this path appear before your eyes.

"The floors of nearly all Buddhist temples are made of yellow polished stone," said the Madame. "It looks like yellow marble. Perhaps it is a freak of the astral vision."

To a cynic, Theosophy was little more than a clever way of marketing Eastern philosophy in the West. After all, this belief system was less than twenty years old and had lifted its major ideas from Buddhism and Hinduism, faiths that were virtually unknown in America. As one of the world's oldest continually practiced religions, Hinduism in particular inspired key Theosophical lessons derived from the Vedas, ancient Sanskrit texts. Americans by and large had never heard of these scriptures.

But with the coming of the world's fair, there would be an opportunity to fully introduce this ancient wisdom in the New World. The nation of India, where these mystical texts were written and revered, had plans to send one special representative to Chicago to lead the teaching. This man was selected to speak at the World's Columbian Exposition as part of an extraordinary event to be called the World's Parliament of Religions. To be convened at the tail end of the fair, beginning in September of 1893, the parliament was being planned with the objective of gathering representatives of all the world's major faiths, "to strike the noble chord of universal human brotherhood" and "to evoke a starry music which will yet drown down the miserable discords of earth," according John Henry Barrows, the Presbyterian pastor who was leading the effort. There was no more perfect place to host this conference than Chicago, he said. "The Western City which was deemed the home of the crudest materialism has placed a golden milestone in Man's pathway toward the spiritual Millennium."

The man whom India selected to address the parliament and to introduce Hinduism to America went by the name of Swami Vivekananda. Unusually tall and magnetically handsome, he was only thirty years old. The swami wore a flowing orange monk's robe, and a yellow turban framed the peaceful gaze of his dark eyes. The tale of how such a young man received such a high honor would become a legend. After studying Western philosophy at Calcutta University, he turned to his own guru, Sri Ramakrishna, a master of spiritual revelations, learning that the path to God is a personal one. The mentor assigned him the mantra "Jiva is Shiva," meaning "Each individual is divinity itself." On his deathbed Ramakrishna anointed the young swami. "I have given you all my spiritual power," he said. "With this great power you will help the people of the world."

With this mission in mind, Vivekananda in July of 1890 embarked on a journey throughout the Indian subcontinent. He had no destination in mind and took with him few possessions. He met the very poor, staying in their grass huts, and he met the very rich, as a guest in their vast palaces. Vivekananda traveled through jungles and deserts. He climbed the snow-covered Himalayas and meditated in the most sacred places of nature. The common sight he saw everywhere in his country was wretched poverty. The swami came to despise the caste system that segregated the population, and he saw a deep need for national regeneration. "I have gone all over India on foot and have seen with my own eyes the ignorance, misery and squalor of our people," he said. "My whole soul is afire and I am burning with a fierce desire to change such evil conditions."

After 888 days of wandering throughout the land, he came to Kanyakumari, the southern tip of India, the meeting point of three great oceans, where white waves crash against giant rocks. On December 24, 1892, Vivekananda swam out to the biggest rock in the sea and sat down upon it. There he meditated for three days about the past, present, and future of India. By focusing intensely on the single thought, *Jiva is Shiva,* he was able to experience incredible visions, to travel to a higher plane of being, and to be at one with India, the Earth, and the universe. "Sitting on that last bit of Indian rock," he later wrote, "I hit upon a plan."

He swam back to shore and returned to a great madras in Calcutta. The swami told the elder Hindu leaders there that India was asleep, like a person who had been slumbering for many years. She must be awakened. He had a plan to go away, to see a place where people had faith in themselves. He would tell these people about India and learn about foreign ways on India's behalf. The swami spoke eloquently about his experience and his vision for India, and he impressed Hindu leaders there to such an extent that they told him about the World's Parliament of Religions, to be held at the Chicago World's Fair. They dubbed him the "Swamiji," selecting him to speak, and then began to raise money for his journey.

The philosophy that Vivekananda planned to share with the American people was quite simple yet profound. "The philosophy of yoga tells us that the root cause of all our sorrows and sufferings is loss of contact with our true Self," the swami said. "Our loss of contact with the Self is due to our ignorance of the Self as the only reality." But the road to the true self is long and difficult, he said. To help people traverse this inner path, one must practice one or more of what the swami called "the Four Yogas," a set of meditations. Each one was demanding, and to learn all four would be a great achievement. "The grandest idea in the religion of the Vedanta is that we may reach the same goal by different paths," he said. "And these paths I have generalized into four."

The first is the Jnâna Yoga, a meditation on what it means for one's brain to receive wisdom.

The second is the Bhakti Yoga, a meditation on what it means for one's heart to know compassion and devotion.

The third is the Karma Yoga, a meditation on what it means to gain the courage to take action.

Finally, there's Rāja Yoga, a meditation on serenity and the achievement of inner harmony.

With grand thoughts of learning from the Americans and teaching them what he knew, the swami boarded a steamship in Bombay on an eastern course. There was one big problem with his mission, however. The swami had not been invited to speak at the world's fair, and no one in Chicago knew he was coming.

13

The Glimmering City

Visitors stroll down the east bank of the Lagoon at
Chicago's Columbian Exposition of 1893.

The streets were lined with beautiful houses all built of green marble and studded everywhere with sparkling emeralds. They walked over a pavement of the same green marble . . . even the sky above the City had a green tint, and the rays of the sun were green . . . Green candy and green pop corn were offered for sale, as well as green shoes, green hats, and green clothes of all sorts. At one place a man was selling green lemonade.

— L. FRANK BAUM,
The Wonderful Wizard of Oz

FRANK BAUM WAS CAUGHT UP in the excitement of living in the country's central destination at a time when all attention gravitated toward the fairgrounds, to the challenge of building a shining city within a city that would live up to America's dream for itself. "Something new and curious was about to happen to the world," Henry Adams wrote about the electric feeling in Chicago on the verge of this transformation. For one of his first assignments at the *Evening Post*, Frank joined the swirl of anticipation. Thomas Alva Edison was coming to Chicago to announce his plans for the world's fair, and it was up to Frank to report on what kind of wonder the great wizard had in store.

If ever a wiz there was, Edison was one because he was already lighting up America. Throughout the 1880s Edison had franchised his electric power system to hundreds of cities and towns. Locally the Chicago Edison Company was run by one of his former laboratory associates. Edison was also the largest shareholder in a manufacturing firm formed around his inventions, the General Electric Company. In the summer of 1889 the wizard amazed the world again when he went to Europe for the Paris International Exposition to host an acre of electricity displays in the Gallerie des Machines. He featured a bank of new machines that played recorded sound, each phonograph fitted with four sets of earphones, so that dozens of people could listen at one time. The invention was a sensation, making Edison's new wonder the second most popular attraction at the fair, after the tower designed and presented by Alexandre Gustave Eiffel. The French fawned. Edison and his wife, Mina, were seated in the presidential box at the city's largest opera house, where the orchestra played "The Star-Spangled Banner" in his honor. Yet Edison didn't return the admiration. "What has struck me so far chiefly is the absolute laziness of everybody over here," he said. "When do these people work? What do they work at? People here seem to have established an elaborate system of loafing. I don't understand it at all."

Edison simply had to pull another rabbit out of the hat for his home country. The organizers of the World's Columbian Exposition were practically demanding it. Indeed, the overriding objective of the expo was to surpass Paris. It was why chief architect Daniel Burnham was in hot pursuit of something more spectacular than Eiffel's tower, an attraction that would "out-Eiffel Eiffel," and he knew that a bigger tower wouldn't do it. He had heard about a new "monstrosity" being proposed by a young Pittsburgh engineer named George Ferris, and the matter was under investigation as to whether the creation would be safe enough and whether enough steel could be obtained in time to build it. In this climate the pressure on Edison was palpable. The organizers were planning the largest electricity and lighting display imaginable, and they insisted on something new and magnificent from Edison to anchor it.

The press conference was set to take place at the Auditorium Hotel, the city's tallest and stateliest building, featuring four hundred rooms, an office complex, a plush theater, and an indoor shopping plaza. Frank Baum waited in the lobby under the giant dome, expecting Edison's entrance. A large crowd wasn't anticipated, as there had been virtually no advance publicity. "Few knew he was coming," Frank wrote. Yet as word spread among people passing through the building, the crowd snowballed. Suddenly the man appeared, and Frank seemed to want to report his every step:

> As he entered the Auditorium Hotel this morning the throng that filled the rotunda parted to let him pass . . . Nearly all recognized his strong, clean-cut features. Of medium height is the wizard of Menlo Park, whose finely shaped head and frank, open countenance, brightened by a pair of gentle intelligent eyes, sits on a frame square-shouldered, stout, erect and sturdy as an oak. He speaks in a low, clear, distinct voice and illuminates his utterances with a smile.

The crowd followed Edison into the theater, where he took the stage. What Frank noticed most about the wizard's appearance before the audience was the sheer size of the man's head in relation to his slight body. "A massive head is his," he observed of Edison, foretelling of a time when Frank would write of the way everyone projected their greatest hopes onto a wonderful wizard, a mysterious figure who first appears only as "an enormous Head, without a body to support it or any arms or legs whatever." To Frank Baum, the encounter was an occasion for his most puffed-up prose. "He is one of those rare men who achieve success and wear it as an ornament," he wrote. "In him indeed the lightning has a kind master."

Getting down to the business at hand, Edison stressed that he held big plans for the expo. "Greatly interested in the world's fair is the wizard," Frank reported. "It has been stated that the invention which Mr. Edison is to exhibit at the fair as his pièce de résistance is something that will surpass in its surprises anything that ever came from his wonderful workshop." Edison began with only a few hints at what this featured invention would be. He didn't seem to have a name for what it was, only a vague description of what it could do, that it would somehow join the magic of the electric light and the phonograph into one machine that would "equal if not exceed the sum of their combined mysteries," as Frank reported it.

At the same time Edison made a disclaimer, warning that "this invention will not have any particular commercial value. It will be rather of a sentimental worth." The anticipation at this point was too great, and listeners now demanded to know: *What is it?* "We-el," Edison said, drawing out his answer. "He hesitated as if loath to part with his secret, then seeing the look of expectancy in the faces of his listeners released a diminutive laugh and said: 'It is not yet completed. But when it is, it will surprise you.'" At this point the audience must have been growing restless, perhaps even doubting that Edison had a great new invention up his sleeve at all. Finally, the inventor tossed out an example of what his new machine could do. "I hope to be able to throw upon a canvas a perfect picture of anybody and reproduce his words," he said, according to Baum's newspaper report. "The invention will do for the eye what the phonograph has done for the [ear] and reproduce the voice as well. I have already perfected the invention so far as to be able to picture a prize fight — the two men, the ring, the intensely interested faces of those surrounding it — and you can hear the sound of the blows, the cheers of encouragement and the yells of disappointment."

Edison attempted to walk an impossible line: he craved credit for devising another fantastic contraption, yet he didn't want to alert others in the field that there was a great fortune to be made from it. He had in fact been tracking the concept of what one French journalist called "a magic lantern run mad" for the past fifteen years, and he even met with the British-born photographer Eadweard Muybridge, who had made the most progress to date in building a machine that would project a sequence of photographs fast enough to fool the eye into seeing fluid motion. But Muybridge had not patented or perfected his invention, and Edison suspected that his rival had little inkling of how much money it was worth. By this time there was a secret building at Edison's West Orange, New Jersey, lab complex devoted to creating what some were calling "motion pictures."

By the close of the press conference there was little doubt that Edison had promised something worthy of the fair. The only question was whether he would be able to produce it in time for the expo's opening. When someone asked Mr. Edison if he knew of any way to get the public to want the kind of machine he had described, the inventor "smiled by way of reply," according to the reporter, "and in a way that all doubts were swept away."

Frank Baum had another front-page feather in his cap. But even though it was well written and produced on deadline, his story in the *Chicago Evening Post* about his brush with the great wizard gained the writer little recognition, as the newspaper carried no bylines. Aside from the excitement of the job itself, his position at the *Post* had little to offer, and it wasn't long before Frank concluded that he had reached another dead end. Twenty dollars per week simply wasn't enough to support his family. Of course, most reporters whom Frank would have met at the press club were underpaid. Many in those days had to take on a second job to support themselves or resort to taking bribes from businessmen and politicians in exchange for favorable notices. This was something Frank apparently refused to do.

Frank lasted only a few months at the *Post* before doubling back to the world of retail, his other area of experience, landing a job in the procurement department at Siegel, Cooper & Company, an eight-story downtown department store that called itself "The Big Store," even though it wasn't as large as Marshall Field's. Frank's new job was to purchase all varieties of fine china and dishware, something he knew how to do from his days of running the Bazaar. It may not have been as exciting as newspaper work, but at least his salary rose to something closer to a living wage.

Like a million other Chicagoans, Frank watched the expo's rising on the waterfront. The press and the public were already calling it "The White City" because all the neoclassical buildings were finished in a bright, gleaming white. By the end of 1891 four hundred new buildings were being built simultaneously and not without significant sacrifice, with four thousand men working through rain, wind, and snow. Four men were killed in separate construction accidents in December of 1891 alone, and there were more such calamities to come. To hasten completion of the Electricity Building, an extra shift worked through the night, under banks of electric lights.

Expectations were intensifying with each passing month, not just in Chicago but everywhere else in America. To honor the spirit of the Columbian anniversary, the editor of the *Youth's Companion*, Francis Bellamy, wrote a poem for all the country's children to recite on Dedication Day: "I pledge allegiance to my Flag, and to the Republic for which it stands, one nation, indivisible, with liberty and justice for all." Although the fairgrounds weren't ready by Columbus Day of 1892, the schedule demanded that the expo was to be officially dedicated then "to the great navigator who four centuries ago set foot on New World shores." The entire premise of the fair was steeped in myth. Not only had the continent already been "discovered" by the people living there before Columbus, but the great navigator himself thought he had landed somewhere near India. He died in 1506, still believing he had arrived in Asia, never knowing exactly where the land in question really was or what it would be called. Yet the legend was so steadfast that it still stirred souls and inspired belief.

It isn't known whether Frank was among the tens of thousands who attended the inaugural ceremony in the Manufactures and Liberal Arts Building. If so, he would have joined the masses inside the largest building ever constructed, with thirty-two acres of floor space, enough to hold the entire Russian infantry and cavalry in full battle array, with the pyramids of Egypt thrown in for good measure. The red-carpeted speaking podium hosted five thousand yellow chairs, one for each member of the choir as a supersize orchestra struck up the "Hallelujah Chorus." When the armylike audience rose to sing and shout along, waving their handkerchiefs in the air, "one had the sense of dizziness, as if the entire building rocked."

Despite the rousing success of this national revival meeting, the fairgrounds were still a long way from being completed, and over the winter came a major setback when a blizzard delivered so much snow to the massive flat roof of the Manufactures and Liberal Arts Building that one day in March 1893 its ceiling collapsed to the floor below. Something else about the fairgrounds wasn't working, or at least it didn't look right to Frederick Law Olmsted. He worried that the sharp whiteness would be blinding. "I fear that . . . great towering masses of white, glistening in the clear hot, Summer sunlight of Chicago, with the glare of the water . . . will be overpowering." He called for an infusion of a different color as a counterbalance. Being a landscape architect, that color, naturally, was green. So as soon as the ground began to thaw, Olmsted led an effort to plant "dense, broad, luxuriant green bodies of foliage." The White City would therefore be tinted with shades of emerald.

In the weeks leading up the fair's opening day, miraculous things were happening. In late March, Alexander Graham Bell placed the world's first truly long-distance telephone call, from New York to Chicago. Soon after, a big black locomotive named Engine 999 rolled away from Syracuse, heading west, and it built up such a head of steam that it set a world speed record of 112 miles per hour. Daniel Burnham was counting on some more miracles. Drenching rains had turned the fairgrounds to muck, causing cascading delays, and even by April's end, on the very day before the fair's official opening, one observer remarked that the whole place was in a state of "gross incompleteness." Ten thousand men and a thousand women worked furiously through the day and night to touch up paint, plant flowers, dispose of garbage, and scrub floors.

May Day broke bright and sparkling, and on this Monday morning more than a quarter of a million fairgoers awoke to dress in their Sunday best—the men in suits and top hats, the ladies in long, flowing gowns. Among them were L. Frank Baum, now nearing his thirty-seventh birthday, and Maud, who was thirty-two. Frank Jr. was nine, Robert seven, Harry three, and Kenneth two. Every few minutes the newly constructed elevated trains, known simply as "the L," rushed thousands of Chicagoans over the procession on foot below, and dozens of bright yellow "cattle car" trains carried thousands more from points farther out. A single line of twenty-three black carriages brought the dignitaries, one for Daniel Burnham, another for Mayor Harrison, and one carting President Grover Cleveland, who was starting his second term after four years away from the White House. Another carriage held Chicago's *grande dame*, Bertha Honoré Palmer, the president of the fair's Ladies Board of Managers, along with a special guest, the duke of Veragua, said to be a direct descendant of Columbus.

For those approaching from the west on the L train, the first major sight to appear was the unfinished Ferris wheel, a disappointment to those who would have to wait about six weeks longer for their promised launch into the sky. The half-constructed wheel anchored the Midway Plaisance, the mile-long thoroughfare that was home to the expo's alter ego, a loose collection of beer gardens, magicians, and lowbrow, carnival-like entertainment that was not part of the main fairgrounds and didn't require an admission ticket. The number of scenes and sights that one could spot from the L stretched endlessly. One moment you could see the stages and cages of the animal show with its trained monkeys and roaring lions, and the next instant you could take in Chief Sitting Bull's preserved cabin, part of Buffalo Bill Cody's fifteen-acre Wild West extravaganza that had already been open for a month and was so popular that it threatened to upstage everything. Finally, the trains would deposit the passengers at the majestic gateway to Jackson Park, where admission to the exposition was set at a half dollar for adults and a quarter for kids.

Inside, Olmsted's otherworldly green gardens created "a sudden vision of heaven." The full rays of the sun burst through the clouds at 10:30 a.m., as much of the crowd moved on for views of the Great Basin, a reflecting pool larger than eight football fields that was stocked with ducks, geese, and exotic birds. Surrounding the water and creating an "inexhaustible dream of beauty" was the Court of Honor, the collection of fourteen white buildings that were designed to recall the architecture of Rome, Venice, Greece, and other empires of history. From a distance the buildings appeared in the reflected light to be fashioned of stone and marble, yet up close it was easy to scratch off the stuccolike covering called staff—mixed from plaster of Paris, jute, and glycerin—that was slathered over planks and plywood. Spray paint was said to be invented for this fair. That the technology of motion pictures would be introduced here was fitting, as the whole place was like a movie set, not meant to last beyond the six months of the spectacle. "What a magnificent ruin they must make when all is finished," remarked William Wallace Denslow, an illustrator on hand to draw pictures for the *Chicago Herald*.

As speakers took to the podium, each burst of rhetoric glided over the water. The fair was "a monument marking the progress of civilization throughout the ages," said one speaker. "Gathered here are the forces which move humanity and make history." The purpose of the fair was "to enlarge the social idea" . . . "to lessen the evils of isolation" . . . "to bring into greater prominence organization in humanity" . . . "to test the intellectual possibilities of man" . . . "to gain an education from the commingling of people and the comparison of things" . . . "promoting harmony in the whole human family." Yet because of the poor amplification, most of these phrases landed in the pond, unheard by the masses.

At noon, President Cleveland stepped up to push a golden telegraph key, which closed an electric circuit that sent thirty thousand machines into motion. Dynamos whirred, steam engines whistled, guns fired, thousands of incandescent lights flickered on, giant flags unfurled; a fountain unleashed dozens of streams of water, whooshing into the sky, illuminated by multicolored lights, casting a rainbow across the sun. At once the massive crowd began to sing "My Country 'Tis of Thee." Like everybody else, Frank Baum and family were inspired—but also overwhelmed. The future had arrived, right before everyone's eyes, but it was far too much to take in at once. Frank would return to the fairgrounds again and again, usually by himself, wandering persistent stretches of exhibits—exploring, gawking, searching. The sights and sound of this joyous atmosphere inspired some of Frank's descriptions of the Emerald City citizens years later. "Everyone seemed happy and contented and prosperous," he would write.

The Columbian Exposition was as vast as the world itself, shrunk into microcosmic form, the past and future converging on the present moment. This being an age of industry and manufacturing, most of the exhibits focused on tangible things or, in the parlance of the fair, "Human Achievement in Material Form." With every step in the cavernous Manufactures and Liberal Arts Building, one was surrounded by the world's finest goods fashioned of silver, granite, leather, silk, and gold.

At every turn there was something superlative or unique. One wouldn't want to miss a collection of the world's oldest paper documents, the world's largest lump of coal, a replica of the Brooklyn Bridge made from soap, a fountain of French perfume that spit out a different scent every day, an immense Venus de Milo statue crafted of chocolate, Tiffany's creation of the world's first toilet smithed from silver, and an entire exhibit devoted to the many uses of Vaseline. The Wisconsin Building featured the world's widest wedge of cheese, weighing eleven tons, and the Pennsylvania Building boasted a map of the United States put together purely of Heinz pickles. Then there was the California Building, which highlighted the state's masterwork: a knight on horseback made entirely of prunes. On most days the light pouring through the walls of windows of the white buildings was so bright that people purchased colored eyeshades. "Because if you did not wear spectacles the brightness and glory of the Emerald City would blind you," Frank later wrote.

If Frank Baum was hoping to find inspiration at the fair, there were plenty of places to look, but if he was expecting to receive that inspiration from the Wizard of Menlo Park himself, he would be disappointed. No doubt the Electricity Building was one of the standouts of the expo, especially in the evenings when it was time to turn on the eighty-foot Edison Tower of Light. Billed as the "brightest thing on Earth," it was a pillar of five thousand blinking incandescent lamps that were fashioned into the shape of an immense bulb, and the whole thing was enveloped by thirty thousand tiny mirrors that served as prisms of magnificent reflections. But the inside of the building looked exactly like what it was: an electrical power plant, cold and forbidding.

And if one wanted to encounter the great Mr. Edison himself there, one would have to come back in August when the inventor would finally be ready to show off what he called the Kinetoscope, a pine box with a peephole fitted with a magnifying glass. Viewers gazed inside at a silvery cylinder that rotated a celluloid strip of photographs. The initial film was a sequence of one of Edison's colleagues waving and doing jumping jacks — a breakthrough for sure, but it would take a giant leap of imagination to picture how this new technology would lead to much of anything. As for the man himself, few visitors could get near the wizard before he skipped town. Edison simply didn't need any more fame and acclaim than he already had. A poll of opinion leaders named him hands down the most likely American who would still be admired a hundred years in the future.

Despite the splendor, the fair was hurting. Right after opening day attendance plunged, down to an average of fewer than twenty thousand people per day, leading to worries that the whole thing would turn into a financial catastrophe, never earning back the investment. Some of the organizers pinpointed a crucial flaw. The exhibitions were endlessly impressive but not necessarily much fun, and the experience was too museumlike, lacking in serendipity. The worries were greatly compounded when a nationwide panic was triggered in early May. A credit crisis at several big banks caused a collapse of trading on the New York Stock Exchange, leading to the worst economic depression thus far in the nation's history. By the following month there were runs on eight banks in Chicago alone. Across America six hundred banks would shut their doors over the coming months, wiping out the savings of tens of thousands of families. Fifteen thousand companies would go belly-up, six dozen of them owners of railroads. Foolish remedies such as high import tariffs made the economy worse, as these Populist taxes boosted the prices of all kind of goods.

As the "convulsion of 1893" was ruining countless lives outside the gates of the fair, the world inside seemed to be viewed as little more than a playground for the idle rich. Henry Adams thought that the fair "falsified history and made unattainable promises." He was not sold on whether the common man would ultimately benefit from the future as presented there. Instead, Adams posed a question as to "whether the American people knew where they were driving." Anyone who visited the exhibits could not help but agree: only a tiny sliver of wealthy people could afford to have what was on display.

If Thomas Edison personified the imagination of the fair, the national figure who most embodied its focus on wealth was John D. Rockefeller Sr., one of the only men in America who was holding on to his fortune in those grim times. The fair's Standard Oil Building was shaped like a miniature oil refinery, intended to turn this controversial image into an icon of prosperity at a time when the Standard Oil monopoly was best known as the catalyst behind the creation of something called antitrust laws.

The oil tycoon knew he needed to repair his reputation, and he was said to be greatly influenced by Andrew Carnegie's credo that "the man who dies rich dies disgraced." In the years leading up to the opening of the world's fair, Rockefeller focused much of his attention on his first major philanthropic project, funding the creation of an esteemed place of higher learning, a Baptist college to be known as the University of Chicago. Land was obtained just north of the Midway Plaisance, and one of the architects of the expo itself was hired to lead the project. The plan worked beautifully, as the new university had welcomed its first class in the fall of 1892. It was hard to tell where the new university ended and the expo began, as "the two projects appeared to blend into a seamless whole."

The year 1893 was also a year in which Rockefeller was beset by his strange illness. Some said it was a nervous breakdown or an ulcer caused by decades of overwork and severe stress. Others said it was the Lord's punishment for being so pious and sanctimonious on Sunday yet so ruthless and greedy from Monday through Saturday. With his severe alopecia, his wrinkled head and shriveled face took on a menacing mien. Frank Baum would one day write of the terrible, mean figure who had "no hair upon his head," as Rockefeller seemed to inspire the second face of the shape-shifting Wizard, a character driven by a belief in strict self-interest. "You have no right to expect me to send you back to Kansas unless you do something for me in return," the Great and Terrible Oz would declare. "In this country everyone must pay for everything he gets. If you wish me to use my magic power to send you home again you must do something for me first. Help me and I will help you."

If the World's Columbian Exposition was lacking in fun for the common folk, Frank Baum would have to supply his own. On the eighth of June he had to go in to work in the morning while Maud took the boys to the fair. The plan was that Maud and the two older boys, Frank Jr. and Robert, would tour the fair's exhibits and buildings. Most likely Maud left the two younger boys, Harry and Kenneth, at the Children's Building, which featured a gymnasium and a child care center, where you could check young children, as if they were coats and hats, get a claim ticket, and pick them up later. Although this sounds like a recipe for trouble, it was modeled on a similar setup at the Paris Exposition, and during the six-month run of the Chicago fair there were no known incidents of anything going wrong with the children. The second part of the plan was that they'd all meet up for lunch with Dad in the Woman's Building. Frank and Maud agreed it would be less crowded and easier to get a table there.

Apparently, however, Frank and Maud guessed wrong, as a major luncheon event was planned at the Woman's Building that day to honor a royal guest, known in the newspapers as the Queen of the Fair. In Spain she was called the Infanta Eulalia, the daughter of exiled Queen Isabel II. She was dressed beautifully and carried herself with grace, but she was terribly self-indulgent, constantly smoking cigarettes and skipping off somewhere, missing her scheduled appointments. When Frank arrived at the Woman's Building, he found it blocked off as the paradelike procession of dignitaries filed inside and curiosity seekers crowded around to catch a glimpse of the queen.

Frank could not even wiggle his way into the building. Instead, he watched the parade of dignitaries pass, and when the last person walked by, he removed his silk top hat, placed it over his left shoulder, imitating the other marchers, and joined the procession to a grand luncheon table, making believe he was part of the official party. "As usual, there were a number of vacant seats and most guests didn't know one another, so father had no difficulty carrying on a conversation with his neighbors," wrote Harry years later. Maud and the boys were apparently annoyed and amused to see him dining on the dais as if he were royalty, too.

Once again Frank showed his knack for transforming life into story. This tale may or may not actually have happened. Harry was only three at the time, and his telling of it years later seems to be enhanced by his father's embellishments. The visit by the Spanish princess, however, was well documented by the newspapers. According to reports, the "queen" never even showed up at her own luncheon, instead opting to dine anonymously in the German Building on bratwurst and beer.

Like many other fairgoers, especially local ones, Frank Baum and family probably spent more time on the Midway than at the official expo itself. Although located side by side, the two places were in many ways polar opposites. The expo was highbrow, stately, and self-important, whereas the Midway was lowbrow, ridiculous, and self-deprecating. The expo charged admission, but there were no gates to enter the Midway. The expo was controlled; you weren't even allowed to take photographs there unless you rented an official camera or paid a $5 fee to register your own. The Midway was chaotic. It was a place that celebrated vice and revelry.

In short, the Midway was far more fun, the kind of place where all day you'd hear barkers in top hats shouting, "Step right up!" and where all night you could dance in a tavern to newfangled ragtime tunes hammered out by a young pianist named Scott Joplin. By late June the Midway was mobbed when the symbol of the fair, the Ferris wheel, was finally up and open for business. At 250 feet in diameter, the steel wheel soared higher in the clouds than the Statue of Liberty, and each of its thirty-six cars was big enough to hold sixty people and host its own dining counter. The Ferris wheel had more than two thousand fairgoers spinning into the sky at any given time, and thousands more lined up.

Open late into the night and on Sundays when the expo was closed, the mile-long promenade was jammed with sideshows, carnival games, fortunetellers, con artists, jugglers, magicians, animal shows, and cheap, unhealthful food of all the best kinds. Frank and Maud were greatly interested in Egyptian culture, and so they had to visit the Street in Cairo exhibit, nearly an entire city block featuring bazaars and belly dancers gyrating their hips to the hootchy-kootchy in the most lascivious ways. The Baums were likely looking for the mythical Egypt of Isis, the fallen goddess whom Blavatsky described in her books. Instead they were surrounded by mystics and mediums advertising palm reading and crystal ball gazing.

If there was any one American who could serve as the ringmaster of the Midway, it would be P. T. Barnum, as this was a place that exhibited a keen sense for getting people to part with their money in return for some momentary excitement. That was exactly the core talent that Phineas Taylor Barnum always proclaimed that he possessed. Known as America's greatest showman, the father of advertising, the inventor of the three-ring circus, Barnum almost single-handedly pioneered the art of making money from cheap thrills and fantastic spectacles. Oftentimes the curiosities that he put on display were fraudulent, such as the fake Cardiff Giant. But people didn't seem to mind paying to see the strange and bizarre because of the terrific stories that went along with them.

However, the self-proclaimed Prince of Humbuggery couldn't make it to the world's fair because he had died on April 7, 1891. In an obituary the *Washington Post* called P. T. Barnum "the most widely known American who ever lived." Yet for a moment it seemed as if even death wouldn't stop Barnum from getting to Chicago and taking his rightful place on the Midway. On May 28, 1893, in the blackness of night, three men with picks and shovels arrived at the cemetery in Bridgeport, Connecticut, where Barnum was buried. The men approached the monument that marked the Barnum grave and started digging. They unearthed a hole next to his vaulted coffin four feet deep when they were spotted by security guards. Shots rang out, and the gravediggers threw down their tools and ran away, uncaught. "Barnum's Body in Peril," screamed a headline in the *New York Times*. Rumors circulated that the men intended to steal the corpse, ship it to Chicago, and charge admission to see the great showman in the flesh. It was exactly the kind of outlandish idea that P. T. Barnum himself might have approved.

Throughout his life L. Frank Baum would always remain fascinated by Barnum and his core insight that Americans not only love to be swindled but will pay money for the privilege as long as the swindle comes with a good story. "Barnum was right when he declared the American people like to be deceived," Frank Baum once wrote. "At least they make no effort to defend themselves. The merchants are less to blame than their customers." In this "age of deception," as he called it, "people accept the most preposterous statements of the purity and honesty of goods without emotion." He seemed to yearn for a world in which a hero pulls back the veil on fraudulent leaders and their self-deceived followers. Why was common sense in such short supply?

One day Frank Baum would write of "a little man rubbing his hands together as if it pleased him" when someone accused him of being a humbug.

"Doesn't anyone else know you're a humbug?" he is asked.

"No one knows it but you four—and myself. I have fooled everyone so long that I thought I should never be found out."

To everyone else, P. T. Barnum was dead. To L. Frank Baum, who had to marvel at just how much money was being spent on nonsense on the Midway, the old humbug was still very much alive, and this was not heartening news at all. So far the world's fair hadn't quite lived up to his expectations. He found it to be wonderful at times, like Edison, but often it was aloof and arrogant, like Rockefeller, and sometimes it was a downright scam, the work of a Barnum. Once again Frank seemed to have created in his mind hopes so high that they could never be fulfilled. Yet there was another side of the fair that had yet to reveal itself, and it was this fourth face that Frank Baum needed to see the most.

14

The Wizard's Challenge

The four faces of the Wizard.

Top left: Thomas Alva Edison, the Wizard of Menlo Park. *Top middle:* John D. Rockefeller Sr., oil tycoon. *Top right:* P. T. Barnum, the Prince of Humbug. *Left:* Swami Vivekananda, the surprise sensation of the world's fair.

"Remember that the Witch is Wicked — tremendously
Wicked — and ought to be killed. Now go, and do not
ask to see me again until you have done your task."

— THE GREAT OZ

THE WORLD'S FAIR wasn't all spectacle, splendor, and diversion. A program of lectures brought an intellectual dimension, with conferences on medicine, education, evolution, history, labor, finance, temperance, religion, literature, architecture, and art. These World Congresses were held not on the fairgrounds but in the center of town at a specially constructed palace fronted by massive stone columns and a pair of iconic statues of roaring lions, a building that would later become Chicago's Art Institute. Inside, brick-lined courts surrounded the central staircase, and the courts served as giant assembly halls. All told, as many as twelve thousand attendees could be mingling about or taking their seats in various meetings there.

The most enduring of these lectures was a history paper delivered by a twenty-nine-year-old professor from the University of Wisconsin named Frederick Jackson Turner. In his talk entitled "The Significance of the Frontier in American History," Turner proclaimed the American frontier "officially closed." He based his conclusion on 1890 census data, which showed that there were no more vast unsettled spaces on the U.S. continent, the census defining such space as having fewer than two people per square mile. The frontier, he said, was where civilization ended and savage wilderness began. American history, he said, is an epic about a new people who pushed the frontier line farther and farther out, and it was this very frontier experience that converted Europeans into these new people called Americans. More than just a physical act, then, the settling of the West is what shaped the American mind—forging a character defined by self-reliance, hard work, restlessness, and imagination. The frontier is where the American identity took root.

It isn't likely that L. Frank Baum attended Turner's history-defining lecture. He didn't have to, for he had lived through the last phase of this history and reported on the final winning of the West as it unfolded in Dakota. But Frank wouldn't have missed the one spectacle that aimed to transform the frontier experience into a lasting mythology. Buffalo Bill Cody's Wild West extravaganza was hands down the most popular attraction of the entire world's fair. Ironically, the show wasn't officially part of the exposition, as the spectacle was denied space at the fair due to "incongruity," which meant that the fair managers believed it simply didn't fit in. First of all, horses weren't normally permitted on the fairgrounds, because of the mess. It was also possible that the panel in charge of the exhibits believed it would be vulgar to host a "Cowboys and Indians" show so soon after the terrible massacre at Wounded Knee and the destruction of native cultures.

Bill Cody took offense at this decision. Undeterred, he leased fifteen acres just north of the fairgrounds and constructed an arena with grandstands for eighteen thousand people. Since it wasn't officially part of the fair, visitors would have to pay a separate admission. Operating seven days a week with two performances per day over the course of six months, the Wild West Show took in nearly $4 million. For the 50¢ price of a ticket, audiences were treated to a big-budget show, featuring a cast of a hundred former U.S. Cavalry soldiers and a hundred Sioux, Cheyenne, and Pawnee. Cody furnished each of them with a horse—and he had eighteen live buffalo shipped in for good measure. The soldiers pitched tents, and the Native Americans set up tepees. There were replicas of a frontier town, a U.S. Army outpost, and Chief Sitting Bull's cabin on the Grand River. There were fields and bluffs and gulches, to represent famous prairie battlegrounds. The most controversial events of the frontier experience were about to be recast as popular entertainment.

Audiences got pretty much exactly what they wanted. In the show, Indians ambushed caravans of settlers and soldiers, shooting and scalping them, and the soldiers retaliated by attacking Indian villages, resulting in more mock mayhem. The cast reenacted the Battle of Little

Bighorn, featuring the heroic "last stand" of General Custer and the savage victory of Chief Sitting Bull. The Sioux performed their mystical Ghost Dance. The scene of Sitting Bull's own death was turned into a Caesar-like drama. The massacre at Wounded Knee of barely three years earlier was depicted as the final triumph. But it was all in good fun. Buffalo Bill told the audience that the cowboys and the Indians played cards together each night to pass the time.

In cheering these frontier scenes as they were ritualized on stage, audiences were taking part in propagandizing the immediate past. The portrayal of the conquering of the continent as nothing but heroic ingrained a bold place called the "Wild West" in American consciousness forever. The show was so successful in every way that Buffalo Bill used the profits to establish his own town called Cody, Wyoming, a place where the frontier spirit would be preserved and a rodeo held every summer night.

Yet there was also a shadowy side of this whitewashing that was left underexplored. In both Buffalo Bill's reenactments and Professor Turner's history paper, the greatness of the Americans justified many misdeeds. Some members of the audience — perhaps even Frank Baum among them — may have been amazed to see so much collective guilt being wiped away by a romanticized rendition of such bloody events. By glorifying violence for the sake of the great cause, a legend can sometimes serve to shackle the human spirit to a hardened "us versus them" viewpoint. This type of thinking reflects what Carl Jung called the "inner split in the psyche," says Gita Dorothy Morena, a Jungian psychologist who is the great-granddaughter of L. Frank Baum, descended through Frank and Maud's youngest son, Kenneth. "Our minds want to separate, to make one side 'good' and one side 'bad.' The bad side becomes the shadow stuff we fear or want to get rid of."

Frank Baum's genocidal editorials are a prime example of this psychic split into good and bad, the wonderful and the wicked. For Frank, watching the Wild West Show may have served as a reminder of the need for of atonement. "When we bring the shadow material out and start to take responsibility for ourselves, we see that we are not perfect," says Gita Dorothy, in talking about her great-grandfather. "Healing comes as we bring both sides into consciousness and find a way to integrate into wholeness."

All the recapitulation at the Chicago World's Fair naturally raised a key question: Where do we go from here? If the geographic frontier is closed and the West has been won, what will be next? The American spirit was more vital, restless, and imaginative than ever. There had to be a new frontier. Where could it be? For Frank Baum, there was only one place to go. "Frank went toward the mind," says Gita. "We'd conquered the land, we'd gone as far as we could go; where else to go but inward? In the United States we have so much. We don't have to worry about getting enough to eat like most of the world does, so it's up to us to go in and develop consciousness. And Frank's story points to that. This is what we needed to do."

Even as Professor Turner was delivering his landmark lecture and even as the Wild West Show was entertaining tens of thousands, a messenger of pure human consciousness was coming to America, in the form of the Hindu monk known as Swami Vivekananda. More than a month at sea, the swami had had plenty of time to meditate, to think, to write, to gaze with both wonder and despair across the Pacific. "Is man a tiny boat in a tempest," he wrote, "raised one moment on the foamy crest of a billow and dashed down into a yawning chasm the next, rolling to and fro at the mercy of good and bad actions — a powerless helpless wreck in an ever-raging, ever-rushing, uncompromising current of cause and effect? The heart sinks at this idea. Is there no hope? Is there no escape?"

On July 25, 1893, the swami's ship, the SS *Empress*, landed in Vancouver, where he boarded a train bound for Chicago, the destination of his pilgrimage. He knew not a soul in America, but the vision of this tall, handsome foreigner in an orange robe, brown trousers, and yellow turban naturally drew all eyes, and he made new friends with great ease. The swami encountered the first of his many American friends on the train. Her name was Kate Sanborn. Fifty-four years old, she was a former literature professor at Smith College and part of a community of transcendentalist writers around Boston. Miss Sanborn was instantly taken by the way the swami walked, with "a lordly imposing stride, as if he ruled the universe," and she was drawn in by his "soft, dark eyes that could flash fire if roused, or dance with merriment if the conversation amused him." The swami told her of his quest to speak at the fair and how he had no place to stay in America during the nearly two months before the World's Parliament of Religions was to open in September. She wrote down her address and invited him to stay with her for a while at her farm in rural Massachusetts. Then they parted ways as they got off the train in Chicago.

When Vivekananda arrived in Chicago, he began to walk the streets of the city, observing its people and places. "The Americans are so rich that they spend money like water," he marveled. He found a hotel he deemed affordable, and day after day the wandering monk paid the steep admission price to attend the expo and soak up its wonders. "It is a tremendous affair," he wrote. "One must take at least ten days to go through it." By the time he located the offices of the Parliament of Religions, however, he was filthy, unshaven, nearly broke, and exhausted. He said he had been sent by his people to speak, yet the managers of the schedule told him that the roster of speakers had already been completed and could not be changed at this late date.

The swami turned away in great disappointment, not knowing what to do next. He had made a promise to the people of India, and he couldn't return home having failed at his quest. He could always try to fulfill his mission in Europe instead, but he felt that America was the one special place for him. "It was reserved for America to proclaim that the Lord is in every religion," he wrote. This was the very same conclusion that Madame Blavatsky said she received from on high.

With little money left, Vivekananda wrote to his new friend Kate Sanborn, telling her that he was taking up her invitation. Then he boarded a train for Boston. Miss Sanborn welcomed him to her farmhouse, which she called Breezy Meadows, and she gave him food and a place to bathe and sleep. When she escorted him around to meet her intellectual friends, the swami began to speak with great humility about the ancient wisdom of India. Vivekananda became such a sensation at Harvard University in particular that one of its leading professors, John Henry Wright, decided he would see what he could do to help the swami achieve his ambition. Soon to be appointed the dean of Harvard's graduate school, Professor Wright held great sway in certain circles. On Harvard letterhead he wrote a special recommendation addressed to Reverend Barrows, urging the leader of the parliament to grant Vivekananda a prime speaking slot.

In the letter Professor Wright remarked that the Swamiji "is more learned than all our learned professors put together," using an expression remarkably similar to that of Frank Baum's Witch of the North, who would whisper that the great Wizard of Oz is "more powerful than all the rest of us together." That Vivekananda's intellect was more powerful than the combined wisdom of the entire Harvard faculty was certainly an example of effusive praise. Yet this kind of remark was repeated again and again by those who would meet the swami, as if he possessed supernatural abilities. "He is not of this world [but] a radiant being who had descended from a higher sphere for a definite purpose," wrote one of his followers. "Others may be brilliant, but his mind is luminous, for he has the power to put himself into immediate contact with the source of all knowledge."

On the eighth and ninth of September, just days before the opening of the parliament, a grateful Vivekananda was back on the train to Chicago. "You are a real mahatma," he wrote to Professor Wright. The train arrived in Chicago after dark. Out of money and having no place to stay, the swami spent the night curled up in an empty boxcar near the depot. In the morning he hiked into the center of the city, once again appearing like a street beggar. He sat down to rest outside a church on Dearborn Street. From across the way a woman named Mary Hale spotted him. She and her husband, George, immediately took him into their home, got him cleaned up and rested for the night, and then the next day took him to see John Henry Barrows about this unusual man's dream of addressing the Parliament of Religions in its opening session the following day. By this time Reverend Barrows was expecting the swami, for he had received the special letter from Harvard.

Matilda Joslyn Gage wouldn't be missing the Parliament of Religions for the world. By August she was already in Chicago, staying with the Baums, and she wrote a letter describing a mystical Theosophy meeting that she, Maud, and Frank had attended. After some debate, Theosophy had been fully included in the parliament as one of the represented faiths, along with Catholicism, Judaism, Islam, Buddhism, Hinduism, and the major Protestant denominations. (Some smaller and newer religions that weren't officially represented sent envoys anyway. For instance, Mary Baker Eddy was in attendance, representing Christian Scientists.) Matilda's long-standing belief in Theosophy told her that every faith holds a portion of the whole truth, and this was an opportunity to see if this were true, as it was the first time in the world's history that leaders of all the religions would be assembled under one roof to seek common wisdom. As members of the Theosophical Society, Matilda, Maud, and Frank would be able to gain seats for many of the sessions of the parliament.

This happened to be a bittersweet time for Mrs. Gage. Her manifesto, *Woman, Church and State*, had just been published. She called it "a book with a revolution in it." This should have been her life's triumph, as the 450-page volume propounded her viewpoint that the Church and the State must cease their suppression of women. The few reviews that appeared tended toward the positive. The *Boston Transcript* dubbed it "the fullest and strongest presentation of the case from the radical woman's standpoint." The *Kansas Farmer*, of all publications, called it a "revelation that ought to be read extensively." Glowing letters of admiration came to Gage from progressive-minded readers everywhere. "I thank you in my soul," wrote one woman. "It throws a light on the dark pages of life, a strong light . . . strong because true." But the book's unpopular thesis assured that it would be largely ignored by the mainstream press.

Her message prompted the women's movement to all but ostracize the author, as her anti-Church positions were seen as a political liability. By now Gage was used to such treatment. Inside the Woman's Building at the fair, she would encounter commemorative statues immortalizing her old colleagues Susan B. Anthony and Elizabeth Cady Stanton. As diminutive characters in the Oz movie would sing, "We will glorify your name! You'll be a bust, be a bust, be a bust, in the hall of fame!" Yet there was nothing there about Matilda, nothing to pay tribute to her lifelong contribution to the cause.

At this point, Matilda exploded with bitterness. She told her son that she was forbidding the publisher of her book to mention her name in connection with the two others in the leadership trio. "They have stabbed me in reputation, and Susan, at least, has stolen money from me. They are traitors, also, to woman's highest needs—and Mrs. Stanton, especially, I look upon in women's battle for freedom, as I do Benedict Arnold during the war of Revolution."

As her old friends were being exalted, she was falling into poverty and obscurity. The cost of publishing her book had exceeded its revenue, and she was now in debt. "I like an active life and one with freedom from money troubles," Matilda wrote. "I like to be independent in every way. But fate or Karma is against me."

Perhaps the Parliament of Religions would provide her with some much-needed spiritual relief. As it turned out, the swami would have much to say to those who blamed karma for their troubles. "We only get what we deserve," he said. "It is a lie to say that the world is bad and we are good. It can never be so. It is a terrible lie we tell ourselves." Frank, too, needed guidance. He continued to suppress his guilt for his Aberdeen editorials against the Native Americans, which was still a touchy subject with his mother-in-law. Maud continued to hold things together between her angry mother and her ashamed husband. Perhaps at this gathering they could all find spiritual clues to help them confront their failings and heal their personal wounds.

At 10:00 a.m. on the morning of September 11, the bells of every house of worship in the city rang out in a beautiful cacophony. The Hall of Columbus inside the World's Congress Auxiliary Building was festooned with flowers as a diverse crowd of devotees from around the globe packed in to take their seats. In the section reserved for Theosophists, Frank, Maud, and Matilda would search for some empty chairs. What a vision they would see. Assembled on the stage were sixty-five scholars from Europe, the Americas, Asia, Australia, and Africa—including bishops, cardinals, clerics, deacons, ministers, monks, pastors, priests, princes, professors, and rabbis. They dressed in silks, satins, and velvets of all colors as well as white cottons and black flannels.

To open the parliament, John Henry Barrows took the podium. A thin, bald man with a thick mustache and large, penetrating eyes, he set the tone with a powerful metaphor: "Religion, like the white light of Heaven, has been broken into many colored fragments by the prisms of men," he professed. "One of the objects of the Parliament of Religions is to change the many-colored radiance back into the white light of heavenly truth." In his view, religion was a rainbow to look beyond.

After his speech Reverend Barrows introduced the opening speakers, who took turns addressing the audience. When it came time for him to single out Swami Vivekananda and present him as the leader of the Hindu delegation, a hush fell over the room as the unknown monk stood up, his orange robe clean and crisp, his yellow turban framing his dark eyes. Of everyone on stage, his was "the face and dress which attracted the most notice, especially from the ladies," according to the *Columbian*, the fair's newspaper. Unfortunately for the ladies, the monk had taken a lifelong vow of celibacy.

As he approached the lectern, the swami felt nervous because he had never before spoken in front of a crowd this big and he had brought no prepared text. But then something extraordinary happened. The simple but highly unusual way he addressed the audience seemed to take people's breath away. "Sisters and Brothers of America," he began.

In a moment the crowd rose to its feet, and thunderous applause erupted through the hall. The simple but audacious thought behind the salutation itself expressed the entire theme of the conference. The clapping and the cheering went on for some time—some say it lasted for a solid three minutes. The commotion drew more and more people into the assembly hall, until it was packed with an estimated seven thousand souls.

When the ovation finally died down, the audience listened with rapt attention as the swami delivered his brief September 11 address of just five hundred words, many of those words inspired by the Bhagavad Gita, the Hindu text expressing the sacred song of God. "The present convention," he declared in his deep, resonant voice, "which is one of the most august assemblies ever held, is in itself a vindication, a declaration to the world of the wonderful doctrine preached in the Gita: 'All men are struggling through paths which in the end lead to me.'" Then came the heart of his message, which was both a prophetic warning and a hopeful dream:

> Sectarianism, bigotry, and its horrible descendant, fanaticism, have long possessed this beautiful earth. They have filled the earth with violence, drenched it often and again with human blood, destroyed civilizations and sent whole nations to despair.

Had it not been for these terrible demons, human society would be far more advanced than it is now. The time has come. I fervently hope that the bell that tolled this morning may be the death-knell of all fanaticism, of all persecutions with the sword or with the pen.

The effect was electrifying, more so than all the volts on the fairgrounds. With this speech and several others to follow, Swami Vivekananda became the surprise sensation of the entire exposition. When his first address was over, the swami later wrote, "I sat down almost exhausted with emotion." For Frank Baum, the speech and the overwhelming reaction must have hit home. The swami's exhortation not to persecute people through the written word had to strike a deep nerve, as Frank's hateful editorials in Dakota constituted just the kind of bigotry the swami was deploring.

After his talk Vivekananda retired to a small meeting room near the assembly hall to quietly meditate and to discuss religion and philosophy with anyone who wished to see him. But the demand to meet with the swami was intense. Delegates and onlookers lined up in long stretches outside the door, and guardians kept tight control of the entrance. "There is a room at the left of the entrance marked 'No. 1 —keep out,'" wrote one newspaper. "The most striking figure one meets in this anteroom is Swami Vivekananda. He speaks excellent English and replied readily to any questions asked in sincerity."

The swami would be speaking several more times at the seventeen-day parliament, his fame and his following growing with each and every appearance, and he'd be conducting more of these intimate sessions afterward. Always there'd be crowds of well-wishers struggling to catch a glimpse of the swami's turban or ask questions while looking into his wise eyes. Peeking into the room, one could spot the swami sitting behind a desk. But the door would always close quickly, to keep the noise out. All day people waited, and most couldn't get inside to see him. Those who did had many questions. At every turn, people presented him with different problems and personal situations, and so each visitor got a slightly different suggestion from the guru.

"There are many paths to realization of the True Self," the swami would say, "just as there are many spokes from the rim of a wheel to its center." To those who needed more knowledge or reason, the swami would suggest the meditations of Jnâna Yoga, the path of wisdom. To those who needed to purify their emotions, to focus on love and compassion, the swami would point to the way of Bhakti Yoga, the path of devotion. To those who expressed fear, that great cause of misery, the swami would prescribe Karma Yoga, the path of courageous action. And to those who had trouble concentrating and achieving serenity, the swami would tell about Rāja Yoga, the path to inner harmony. But bringing all four paths together into one road to the True Self "is a long process," the swami warned, "and most seekers do not have the patience."

Whether or not Frank Baum got the opportunity to enter the door of the swami's meeting room didn't matter, for the door itself was only a metaphor. "The world is ready to give up its secrets if we only know how to knock," the swami said. The main question for Frank was which of the four paths he needed to travel the most. Choose the yoga path that best suits you, said the swami, and you choose the way to know God. For Frank, the answer wasn't clear. Like most people, he needed them all. He was certainly seeking the wisdom to realize who he really was. He especially needed to enlarge his circle of compassion, to purify his heart of any remaining bigotry and prejudice. But he also needed to face the results of his actions, to have the courage to make up for the bad karma he had already created, to compensate for becoming a messenger of a destructive ideology. Joining all these together with the path of meditation and harmony would lead to transformation and bliss.

But exactly how he would accomplish all this was something he needed to figure out on his own. The task was difficult, for it meant that he must find himself, purify himself, and cast away his own inner demon, his fear of failure, then move on to doing something in direct opposition to that which had brought all the bad karma into his life. In mythology this great test is often called "the Wizard's Challenge," as it is presented to the hero by a figure from the mystical realm. It could be pulling a sword from a stone, slaying a sea serpent, entering a cave to destroy a dragon, or going into a territory from which no one has ever come back alive.

"It's doing something that looks impossible to do," says Gita Dorothy Morena. "In the psychological realm, it's really confronting your shadow. That's the most serious and awful thing to do. If we seriously look at our shadow, we're afraid we'll disappear into it. If I look at how much of a failure I've been, I'm afraid I'll only be more of a failure. If I look at how cruel I am, I'm afraid I'll only become more cruel."

In Frank Baum's fiction, Dorothy would need to confront her own shadow—the fear of wickedness. In the book, Aunt Em first embodies the fear. "When Dorothy, who was an orphan, first came to her, Aunt Em had been so startled by the child's laughter that she would scream and press her hand upon her heart whenever Dorothy's merry voice reached her ears; and she still looked at the little girl with wonder that she could find anything to laugh at." In the movie, the darkness is embodied by a separate character, Elmira Gulch, the bicycle-riding shrew who confiscates Toto and later morphs into the most frightening female in filmdom. "I'll get you, my pretty," she shrieks, "and your little dog, too!" And so Frank would create perhaps the most famous Wizard's Challenge in all of American literature. "Kill the Wicked Witch of the West," the Great Oz commands. "Now go, and do not ask to see me again until you have done your task."

Back in 1893, as the Parliament of Religions was drawing to a close, the Swamiji's sayings were suddenly everywhere, his photograph and words appearing in every newspaper, the city plastered with full-color posters of his image advertising his lectures. "Karma Yoga is the way to freedom," he said. "It is a way of life that's dynamic, positive, and creative. We must seek freedom *in* action and not *from* action." On the strength of such wisdom the swami was invited to be the guest speaker at Hull House, the famous community center for the poor founded by Jane Addams, and receptions in his honor were thrown at the Woman's Building and at the stately home of Mrs. Palmer, the city's wealthiest lady.

The Parliament of Religions ended on September 27 with Vivekananda's concluding address, calling for religious harmony. "If anyone here hopes that this unity will come by the triumph of any one of the religions and the destruction of the others, to him I say, 'Brother, yours is an impossible hope.'" The swami's overall message was that one must instead become the change in the world that one seeks. This idea sparked such broad curiosity that the swami was suddenly flooded with speaking offers nationwide. He signed a three-year contract with a top lecture agency and crisscrossed the country, from Minneapolis to Memphis, from New York to Los Angeles, earning upward of $80 per appearance. The impoverished monk soon became a man of great wealth, an outcome he never anticipated. He had found a way to turn ancient ideas into certificates of gold, and he would give away all the certificates he did not need. "To work, alone, you are entitled, but never its fruit," says the Gita. "Never let your motive be the fruit of action."

Frank Baum now had a great task set before him. He was not at the mere mercy of the Law of Karma but could gain control of his own destiny, just as the swami had challenged: "Come up, O lions, and shake off the delusion that you are sheep . . . Be not afraid of anything. You will do marvelous work. But the moment you fear, you are no-body. It is fear that is the great cause of misery in the world. It is fear that is the greatest of all superstitions, and it is fearlessness that brings heaven even in a moment. Arise, awake, and stop not 'til the goal is reached."

15

The Witch Is Dead

Matilda Joslyn Gage painting in watercolor in the
back parlor of her Fayetteville, New York, home

◆

"I have been wicked in my day, but I never thought a little girl like you would ever be able to melt me and end my wicked deeds. Look out — here I go!"

— THE WICKED WITCH OF THE WEST

F

OR FRANK BAUM and countless others, the final month of the world's fair served as a sendoff into an uncertain future. October 9 was Chicago Day, a celebration to honor the host city on the anniversary of the Great Fire of twenty-two years earlier. The event drew an overwhelming crowd of seven hundred thousand people, by far the expo's biggest day. The fairgrounds by now had become something they hadn't been at the outset: great fun. By cross-pollinating the expo with some of the things one expected to find on the Midway — live music, magicians, jugglers, inexpensive food — the fairgrounds had become more festive and more democratic. By now even the fair's critics had to acknowledge that it had been a rousing success. "Was the American made to seem at home in it?" Henry Adams asked. "Honestly, he had the air of enjoying it as though it were all his own; he felt that it was good; he was proud of it."

The Columbian Exposition would implant in those who saw it a set of unforgettable images: the majestic arches of the Transportation Building's Golden Doorway, the General Electric searchlight dancing across the Lagoon at night, Mary Cassatt's inspirational wall mural in the Woman's Building of mothers and daughters picking apples together, the original Liberty Bell on display inside the Pennsylvania Building, the replica of the *Santa Maria* floating on the lake, and, of course, the Ferris wheel, which wasn't the only way at the fair to go aloft; one could also climb into the basket of a giant hydrogen-filled balloon and soar into the sky, at least until the tether ran out and you were pulled back to Earth.

The closing ceremonies on Halloween were muted, as Chicago's Mayor Harrison had been assassinated in his home by an angry lunatic just days earlier. But the final numbers were nothing less than impressive. There had been more than twenty-seven million admissions to the fairgrounds, not bad for a nation with a population of about sixty-five million people. It was estimated that nearly one in four Americans came for at least one day. The total cost of producing the expo was $30,500,000, yet total receipts surpassed that; the final tally was pegged at $32,750,000. A dividend of 10 cents per share was paid out to investors who had purchased stock in the enterprise.

But when the gates of the expo closed for good and all the jobs that the fair had provided disappeared, the nation's economic depression finally got hold of Chicago, too. Unemployed men flooded the streets of the city, and the fair was no longer there to serve as a source of hope. The White City went black, disappearing like a mirage in the desert. In the months after the expo ended, the fairgrounds were ravaged by a series of fires and professional wrecking and salvage companies, until only a few of the buildings were left standing.

The Gilded Age, as originally defined by Mark Twain, was now nearing its height. Money disappeared from the hands of the poor and middle classes at an alarming rate and became concentrated in the hands of a few robber barons who created monopolies to control the price of everything from oil to train tickets to paper to sugar. This fueled anger among the masses, who wanted the government to sever the dollar's attachment to the gold standard—why not use silver, too, in order to print more money and stimulate the economy? The men of Washington refused, on the grounds that only gold-backed dollars assured complete confidence. Like everyone else, Frank Baum read the newspaper reports on how the Populist insurgency was swelling around the country, but he was not taken in by it. By default, he remained a lifelong member of the party of Lincoln and never showed much interest in national politics or the Populist cause.

His attention was focused on matters closer to home, such as survival. After the closing of the fair, Frank Baum was left facing a mighty challenge, yet he had no clear way of meeting it. Despite the swami's exhortation to conquer his fear, that was easier said than done, as Frank's fear of failure at this point only grew more intense. Unable to support the family with his job *buying* fine china at the department store, he decided to switch to a job *selling* the very same sorts of products. His new position as a traveling salesman for a firm called Pitkin & Brooks entailed finding his own way in a sales territory west and south of Chicago that encompassed Iowa, Missouri, and the lower half of Illinois. He'd have to pack up trunks of delicate, breakable objects and transport them on the train, wheeling his china bundles to an empty display room, where he would set up his wares. Buyers would file in to view it all and place their orders. In this heyday of the traveling salesman, Frank was in the same line of work, using the same mode of travel, and in the very same territory that would later inspire composer Meredith Willson to create the hit show *The Music Man*.

To Frank, everything about this new job was stressful—being away from Maud and the boys, being careful not to break any china, and managing to make his sales quota and earn enough in commissions. He'd often have dinner alone and retire to a hotel room, his expenses being picked up by the firm. Fighting his frights became a daily battle, as this was a worry of the worst kind, angst about his kids having enough to eat and whether his weak heart would be able to withstand the stress of his new, more physically demanding line of work. Frank would later allude to this critical point of departure in his life by writing of the four companions as they headed into the dangerous Winkie country to find the castle of the Wicked Witch of the West and to destroy her before she destroyed them. "The Emerald City was soon left far behind," he would write, and since there was no longer a clearly marked road to take them where they needed to go, "the ground became rougher and hillier."

This new situation in the land west of Chicago was so precarious that Frank's own mother tried to intervene, writing a letter to him with an offer to take her son and his family in with her. But turning away from his duty was an option that Frank would under no circumstances consider. What's more, Cynthia Baum's health was not good and her own finances were shaky. She herself was living with Frank's sister Hattie back in Syracuse. Worst of all, the prospect of giving up his independence would deal a fatal blow to his pride as a man. In

January of 1894, from a hotel in a town called Galva, Illinois, Frank downplayed his fears in his reply to his mother. "My present job is until April 1 and if everything is satisfactory they will keep me the whole year," he assured her. "I am starting in very well and have not much to fear now [about whether] I shall be able to get bread and butter . . . although I'm afraid we can't indulge many luxuries."

For the time being, Frank's fear seemed to serve as a powerful motivator, as he started off strong in his new job, just as he had with all his past ones. "Because he had no idea what his sales should be, he secured orders for an amazing volume and became almost overnight the firm's leading salesman," his son Harry would later write. Although he couldn't tell whether he could keep up this pace, Frank gently told his mother in no uncertain terms that he must decline her offer: "You are very kind, dear, to offer me a home but I shall not need that. While I live I shall *somehow* manage to provide for those dependent on me, and I shall never burden you, although I know your love would not consider it a burden."

Frank managed to do well enough at Pitkin & Brooks that his contract was renewed. Still, the job only grew more demanding. Missing his father, Kenneth one day broke down into unstoppable sobbing, repeatedly wailing, "I want my daddy!" Maud carried the toddler over to a picture of Frank on the wall. "There's your daddy," she said, in a soothing voice. For a second the boy stopped crying. Then he blurted, "I-want-a-daddy-with-legs!" and resumed being inconsolable. Frank's many trips away from his family only made him cherish the time he spent at home with the boys even more. Always, he returned home with stories that made his tedium seem like an adventure, often telling his tales with Harry on one knee, Kenneth on the other, and the two older boys gathered around them. Sometimes neighborhood friends would come over, too, and they'd cook molasses taffy and pop corn on the coal stove.

Frank created a colorful land called the Dainty China Country, in which all of the houses, barns, and fences were made of delicate china. "And, strangest of all, these people were all made of china, even to their clothes," Frank would one day write. This episode, which didn't fit into the movie adaptation, shows just how autobiographical many of the symbols and images in the Land of Oz really were. In life, the china country served as one of Frank's final obstacles. So it was in the story, too, as the four companions were caught up there on their way to meet Glinda, the Good Witch of the South. "We must cross this strange place in order to get to the other side," as Dorothy would say.

At the beginning of May a new public playground opened at the Polk Street School near their home. Frank and Maud must have joined in the festivities, which included sack races, three-legged races, and exhibitions of Frank's favorite pastime, baseball. But such respites didn't mean that his worries had subsided. Frank was always in danger of becoming a slave to his fears, not unlike the famous traveling companions who enter the perilous land outside the Emerald City, where they press ahead in constant fright of both the known and unknown forces of the forest.

Matilda Joslyn Gage was battling anxieties of her own. Her book was banned from many libraries, including the school library in her very own hometown of Fayetteville. Anthony Comstock, leader of the New York Society for the Suppression of Vice, called the book "salacious" and declared he would bring criminal proceedings against any person who should place it in the school library. "Anthony Comstock misrepresents all works upon which he presumes to pass judgement, and is as dangerous to liberty of speech and of the press as were the old inquisitors," Matilda retorted. "Buddha declared the only sin to be ignorance. If this is true, Anthony Comstock is a great sinner." What's more, Matilda was arrested for trying to vote in a school board election in Onondaga County, not far from her home. Her anger flared to an all-time high as she took her case to New York's court of appeals.

In her public speeches she articulated exactly how she felt. Introduced at a meeting of the New York City Women's Suffrage League as "the most disfranchised woman of us all," Gage let it rip in a lecture covered by the *New York Times*: "When the world is in the hands of women, justice will be done, and one sex will not be punished for the sins of the other." The source of her fury at this time was a statement made by a preacher named Parkhurst, a leader of the Social Purity Society, who said that prostitutes who do not embrace the Lord and repent for their sins deserve to "starve or freeze on the streets." In response, Gage took the *Times* reporter aside and gave him an earful. "It is outrageous, it is cruel and wicked to turn these poor creatures to the streets," she seethed. "If Dr. Parkhurst wishes to suppress this great evil he should turn his attention to the men . . . the pillars of the country . . . He can have every disorderly house watched, and every man entering arrested, fined, and his name published. That would put a stop to it speedily."

Matilda was now sixty-seven years old, and at this point in her life she must have known that she would not live to see the changes she fought for come about in America. So she decided to join a society where women already had their civil rights. She longed to identify with a culture that valued the same things she valued. And she knew of one. She had never forgotten her old friendships with the Native Americans of the East, how the Iroquois of New York State had inspired her own vision of a future in which the rights of women were recognized and the sexes were "nearly equal," as she once wrote. "Never was justice more perfect, never civilization higher."

Matilda Joslyn Gage wasn't the only great American who was inspired by the social and political sophistication of the Iroquois. Some of the Founding Fathers of the United States of America picked up key ideas for the U.S. Constitution by studying the ways in which the Six Nations of the Iroquois confederation were able to balance the roles of men and women while keeping peace among opposing factions. The tribes accomplished this by creating the Iroquois League, a council of fifty representatives. Each of the Six Nations — Mohawk, Oneida, Onondaga, Cayuga, Seneca, and Tuscarora — selected a number of "sachems" to attend regular council campfires to work out conflicts. Although the sachems, or sages, were older men, they were chosen by the women, the matriarchs, who governed each longhouse, where groups of extended families lived. Benjamin Franklin made a particularly detailed case study of the Iroquois system:

> The Indian Men when young are Hunters and Warriors; when old, Counsellors; for all their Government is by Counsel of the Sages; there is no Force, there are no Prisons, no Officers to compel Obedience or inflict Punishment. Hence they generally study Oratory; the best Speaker having the most Influence. The Indian Women till the Ground, dress the Food, nurse and bring up

the Children & preserve & hand down to Posterity the Memory of public Transactions.

This was a culture that Matilda could embrace. Not long after her arrest she paid a series of visits to a Mohawk reservation based north of Syracuse. Out of her friendships there came the possibility that she could be "adopted" into the Mohawk Nation as an honorary member with voting rights for council sachem. The Mohawk themselves were organized into a series of clans, each composed of groups of related families and named after an animal, such as the Bear, the Wolf, and the Turtle, and each clan was governed by a women's council.

In a ceremony that likely involved the bestowing of a special wampum belt that recorded and commemorated the transaction, Matilda was adopted into the Wolf Clan of the Mohawk Nation and given a special Mohawk name. "I received the name of Ka-ron-ien-ha-wi," she wrote to her daughter. "This name would admit me to the Council of Matrons where a vote would be taken, as to my having a voice in the Chieftainship." Roughly translated, Matilda's new name was "She Who Holds the Sky."

From her Native American friends Matilda learned the practices of the medicine women. To heal the sick, the women of the tribe used a combination of ritual prayers and mixtures of natural plants and herbs. Their meditations and their medicines were handed down from generation to generation and adapted over time. In learning the wisdom of these kinds of remedies, Matilda was in a way living up to the wishes of her own father, Hezekiah Joslyn, the wise doctor who believed in natural medicines and holistic healing. Dr. Joslyn had hoped that his only child would also become a doctor, one who practiced the sorts of homeopathic treatments that had long been anathema to white society. The all-male medical establishment believed they knew much better, yet doctors then often prescribed remedies that contained arsenic and mercury. Author Louisa May Alcott was one of the most prominent to die from the effects of mercury treatment, passing away at age fifty-five in 1888.

Matilda's obsession with holistic medicine threaded through her letters. Whenever one of her children or grandchildren became sick, Mrs. Gage would demand an account of all the symptoms and then reply with a detailed treatment. When her granddaughter Leslie in Aberdeen fell ill in 1895, Matilda prescribed positive thought energy. "I am sorry to hear of your illness & head trouble," she wrote.

> You must continually think that you are going to be well. Say to yourself "I am well." Your real self is well. It is only your body that is ill. Take five minutes three or four times a day to think of health and when you go to bed at night keep saying to yourself "I am well." Grandma knows by *experience* that a great deal of good comes from concentration of thought. If your mother [Helen] would think of good things instead of bad things *which cannot be helped* she would see a change in her fortunes.

For extra inspiration, Grandma sent Leslie a framed portrait of Hypatia, who lived a great many centuries ago in Alexandria, Egypt. Born around the year 370, Hypatia was the first woman to make breakthroughs in the development of mathematics. She was taught by her father that there is an "ultimate reality which is beyond the reach of thought or language." Because Hypatia came to symbolize the learning and science that threatened the powers of the Church, the early Christians accused her of heresy and paganism. Her brutal murder at the hands of a mob of fanatical religious zealots came to be viewed as marking the end of the Hellenistic age. And so it continued throughout history. The very same women who could serve as role models for smart girls could also been seen as examples of wicked witches, especially to men who felt threatened by unfamiliar knowledge of medicine or spirituality.

Some months later Leslie developed a different ailment, and Matilda reprimanded her daughter Helen for not being forthcoming enough about the symptoms. "In regards to Leslie, I am very angry you did not let me know when the swelling began," she wrote. Matilda the medicine woman prescribed a mixture of natural mint and Vaseline. "Best to mix together into an ointment," Matilda added. "I know you have small faith in my treatment but everyone else seems to have. Even Mrs. Moore sent for me when she was sick as she would rather have me than the doctor. I have helped her before, but I do not like to take responsibility. I very much dislike for Leslie to take 'Fowlers Solution' [arsenic]. It is a poison, strange for a doctor to prescribe it. I know two people who are very great sufferers from medicines prescribed by doctors. If she once gets mercury into her system, she is liable to have a life of suffering." In one letter about another cure, Matilda enclosed 10¢ "to get witch hazel," a natural astringent.

To Frank Baum, it must have seemed as if his mother-in-law were actually two opposing characters. Her public persona was that of an old shrew, an angry, half-crazed widow who mixed her own secret potions, believed in impossible notions such as thoughts that heal, and who railed against the Church at every opportunity. In other words, she had grown into the exact persona of the medieval witch, the ugly sorceress whose magic herbs were often seized by church leaders and presented to judges as evidence of their wicked ways. As ancient as the Bible itself, this image of darkness had been implanted in the minds of children for centuries. "Of all Bible stories, none is more popular with children than the tale of the Witch of Endor," wrote the *New York Times* in 1894. Traditionally, this mythical witch was portrayed in paintings as a toothless, hunchbacked hag.

Yet in private Matilda reigned as the loving matriarch of her extended family, a wise mentor to her children, and a courageous role model to her grandchildren. When she stayed with the Baums, Matilda helped Maud keep up the house while Frank was away. "Frank came in and kissed me goodbye, as he always does," wrote Matilda. "He is very kind to me." She spent much of the time enjoying ordinary activities, such as embroidery and needlepoint with her daughter, as well as quietly reading and writing.

Of course, her thinking powers were anything but ordinary, and she knew it. Indeed, she was so far ahead of her time in so many ways that this woman with the snow-white hair came to believe she had been granted something akin to supernatural gifts. This aspect of her reflected the flip side of the witch duality, as the very same Witch of Endor was sometimes depicted in paintings as a lovely lady in a white robe, casting magical spells for those who sought her protection. The mythical white witch was a force for good.

In February of 1895, while wintering in Chicago, Matilda ran across a contest announced in the *Youth's Companion*, the nation's largest magazine for young adults. A rich prize of $500 was being offered for best original story; $250 was offered for second place and $100 for third. These extraordinary sums seized her attention, and she naturally thought of her daughter Helen and her son-in-law Frank, who were considered the best writers in the extended family. Mrs. Gage had always urged Frank to write down the stories he would tell to his sons and other children in the neighborhood. But now her insistence turned into beseeching.

The deadline for receiving the entries was the first of March, and it was already February 11. Mrs. Gage specified the same instructions in a letter to Helen that she must have read aloud to Frank. "Keep in mind it is not a child's paper but a paper for youth and the older members of the family," she wrote. "No love or religion . . . or political or purely sensational stories will be accepted. The moral tone and literary character of these stories must be exceptional." Dramatic and humorous stories were desired, "not narration or passages from history, but *stories*," defined as tales with "a dramatic arc from the beginning to the end." The word count was very specific — at least 2,200 but no more than 3,000 words — as were the instructions to submit entries written only on nine-by-eleven-inch manuscript paper.

"Now you are a good writer and I advise you to try," Matilda urged. "Of course you have but a little time, but ideas may flow!" She went so far as to suggest a topic. "If you could get up a series of adventures or a Dakota blizzard adventure where a heroic teacher saves children's lives." Maybe instead of a blizzard, she wrote, you could "bring in a cyclone . . . from North Dakota," perhaps recalling the story of the rising house that Helen had written seven years earlier. But stay away from writing stories that have actually happened, she stipulated, and create "a fiction which comes with a moral, without however any attempt to sermonize."

What especially captured Matilda's interest was the magazine's hint that there was such great demand for these kinds of stories that it would even purchase many of the best ones that didn't win the prizes. Apparently young people were so hungry for inspirational reading that it was actually possible to make something of a living writing for this market. "First, get an idea and write it out," Matilda urged. "Then count the words and if too long cut down, but do not delay. Write some story anyway. I can find other chances for you. You can write beautifully.

Now do try for this $500 or $250, as it is worth the effort. And even if you don't win the prize the story will be bought at a liberal rate."

As usual, Helen did not listen to her mother, much to Matilda's endless frustration. But to Frank, this information seemed to come as a revelation. He had always thought in terms of demand, what people wanted and needed. Do people want chicken and eggs? Do they want oil and lubricants? Do they want novelty items, toys, bric-a-brac, trinkets, and sporting goods? Do they want a better newspaper? Do they want fine china and figurines? Frank gave only secondary consideration to whether his talents were well suited to any particular line of work. He believed he could do most anything, and he was usually right. He proved to be competent across many different fields. Yet there was something special about this idea of getting paid to write stories for children. It seemed too good to be true.

Frank could not meet the looming deadline, as he was traveling too much and working too hard at his trade to conceive and write a story in just a couple of weeks. But it was indeed around this time that he began a new routine. Every evening, no matter where he was, he would write down the ideas he had thought of that day, on old envelopes and scraps of paper. He was always thinking of stories, and when he was away at hotels, he had nothing much to do at night, so he might as well use the free time wisely. Soon he began submitting his poems and tales to newspapers and magazines.

At first Frank received so many more rejection letters than acceptance notices for his stories that he kept tabs in a little book that he called his "Record of Failure," something he could very well have been keeping mentally his whole life. But over the coming months Frank did write a number of short pieces that were published. A comical poem called "La Reine est Morte—Vive la Reine!" (The Queen Is Dead—Long Live the Queen) was picked up by the *Chicago Times-Herald*. In it Frank focused his sharp pen on feminists like his mother-in-law:

> Shout hurrah for the woman new.
> With her necktie, shirt and toothpick shoe.
> With tailor-made suit and mien severe.
> She's here!

Another story, "The Heretic," a lampoon of the hypocrisy of preachers, argued that if freethinking labels a person a heretic, then he, the writer, pleaded guilty.

The stories kept coming, always twisting the real into the poetic. He placed third in a *Times-Herald* contest for "Yesterday at the Exposition," a futuristic take on a world's fair in the year 2090, in which he predicted that Ireland would be independent and England would be led by a female. He published a poem supporting the gold standard and presidential candidate William McKinley in the 1896 election ("Great will be our satisfaction, when the 'honest money' faction, seats McKinley in the chair!"), the most direct evidence showing that Baum was not a Populist. A story called "The Latest in Magic" mythologized the recent discovery of x-rays. Another piece, called "Two Pictures," told of the baseball hero Cap Anson of the Chicago White Stockings, contrasting the crowd reactions to a winning game and a losing game.

Frank was doing well enough at his sales job—and was so optimistic about the extra income from writing—that he decided it was time to move the family to a somewhat better place, relocating just a couple of blocks away to a house at 120 Flournoy Street. This home was not only larger, but it came with the luxuries of flushing toilets, running water, and gas lighting. It was at this time that a doctor who examined Frank told him in no uncertain terms that his heart was too weak to withstand much more of the constant stress of traveling. The caution arrived around the day that Frank turned forty years old—the very age when his childhood doctor had warned that his heart valves would begin to deteriorate dangerously. Frank accepted this advice and cut back on his travel, apparently relying more on letters and telephone calls to sell to established clients. He threw himself more fully into his writing, deciding in 1896 that there was indeed a future for him in crafting tales for children.

In doing so Frank took a giant step down the Eightfold Path of Buddhism. Choosing the right livelihood to match one's talents is considered the fifth step on the path, although the order of the steps isn't important. The ultimate goal is to practice simultaneously all eight elements—the right view, the right intention, the right speech, the right action, the right livelihood, the right effort, the right mindful-

ness, and the right concentration. Mrs. Gage was constantly remind-
ing everyone in the family of these kinds of lessons. "We are placed
here for the purpose of self-development," Matilda wrote. "We must
make use of talents entrusted to our care, for our own benefit first of
all, then for the good of others. Self sacrifice, although noble when absolutely called for, is not the first option in life. The first task of every
human being is to do good to himself/herself, to make use of their own
powers. All shall educate themselves in spiritual things, to gain spiritual growth."

But Frank on his own path was still unable to conquer his persistent fear of failure. Indeed, his fear may have grown even more intense now that he was trying to switch to a riskier line of work and
now that his expenses were increasing. Everyone in the extended family was plagued with dire money troubles. The publisher of *Woman,
Church and State* was paying Matilda her meager royalties not in cash
but in her choice of other books, and Matilda was in danger of losing
her house because she was unable to keep up with her property taxes.
Indeed, the entire country was mired in a depression that had already
lasted three years.

Kids, of course, never want to hear about the economy. At this
point Frank Jr. was thirteen, Rob was ten, Harry was seven, and Kenneth was five. Now that they were older, the boys wanted bicycles, especially after Uncle Clark and family visited from Aberdeen and insisted on having a group lesson to show the Baums how much fun it
was to ride. Frank Jr. and Rob joined a fife-and-drum corps, which involved the purchase of blue blazers and drumsticks. Maud was helping
out, earning some extra money by giving embroidery lessons at 10¢
per hour, and she had about twenty students. For their own home she
made a beautiful violet tablecloth. But often such projects required the
purchase of expensive threads and materials.

After one extended business trip, Frank came home in a grumpy
mood. He was struggling to succeed at his day job while cutting back
on travel, and at the same time he was figuring out how to make a living as an independent writer. About this time he was hit by a whop-
ping tax bill. Apparently there were overdue taxes and penalties that
Frank had failed to pay years before when he was running the store
in Aberdeen, and local authorities were shaking down Helen Gage,

who was still operating Gage's Bazaar at the same location. "L. F. is home but not in good humor," Matilda wrote to Helen, "and I do not like to ask him myself about the taxes." Something had to give. Frank couldn't stand living so close to the edge of poverty any longer. It was time he took a leap of faith.

He came up with an ingenious idea for his first published book. A nasty tornado had swept through Kansas that spring, destroying farms and launching an entire opera house through the air. But that had absolutely nothing to do with Frank's current book idea. Instead, his notion was to take a new and different look at the most popular children's stories of all time, the famous rhymes of Mother Goose. How did these poems come to be? Who created them? What did all those strange verses mean? For some time he had been making up his own silly explanations of why someone would bake blackbirds in a pie, why the mice in "Hickory Dickory Dock" kept running up the clock, who Little Bo Peep was and where her sheep may have gone, what Jack Horner did to get himself into the corner, exactly why Old King Cole was so merry, what really prompted the cow to jump over the moon, and why people kept asking Little Boy Blue to blow his horn. He had been putting these zany questions to his own boys at story hour on most evenings, and now he decided to provide a whole book full of answers.

Frank researched the origins of these rhymes at the library as best he could. Like a storytelling Darwin, he studied the Galápagos of fairy tales—to uncover evidence of how each legend evolved over eons of bedtimes. When he couldn't find the answers, he'd simply make up dialogue and situations to fill in the gaps. He wrote an introduction, marveling how these verses are never forgotten and how through these bizarre poems "one generation is linked to another by the everlasting spirit of song." Although the rhymes came from many different places, there were three countries—France, England, and the United States—that spawned creation myths about who this "Mother Goose" person actually was, according to Frank. The American version told of a Boston woman named Eliza Vertigoose who married a printer named Thomas Fleet, who thought the nursery rhymes that his wife sang to their children were good enough to put into a 1719 book,

Mother Goose's Melodies for Children, showcasing an image of a goose on the title page.

Frank copyrighted an early draft of his own book, *Mother Goose in Prose*, in June 1896 and sometime later was introduced at the Chicago Press Club to a distinguished gentleman named Chauncey Williams, of the Williams & Way book publishing company. Mr. Williams spent a week reviewing the manuscript and thought Mr. Baum's creation myths were so clever that he agreed to assign a young illustrator named Maxfield Parrish to draw pictures to complement many of the tales. The handsome book would be published in time for Christmas 1897 with a price tag of $2.

But even before his first book rolled off the press, Frank was so encouraged that he quit his job in china sales and began writing more books for children as fast as he could. He had an idea for his own nonsense verses: if children like Mother Goose so much, Frank thought, why can't I invent Father Goose? And so he did. Another one of his book ideas was even further along. *Adventures in Phunnyland* told of a fantasy land where there's no money, everything anyone could want grows on trees, there's a river of milk, it rains only lemonade, no one ever dies, and all people remain young and beautiful. But perhaps because this tale contained no conflict, it came across as wonderfully boring and was rejected by publishers for years.

Not yet ready to depend solely on writing books, Frank approached Mr. Williams with an idea for a new venture that would combine his own lifelong interests in retail, publishing, and storytelling. To be called the *Show Window*, it would be "a monthly journal of practical window trimming" and would showcase the best ideas and artwork from store display windows around the country, with a focus on New York and Chicago. Every window can tell a story—that was Frank's view. Mr. Williams liked the idea well enough to bankroll the magazine, which set up offices in the Caxton Building in a corridor of tall structures on South Dearborn Street known as Printing House Row. In Frank's mind, every retailer in the nation would need to subscribe, at $2 per year, and the advertising possibilities were endless.

And so there he was, in October 1897, on the verge of finding out whether any of his ideas would become hits. *Mother Goose in Prose* was just arriving in stores, and the *Show Window* was about to make its debut. The forty-one-year-old L. Frank Baum was now a budding author and magazine editor, and he could hardly take the stress. "I have been more worried than usual about business matters this summer, and have scarcely spent time to sleep and eat from my business," he wrote his sister Mattie on stationery from his magazine. "Writing of all kinds I have been forced to neglect the result, after all my labors, [it] has profited me but little." Wonder of wonders, he was following the swami's exact advice, probably unconsciously. "To work, alone, you are entitled, but never its fruit," says the Gita. "Never let your motive be the fruit of action." That may have been all well and good, but it didn't pay the bills and it didn't quell the fear.

Staying with the Baums for her final winter, Matilda Joslyn Gage was now confined to bed, as her health had totally deteriorated. Mostly it was her lungs, throat, and stomach that caused her pain, but she also suffered kidney attacks. It didn't much matter what the physicians said, as Matilda was her own doctor and she usually prescribed little more than the drinking of hot water. She knew her body and she knew her self. These were two different entities, in her view. "We all must die and I pray to go quickly when I leave," she sighed. "I would a thousand times prefer Black Death to long-term paralysis . . . The real suffering comes from lack of knowledge of real things—the spiritual."

Since she realized that her nearly seventy-two-year-old shell would soon expire, Matilda had begun writing down pearls of wisdom to leave to her children and grandchildren. "I lived through some of the most important events of the century and the world," she began, "and I want now to impress some things indelibly on your mind." To her dear son, Thomas Clarkson, named for the abolitionist, she would leave the family legacy of fighting slavery. "Your grandfather Joslyn's house was a station on the Underground Railroad," she wrote of her father. "It was a magnificent time in the history of the world and later will be more fully recognized than at present. We are now too near for a clear view. Following in your grandfather's footsteps, I have had grand experiences on the question of human liberty during my life, and if I must live I hope to do more for human freedom just yet."

To her colleagues in the movement Matilda left a message to carry on the good work. Susan B. Anthony paid Matilda a private visit in these final months, and after years of strain in their relationship, "the two women may have found some resolution." In Washington, DC, thousands of activists were gathering in February 1898 for a convention to commemorate the fiftieth anniversary of the first women's rights conference—Seneca Falls, 1848. Matilda could not be there, and there was a rule preventing papers from being delivered by anyone other than the author. To honor her, however, an exception was made, and so Matilda's final speech, "Woman's Demand for Freedom and Its Influence on the World," was read on her behalf, with great grace, by her friend Mary Seymour Howell.

To Maud and her other daughters and granddaughters she left what she called "the divinity of the feminine." This divinity, she said, can be found only inside oneself. "I want you to try to turn the current of your thoughts into a different channel," Matilda suggested. "You have got to do it for yourself, no other person can. *Look within your own soul for light.* Purify yourself. The kingdom of heaven is within you . . . *By and by you will get the light* . . . and learn the secret of the universe."

To her son-in-law L. Frank Baum she left her mystical powers. "I am one of those that are set for the redeeming of the Earth," Matilda relayed, in a moment of transcendence. "I am to live on the plane that shall be above all things that dishearten. I shall have courage and [gain] force out of the Unseen to do the things that I am asked to do. When I receive instructions from those who are in the Invisible, I will receive them willingly, with a desire to put them into practice to the extent of my spirit light and potency." She was writing as if she were about to become a mythological character living in the world of the Astral light.

Watching his mother-in-law die in such courageous fashion seemed to have a great effect on Frank Baum, for it was around this time that he wrote a remarkable poem that indicated he had finally conquered his own fear, and he, too, did it through myth. The piece was called "Who's Afraid?" and it showed how fear can be packaged as a villainous character, and when that metaphorical character is banished or killed, the fear is gone along with it.

Ev'ry Giant now is dead—
Jack has cut off ev'ry head.
Ev'ry Goblin, known of old,
Perished years ago, I'm told.
Ev'ry Witch, on broomstick riding,
Has been burned or is in hiding.
Ev'ry Dragon, seeking gore,
Died an age ago—or more.
Ev'ry horrid Bogie Man
Lives in far-off Yucatan.

In the middle of March of 1898, Matilda suffered a serious stroke. "I think the matter is near the end," Frank wrote to his brother-in-law. "It is now ten hours since she was stricken, and she is still in the same semi-conscious condition. The only sound she can make is a kind of moan, and we cannot understand it."

Matilda must have been communicating with herself in these final moments. She had come a long, long way, traveling the paths of wisdom, compassion, and courage as completely as anyone who had ever lived, but she struggled until the end to finish the fourth path, that of inner peace. "Harmony with oneself should be sought, a feeling of calmness, the putting away of fretfulness, of restfulness, of coming into oneness," she wrote toward the very end of her life. "First, last and all the time, harmony is absolutely essential."

Matilda Joslyn Gage passed away on March 18, 1898. Her brief, four-paragraph obituary, appearing in the *New York Times* and elsewhere, said "her death was caused by apoplexy," which was an old medical term for a seizure but also means a state of extreme rage. Finally, the newspapers got something right about Gage. She was indeed apoplectic, furious at the world for not changing according to her desires. She would not rest in peace, not dear old Matilda. "Your mother," Frank concluded, "will never be able to go home." A believer in the reincarnation of spirit, she would "live on the plane above all things that dishearten," just as she said she would. With her passing she revealed herself as the mythic white sorceress. As such, Frank was greatly moved, so much so that he likely took the honorific of Good Witch Matilda and shortened it—to Glinda.

16

This One Story

A 1900 poster promoting the new children's book by *Father Goose* author L. Frank Baum and illustrator W. W. Denslow

◆

"We must go back to Oz, and claim his promise."

"Yes," said the Woodman, "at last I shall get my heart."

"And I shall get my brains," added the Scarecrow joyfully.

"And I shall get my courage," said the Lion thoughtfully.

— L. FRANK BAUM,
The Wonderful Wizard of Oz

A S ONE WOULD EXPECT of Matilda Joslyn Gage, she had drafted a last will and testament that spelled out specifically what should be done upon her death, including the upkeep of the flower garden at her house in Fayetteville. Her home and assets were to be divided equally among her four children—Clarkson, Helen, Julia, and Maud—with one exception: "I give and bequeath all of my woman suffrage papers, books and documents . . . to my youngest daughter, Maud Gage Baum." And at the very top of her final to-do list was her desire to have her body cremated, "as I deem cremation to be a much more . . . healthful method . . . than of burial in the ground."

After conducting a small memorial ceremony in Chicago with Frank, their four sons, and the families of her Dakota siblings, Maud knew what she had to do next: carry her mother's ashes back to Fayetteville, to be interred in the graveyard near her childhood home, alongside the grave of her dearly departed father, Henry Gage. Maud would complete this difficult task alone, as it would be too expensive and disruptive to bring the entire family with her during a school term. This is when the magic happened. While the spirit of Matilda Joslyn Gage was ascending to a different realm, and while Maud was taking this deeply emotional trip to return her mother's mortal remains to the earth, Frank experienced a singular moment unlike any other in his life.

"Suddenly, this one [story] moved right in and took possession," Frank later wrote to his publisher. The moment came toward the end of a snowy winter's day. Frank had probably spent the day at home trying to do some reading and writing. He had put on his boots and hat and coat to go outside on an errand, probably to buy some food to cook for the family's dinner. A gaggle of guys—including Frank Jr., Rob, Harry, and Kenneth—was returning from playing outside, most likely dragging sleds, and probably accompanied by the family dog. It was twilight, a moment between light and shadow. It was also a time between a fresh burial of the past and a sudden vision of the future, in the form of his fast-growing sons. When the boys spotted him coming out of the house, they at once demanded a story, as they often would, forcing Frank to turn back through the door and into the front hall.

The vision arrived with such clarity that Frank was hardly able to speak. He was not going to be telling the children a coherent story that day. "I shooed the children away." What he was experiencing in the entrance to his home was a moment of transcendence, an instant in which the body is fully awakened yet given over to the subconscious, an extraordinary encounter with the visionary mind.

Ralph Waldo Emerson was one of the few who did justice to describing this mystical phenomenon, in one of the most famous passages in transcendentalist literature. Emerson was able to capture on paper an experience he had had during a similar time of day and year. "Crossing a bare common, in snow puddles, at twilight, under a clouded sky, without having in my thoughts any occurrence of special fortune, I have enjoyed a perfect exhilaration," he reported. Emerson described it as a transformation, when the fear of terrible things is replaced by "almost a fear" of "how glad I am," knowing finally "that nothing can befall me in life—no disgrace, no calamity . . . which nature cannot repair."

At such a moment of being "uplifted into infinite space," Frank left behind the fear that had long been blocking his own passage, and in doing so he was granted access to something wonderful, a portal of return to childhood. This is an instant in which "all egotism vanishes,"

Emerson continued, and "a man casts off his years, as the snake his slough, and at what period so ever of life is always a child." Emerson finished with one of his most memorable images: "I become a transparent eye-ball. I am nothing. I see all. The currents of the Universal Being circulate through me; I am part or particle of God."

This is the same experience that poets, painters, musicians, scientists, seekers of the spiritual, and other creative thinkers have had throughout the ages, a moment of eternal inspiration. The poet William Blake described this meeting with "the divine imagination" as an instant in which "we access infinity" by entering "through the doors of perception." Only at rare times did Madame Blavatsky claim such spiritual ecstasy, as did Swami Vivekananda, most notably while meditating on the big rock in the ocean off the tip of India. To them, this state of mind was *samadhi*, the ancient Sanskrit concept of the gap in consciousness in which matter, space, and time all converge into one point where the universe becomes transparent to thought.

Years later, asked how he came up with this story, Baum in an interview described his extraordinary moment in the simplest terms he could. "It was pure inspiration," he said. "It came to me right out of the blue. I think that sometimes the Great Author has a message to get across, and He has to use the instrument at hand. I happened to be that medium, and I believe the magic key was given to me to open the doors to sympathy and understanding, joy, peace and happiness."

Frank Baum not only realized his own *samadhi*, but he conceived an entire story based around a character on the same kind of flight, one of pure inspiration. He picked up a pencil. "I grabbed a piece of paper that was lying there and I began to write. The story really seemed to write itself. Then, I couldn't find any regular paper, so I took anything at all, including a bunch of old envelopes." But instead of scribbling highly intellectual thoughts like those of Emerson, Blake, Blavatsky, and Vivekananda, he rooted his vision in American images that were so vivid and concrete that they could capture the attention of children. Things he had seen in his life and had filed away for some later use were now rushing back and coming out onto scraps of paper.

Among the first images he jotted down that day was that of a tornado. In Dakota, Frank had been confronted by the power of these terrible storms, and he saw how homes and barns could be lifted up and taken away. "The house whirled around two or three times and rose slowly through the air," Frank wrote. In mythology, a tornado can serve as a time tunnel, a spinning vortex that can transport someone into another dimension of perception. In storytelling, a tornado can be a call to adventure, the catalyst that sets an epic in motion, taking the character from the ordinary world into the special world, much like Odysseus being swept away by the tidal swirls of Poseidon. In life, one can be struck by a symbolic tornado, a sudden twist into a new realm—as Frank experienced when he was sent away to military school, or when his father died around the time he became a father himself, or when he uprooted himself from the place he grew up and headed west.

But Frank didn't call it a tornado, not once. "There's a cyclone coming, Em," Uncle Henry shouts. The two storm names are often used interchangeably, but *tornado* is most commonly used for twisters on lands such as the Great Plains, whereas *cyclone* is used for those forming at sea, especially Asian seas. This was fitting because the eye of this twister would be taking the reader on a journey guided by Eastern philosophy.

Frank jotted down *Kansas*. Kansas is only one of several states where twisters rip through the landscape each spring, and so Frank must have chosen it for a reason: Kansas was the bleakest, grimmest place he had ever been. He and Maud were there only once, while traveling with the *Maid of Arran* troupe after their honeymoon. Maud had declared it no good, writing that she "couldn't be hired to live here." Frank needed a place he could portray as flat, dull, and colorless—to maximize contrast with the dimensional, dynamic, and colorful place where the story was going. "Not a tree nor a house broke the broad sweep of flat country," he wrote. "The sun had baked the plowed land into a gray mass, with little cracks running through it." Sixteen times in the story's opening Frank would use the word *gray*. The house was gray, the sky was gray, the people were gray.

He imagined a girl on a journey of discovery. The father of four sons, Baum would be naturally inclined to make his main character a boy and to write from a boy's point of view. His decision to create a female protagonist was therefore significant, as well as essential to the story. The character would embody a message so powerful that the author would never need to state it. As the writing contest in the *Youth's Companion* once commanded, the best stories for children come with a strong moral but contain no sermonizing. As created by Frank Baum, this lively girl represents the human spirit, which resides in females as well as males, a concept that needed to be brought into full consciousness. This spirit had been on dramatic display ever since Frank met Maud when she was a lively college coed, and he acknowledged only her on the dedication page. "This book is dedicated to my good friend and comrade, my wife."

Although the girl is introduced as an orphan living in a grim household, there's no explanation of what happened to her parents. Instead, she lives with her domineering Aunt Em — the letter M an apparent reference to the lost matriarchy of the ancient world and perhaps a nod to the important women with M names in his life. Uncle Henry, meanwhile, was modeled in part after father-in-law Henry, Maud's compliant father. But this farmer and his wife were also inspired by the hard-working, humorless, and narrow-minded couples that Baum had met during his stint living in South Dakota and writing his "Our Landlady" column. Aunt Em "looked at the little girl with wonder that she could find anything to laugh at," and Uncle Henry "worked hard from morning till night and did not know what joy was."

The story called for a dog, one that makes the girl laugh, saving her from "growing as gray as her other surroundings," as Frank wrote. "He was a little black dog, with long silky hair and small black eyes that twinkled merrily on either side of his funny, wee nose." Behaving the same in Oz as he would in Kansas, this spiritual guide dog would unite both worlds of the story, just as the Eastern philosophy of *totality* speaks to the unity of all space and time. Madame Blavatsky told of how the physical world and the world of the spiritual are not separate but are indeed part of one another, viewing "the Eternity of the Universe *in toto* as a boundless plane." And so Frank decided upon a name for this intuitive creature: Toto.

The special world itself was inspired by Theosophy and its concept of the mystical realm known as the Astral. This is "a plane of existence created by the uncontrolled use of the creative imagination," wrote Charles W. Leadbeater, one of Blavatsky's most ardent followers. In 1895 this former Anglican priest published a book called *The Astral*

Plane: Its Scenery, Inhabitants and Phenomena. The short book was so popular in the Baum and Gage families that a letter written by Matilda indicated there may have been three copies of this "very interesting" work circulating, one owned by Frank, one owned by Clarkson, and one that Matilda sent to her daughter Helen. In the book Leadbeater explains that one's thought energy can create a temporary Astral body to be projected onto the Astral Plane. This was not a dream world, but "a realm of nature within our solar system," a place "as real as our bodies, furniture, and houses" and "visited exactly as a foreign country might be visited, like Greenland."

As noted by mythologist Joseph Campbell, a common element of every mythology and religion is an invisible plane of transcendence that supports the physical world. In Western religions that plane is heaven, entered in the afterlife. But in Theosophy, as well as in Eastern religions, that secondary realm can be reached in the here and now. "Only the trained visitor from this life who is fully conscious on both planes can depend upon seeing both, clearly and simultaneously," wrote Leadbeater. Frank Baum adopted many of the rules of this "realm of illusion," as they were defined by Leadbeater: inhabitants can change their forms with Protean rapidity, sight is different here, as objects are visible from all sides, and every physical object in common space has its Astral counterpart. In the Astral light one meets with experiences of all kinds, both pleasant and unpleasant.

Clearly inspired by the White City of the World's Columbian Exposition, Frank created the Emerald City as the story's central destination. Just as the world's fair popped up in the center of America in 1893 and served as the place of transformation in Frank Baum's life, so would the Emerald City serve in this new realm. His main characters yearn to get to this city glimmering in the distance, even though no one knows anything about what will be inside or what will happen there. "It is a long way to the Emerald City, and it will take you many days," warns one of the story's heralds, Boq the Munchkin. "The country here is rich and pleasant, but you must pass through rough and dangerous places before you reach the end of your journey."

A yellow brick road appeared in his mind's eye. Physically it may have been inspired in part by the old Plank Road, the unique tollway leading from Frank's childhood home into the heart of Syracuse, and in part by the path of yellow paving bricks that led to the hilltop campus of the Peekskill Military Academy that Frank traversed in his youth. But this path is much more than mortar and brick. In his fiction this would be the path where the spiritual adventure unfolds on the way to the city of emeralds. One of the most memorable metaphors ever put to paper, this long and difficult path of tests and trials was inspired by a concept central to Theosophy, Buddhism, and Hinduism. Even the color is significant, as yellow is the hue of sunlight, the daily process of awakening and awareness representing consciousness itself. "The road to the City of Emeralds is paved with yellow brick," says the story's mentor figure, "so you cannot miss it."

To embark on her journey, the girl would have her own *samadhi* moment, projecting herself through the eye of the cyclone into the mystical realm where she would meet all kinds of strange and interesting characters who would either help her work out her problems or block her from reaching her goal, which was simply to get back to the safety and comfort of home.

Frank understood from the start that the entire premise was absurd, which is why he presented the goal of his main character with humor, the real lessons of the journey to be learned from encounters with comedic characters. "I cannot understand why you should wish to leave this beautiful country and go back to the dry, gray place you call Kansas," says one of these characters, a Scarecrow, who would embark on his own quest, for a brain.

"That is because you have no brains," answers the girl. "No matter how dreary and gray our homes are, we people of flesh and blood would rather live there than in any other country, be it ever so beautiful. There is no place like home."

The Scarecrow sighs. "Of course I cannot understand it," he says. "If your heads were stuffed with straw, like mine, you would probably all live in the beautiful places, and then Kansas would have no people at all. It is fortunate for Kansas that you have brains." Frank scribbled much of this and maybe more on assorted scraps of paper during that twilight experience in late March of 1898. To him, the story was quite funny and special. The main question was whether anyone else would agree.

• • •

L. Frank Baum had finally embraced his true self, an author of children's books. Although he was never meant to be a chicken breeder, an oil salesman, a storekeeper, a newspaper publisher, a peddler of fine china, or even a magazine editor, those experiences turned out to be quite useful to him. Now that he had the wisdom to see who he really was, now that he had enlarged his circle of compassion, now that he had dissolved his fear, he was finally able to approach his own climactic moment. His confidence had already been affirmed by others. His publisher was promoting *Mother Goose in Prose* as "the children's book of the year" in advertisements, and a reviewer in the *Chicago Tribune* called it "ingeniously constructed." He probably received his first substantial royalty check in the spring of 1898, for at least $100, representing solid sales during the past Christmas season. He was now ready to look and act the part of an author.

Soon after Maud returned to Chicago, she and Frank decided that the family now deserved to move into a residence befitting a published author. It would be the first truly nice house that Frank or Maud had lived in since their childhood homes. On May 1 the Baums moved, again, for the eighth time in sixteen years. Perched on a corner lot near a big green park, their two-story Victorian at 68 Humboldt Park Boulevard was rigged with electric lights and full indoor plumbing. It also featured a covered porch out back, where Frank could tell stories to his sons and their friends while Maud served them lemonade. The house had a den, where Frank set up a writing desk, plus a master bedroom cocooned inside a whimsical domed turret, and a basement, where Frank took up the hobby of woodworking, making some of the home's furniture.

The modest success of his first book didn't mean that the completion of his great task would be easy, though. Now that his expenses had greatly increased, he still had to keep his commitment to his day job editing the *Show Window*. The endeavor had him taking the train to his downtown office several days per week, where he would write articles and evaluate photographs sent in by storeowners, in his effort to cover each new season of store displays as if they were the premieres of new stage productions. Frank saw interest in this art form growing so high that he formed the National Association of Window Trimmers of America, proclaiming the *Show Window* as the association's "official organ." He opened a bureau in New York and planned an annual convention, to be held in the summer at the Palmer House, Chicago's fanciest hotel.

Once again Frank had hit upon a promising new enterprise, only to face challenges on the business end of things. The first calamity hit when his financial backer, Way & Williams, went belly-up. Since this company was also the publisher of his first book, the bad news also meant that *Mother Goose in Prose* was suddenly out of print, with no more royalty checks forthcoming. To make matters worse, Frank's magazine was being ripped off by phony sales agents, who promised subscriptions to people and pocketed their money. "Heretofore, the Show Window has made good these losses, and has sent the magazine to all parties claiming to be victimized," Frank wrote. But "the losses have grown unbearably great," and at one point Frank told his readers he could no longer guarantee subscriptions to the defrauded.

But now that he had conquered his fear, he saw new doors that didn't seem to be there before, and he felt assured in entering them. At the Chicago Press Club, Frank was introduced to a gruff, pipe-smoking man with a walrus mustache named William Wallace Denslow, one of Chicago's most talented and esteemed illustrators. "Den" to his friends, he had traveled the country working freelance before coming to Chicago in 1893 to draw pictures of the Columbian Exposition for the *Herald*, at a handsome salary of $70 per week. Frank showed Den a copy of his first book and said he was working on a couple more manuscripts that needed just the right kind of illustrations. Den was impressed enough to agree to collaborate. Nearly the same age, they found a lot in common.

The two began working more and more together, Frank smoking cigars, Den puffing a corncob pipe and wearing a red vest. Sometimes they'd meet at Frank's house, where he had reverted to one of his childhood hobbies and set up a foot-powered printing press. Den contributed a number of illustrations to a book of verse that Frank fixed directly in type—skipping over pen and paper. The self-published work, entitled *By the Candelabra's Glare*, contained many of the poems and tales he had already written for the newspapers. Only a handful of copies were bound and distributed to friends and relatives. Sometimes Frank would meet with Den at his eighth-floor office in the Fine Arts

Building, on South Michigan Avenue. The building had been converted into studio space in 1896, and the motto "All Passes. Art Alone Endures" was posted on a sign near the entrance. In one of the building's studios, daily classes had been given by none other than Swami Vivekananda. It is not known whether Baum or Denslow attended any of these sessions, but neither could have missed the swami's continued presence in Chicago in the late 1890s. Vivekananda used Chicago as his home base as he continued to lecture across America and the world.

The first major project that Frank and Den worked on together was Frank's collection of original poems for children that he called "the tales of Father Goose." By inventing this new storytelling character, Frank was taking a soft jab at feminism. "Old Mother Goose became quite new and joined a Women's Club," he joked. "She left poor Father Goose at home to care for Sis and Bub. They called for stories by the score . . . When Mother Goose at last returned, for her there was no use; The goslings much preferred to hear the tales of FATHER GOOSE." Den's illustrations were brilliant and brought an added dimension of humor to Frank's verses. The two took sample pages of their work to the George M. Hill Company, on South Clinton Street, where Den had contacts. Mr. Hill said he was willing to publish the work, provided that the collaborators would agree to pay the cost of having color plates made. Entitled *Father Goose: His Book*, the story collection would be readied for release in time for Christmas of 1899.

Meanwhile, Frank's adventure tale—the one about a yellow brick road leading to a city of emeralds—simmered on the back burner. Since it was intended as a novel, not a book of verse, there was much more writing involved, and so it would take much longer to finish than the two other books he was completing. Yet Maud knew when Frank was traveling on the Yellow Brick Road, because he would go into a trance, totally absorbed by the fantasy. "His best friends could speak to him at such times and he wouldn't recognize them," she said. At one point Frank grew frustrated with the story. "My characters won't do what I want them to do," he lamented to Maud. Days later, she checked back and found out that Frank had solved the problem. "How?" Maud asked.

Frank threw up his hands. "By letting them do what they wanted to do." This kept happening over and over, and Frank just went with the flow. "The characters surprised me," he said. "It was as though they were living people."

On June 11, 1898, Maud's brother, Clarkson, and his wife, Sophie, welcomed another child into the world. They named the baby Dorothy. Clark and Sophie had recently moved from Aberdeen to Bloomington, Indiana, and so the two families were now able to spend more time together, as this new location was five hundred miles closer to Chicago. Maud enjoyed visiting with her brother that summer and cradling the baby in her arms, perhaps a little enviously, since she never had a daughter of her own. It was now clear that at age thirty-seven, the mother of four sons, she never would. Dorothy's big sister, Tillie, was now twelve and delighted to have a baby girl in the house as well.

But over the coming weeks Dorothy became ill. She ran fevers and failed to recover. On November 11, at the age of five months, Dorothy died, her brain swollen from fever. Dorothy Louise Gage was "a perfectly beautiful baby," Maud mourned. "I could have taken her for my very own and loved her devotedly." So hysterical and distressed was Maud that she needed to seek medical treatment. One can only imagine what Matilda would have done if she were still alive. She may have been better able to diagnose what was wrong and apply treatments that could somehow have prevented the baby's death.

Frank tried to comfort Maud as best he could. It may have started as just a small gesture, a way of imagining a child who never had the chance to grow up, but Frank began calling the main character in his Emerald City story by the name of Dorothy. In this way the baby's spirit was resurrected. Her last name eventually became Gale, a double reference, to the gale-force cyclone of the story and to the family name of Gage. This more fully fleshed-out character of Dorothy also took on idealized attributes that Frank had projected onto the women of the West when he first moved to Dakota, where females were known for their "good judgment, active minds and independence," as he once wrote in his Aberdeen newspaper.

As for the strange but beautiful realm to which Dorothy traveled, the land itself also needed a name. While Frank was telling a version of the story to a gathering of kids in his study one day, one of the girls asked what this magical world he was describing was called. The storyteller looked around the room for a clue. His eyes stopped at a nearby file cabinet. "The land is called . . . the land is called . . ." On the cabinet, underneath the drawers labeled *A–G* and *H–N*, was one that naturally said *O–Z*. "The land," said Frank, "is called the Land of Oz."

This explanation grew famous, but it is almost certainly apocryphal, made up after the fact. Frank first told the filing cabinet anecdote in an interview in 1903, five years after it supposedly happened. And Maud angrily denounced it many years later as the fanciful fabrication of an author who may have been trying to emphasize the pure entertainment value of his story, rather than its more spiritual origins. "The word OZ came out of Mr. Baum's mind," Maud insisted. "No one or anything suggested the word. This is fact." The name Oz may indeed have simply been a nonsense word, with the special feature of having a *z* for alliteration with *Wizard*. Some have speculated that Frank was inspired by Percy Shelley's short poem "Ozymandias," about an Egyptian pharaoh. Or perhaps it has something to do with the meaningful shape of the letters—the eternal circle of life's journey fused with the constant zigzag of the wandering soul. Where he got the name didn't much matter. Maud knew better than anyone how personal this story was to Frank, how the characters and symbols were inspired by significant people, events, and beliefs, not random nonsense.

Frank's conception of the four witches of Oz was anything but nonsense. Significantly, the cyclone gets formed by the north and south winds, the directions associated with the good witches in the new dimension—not the east and west winds, associated with the wicked ones. This dual view of witches was something Frank witnessed firsthand; his mother-in-law, Matilda Joslyn Gage, was caricatured in the press as a wicked witch–like figure, appearing throughout her lifetime as a threat to the many tradition-bound men she combated in her years of "moral warfare" for an impossible cause.

Yet to her family and to the many supporters of her fight, Matilda was good, a wielder of the lightning rod of liberty, able to transmit her goodness to others in a powerful way, as if by magical thought energy. To Frank and Maud, who believed in communication with spirits from the Great Beyond, Matilda's karma was still very much alive, and she had plenty more work to do. Her spirit would live on, forever, in story, as the inspiration for the legendary witches of Oz. "One of my greatest fears was the Witches," says the Wizard, "for while I had no magical powers at all I soon found out that the Witches were really able to do wonderful things. There were four of them in this country, and they ruled the people who live in the North and South and East and West."

Dorothy and Toto arrive in the Land of Oz riding in a house that happens to crush the Wicked Witch of the East to death—perhaps by accident, perhaps not. The Good Witch of the North then appears to explain the significance of this, bestowing on Dorothy the magical silver slippers that the freshly dead witch had worn. It's the northern witch who gives Dorothy the kiss on the forehead, leaving a mark that protects her from harm, shielding her from the evils of the dreaded Wicked Witch of the West. This first good witch is the old, wrinkled, white-haired sister of the young and beautiful Glinda—likely a contraction of Good Witch Matilda—who appears only toward the end of the story.

This classic theme of mythology, that good shall triumph over evil, was also a reflection of Theosophy, as Leadbeater ends his book *The Astral Plane* with a poem:

> Hour after hour, like an opening flower,
> Shall truth after truth expand;
> For the sun may pale, and the stars may fail,
> But the LAW OF GOOD shall stand.

Dorothy encounters a strange group of little people who appear very old and walk rather stiffly. Sporting round, pointy hats "with little bells around the brims that tinkled sweetly as they moved," the little men were dressed in blue and the women in white. Dorothy's own dress is "a pretty frock," with "checks of white and blue"—no coincidence as she is well received here. One of the small women steps forward. "You are welcome, most noble Sorceress, to the land of the Munchkins," she says. "We are so grateful to you for having killed the Wicked Witch of the East, and for setting our people free from bondage."

The name Munchkins may have been a nod to the Baum family's ancestral homeland of Germany, taken from *Münchner Kindl*, meaning "Munich child," the symbol on the coat of arms for the Bavarian capital and the mascot for Oktoberfest. Baum insisted in his introduction that "the stereotyped genie, dwarf and fairy are eliminated" in his story, and indeed the Munchkins do have some unique attributes. Some of the blue-suited males of the land appear to be inspired by the boy cadets of the Peekskill Military Academy, especially in the movie version, where they are shown marching in order with guns; but the big clue arrives when the author refers to "the four nations that inhabit the Land of Oz." The Munchkins of the East, the Winkies of the West, the Quadlings of the South, and the Gillikins of the North are each a different people, with their own customs, their own identity, and their own national color. Baum also entitles the chapter introducing these small people as "The Council with the Munchkins." *Tribal council* is the signature term for a Native American political structure.

All this seems to be Baum's way of giving the native peoples he had wronged in his own life a place in his mythical land—where they would be set free from bondage and oppression. The Iroquois, the Sioux, the Navajo, the Apache, among many other native peoples, view themselves not just as tribes but as sovereign nations, yet still subjugated. As Matilda once wrote, "our Indians are in reality foreign powers, though living among us." The Quadlings in particular are a red people, and it is in this red land that the Lion is restored to the throne as the King of the Forest at the story's end, perhaps a nod to the spirit of Sitting Bull, the Lion of the Lakota who was at various times viewed as courageous and cowardly. Clearly, Frank would have to disguise any positive portrayal of native peoples, as most Americans still viewed them as savages. What's more, any novel that depicted Indians tended to be classified as a cheap dime novel, and Frank needed to stay clear of that genre, or he would destroy his ability to make much money from his efforts. But if writing fiction is an author's way of working through his or her own psychological problems, this nod to the Native Americans may indeed have been Frank's way of rectifying the bad karma of his terrible deed in Aberdeen.

The way the author describes the Land of Oz as a "place of marvelous beauty" seems to evoke a lost and idealized America—a bountiful, preindustrial land of great natural wonder. In the Land of Oz, the

West is the frontier, the most dangerous territory, dominated by the one remaining Wicked Witch, who rules the land from her castle and has enslaved the yellow Winkies. This is not unlike the way U.S. soldiers built frontier forts to lord over the Native Americans and corral them onto reservations. Like all captive peoples through eternity, the Winkies long to be free, just as the Sioux of the Great Plains yearned to revive their own freedom of "long-ago times" through their Ghost Dance ritual.

To reach her goal, Dorothy must embark on her difficult journey, and she cannot do it alone. Each of the comical companions that she meets along the Yellow Brick Road ends up joining her, to complete their own quests. The Scarecrow, an icon of farm country, was partly inspired by the brainless populists of the Farmers' Alliance who wouldn't vote for women's rights in the South Dakota campaign of 1890, just as the Tin Woodman was partly inspired by the heartless industrial workers of the Knights of Labor. The Tin Man also needs to be oiled constantly, something Frank learned a lot about doing the job of selling his brother's axle grease at Baum's Castorine. Taken together, the three companions also seem to symbolize the three kingdoms of nature in the world of the Astral—the Lion is animal, the Scarecrow is vegetable, and the Tin Woodman is mineral. As *The Secret Doctrine* states, human consciousness "has to pass through its mineral, vegetable, and animal forms before the Light of the Logos (the spirit of the universe) is awakened in the animal man."

Even more significant than the outward appearance of the comical trio is, of course, the symbolic goal of each character. The Scarecrow wants a brain, the Tin Woodman a heart, and the Cowardly Lion some courage. Dorothy herself, on her quest to get back to her home, would lead them all to the Emerald City to ask the Great Wizard to grant them these things. These goals are reflections of the Four Yogas of Swami Vivekananda, detailing the four paths to one's true self. But since this is a journey of self-discovery, each character needs to learn from experience, not from someone else. Neither a swami nor a wizard can give them what they want, for they already possess it inside.

Just as life wasn't easy for Frank or Maud or anyone else, the Yellow Brick Road isn't an easy path for Dorothy and her new friends. Their most difficult barrier stretches in every direction, blocking their approach to the Emerald City. It's the field of beautiful scarlet poppies whose "odor is so powerful that anyone who breathes it falls asleep . . . forever." This symbolic field of blood is inspired by the red poppies that seemed to grow from the blood of the fallen soldiers on the battle-fields of the Napoleonic Wars. The brilliant flowers were said to com-memorate the dead. This is why Armistice Day in Europe (Veterans Day in the United States) is sometimes called Poppy Day. After the Scarecrow and the Tin Woodman rescue Dorothy from the seductive flowers, her brain and heart won't let her fall for the poison of the pop-pies ever again—just as Frank Baum wouldn't succumb to the terrible allure of racism and prejudice ever again. And just as Frank began his own spiritual awakening during the time of the World's Parliament of Religions, Dorothy in the story is thus awakened.

This concept of an awakening is also central to Eastern philosophy. As Buddhism states, the natural state of humans is one of sleepwalking through life; indeed, *Buddha* means "awakened one." After their res-cue from the poppy field, the companions who are made of flesh and blood find themselves fully awake, ready and eager for their first ap-proach to the Emerald City.

A glimmering place of promise and splendor, bursting with all the lat-est gadgetry, the Emerald City is heavily guarded by those who state the rules of entry. To go inside the walls, for instance, one must put on green eyeglasses. In a twist on the proverbial "rose-colored glasses," Frank had already referenced green glasses in one of his "Our Land-lady" columns, when it was suggested that the horses should wear them to convince them that sawdust was actually grass during a time of drought. Colored eyeshades had also been sold at the Chicago World's Fair for the very purpose of blocking the blinding brightness of the White City.

Once admitted to the city, Dorothy and her friends are at first daz-zled by the brilliancy. And after much ado they are ushered inside the Throne Room, to finally see the Great Wizard. Eventually they will come to see that there are four distinct sides to this mysterious charac-ter, each inspired by a historical figure with whom Frank Baum crossed paths in real life. At first the Wizard is a figure of pure wonder and imagination, not unlike the Wizard of Menlo Park, a wonderful man capable of great feats, including an ability to project a photorealistic moving image of himself onto a screen—the very same invention that Thomas Edison himself promised he would reveal at the Columbian Exposition. Significantly, Edison is the only living figure that Baum mentions in any of his Oz novels.

But the Enormous Head quickly turns mean and terrible. Dorothy notices that "there was no hair upon this head," a likely reference to John D. Rockefeller and his alopecia. The world's richest man was the most reviled robber baron of the Gilded Age and a personal foe of Baum's father in the oil business. The all-consuming greed and materialism of Rockefeller also seem to be referenced when the Great Oz demands payment for granting any request. "In this country everyone must pay for everything he gets," he bellows. This turns out to be the mythical Wizard's Challenge, the classic impossible task.

Reluctantly and with great trepidation, the companions accept the challenge to annihilate the Wicked Witch of the West, and after a time of preparation they head westward from the Emerald City on their witch-hunt. Their assignment is especially difficult because there is no road leading west to the Witch's castle, and the wicked one has many tools at her disposal to thwart those who approach her. She will either destroy you or make you her slave, the companions are warned. Chief among the witch's terrible weapons is a flock of evil-eyed Winged Monkeys that could be instructed to do most anything—not unlike the fabled *wakinyan*, the multijointed Winged Ones of Lakota legend.

Anyone can command these terrifying monkeys. But first one needs the Golden Cap, which grants the holder three wishes. In other words, the flying monkeys can be a force for ill or good, depending on who possesses the controlling talisman. In the case of the Wicked Witch, she has already used two of the three commands granted by the Golden Cap to order the Winged Monkeys—one to enslave the Winkies and one to drive the Wizard from her land. She invokes her third command to thwart Dorothy and her friends. Obeying the witch, the Winged Monkeys proceed to unstuff the Scarecrow, take apart the Tin Man limb from limb, harness the Lion for hard labor, and capture Dorothy, bringing her back to the castle as the witch's slave.

Face-to-face with her worst fear, Dorothy soon notices unusual things about the Wicked Witch: that she covets the Silver Shoes, that she does not bleed when the brave Toto bites her leg, and that she never goes anywhere near water. Once, while Dorothy is scrubbing the kitchen floor, the witch uses trickery to steal one of the Silver Shoes, and Dorothy is forced into an uncharacteristic rage. "You are a wicked creature!" she cries. "You have no right to take my shoe from me."

"I shall keep it, just the same," says the Witch, laughing at her, "and someday I shall get the other one from you, too."

In the single most important moment in the story, Dorothy picks up the bucket of water and dashes it over the witch. The witch shrieks and begins to melt away, like "brown sugar."

"Didn't you know water would be the end of me?" wails the Witch in her final despair.

The sign of a truly great climactic scene is that one single action accomplishes many transformations all at once. There's no finer example than the melting of the Wicked Witch of the West. By destroying the Witch, Dorothy at once conquers her fear, takes control of her fate, gets back her shoe, frees the Winkies from bondage, and turns them into her eternally grateful friends. She also gains control of the Golden Cap. Now in command of the Winged Monkeys, she is able to rescue, reconstruct, and reunite her companions, and since she has accomplished the impossible task set forth by the Wizard, she can now go back to him, demanding that everyone's requests be granted.

But it's the symbolic meaning of the melting of the Wicked Witch that elevates this one story to the highest level. In myth and in dream, water often represents the subconscious. That it was so easy to wash away the Wicked Witch with a dash of water speaks to the fact that there wasn't much to her to begin with. Her crimes "never existed save for the imagination of her persecutors," as Matilda Gage once wrote of a woman accused during the Salem Witch Trials. Only when others assigned her evil powers did she appear evil. In this way the Wicked Witch is a metaphor for all irrational fears that exist primarily in one's mind. Not only are individuals often held captive by their own fears, but entire nations can be controlled by the rule of fear, just as it was in the Land of Oz. This lesson, if properly learned, holds the power to change America or any country, one individual at a time. "In the last analysis," asks Carl Jung, "what is the fate of great nations but the psychic changes of individuals?"

After this moment of supreme transformation, Dorothy and her companions return to the Throne Room, where they discover the other two sides of the Wizard's character. The first is revealed when Toto notices something behind a screen in the corner and essentially pulls away the curtain, uncovering "a little old man . . . who seemed to be as much surprised as they were." The Great Wizard is now exposed as a fraud who breaks down and admits, "I am a humbug!"

With this revelation the story evokes P. T. Barnum, that most famous purveyor of fraudulent amusements, the self-proclaimed Prince of Humbug. "I have fooled everyone so long that I thought I should never be found out," says the Wizard. In this light the Giant Head in the Throne Room seems to recall the Cardiff Giant, the great hoax of the nineteenth century. Now that his mask is off, the Wizard delights in showing his visitors the secrets of his best tricks, and he's relieved to tell the story of how, as a young man, he accidentally floated away in a hot-air balloon, from a circus in Omaha over the sands of the desert to the Land of Oz.

The Wizard's confession raises doubt as to whether the companions will be able to collect on his lofty promises, and it seems for a moment that they'll never get their wishes granted. It's now time for the fourth side of the Wizard's character to be revealed, the one inspired by Swami Vivekananda, the surprise sensation of the Chicago World's Fair. The guru had become famous for his lectures on the Four Yogas, meditations on wisdom (Jnâna Yoga), compassion (Bhakti Yoga), courage (Karma Yoga), and serenity (Rāja Yoga). The three companions that Dorothy meets on the road of yellow brick are magical incarnations of the first three of those spiritual quests. The Wizard now bestows token gifts on the Scarecrow, the Tin Man, and the Lion, making it clear that they already possess what they want the most. Their positive thought energy has already made it so. As the swami once said, "the Self is revealed in the mirror of the mind."

As for Dorothy's quest to return home, the Wizard comes up with the idea of traveling in a hot-air balloon back over the sands surrounding the Land of Oz. As a boy, Frank Baum had once witnessed a hot-air-balloon demonstration when visiting Professor Coe took off from the center of Syracuse, and ballooning had since become a romantic activity all over the world. In the Emerald City it takes three days for everyone to pitch in and make a balloon from silk and thread and various epoxies and glues. A large crowd gathers for the great sendoff. But Dorothy's hope of going back home seems to vanish forever when Toto decides to scurry away from the launch pad. Dorothy chases after her pet as the balloon rises into the air without her, carrying the Wizard away and out of reach.

As it so happened, Swami Vivekananda himself developed a keen interest in hot-air balloons, as ballooning to him represented an experience of transcendence, another way to achieve his preferred state, what he called "superconsciousness." He lectured one evening in England at the London Balloon Society, composed of scientists interested in the fledgling field of aeronautics, and he learned a little about the concept. Later, the swami decided to try it for himself. While in Geneva in the summer of 1896, he happened to be accompanied at a meeting by England's counterpart to Matilda Gage. She was Henrietta Muller, a women's suffrage leader who was also a member of the Theosophical Society and the first female president of the London School Board. In the midst of a magnificent sunset, the swami and Ms. Muller entered the door to the basket and the balloon was launched. As the giant orb rose higher and higher, the two friends took in a full view of the beautiful city as the bending rays of yellow, orange, and red played over the pristine waters of the lake.

After his world travels and his balloon rides, the swami decided to donate all the profits from his years of lecturing to the establishment of Vedanta Societies, temples and schools devoted to the study of the Vedas. Also called Vivekananda Centers, they were established in Chicago, New York, and Los Angeles, as well as several other locations, including Geneva, England, and the swami's home country of India, where he would spend the rest of his days teaching. "We think symbolically," he would tell his students. "All our words are symbols of thought. But all our knowledge is based on experience."

Each of the Vivekananda Centers would be marked by a special seal, a symbolic logo emblazoned on the doorways designed by the swami himself. The seal is formed by two shapes: a yellow cobra forms a perfect O, and inside it a Z-shaped white swan swims by an open lotus on the blue waters at sunset. The seal is a symbolic expression of the central goal of Vedanta philosophy: the finding of divinity within oneself.

But even though the swami was an enlightened man of exalted character, some of his own followers, including Henrietta Muller, became disenchanted with him. She was a major contributor to the purchase of land in eastern India for the swami's main Vedanta Society, a place called Belur Math. On May 15—coincidentally Frank Baum's birthday—in 1899, a newspaper report stated that Ms. Muller had come "face to face with the unavoidable conclusion" that the Belur Math "is utterly rotten and corrupt from beginning to end and full of danger to the unhappy people who place their faith in it." Although the swami's campus would go on to become successful—and today remains a thriving center of spirituality—the lesson was clear: one must place one's ultimate faith in oneself, not in someone you hardly know.

Imparting this same lesson, Frank Baum's Wizard finally comes clean when Dorothy confronts him with his own failings. "I think you are a very bad man," she grumbles.

"Oh, no, my dear," the Wizard concludes; "I'm really a very good man, but I'm a very bad Wizard, I must admit."

17

Home Again

Maud Gage Baum in 1900 with sons (from left) Robert,
Harry, Kenneth, and Frank Jr.

T HE LEFT-HANDED AUTHOR wrote the original draft of his
Oz story in pencil, his elegant lettering leaning backward
on sheets of white typewriter paper fastened by a clipboard.
Frank did most of his writing while sitting comfortably in a big upholstered armchair in the den of his Humboldt Park Boulevard home,
often folding his legs over one side, but he also would write while sitting out on the back porch or anywhere else there was a nice chair.
There is a grainy photograph from this time of Frank perched in his
living room chair, wearing slippers, enjoying a book and a cigar. Harry,
with his arm on the chair back, seems to be talking to Kenneth, who
is sitting down and holding the family cat. Gathered on the sofa are
Frank Jr. and Robert, who is also reading a book. One can imagine Dad
putting down his book and sharing a story with the boys. These were
Frank's three favorite modes of being: reading, writing, and telling.

By the summer of 1899, Frank felt that the manuscript for the book
he was calling *The City of Oz* was ready enough to show to Denslow.
The illustrator was a tough critic, always carping and bellowing something in his foghorn voice, but he also had an uproarious laugh and a
twisted sense of humor. Den enjoyed Frank's unusual story well enough
to agree to illustrate it. The two men forged a contract similar to the
one they had made for their *Father Goose* book. Once again showing his less than keen business acumen, Frank agreed to split royalties
equally with Den and to chip in with him to pay the extra cost of pro-

ducing color illustration plates. Frank never typed out the story, and the only complete manuscript was written by hand.

By the fall Frank was calling the book *The Emerald City*. He framed the original pencil stub he had used and hung it above his writing desk in his study. He dated this memento October 9, 1899. But it was very likely that he had completed the writing weeks before then. The date of October 9 held significance because it was Chicago Day, the anniversary of the Great Fire of 1871. Frank had grown so fond of his adopted home city, the place of his great inspiration, that he apparently wanted to honor it by creating the impression that this was the day he finished the book.

Frank and Den presented the manuscript along with sample full-color illustrations to George M. Hill, their publisher. Years later, legend told that the book was rejected by every major publishing house in the country, but with only a handwritten manuscript, that would have been unlikely, and there's no evidence it was widely submitted. Apparently, though, George M. Hill himself wasn't sure about this unusual story, so he gave copies to two children and a kindergarten teacher, and they all liked it very much. By November 16 Baum and Denslow signed a contract with Hill to publish the work and offer it for sale at $1.50 per copy, with a royalty rate of 9¢ per copy. They were also supposed to receive $500 each as an advance. The title kept changing. At one point it was called *From Kansas to Fairyland*, then *The City of the Great Oz*, then just *The Great Oz*, and then *The Fairyland of Oz*. When preparing the title page, Denslow changed it to *The Land of Oz*.

Sometime in early 1900 Frank arrived at Denslow's studio with yet another new title, *The Wonderful Wizard of Oz*. They took this title to press, along with Denslow's set of twenty-four full-page, brightly colored illustrations. Den also supplied dozens of smaller monochrome drawings to adorn many of the pages of text. There would be nothing on the market quite like it, as this was shaping up to be the most lavishly illustrated children's book yet to appear in print.

During the time that Baum and Denslow were preparing *The Wizard* for publication, something amazing and unexpected happened: *Father Goose* began selling like hotcakes; copies flew off the shelves of the nation's bookstores by the thousands. When the numbers came in, it was determined that *Father Goose: His Book* was the best-selling children's book of the Christmas season. It would go on to become the number-one picture book in America for the year 1900. All of a sudden Baum and Denslow had a built-in fan base of kids and parents all across the country who were eager to receive their next creation. The attention surprised Frank, who didn't view *Father Goose* as a good example of his work. Indeed, it was the pictures, not the poems, that seemed to be drawing the most acclaim. This sowed the seeds of an imbalance in the relationship between the author and the illustrator.

In classic myth, stories rarely end abruptly. Instead, the hero must complete a final journey, the return home to the ordinary world, and this last leg is fraught with its own challenges. Sometimes the hero who has already slain the dragon doesn't even make it back home alive but dies for a greater cause. In the case of Dorothy, Toto bounding away from the Wizard's hot-air balloon represents the "refusal of the return," a telling element in many myths. Dorothy sees what Toto senses: that the Wizard isn't trustworthy and has little idea what he's doing. She must complete her own journey herself, on her own steam.

Before he departs, the Wizard proclaims the Scarecrow the new ruler of the Emerald City, and so the Scarecrow convenes a meeting with Dorothy, the Tin Man, and the Lion in the Throne Room, to brainstorm a way for Dorothy to realize her wish to go back to Kansas. "Why not call the Winged Monkeys, and ask them to carry you over the desert," suggests the wise Scarecrow. It seems like a smart idea, but when summoned, the leader of the monkeys says this is not possible, for the Winged Monkeys belong to the Land of Oz and cannot leave it. Yet because the monkeys answered her call, Dorothy loses one of her three commands.

It is one of the soldiers of the Emerald City who suggests that Dorothy go see Glinda. None of the companions has ever heard of Glinda. She's the Witch of the South, explains the soldier, "the most powerful of all the Witches, and rules over the Quadlings. Besides, her castle stands on the edge of the desert, so she may know a way to cross it."

"Glinda is a Good Witch, isn't she?" asks Dorothy.

"The Quadlings think she is good," replies the soldier, "and she is kind to everyone. I have heard that Glinda is a beautiful woman, who knows how to keep young in spite of the many years she has lived."

But unlike the film interpretation, Glinda of the book can't just jet around Oz in a bubble and meet Dorothy in the Emerald City. The companions must go to her, so they set out on their final perilous journey from the Emerald City, heading south this time. Along the way they have to battle fighting trees, and then they come upon a high wall that they must climb. This is when they find themselves trapped in the region known as the Dainty China Country. This fragile zone is filled with jokes that only Frank Baum and those who knew him would get. His work as a traveling salesman of fine china was probably the most stressful of all his many careers, and breaking free of this job was also one of the final barriers in the way of his return to his true self. All the figures in the china country, including a princess, a clown, and a chicken, are terrified of being broken. The travelers almost make it across without incident. But with a wag of his tail, the Lion ends up smashing a tiny church to pieces before they bound over the far wall and escape.

After the Lion does battle with a fierce giant spider and earns his title of King of the Forest, the companions next encounter a deadly tribe of Hammer-Heads, forcing Dorothy to call on the Winged Monkeys one final time, to carry them to the far end of Quadling country, where they find a good-natured tribe of stocky people dressed all in red, perhaps the clearest reference to Native Americans in the tale. Inside her castle the lovely red-haired Glinda sits on a throne of rubies. "What can I do for you, my child?" she asks.

After telling her story, Dorothy presents the Golden Cap to Glinda, who promises to use her own three commands in a completely unselfish way. She instructs the Winged Monkeys to escort the Scarecrow back to the Emerald City, the Lion to his new kingdom in the Quadling forest, and the Tin Woodman to his requested post of ruling the Winkie country. Dorothy is happy for her friends but is still waiting to learn how she can get back to Kansas. "The Silver Shoes," says Glinda, "have wonderful powers . . . All you have to do is to knock the heels together three times and command the shoes to carry you wherever you wish to go."

As she hugs each of her dear friends goodbye, Dorothy cries tears of great sorrow, knowing that they will remain a part of her forever. "I think I'll miss you most of all," says the movie Dorothy to the Scarecrow. Then she gathers Toto in her arms and clicks the silver shoes three times, saying, "Take me home to Aunt Em!" This sets her whirling along into the next brief phase of classic mythology, the magic flight. During this flight, the wind whizzing around her ears, her slippers fall off and are lost in the desert. The silver cord tying Dorothy's physical body to her Astral body is now recoiled.

Unlike in the movie, in the book she doesn't simply wake up, because she was never asleep, and she is not in a bed. Her adventure was not a dream. Instead, Dorothy is now sitting on the grass of the broad Kansas prairie, as if back from *samadhi*. Toto leaps out of her arms, barking. As the dog darts toward the house, Dorothy gets up and runs after him. Aunt Em comes outside to water the cabbages and sees Dorothy running toward her. "My darling child!" she cries, welcoming Dorothy into her open arms. "Where in the world did you come from?"

"From the Land of Oz" is all Dorothy says by way of explanation. "And here is Toto, too. And oh, Aunt Em! I'm so glad to be at home again!"

And so the book ends, in a way that is anything but sentimental and sappy. This is less a coming-of-age story, as some have suggested, and more a transformation-of-consciousness story. Like the Buddha, Dorothy attains enlightenment. In bringing together two worlds that now cease to appear contradictory, she becomes the master of both, an accomplished "cosmic traveler," in the language of mythology.

Her adventure and her encounters with both the good and wicked witches make a powerful statement about the rescue of the divine feminine. "In the picture language of mythology," the female "represents the totality of what can be known," says Joseph Campbell. She is "the guide to the sublime acme of sensuous adventure. By deficient eyes, she is reduced to inferior states. By the evil eye of ignorance, she is spellbound to banality and ugliness. But she is redeemed by the eyes of understanding." Those eyes belong to the readers.

In the story Dorothy does not perform acts associated with male heroes. She does not enter into any fights—no hand-to-hand combat, no swords, no guns, no spears. She is never put in any real physical danger, for she is always protected from harm by the kiss of the northern witch. Her two acts of killing are single strikes — one with a house, the other with water — and what she really kills are mythical symbols, not beings of any real flesh and blood. In all her deeds the character of Dorothy is presented as entirely nonthreatening to all. Only the Wicked Witch of the West shows any trepidation over her, and that has more to do with jealousy over a fetching pair of shoes.

All Dorothy wants is to go home. She could easily have chosen to stay in the Land of Oz but never shows any interest in doing so. She is patient, determined, and admirable, helpful when called upon, but she doesn't overstep her bounds. In terms of gender, her whole story seems more a matter of principle, not a matter of changing the balance of power. And so Dorothy becomes a new kind of hero, a feminine one, sharing her duties with her three traveling companions, who do indeed put themselves in danger and sacrifice themselves again and again. They do it all for the sake of Dorothy, and in the end they become part of her and give her what she needs to take back into the world of common day.

"The hero," says Campbell, "is the one who produces the means for the regeneration of the society." In Oz, the Scarecrow, the Tin Man, and the Lion all do this by ascending to new positions of leadership. But what about back in the ordinary world, the one with Kansas in it? Dorothy does not seem intent on changing that world. She changed only herself, and if that changes the world, so be it. However, there is another hero in the ordinary world, one who indeed produces the means for regenerating society, and this hero does so by creating a mystical land so vivid that you don't just read about it, you enter it, and then that world becomes a part of you forever.

This other hero is L. Frank Baum. By encoding life in mythical forms and symbols, he discovered a story that would hold up an eternal truth: "divinity within oneself," the belief that all humans, even girls, have a sacred obligation to think for themselves, to feel compassion in their hearts, and to gain the courage of their convictions. With that, harmony is achieved. As it turns out, *The Wonderful Wizard of Oz* is the book "with the revolution in it," and it was Baum who brought this previously unpopular idea of human divinity into American consciousness. Emerson during his lifetime was lambasted for saying that "as long as the soul seeks an external God, it can never have peace" and for focusing on the idea that "the kingdom of God is within you," even though he was only quoting Jesus (Luke 17:20–21). Frank Baum was not known to engage in such arguments. This idea wasn't his personal agenda at all, and spreading it isn't what he consciously set out to do. In his words, it was "the Great Author who had a message to get across." But once he was given the magic key to understanding, he fought hard along his own road to complete the challenge.

And then came the time for this brave man to make his journey back to his childhood home. At the printer, the plates were pressing the rainbow of colorful inks onto paper, as *The Wonderful Wizard of Oz* would be set and bound during the month of April 1900. By the eighth day of that month, Frank was preparing himself for his return. "The boys are growing wonderfully, and I sometimes think I must be a kid no longer, when I behold the stalwarts around me and hear them call me 'dad,'" Frank confided, in a rare letter to his brother, Dr. Harry Baum. "There's a mistake somewhere, for I have failed to grow up — and we're just five boys together." Frank had a theory, Maud once explained, "that people who remain young are those who never forget their childhood."

Curiously, Frank announced that he was sending his oldest son off to a military academy, despite his own intense aversion to that experience when he was a boy. Perhaps he had realized that this difficult experience did him good, or perhaps the son made the decision on his own. But it seemed to be part of the completion of his own circle, a final way to erase any lingering guilt about leaving behind his fellow cadets. Frank Jr. would end up serving with distinction in Europe during the Great War.

The author's own past was on his mind as he penned this letter, as he also recalled his days at Rose Lawn, and how he missed the closeness of family and childhood friends. "Here I have many acquaintances," he confessed, "but outside my home, no intimates. I do not make friends easily, nor does Maud."

Turning to the immediate future, Frank wrote about his forthcoming books. On the strength of a few months of strong sales for *Father Goose*, publishers were now eager for all his works. The first book he ever wrote—the one about the place called Phunnyland—had been repeatedly rejected but was now accepted by a New York publisher, illustrated by someone he had never met, and retitled *A New Wonderland*. "The work is splendid," Frank wrote. (No, it wasn't. It was seen as an attempt to imitate the freshly deceased Lewis Carroll, who "had a real distinction of style which is wholly lacking here," according to one reviewer.) A musician had written songs to go along with the verses of *Father Goose*, to be published soon as well. Frank had also penned a pair of books—*The Army Alphabet* and *The Navy Alphabet*—that seemed to honor the armed services from a child's point of view. "One of those books *ought* to catch on," Frank figured. Neither did.

"Then there is the other book," Frank continued. "The best thing I have ever written, they tell me, *The Wonderful Wizard of Oz*. Denslow has made profuse illustrations for it, and it will glow with bright colors. Mr. Hill, the publisher, says he expects a sale of at least a quarter of a million copies on it. If he is right, that book alone solves my problem. But the unreliable public has not yet spoken. I only need one hit this year to make my position secure, and three of these books seem fitted for public approval. But who knows anything?" In the meantime, he concluded, "I'm working at my trade, earning a salary to keep my family and holding fast . . . until the fiat has gone forth."

He concluded by telling his brother that he and Maud were coming to Syracuse, arriving the tenth of May. "I want to be with you on my birthday," he wrote. "Then we will have a big talk and get acquainted."

Frank really meant to say reacquainted, but the point was well taken. His brother Harry and his two sisters, Hattie and Mattie, had never been able to make the long trip to Chicago for a visit. His mother had visited only a few times. Unlike the Gage family, the Baums didn't even correspond very much. Since leaving Syracuse twelve years earlier, Frank had been back only a couple of times. He was always so busy, attending to his struggling businesses, raising his boys, searching for new opportunities. Plus, he didn't have the money to travel. His mother would have to pay his way, and so the prospect of going back for visits had always been somewhat depressing.

Not anymore. He not only had the money to travel, but he was arriving in his old home city as the best-selling children's book author in America. Of course, claiming such a distinction was like saying you were the tallest person in Munchkinland. To a close approximation, there *were* no successful children's book authors in America. Children in America had mainly read European literature—from the old stuff like Grimm and Andersen to the more recent stuff like Carroll and Kipling.

In myth, the hero returns with the "boon," the special object or piece of wisdom that signifies transformation. Frank and family arrived in town with an armful of the very first copies of *The Wonderful Wizard of Oz* to roll off the press, to be given as special gifts. No one could have known then all of what the Oz story would go on to become, but that didn't matter. What mattered now was the sheer joy that Frank attained by bestowing these first editions on his siblings, while writing personal inscriptions inside each. It had been said of their father's time that money was the poetry of the age. The son had inverted the world of his father. For Lyman Frank Baum, poetry would become the money of the age.

Frank honored Mattie first. Her book wasn't even bound but was hand-stitched from pages that Frank literally grabbed as he watched them coming off the press, "really the very first book made of this story," he wrote. The first bound copy went to his brother Harry, and the next ones to Hattie and his mother, Cynthia. The entire Baum family reunited to celebrate Frank's birthday. Since the number 4 was an auspicious figure that kept cropping up again and again in both life and story—there are four companions and four witches and four nations in the Land of Oz—his forty-fourth birthday seemed especially significant. "It's a number of totality," says great-granddaughter Gita Dorothy Morena. "You have to overcome the obstacles in all four directions to find wholeness."

Back in Chicago advance requests for the book were already pouring in, the first five-thousand-copy printing having been pre-ordered by stores months before the publication date, resulting in an immediate second printing. In July the work was first shown publicly during the Chicago Book Fair, at the Palmer House, and the publisher at that point began taking back orders. Frank resigned his position as the editor of the *Show Window* in October. "The generous reception of the American people of my books for children has resulted in constant demands of my time," he explained.

When the reviews started rolling in, some critics compared *The Wonderful Wizard of Oz*—favorably this time—to *Alice's Adventures in Wonderland*, an assessment that flattered Baum. But many reviewers gave more credit for the book's overall splendor to the illustrator than to the author. One newspaper said it was "remarkably illustrated by W. W. Denslow, who possesses all the originality of method which is denied by his collaborator." At last, when the *New York Times* reviewed the book on September 8, Frank knew at least someone saw the story for what he meant it to be—a modern fairy tale for a new world:

> The book has a bright and joyous atmosphere. The story has humor and stray bits of philosophy that will be a moving power on the child mind . . . It's impossible to conceive of a greater contrast than exists between the children's books of antiquity and the modern children's book, of which *The Wonderful Wizard of Oz* is typical . . . The time when anything was good enough for children has long since passed, and the volumes devoted to our youth are based upon the fact that they are future citizens: that they are the country's hope.

Yet as happy as the *Times* review must have made Frank, Christmas was fast approaching and he had little idea how the book was faring among actual readers. When it became clear that the Baums did not have enough money to buy their children Christmas presents, Maud suggested, then demanded, that Frank go to the publisher and insist upon some sort of advance payment. They needed at least $100 to buy proper gifts and get through the expensive Christmas season. As usual, Frank did as he was told.

The George M. Hill publishing company was housed in an antiquated eight-story factory where books were both edited and manufactured. When Frank marched in to confront Mr. Hill, he was surprised to be greeted more warmly than ever before. When he demanded an advance against a scheduled January royalty payment, Mr. Hill agreed and instructed his secretary to write Mr. Baum a check and seal it in an envelope. Frank put it in his pocket without opening it and went home.

Maud was standing in the kitchen doing some ironing when Frank walked in. He opened the envelope and looked at its contents without expression. He then handed the check to Maud, who hoped against hope that the check would be for at least $100. After setting the iron down on Frank's shirt, Maud peered at the check and nearly jumped out of her skin when she saw the actual figure: $3,432.64. As they embraced in laugher and tears, Maud forgot about Frank's shirt, burning a hole right through it. That only caused more shouting and laughter, attracting Harry, Kenneth, Frank Jr., and Robert downstairs to join in the celebration.

After so many years of being deprived, Frank unleashed himself on Chicago's decked-out department stores for Christmas of 1900. He purchased four Christmas trees, one for each of the four boys, setting them up in the four corners of the living room, wrapping piles of presents to place under each tree. To Maud, Frank would give a sparkling emerald ring, a cherished gift that remains in the family to this day. Frank also presented Maud with a two-pound box of the finest chocolates, despite her insistence years before that he was never to bring food into the house. Maud thenceforth changed her policy. "I am very fond of candy," she admitted.

The festivities continued as *The Wonderful Wizard of Oz* became the number-one best-selling book in America for the holiday season. For New Year's Eve, Frank and Maud joined Bill Denslow and his wife, Ann, in a festive splurge, inviting friends and colleagues to Rector's, one of Chicago's fanciest restaurants. Seated at a giant round table whose centerpiece was a model of the Tin Man surrounded by red roses, they feasted and drank glass after glass of Champagne. At midnight L. Frank Baum asked the group to raise their goblets to ring in the official first year of the twentieth century, a simple toast to a world renewed. "So everything conspires to make *me* glad," the newly famous author remarked, "and I send the heartiest wishes for a glad New Year—and century—to you and yours."

EPILOGUE

A Great Awakening

L. FRANK BAUM telling "OZ" stories at Coronado

After becoming a famous author, Baum and family spent several winters at Hotel del Coronado near San Diego.

The Silver Shoes had fallen off and
were lost forever in the desert.

— L. FRANK BAUM,
The Wonderful Wizard of Oz

AND SO L. FRANK BAUM achieved true happiness, a state of bliss available to everyone in this life even though only the lucky few ever reach it. Frank radiated his happiness for the rest of his days, creating concentric circles of joy, spreading from Maud and the boys, to his extended family, rippling through space and time, continuing for eternity. "Every one loved him, he loved every one, and he was therefore as happy as the day was long," Frank wrote of the Tin Woodman.

Returning to his roots as a playwright, Frank adapted *The Wonderful Wizard of Oz* into a musical stage extravaganza, adding comedy and costumes not found in the book. The producers of the show piled on all kinds of unrelated characters, silly love songs, and utter nonsense that Frank wasn't pleased with but ultimately accepted. The show opened in Chicago in the summer of 1902 and traveled to New York and twenty other cities over a remarkable eight-year run that turned Frank Baum into a rich man. The family summered at their breezy cottage on Lake Michigan and wintered on the California beach, at San Diego's castlelike Hotel del Coronado. "Mr. Baum settled back in an easy chair in the sunshine," wrote one reporter who came for an interview, "and he looked in a supremely happy way at his wife and sons."

Aside from achieving happiness and harmony, Frank didn't change much. He retained his tendency to overdo things. The children of America demanded that he write sequels about the Land of Oz. He hadn't planned on this, but write them he did, filling the pages of thirteen more Oz novels with endlessly delightful moments and images. Some were significant to the saga, such as when a young princess named Ozma ascends to the throne to rule the Land of Oz, a restoration of the ancient matriarchy. But some of the books feel disjointed, written in haste. Clearly, all of Baum's Oz books derived their magic from the original one, and nothing else that Frank created would ever approach the brilliance of *The Wonderful Wizard of Oz*. It was as if he had possessed for only a very short time a special mystical object—not unlike Dorothy's magic slippers that were forever lost when she returned home to Kansas.

Seeking warmer climes year-round, Frank and Maud moved in 1909 to California, where they lived in style in their custom-built Victorian, which Frank named Ozcot. They selected a neighborhood called Hollywood because of its charm, not because there was any special industry forming there. By then their four sons had grown and were off on their own journeys. Maud embroidered and Frank sat in the backyard writing, often taking long breaks to plant and cultivate flowers. Tending his gardens at Ozcot, Frank named a strain of chrysanthemums "Matildas." He experimented with making silent films, forming with his eldest son the Oz Film Manufacturing Company—but those movies seem unwatchable now. He also produced more plays made from his works, including the ill-fated *Woggle-Bug* and the disastrous *Fairylogue*. These expensive productions forced him into bankruptcy in 1911. But he recovered quickly by writing yet another Oz novel. He was probably the most prolific author in America, tossing off an average of one new book every four months, for both kids and adults, many written under curious pen names like Floyd Akers and Edith Van Dyne. He kept up this pace for nearly twenty years and created entirely new lands, such as Ev, Ix, and Mo, but nothing clicked quite like Oz.

Before long the generation of childhood readers of *The Wonderful Wizard of Oz* grew up and began having kids of their own. In 1918, while completing the manuscript for *Glinda of Oz*, his fourteenth Oz novel, Frank fell ill. In February 1919, on his deathbed, he learned that the first Congress convened after the Great War would have enough votes to pass the Nineteenth Amendment, also known as the Susan B. Anthony Amendment, guaranteeing women the right to vote. It would be ratified by the states the following year. But as his mother-in-law, Matilda, would have said, it would be only one step along the long road to justice and freedom. Future storytellers would have to create more myths that expanded consciousness to ensure that the American dream could come true for everyone.

As he lay dying, Frank had a quiet chat with his wife of thirty-six years. "This is our house, Maud," he whispered. "I would like to think you are staying here where we have been so happy." Maud nodded. "I shall stay here as long as I live," she replied. Frank's heart stopped beating on May 6, 1919, about a week shy of his sixty-third birthday.

In 1933 the eldest son sold the movie rights to his father's book to MGM for a reported $40,000. There was no provision for royalties if the movie did well. Aside from that, Maud made just a small consulting fee during production of the 1939 classic starring Judy Garland. Nevertheless, she loved how it all turned out and said Frank would have, too. Over time, more people would see *The Wizard of Oz* than any other film in motion picture history.

POSTSCRIPTS

Maud Gage Baum reading her late husband's book with
Wizard of Oz star Judy Garland, 1939

◆

"Rainbow" has always been my song. Everybody has a
song that makes them cry. That's my sad song.

— JUDY GARLAND

L FRANK BAUM never intended *The Wizard of Oz* to spawn
a series, and so he moved on, telling tales that took place
in other lands. But the surprising success of the musical extravaganza based on his book—coupled with more than a thousand
letters from children requesting "more about Oz"—soon convinced
him otherwise, and in 1904 he finished *The Marvelous Land of Oz*.
He called it a sequel, even though Dorothy is entirely absent from
the adventure, as she remains in Kansas for the time being. The new
story instead focuses on Tip, a boy from the Gillikin country in the
north of Oz, and his adventures with the Scarecrow, the Tin Woodman, and several new characters. The book sold well enough to assure
that Frank wouldn't be escaping Oz anytime soon.

Baum worked with a talented new illustrator named John R. Neil
for the rest of the Oz series. This new partnership was necessary because Baum had split with W. W. Denslow after disputes over money
and credit. "Denslow got a swelled head, hence the change," quipped
Maud. Although Frank was always ambivalent about Denslow's contribution, Maud was firm. "I have always disliked Denslow's Dorothy,"
Maud admitted years later. "She is so terribly plain." With his Oz royalties, Den purchased a tiny piece of land off Bermuda and proclaimed
himself King Denslow of Denslow Island. He continued illustrating
children's books but also took to heavy drinking, and he ended up divorcing three times. Denslow's death came in 1915, after he caught
pneumonia while out celebrating his sale of an illustration for the
cover of *Life*.

The split-up of Baum and Denslow was complicated by the fact that their publisher, George M. Hill, was unprepared for the initial Oz boom and then expanded operations too suddenly, moving into expensive new offices. Hill was leveled, filing for bankruptcy in 1902. Legal wrangling ensued. The plates of all of Baum's books to date were soon auctioned off, picked up by the Bobbs-Merrill Company of Indianapolis. Frank was unhappy with how the new owner treated his work and his accounts, and so he ended up publishing his Oz sequels with Reilly & Britton, a startup publisher formed by a pair of trusted colleagues from the old Hill company.

One of the most striking themes threading through the entire Oz series is the tension between home and away. Baum typically presents homes as either destructive (after all, Dorothy's house kills a witch) or the kinds of places from which one must escape or be rescued. Baum did use the now famous line "There's no place like home" in the first Oz book, but Dorothy seems to say it in jest. Still, although Dorothy does not repeat this sentiment at the end of the story, she is clearly glad to be back at home with Aunt Em. However, when Dorothy Gale returns to the series in the third book, *Ozma of Oz*, she immediately sets out again for the Land of Oz, this time leaving Toto behind, traveling to Oz on a ship with a talking yellow hen named Billina. In this story the Gillikin boy Tip never returns home. It turns out he wasn't even a boy but had been transformed into one by a wicked sorceress. Glinda changes Tip back into the secret lost princess, Ozma. She now ascends to the throne, ruling Oz as its queen from the Emerald City.

In the fourth book, *Dorothy and the Wizard in Oz*, we learn that the Wizard never did make it back to Omaha. Instead, he's in San Francisco, where the characters journey beneath the crust of the Earth. In the fifth volume, *The Road to Oz*, Dorothy falls in with all kinds of homeless characters, including the Shaggy Man and Polychrome, yet she does manage to reunite at the end in Kansas with her aunt and uncle.

Baum intended to conclude the series with the sixth book, *The Emerald City of Oz*, in which Dorothy is asked to stay at home and do chores. "Wouldn't it be funny for me to do housework in Kansas when I'm a Princess in the Land of Oz," she muses. The solution is that they all relocate to Oz and abandon Kansas forever. Even though Oz is about to be attacked by the Nome King, Auntie Em at this point seems ready to get away from home and farm. "I've been a slave all my life, and so has Henry," she declares. "I guess we won't go back to Kansas, anyway. I'd rather take my chances with the rest of you." Once settled in Oz, Auntie Em smiles — she's finally happy. But even in Oz, Dorothy does not live with her aunt and uncle, as there are no traditional households in this land. The characters take joy in living nomadic lives and experiencing adventures. Home is only a temporary place of respite, and happiness comes from going away.

In real life the Baum family kept on the move, relocating two more times to nicer homes in Chicago — the ninth and tenth moves for Frank and Maud as a couple. They also took off on their first and only foreign trip, a six-month excursion to Europe and Egypt, where they visited the pyramids and the sacred crypts and tracked down Theosophical symbols and lost goddesses such as Isis. Maud's many descriptive letters on the trip formed the basis of her own book, called *In Other Lands than Ours*. In 1907 Frank and Maud hosted a party for their silver wedding anniversary, Frank writing on the invitation that "Father Goose and wife have not quarreled in twenty-five years."

In 1909 the Baums moved to California for good and ordered the construction of Ozcot, a whimsically designed house located off Hollywood Boulevard. After a series of ambitious stage adaptations of his stories failed to pan out, and after his investments in silent film production ate up the rest of his funds, he transferred all his property and literary rights to Maud and declared personal bankruptcy in June of 1911, claiming that his assets consisted of only his clothing and an old typewriter. Only Oz could save him. But in his series ender he had declared that Ozma had sealed off Oz forever, rendering it invisible to the outside world. "But how can you do it," asks Dorothy. "How can you keep everyone from ever finding Oz?"

Picking up on a suggestion from a child's letter, Frank reestablished contact with Dorothy by way of wireless telegraph, and he resumed the series with *The Patchwork Girl of Oz*. Frank continued to add characters and plot devices directly suggested by his legions of young fans. He appointed himself the "Royal Historian of Oz," as he now saw himself as more of a curator than a traditional author. This method helps explain why many of these later books are often jumbled and nonsensical. He rarely edited or revised, and he never went back to reread his prior books to assure consistency and avoid contradictions in the overall epic. He was happy to keep writing, prolifically, but Frank seemed never again to experience the kind of *samadhi,* a moment of visionary inspiration, that sparked his initial discovery of Oz.

As grandparents, Frank and Maud spent as much time as possible with family, at Ozcot and elsewhere. Their youngest son, Kenneth, married a beautiful young woman who happened to be named Dorothy, and when their daughter was born, they named her Frances. Grandpa Baum thought this name would not do. He held up the baby, looked in her eyes, and decided that Frances was not her name. Her name was Ozma. And so the baby's name was changed to Ozma. Frank presented his granddaughter with a special Oz pendant that she would treasure the rest of her life. When Ozma grew up and had a daughter of her own in 1948, she named her Dorothy. This Dorothy grew up to earn a PhD and become a Jungian psychotherapist. But after a crisis in her own life, she gave up her home, stopped her practice, sold all her possessions, and entered an ashram in Oregon, where she lived and meditated for months. Her guru there gave her the name Gita, which means "song." But she eventually returned to establish a wonderful new home and restart a thriving practice. Gita Dorothy now embraces both names and carries on the spiritual traditions of Oz. "Our family is very at ease with the world of spirit," she says. "The spirit world is all around us. We have an interface with it. Frank lived in that space. Matilda certainly lived in that space."

Despite creating America's first successful series of children's books, stories that had become overwhelmingly popular around the world, Frank was never able to manage his business affairs in a profitable way. He left Maud with cash in the bank amounting to exactly $1,072.96. "L. Frank Baum made balm of failure," said his obituary in his hometown *Syracuse Journal.* "He kept everlastingly at it." Of course, his legacy would transcend anything that financial success could possibly bring. "He was a man who knew the heart of a child," the newspaper concluded.

Money woes continued after Frank's death. Maud felt she was being cheated out of royalties by Bobbs-Merrill, as the publisher had licensed cheap versions of the first Oz book without her consent. The total amount of royalties she received between 1919 and 1931 amounted to less than $15,000, despite the fact that millions of copies were in print. Maud did earn additional income by granting radio rights to NBC, to produce a series of fifteen-minute plays based on adventures from the first six Oz books. Sponsored by Jell-O, the programs ran three afternoons per week in the early years of the Great Depression.

The film rights to *The Wonderful Wizard of Oz* were highly sought after. An internal memo at the Walt Disney Company stated that "an analysis of our fan mail . . . reveals that there have been more requests for us to adapt the Oz books than for any other material . . . We are currently investigating the rights to these books." One Disney treatment had Mickey Mouse in the Dorothy role, and he would be transported to Oz along with Donald Duck. For avoiding this most awful of fates we can thank Maud. "I have never met Mr. Disney, but several times he has sent his representative to see me," Maud wrote. "I was not interested in his proposition." When it came to negotiating a deal, she left the matter to her eldest son, Frank Joslyn Baum, who in 1933 sold the film rights to Samuel Goldwyn for a flat $40,000 fee. The business of talking pictures took off during the Depression, and Goldwyn ended up reselling the rights to the company he cofounded, MGM, for $75,000, in 1938. It was considered the perfect starring vehicle for the child superstar Shirley Temple.

MGM producer Mervyn LeRoy and his associate Arthur Freed (lyricist for "Singing in the Rain" and "You Are My Lucky Star") nixed Miss Temple in favor of the less well-known sixteen-year-old Judy Garland, perhaps the most fortunate casting decision in movie history. Ray Bolger was originally cast as the Tin Man, but he pleaded and "fought and fought and fought" with Louis B. Mayer himself for the role of the Scarecrow instead, as he wanted to show off his dancing. Negotiations with Bert Lahr for the role of the Cowardly Lion almost broke down because he demanded a contract that guaranteed him six weeks' pay while the studio insisted on just five weeks. Shooting began in September of 1938 and ended up stretching out for nearly nine months, much to Lahr's discomfort, as he had to endure hours of makeup and climb into his eighty-pound costume almost every day.

In crafting the screenplay, lead writer Noel Langley benefited, perhaps without realizing it, from two new schools of thought that didn't yet exist when Frank Baum created his masterwork. One was the Freudian analysis of dreams. Sigmund Freud was born in the exact same month as Frank Baum, and his breakthrough work, *The Interpretation of Dreams*, about "the royal road to the understanding of unconscious mental processes," appeared in the very same year as *The Wonderful Wizard of Oz*. Langley greatly expanded Baum's sparse opening Kansas sequence, adding strong suggestions of Freudian wish fulfillment by creating mirror characters in Kansas that would appear in different forms in the Land of Oz.

Freud's work also helped inspire the art movement of Salvador Dalí, Joan Miró, Max Ernst, and Man Ray known as surrealism, a way of commenting on reality by creating images that sit "on top of reality," as the term implies. Baum's book certainly contained many surreal juxtapositions—a house that flies, a bright yellow road in an unsettled forest, a scarecrow that talks, a lion without any nerve, trees that fight. But Langley added even more—a series of evocative images flashing in Dorothy's window as her farmhouse flies to Oz, an astonishing Munchkinland sequence that is totally out of this world yet seems strangely real, a good witch floating in a bubble, a "horse of a different color" that morphs among different hues, and in a very late draft of the script, it was Langley who changed the slippers from silver to a surrealistic ruby so they would pop better in Technicolor along the Yellow Brick Road.

When it came to creating the music, there was a feeling among some studio people that the movie should simply make use of the songs from *The Wizard of Oz* stage production. But most of those songs were filled with random nonsense that had nothing to do with the story, and Freed wanted to make use of an innovation pioneered in 1927's *Show Boat*—the idea that songs in a musical should support the plot and be integral to the characters. That the composer and lyricist duo of Harold Arlen ("Get Happy") and E. Y. "Yip" Harburg ("Brother, Can You Spare a Dime?") were able to create a dozen numbers along these lines in just fourteen weeks seems like a miracle. Yet "it really was no miracle, what happened was just this." First, they wrote what they called the "lemon drops," the easy songs ("Ding Dong! The Witch Is Dead," "We're Off to See the Wizard," and "The Merry Old Land of Oz"). Then they reused a melody of theirs (cut from a show called *Hooray for What?*) for the "If I Only Had Brain . . . a Heart . . . the Nerve" trio. For the Munchkinland medley, they were guided by the stage play's eight-part format.

Still, each new tune of theirs was a revelation. If the sheer joy gained over the years from the Munchkinland sequence that begins with "Come out, come out, wherever you are" could be measured in pounds, the grand total by now might outweigh the Earth. Arlen was most challenged in his quest to write "a song of yearning" that could unite the worlds of Kansas and Oz. He was inspired by Baum's original description of Kansas, in which everything was gray. Suddenly, he got the idea that the only colorful thing that Dorothy might ever see there would be a rainbow. Famously, he had to fight to keep the resulting song, "Over the Rainbow," from being cut from the final film, because Mayer felt the movie was too long. That he narrowly won his battle might be explained by the Law of Karma. Another terrible decision was averted, and Hollywood would now have its most memorable musical moment. The Recording Industry Association of America ended up voting "Over the Rainbow" the number-one song of the twentieth century.

Many a dispute in the making of *The Wizard of Oz* was settled by "going back to Baum." Costume designers spent two months creating endless designs and colors for Dorothy's dress, and Judy Garland had to be photographed wearing each one. In the end they simply went back to Baum's sparse description: "It was gingham, with checks of white and blue; and although the blue was somewhat faded with many washings, it was still a pretty frock." The screenwriters also used stray lines from the book. "I'm Dorothy, the small and meek," Judy Garland tells the Wizard. Frank Morgan's Wizard admits, "That's exactly so! I'm a humbug!" and "Oh, no, my dear; I'm really a very good man, but I'm a very bad Wizard." For the song "We're Off to See the Wizard," the songwriters brought back the word *wonderful,* which had been dropped from the title in later editions of Baum's book. They even added references from Baum's own family life that weren't in his first Oz novel, such as the chicken farm and Professor Marvel's incantations about the goddess Isis. Best of all, the opening screen credits pay tribute to the triumph of the original author. "For nearly forty years this story has given faithful service to the Young in Heart; and time has been powerless to put its kindly philosophy out of fashion. To those of you who have been faithful to it in return . . . and to the Young in Heart . . . we dedicate this picture."

The production was fraught with difficulties and mishaps. Perhaps the toughest job was locating 124 little people to serve as Munchkins. Many were recruited from eastern Europe and couldn't speak of word of English, so their voices had to be dubbed. They each earned $100 per week, less than the salary of Terry, the star terrier who played Toto. Meanwhile, special aluminum-flake makeup made Buddy Ebsen, the Tin Man, so violently ill that he was hospitalized, famously, and had to be replaced, magnificently, by Jack Haley. The Wicked Witch of the West, played by Margaret Hamilton, often arrives in a fireball, and during one take Hamilton actually caught fire and had to be hospitalized to treat major burns. But the production has also spawned countless urban legends. Although it is true that many of the Munchkins had crushes on Judy Garland, nothing actually happened, except for a few getting caught under her dress, and no Munchkin committed suicide or died during the production of the film, although one got stuck in a toilet.

To criticize the movie, of course, is to toss pebbles at a castle, as *The Wizard of Oz* is one of humanity's most enduring and beloved pieces of motion picture art. However, there is one giant "however": the way the film ends. "If I ever go looking for my heart's desire again," Dorothy tells Glinda, "I won't look any further than my own backyard." The true Baum devotee detests the way Dorothy wakes up in Kansas from her dream and is laughed at by all the adults. "I hate it," says Gita Dorothy Morena, "and I even hated it when I was a kid." Dorothy vows that "I'm not going to leave here ever, ever again . . . And oh, Auntie Em, there's no place like home." Not only is it hard to believe that Dorothy would prefer staying in gray Kansas after her colorful adventure, but this comforting message runs precisely opposite to Baum's view of home. The overemphasis on the outer goal of home seems to undercut the story's internal message, about discovering one's true self through experience.

The sentimental scene was insisted upon by LeRoy and Freed over the objections of Langley and Harburg, who called it "tripe." But the syrup was poured on for a reason: this was a theme Hollywood felt America wanted and needed at the time. Another of MGM's Freed-produced musicals of the era had pretty much the same "It's all right in our own hometown" ending. In *Meet Me in St. Louis*, Judy Garland delivers the final line: "I can't believe it, right here where we live, right here in St. Louis!" But considering all the terrible ways that *The Wizard of Oz* could have been tragically ruined, the sappy ending isn't so bad after all.

MGM pulled out all the stops to promote its $3 million master-piece. Cast members sang songs live on the radio. "The Wizard of Oz is a world's fair in itself," said one ad, "a World's Fair in Technicolor." Cartoons and pictorials were created for newspapers. "The greatest bestseller of modern fiction (9,000,000 copies) . . . long remained untouched by Hollywood producers," said another ad. "The Wizard of Oz —filmed as L. Frank Baum himself would have wished it." The seventy-eight-year-old Maud Gage Baum was hired to pitch in, and she was interviewed on the radio show *Ripley's Believe It or Not!* about the origins of her husband's story, reading in her high-pitched voice copy that was half-fictionalized by the MGM publicity department. Maud had lunch with Judy Garland, and the two were photographed sitting and reading the book.

At the premiere at Grauman's Chinese Theatre on August 15, 1939, Munchkins in full costume greeted LA filmgoers. Wearing a corsage on her dress, Mrs. L. Frank Baum attended the gala, mingled with director Victor Fleming and Billie Burke (Glinda), and was photographed with Ray Bolger and other luminaries. The newspapers referred to her as one of the "celebrities." Maud was enchanted by the movie. Afterward Mr. LeRoy sent her a note of thanks. "Success is complete knowing that you loved it as I do," he wrote. "We are grateful for Mr. Baum's wonderful and remarkable imagination which made the picture possible."

Maud Gage Baum lived until age ninety-one, dying in 1953. She was buried next to her husband not far from their home in Hollywood.

Despite all the hoopla surrounding the movie's release, despite rave reviews, and despite record-breaking attendance in most cities, *The Wizard of Oz* lost money on its initial release. L. Frank Baum wouldn't have had it any other way. Among the reasons were the high promotion and advertising costs and the fact that a third of the audience was made up of children, who paid very little to attend. The film finally turned a profit after the war, in its 1949 worldwide rerelease.

The story began an entirely new phase of life one hundred years after the birth of L. Frank Baum. On Saturday, November 3, 1956, the movie debuted on television, airing on CBS's *Ford Star Jubilee* in a two-hour presentation, hosted by Bert Lahr and the ten-year-old Liza Minnelli. An astounding forty-five million people watched, despite the fact that most households, if they had a TV, had only black-and-white sets. CBS aired it again in 1959, attracting an even larger audience, and thus began the tradition of annual showings. More and more people every year got color sets and were now able to witness the moment of wonder, Dorothy's arrival in Oz, the breathtaking switch from sepia tones to Technicolor. "That's when all the fuss began," remarked Margaret Hamilton.

More than a movie, Oz became a cultural touchstone, a way to initiate young children into American life. Because of the monster ratings, the annual airing became known as the "Children's Super Bowl," and a debate raged over the appropriate age (nine? six? three?) for a child's first encounter with Hamilton's deathly scary Wicked Witch and her flying monkeys. In 1967 NBC agreed to triple the license fee, taking over the annual ritual. In 1970 the most emotional of these audiences assembled for the first showing after the death of Judy Garland, at the age of forty-seven. Upon hearing the sad news, Ray Bolger said he cried like a baby. The movie kept attracting a cultlike following, only virtually everyone was in the cult. After a dozen more annual showings, it was estimated that more than a billion people had seen *The Wizard of Oz*, more than any other motion picture.

The Wizard of Oz remained so popular on television that MGM was able to increase its broadcasting fee to $1 million per showing. However, to justify such a high price, the network proceeded to cut segments of the movie in order to maximize the time for commercials. One of the first things to go was the tribute to L. Frank Baum's original book in the opening credits. And so it became possible for millions of people to watch *The Wizard of Oz* and not even realize that the film is based on a book.

Throughout the network TV years, other strange things happened to Baum's legacy. Most of his books went out of print, and in many locations *The Wonderful Wizard of Oz* and its sequels were banned by schools and public libraries. Religious groups were offended by the concept of a "good witch," by Glinda's devotion to the "secret arts which we have learned from Nature," and by the teaching to children of the lesson of self-reliance rather than reliance on God. Some followers of Senator Joe McCarthy proclaimed Baum's books socialist, in part because of the Tin Woodman's comment in the fifth book that "money is not known in the Land of Oz. We have no rich, and no poor; for what one wishes the others all try to give him, in order to make him happy."

The Florida Department of State put the works of Baum on its list of "Books Not Circulated" because they were "unwholesome for the children." Similar edicts were issued in other states, districts, and counties. "Lessons drawn from *The Wizard of Oz* undermine religious education," stated seven fundamentalist families who challenged its inclusion on a school reading list before a U.S. District Court in eastern Tennessee. "Females assumed traditional male roles in the book, and it projected witches as being good." (The families actually won this case, but the ruling was overturned.) Remarkably, the very same issues that Matilda Joslyn Gage fought over were being stirred up again in the era of ERA, the Equal Rights Amendment that was shot down in the 1970s.

A new theory was hatched to explain what *The Wizard of Oz* was really about. A high school history teacher named Henry Littlefield was trying to get his students interested in learning about the Gilded Age, and so he developed "a teaching mechanism which is guaranteed to reach any level of student." L. Frank Baum wrote *The Wonderful Wizard of Oz*, he said, as a "Parable of Populism," the political movement that spread through America in the 1880s and 1890s. All the references were there, he said, between the lines. The Yellow Brick Road represents the gold standard, and Dorothy's silver slippers represent the Populist effort to use silver to back the dollar, so more money could be issued. The Scarecrow is the western farmer, the Tin Man the eastern industrial worker, and the Cowardly Lion is Williams Jennings Bryan, the Populist candidate marching to confront President McKinley, the Wizard, who lives in Washington, the Emerald City. Someone else pointed out that Oz must stand for ounce, a measure of gold. Littlefield published his notion in an academic history journal in 1964, just as America's appetite for political conspiracy stories was ratcheting up, and the strange theory took root and spread over the years.

In 1992, in response to an article about the theory in the *New York Times*, leading Oz scholar Michael Patrick Hearn wrote a letter saying that there was "no evidence that Baum's story is in any way a Populist allegory." Littlefield, in turn, agreed that he intended it only as a teaching mechanism, acknowledging that "there is no basis in fact to consider Baum a supporter of turn-of-the-century Populist ideology." But then came the Internet. Among the Internet's many wonders is its ability to spread seductive misinformation, and if you look online, you'll see that the Parable of Populism theory of Oz has been received in many quarters as conventional wisdom.

Yet it's always been the case that *The Wizard of Oz* has meant different things to different people, and that meaning changes with repeated viewings. On videocassettes and later DVDs, the movie became a gigantic seller, and this meant that people no longer had to wait to see it once per year. Since children are naturally inclined to watch their favorite movies again and again, the new generations devoured it, committing the classic to memory in a way their parents and grandparents never could.

There have always been new interpretations of the L. Frank Baum story, but they almost always fail because of the inevitable comparison with the original. Many attempts have been made, for instance, to reinterpret Oz in a more adult context by sexualizing Dorothy, but this is always seen for what it is: a form of literary child abuse. Once in a while, however, creators get it right by reinterpreting the story while remaining true to Baum. *The Wiz* recast the tale as an African American dream, taking Broadway by storm in the late 1970s—although the film version staring Diana Ross as Dorothy and Michael Jackson as the Scarecrow bombed at the box office. *Wicked*, Gregory Maguire's best-selling book, tells the ingenious backstory of the Wicked Witch of the West, and the stage adaptation has gone on to become the most successful musical extravaganza in recent times, a phenomenon on Broadway and in dozens of cities worldwide. It seems that audiences admire not only originality but also respect for the spirit of the original.

As *The Wizard of Oz* has captivated more and more people over the years, there is one group that has never forgotten the darkest episode that figured into the story's creation. Those people are the Lakota Sioux. Few Americans realize that L. Frank Baum wrote those terrible things back in 1890, but the Native Americans living on the reservations in South Dakota are more aware of it than ever before. Today the area that encompasses the Standing Rock and Pine Ridge reservations remains the most impoverished region of America, an area of dumping grounds and toxic uranium mines.

Some of Frank Baum's descendants have tried to reconcile how those editorials could have been written by the same man who created America's greatest story for children. "How is it possible?" asks Mac Hudson, a great-great-grandson. Hudson concluded that Baum was "an ordinary racist" who was saying the same things that most white people of the time were saying, yet that explanation didn't provide any comfort to him. So in the summer of 2006, Hudson and his cousin Gita Dorothy Morena traveled to Pine Ridge to apologize to the descendants of the Wounded Knee massacre on behalf of the Baum family. "We're here to say we're sorry," Hudson said. "I just wanted to talk to the survivors and to feel what they've gone through," recalls Gita.

Gita came to realize that the general attitude toward Native Americans "is a big problem, way bigger than our family, and way bigger than L. Frank Baum." She arrived on the Lakota lands with the message that her great-grandfather "is accountable for his actions, words and attitudes, just as we all are. Our actions, words and attitudes are what create the future." The Baum family members then offered their heartfelt apology. "An apology," says Gita, "is an atonement," a way to become at one with the wrong you have done, to bring it into consciousness and to deal with it. The Lakota at the ceremony accepted the family's apology. Then they all celebrated, with a spirited drum ceremony around a campfire that reverberated into the night.

Many of the sights that inspired key elements of L. Frank Baum's story or changed his life are still there. In Syracuse, Hattie's house, where Frank first met Maud, remains standing, and a segment of the old Plank Road remains preserved in the north of the city.

In Peekskill, New York, a stretch of yellow brick road is still there, and by the town historian's account, these are probably the very same bricks that the teenage Frank traversed on his way to the old military academy on top of the hill, now home to an elementary school. At Cornell, Maud Gage's old dormitory, Sage College, still stands but was converted into the university's business school. The parlor remains preserved as a nineteenth-century room, and in a bureau drawer there one can find a transcript of the letters of Maud's classmate Jessie Boulton.

Baum's Castorine is still going strong after more than 130 years, making innovative lubricating products out of its factory in Rome, New York. In Fayetteville the Greek Revival home of Henry and Matilda Gage still stands and is being restored by the Matilda Joslyn Gage Foundation to match a set of photographs taken in 1887 by her son-in-law. In Aberdeen, South Dakota, the Dacotah Prairie Museum contains exhibits relating to the Baum family's time living there and also hosts a preserved version of the Gage family's front parlor from Fayetteville. A different house stands on the site of the Baum home on South Kline Street, across from the library where many of the family letters and papers are held. North of town one can visit Storybook Land, which contains a Land of Oz theme park, complete with a hearty tribute to Baum as well as a winding Yellow Brick Road surrounded by all the characters and scenery from the story. In Bloomington, Indiana, one can find the gravesite of baby Dorothy Louise Gage, discovered in recent times by Sally Roesch Wagner, the director of the Gage Foundation.

In Chicago none of the locations where the Baums lived exist in any recognizable way, but many remnants of the Columbian Exposition remain, including the grounds of the Midway Plaisance and the expo's Palace of Fine Arts, which is now the Museum of Science and Industry. One can also visit the Fine Arts Building where W. W. Denslow had his studio as well as the Art Institute of Chicago, which held the World's Parliament of Religions. Swami Vivekananda's Vedanta Society is located near the old fairgrounds, but has plans to move to an expanded temple in the suburbs. The swami spent many weeks staying at the Hales' home near Lincoln Park, and he spent many hours meditating at the park's entrance. Today that entrance is guarded by a magnificent statue of the Tin Man, in a zone that has been renamed Oz Park. Statues of the Scarecrow, the Cowardly Lion, and Dorothy and Toto have also been put up, funded by citizens who donated money for engraved yellow bricks. The whole park pays tribute to the man who created *The Wizard of Oz* not far from there.

In Los Angeles, Ozcot is no more, but on the nearby Hollywood Walk of Fame one can find sidewalk stars honoring most of the principal players in the MGM movie. The latest to receive their star were the Munchkins, with several surviving little people attending a glorious unveiling ceremony in 2007. But there's something missing on the walk: a star for the man who discovered the Land of Oz and made all the others possible.

When it comes to legacies, perhaps no one has been more overlooked than Matilda Joslyn Gage. Her two colleagues and coauthors, Elizabeth Cady Stanton and Susan B. Anthony, were named the two most influential American women who ever lived on a recent list of the "100 Most Influential Americans," published by the *Atlantic*. Yet Gage, who fought a more principled fight than either of them, is rarely mentioned in histories of the movement. She remains obscure outside her old hometown, where her house has been designated a landmark by the state of New York.

Also remarkable about the *Atlantic*'s list is how a quarter of all the figures on it factored in this book's story — including Edison, Rockefeller, Barnum, Twain, Emerson, Olmsted, and Samuel Goldwyn, the man who purchased the film rights to Baum's novel. It's true that Frank Baum wasn't one of America's Founding Fathers, and he didn't hold the Union together. He didn't invent a ubiquitous technology, and he wasn't a great captain of industry; he never ran for president, and he probably didn't start a new religion or faith. But America is also a nation of storytellers, and few Americans have created stories powerful enough to join together five generations and counting. Certainly, no one on any list of American luminaries has ignited the imagination of the world quite like L. Frank Baum. *Ain't it the truth? Ain't it the truth?*

ACKNOWLEDGMENTS

NOTES

CREDITS

INDEX

ACKNOWLEDGMENTS

My very earliest memory is being scared out of my wits by the Great and Powerful Oz and those flying monkeys and that Wicked Witch of the West as she cackled and wailed, then melted away. And like most Americans and millions of others around the world, I've been hooked on *The Wizard of Oz* ever since. I read L. Frank Baum's classic novel a long time ago, and since my career has been focused on the understanding of creativity, I've long been intrigued by the question of how one man was able to come up with so many icons of the imagination and pack them into one story.

But the journey of this book really began one evening a few years ago, while rereading *The Wonderful Wizard of Oz,* this time aloud at bedtime with my seven-year-old daughter Lily. In seeing her reaction to the century-old novel, and in being amazed at how fresh it still seemed, that question was brought into sharp focus. We turned to Baum's brief biography page in the back of the book. He was in his early forties when he began writing it? That was my age. His career had been littered with disappointments? Who couldn't relate? His greatest achievement was just around the corner? Who wouldn't want to believe that?

I ended up on a road of research that took me on seven separate trips to the Syracuse area, where Baum spent his first thirty-two years, and I traveled to his other stomping grounds: to Aberdeen, South Dakota, and to Chicago and Los Angeles. Along the way I encountered a minefield of misconceptions about Baum and Oz on one side and untold aspects of his experiences on the other. It seemed to me that what I could contribute was not a complete biography of Baum's life but rather a story. It's the story of his own journey of self-discovery and how this process of finding himself inspired and paralleled the universal myth we all know and love. That specific quest unfolded, mainly, over just twenty years of his life.

My thanks begin with my agents, the incomparable duo of Lane Zachary and Todd Shuster, and to Rachel Sussman, who was so perceptive during the writing of the proposal. Thanks to my colleague Doug Starr for introducing me to them. My gratitude goes to everyone at Houghton Mifflin, but especially to Deanne Urmy, for her fine judgment, and to my editor Nicole Angeloro, who championed the book and improved the manuscript in countless ways. Shouts also go out to Jane Rosenman, who first spotted the golden path, and to Eamon Dolan, for his brief but brilliant role as the guardian of the gate.

My research was enriched at the Wonderful Weekend of Oz, an annual event put on by the Matilda Joslyn Gage Foundation. Attending the first and second of these Oktoberfests for Oz scholars, in 2006 and 2007, I was able to spend time in the Gage House in Fayetteville, New York, and visit other historical sites. By the third Oz weekend, in 2008, I was given the chance to present some of my research to the group. Thanks go to Sue Boland and everyone at the foundation, but special thanks are reserved for Sally Roesch Wagner, its founder and director, as she is the one who has rescued Matilda from history and has been working to restore Gage and the Gage House at the very same time.

These weekends brought me in contact with descendants of L. Frank Baum. I have learned a great deal from great-grandson Robert A. Baum and from great-great-grandson Mac Hudson. I am grateful to them, and to great-granddaughter Gita Dorothy Morena for her wisdom, her awareness, and her generosity of spirit. I also thank Michael Patrick Hearn and John Fricke, the two best Ozologists on the planet. However, no endorsements by any of these great and powerful people are implied. I'm responsible for any errors in this book and any shortcomings are entirely my own.

Thanks continue to flow, to Barb Evans and the producers of the annual Oz-Stravaganza weekends in Baum's birthplace of Chittenango, New York, and to Linda Ryan and staff at the Fayetteville Free Library, to Nicolette and staff at the Syracuse University Library, where I spent dozens of hours with the L. Frank Baum Papers, to John Curran at the Peekskill History Museum, to Michael Flanagan at the Onondaga Historical Association, to Charles F. Mowry at Baum's Castorine, whose grandfather invested in the firm that purchased the company from Frank Baum in 1888, to the people who preside over the Matilda Joslyn Gage Papers at the Schlesinger Library at Harvard's Radcliffe Institute, to Shirley Arment and staff at the Alexander Mitchell Public Library in Aberdeen, to those who dwell at the Chicago History Museum, and to a mysterious man in a flowing robe, the current swami at the Vivekananda Vedanta Society of Chicago.

My gratitude also goes to the members of the International Wizard of Oz Club, now residing at ozclub.org, an incredible network of Baum fans, especially to Peter Hanff and Marcus Mebes for all their help with photographs and images, and to Jay Walker and everyone at Walker Digital for all their encouragement and support, to the inspirational members of the TED community, to the writing teachers of my past, Drew Yanno and John Maguire, to the members of the Ridgefield Starbucks Writing and Drinking Society, to Christina Nolan at the Ridgefield Public Library, for putting up with me camping out for hours every day in the area I came to call "the Nineteenth-century Room," and to a librarian who kept vigil over the book stacks and wore a nametag that simply said "Dorothy."

A big bowl of wholesome crunchy thankfulness goes around to my friends, my parents, and my family, but first to Lily and Michaela, who somehow changed into lovely young ladies while I was writing this book, and foremost to my wonderful wife, Amy, for all her love and cooking. And to our little dogs, Buddy and Frankie, too. Finally, a tip of the hat to all the fans of *The Wizard of Oz* everywhere, for keeping the Baum fire burning.

by Lily Isabel
Schwartz, age 8

NOTES

The following handles are used for the author's primary research locations:

ABERDEEN: L. Frank Baum Papers, Alexander Mitchell Public Library, Aberdeen, SD

BARNUM: P. T. Barnum Museum, Bridgeport, CT

CASTORINE: Baum's Castorine Company, Rome, NY

CHICAGO: Chicago History Museum

CHICART: Art Institute of Chicago

CHICSCI: Chicago Museum of Science and Industry

COLUMBIA: The Wizard of Oz Club Papers, Butler Library, Columbia University

CORNELL: Rare Books and Manuscripts Collection, Kroch Library, Cornell University

DAKOTA: Dacotah Prairie Museum, Aberdeen, SD

ERIE: Erie Canal Museum, Syracuse, NY

FAYETTE: Matilda Joslyn Gage Archive, Fayetteville (NY) Free Library

GAGE: Matilda Joslyn Gage Foundation and House, Fayetteville, NY

HARVARD: Matilda Joslyn Gage Papers, Schlesinger Library, Radcliffe Institute, Harvard University

ONONDAGA: Onondaga Historical Association, Syracuse, NY

PEEKSKILL: Peekskill (NY) History Museum

SYRACUSE: L. Frank Baum Papers, Bird Library, Syracuse University

THEOSOPHY: Theosophical Library Center, Altadena, CA

UCHICAGO: University of Chicago Library

VEDANTA: Vivekananda Vedanta Society of Chicago

WALKER: Jay S. Walker Library, Private Collection, Ridgefield, CT

YALE: L. Frank Baum Collection, Beinecke Rare Book and Manuscript Library, Yale University

Abbreviations for principal figures:

LFB: Lyman Frank Baum

MGB: Maud Gage Baum (wife)

TCG: Thomas Clarkson Gage (brother-in-law)

MJG: Matilda Joslyn Gage (mother-in-law)

SBA: Susan Brownell Anthony (mother-in-law's colleague)

WWOZ is used to abbreviate the primary text:

L. Frank Baum, *The Wonderful Wizard of Oz* (Chicago: George M. Hill, 1900; repr. New York: HarperCollins/Books of Wonder, 1993).

Prologue: America's Adventure

x   *"Then a strange thing happened"*: LFB, *WWOZ*, 17.
"The story really seemed to write itself": LFB quoted in Jeanne O. Potter, "The Man Who Invented the Wizard of Oz," *Los Angeles Times Sunday Magazine*, August 13, 1939, 12.
"With this Pencil I wrote the ms.": SYRACUSE.
"books with jewel names": "The Oz Timeline," an LFB and Oz chronology compiled by the Centennial Committee of the International Wizard of Oz Club, www.oz-club.org; also see Frank J. Baum and Russell P. MacFall, *To Please a Child* (Chicago: Reilly & Lee Co., 1961), 114.

xi   "somehow *manage to provide*": LFB letter to Cynthia Stanton Baum, January 16, 1894, ABERDEEN.
"infidel" . . . *"satanic"*: Sally Roesch Wagner, *She Who Holds the Sky* (Aberdeen, SD: Sky Carrier Press, 1999), 3. Also see *History of Woman Suffrage*, vol. 1, ed. Elizabeth Cady Stanton, Susan B. Anthony, and Matilda Joslyn Gage (New York: Fowler & Wells, 1881), 543.
"damn fool": Baum and MacFall, *To Please*, 44.

xii   *"vital powers disintegrate"* . . . *"locked in the labyrinth"*: Joseph Campbell, *The Hero with a Thousand Faces* (New York: Pantheon, 1949; repr. New York: Holtzbrinck, 1989), 50; full quote on five-CD set (Audio Renaissance, 2000), read by Ralph Blum.
America's first native fairy tale: LFB called it a "modernized fairy tale" in the introduction to *WWOZ*. Michael Patrick Hearn cites the demand in the 1890s for "an indigenously American literature" in LFB, *The Annotated Wizard of Oz*, ed. Michael Patrick Hearn (New York: Clarkson Potter, 1973; repr. New York: W. W. Norton, 2000), 5.

xiii   *"greatest bestseller in modern fiction"*: Jon Fricke, Jay Scarfone, and William Stillman, *The Official 50th Anniversary Pictorial History of The Wizard of Oz* (New York: Warner Books, 1989), 125.
among the American Film Institute's all-time top ten: For complete AFI lists see www.afi.com/tvevents/100years/movies10.aspx. In 2008, the AFI named it the number one fantasy film of all time.
eyes stopped on a filing cabinet . . . *"the land is called"*: Baum and MacFall, *To Please*, 110. See chapter 16, notes for p. 273 for more information.

xiv   *"private Pantheon of dreams"*: Campbell, *Hero*, 2.

1. No Place Like Home

4   *"There were lovely patches of greensward"*: LFB, *WWOZ*, 22.
still living with his parents: SYRACUSE.

5   *there were six bedrooms*: Baum and MacFall, *To Please*, 21.
rail-thin man with dark circles: Photographs, SYRACUSE.
devout Methodist turned Episcopalian: SYRACUSE.
purchased this nearly four-acre estate in 1866: ONONDAGA.
"the Rose Kingdom": LFB, *Tik-Tok of Oz* (Chicago: Reilly & Britton, 1914), 40.
clusters of apple, pear, and plum trees: Baum and MacFall, *To Please*, 20.
nearly three hundred acres: ONONDAGA.
"Few may be able": "Extensive Ornamental Barn," *Cultivator & Country Gentleman*, August 29, 1972, 554, ONONDAGA.

hired a cook . . . and a gardener: ONONDAGA.

6   *Hattie . . . married*: SYRACUSE.
having been stricken: Baum and MacFall, *To Please*, cite congenital heart disease as the cause of LFB's heart problems, but the fact that he was able to live for so long indicates rheumatic fever. According to the Mayo Clinic, the disease permanently damages heart valves but often goes into remission for long periods.
schooled at home: SYRACUSE.

7   *Dickens . . . Thackeray . . . Shakespeare*: Baum and MacFall, *To Please*, 24.
"longed to write a great novel": LFB inscription inside *Mother Goose in Prose*, to Mary Baum Brewster, 1897, ABERDEEN.
calling it Spring Farm: ONONDAGA.
"Kut-kut-kut, ka-daw-kut" . . . "yellow hen squatting in the opposite corner": LFB, *Ozma of Oz* (Chicago: Reilly & Britton, 1907), 24–25.

8   *"Can't you see, we're busy?"*: Aunt Em, in *The Wizard of Oz* (MGM, 1939) on DVD (Warner Brothers, 1999).
Plank Road . . . the first passageway of its kind . . . Completed in 1846: www.northsyracuse.org/history/.
travelers had to pay a series of tolls . . . the very first tollgate . . . spy horses of all different colors: Susan Ferrara, *The Family of the Wizard: The Baums of Syracuse* (Philadelphia: Xlibris Corp., 2000), 75–78.

9   *Syracuse Weighlock Building*: ERIE.
"rich and pleasant" . . . "beautiful and wonderful" . . . "green glow": LFB, WWOZ, 42, 137.
"beautiful homes, splendid clothes, and ample food" . . . "something was wrong": LFB, *Glinda of Oz* (Chicago: Reilly & Britton, 1920).

10   *"That's all it is!"*: Glinda, in *The Wizard of Oz* (MGM).

2. An Unexpected Journey

12   *"There were several roads . . . paved with yellow bricks"*: LFB, WWOZ, 37.
enroll his son in the Peekskill: Baum and MacFall, *To Please*, 23.
Frank resisted: Ibid., 23.
Her empty religious piety: Ibid., 84.

13   *traveling down the Hudson River*: PEEKSKILL.
stepped onto one of the many roads: PEEKSKILL.
Thousands of these bricks: Author interview with John Curran, town historian, Peekskill, NY, August 2007. Also see Tony Seideman, "The Yellow Brick Road—Underneath Our Feet," *Peekskill Evening Star*, December 12, 2002, 6.
there were yellow brick roads all around town: Ibid.
still survives today: Author visit, August 2007.
original military headquarters: PEEKSKILL.
By the center staircase . . . gold-plated insignia: Peekskill Military Academy alumni website, www.pma-alumni.org.

14   *Upton's Tactics*: *Academician*, newspaper of the Peekskill Military Academy, May 12, 1868, PEEKSKILL.
"The government made treaties": Albert Marrin, *Sitting Bull and His World* (New York: Dutton, 2000), 7.
"I complained to my father" . . . "The teachers were heartless": Baum and MacFall, *To*, 23.

15 *clutched his chest . . . Frank's time at Peekskill . . . Mr. Baum bought his son:* Ibid., 24.
16 *the* Rose Lawn Home Journal: SYRACUSE and ABERDEEN.
    "Wit and Wisdom" . . . "In ancient days": SYRACUSE.
    "the poetry of our age": William Dean Howells, *The Rise of Silas Lapham* (1885; repr.
    New York: Signet Classics, 2002), 57.
17 *"It was such a period as seldom occurs":* Thomas Mellon, *Thomas Mellon and His
    Times* (1885; repr. Pittsburgh: University of Pittsburgh Press, 1996), 238.
18 *A mad gusher:* Ron Chernow, *Titan: The Life of John D. Rockefeller, Sr.* (New York:
    Random House, 2004), 85.
    "vast stores of wealth": Ibid., 76.
    "Baum has gone to PA": Ferrara, *Family,* 51.
    Cherry Tree Run: "Accident to a Merchant," *New York Times,* October 20, 1885.
    the Cynthia Oil Works: SYRACUSE.
    Second National Bank: ONONDAGA.
    bank run by Jay Cooke: Chernow, *Titan,* 160.
19 *"close application to business":* obituary in *Syracuse Courier,* February 15, 1887: SYR-
    ACUSE.
    put Rose Lawn up for sale: ONONDAGA.
    "The elegant country residence" . . . family was forced: ONONDAGA.
    the highest bidder: Ferrara, *Family.*
    turn Spring Farm: ONONDAGA.
20 *a series of inquiries:* Natalie Flynn, "The Historical Evolution of Dating in America,"
    www.oberlin.edu/faculty/ndarling/transition/group21/history.html.
    "B. W. Baum and Sons": Brochure cover, ONONDAGA.
    "first prize for Houdan Fowls": Ferrara, *Family,* 124.
    The Poultry Record: ONONDAGA.
    The Book of Hamburgs: Published by Stoddard, 1886; copy at the New York Public
    Library.
21 *bank had finally auctioned off:* Ferrara, *Family,* 86.
    only a small fraction: Article from ONONDAGA.
    her own School of Oratory: SYRACUSE.
    Mother Goose Entertainment . . . *portrayed by Cynthia Baum . . . one of their shows
    to Chittenango:* Ferrara, *Family,* 121.
22 *"Uncle Doc," Dr. Adam Clarke Baum:* SYRACUSE.
    border town called Bolivar: Ferrara, *Family,* 126.
    first Baum Opera House: SYRACUSE.
    drafts of five scripts . . . registered three of these plays: Ibid.
23 *premiered at the Baum Opera House:* SYRACUSE.
24 *"the Devil's Synagogues" . . . Astor Place Riot . . . "God punishing them":* Wikipedia,
    "Theater in the United States."
    In the eyes of many churchgoers: Thanks to the theater historian Oscar Andrew
    Hammerstein for improving this passage on theater history and reviewing its accu-
    racy.
    under the name George Brooks: SYRACUSE.
    a young Samuel Shubert: "The Shubert Brothers," in *Encyclopedia of World Biography,*
    vol. Sc–St, 2nd ed. (Farmington Hills, MI: Gale Research, 2006).
25 *Christmas holiday of 1881:* SYRACUSE.
    wife of the dry goods merchant: Ibid.
    worked part-time at the store: Ibid.

26 Hattie extended an invitation. . . "Show business doesn't leave me much time" . . . "different from the girls" . . . "pretty but independent": Baum and MacFall, To Please, 42–43.

3. A Girl in a Man's World

28 "Won't you go with me?": LFB, WWOZ, 31.
aboard the train: Maud's trip was likely on the Ithaca, Auburn & Western Railroad; Ontario & Western Railway Historical Society, www.nyow.org. See nyow.railfan. net/nyow/auburn.
Cornell was the first major: Charlotte Williams Conable, Women at Cornell: The Myth of Equal Education (Ithaca and London: Cornell University Press, 1977).
29 Sage College was fashioned: Ibid., 54.
interior featured: Ibid., 81.
Thick area rugs . . . fireplace mantel trimmed: Photograph of old parlor interior hanging in current parlor, author visits, 2007 and 2008.
Clarkson, had made it through Cornell: SYRACUSE.
Her mother wished for Maud: SYRACUSE.
"I dearly love dancing": Letters of Jessie Mary Boulton while at Sage College, 1879–1883, CORNELL, September 15, 1880.
30 "Her name is Gage and she is lively": Ibid.
"A girl scarcely dares": Boulton letters, October 6, 1880.
tuition . . . set at $25: Cornell University Register, 1878–83, CORNELL.
roommate by the name of Miss Josie Baum: Baum and MacFall, To Please, 42.
Their room was bare: Ibid.
entrance examinations: Cornell Register, 1878–83.
31 listed on September 16, 1880: Cornell Sun, CORNELL.
"Boys or young men" . . . "are quite rude here": Boulton letters, October 8, 1879.
"Dictionary of Slang": Cornellian, 1878.
the typical meal: Boulton letters, October 4, 1879.
32 came down to eat seven minutes late: Boulton letters, January 30, 1881.
only thirty women living at Sage: Conable, Women at Cornell, 84.
were to leave before 10:00 p.m.: Boulton letters, October 4, 1879.
Charlie Thorp, to dine at her table . . . Jessie invited Maud Gage: Boulton letters, October 17, 1880.
33 "Cornell was no place for lively girls" . . . Maud Gage for the position of class marshal . . . "We have had a sensation here": Boulton letters, October 6, 1880.
34 "No one will dare injure a person": LFB, WWOZ, 31.
"I'm glad all the girls are not like": Conable, Women at Cornell, 116.
"The Sage Maidens": Cornell Sun, November 30, 1880.
"Matilda, may I ask your age?": Cornell Sun, September 29, 1880.
35 "I am alarmed for the future": Boulton letters, October 6, 1880.
"A great many students will go home": Cornell Sun, October 29, 1880.
"The excuse that the mock ticket": Ibid.
36 Matilda Joslyn Gage herself was scheduled: Cornell Sun, February 15, 1881.
personally petitioned Ezra Cornell: Conable, Women at Cornell, 36–37, 58.
"would sink at once from the rank": Ibid., 77.

"Women's Rights monomaniacs": Cornellian, 1871.

"Those condemned as sorcerers and witches": MJG, Woman, Church and State (1893; repr. New York: Humanity Books, 2002), 246.

A chronicle of women's struggle: The Concise History of Woman Suffrage: Selections from the Classic Work of Stanton, Anthony, Gage and Harper, ed. MariJo and Paul Buhle (Chicago: University of Illinois Press, 1978; excerpts from the six volumes originally published from 1881 through 1922).

the only child of the town's only physician: "Matilda Joslyn Gage," in Notable American Women 1607–1950: A Biographical Dictionary, ed. Edward T. James, Janet Wilson James, and Paul S. Boyer (Cambridge, MA: Belknap Press, 1974), 4.

37 *Dr. Joslyn . . . was a bona fide freethinker*: Ibid.

one of the earliest outposts of the Underground Railroad: Ibid.

set off for the Clinton Liberal Institute: See historical sketch of the school at Mohawk Valley Library System website, www.mvls.info/lhg/fortplain.

building a hospital: Obituary of Henry Gage, FAYETTE.

smart location by the docks of the feeder canal: Author tour of Gage neighborhood in Fayetteville, conducted by Sue Bolton of the Gage Foundation, October 2007.

38 *"The true religion believes in"*: Report of the International Council of Women, Washington, DC, March 25 to April 1, 1888 (Washington, DC: National Women's Suffrage Association, 1888), 347, HARVARD.

"Do not let the church or the state": MJG, preface to Woman, Church and State.

"with a palpitating heart": Report of the International Council of Women, 347.

"There will be a long moral warfare": MJG speech at the Third National Women's Rights Convention, Syracuse, NY, 1852, quoted in Wagner, She Who Holds, 2.

"satanic": Ibid., 3.

"a woman that feareth the Lord": Rev. Byron Sunderland, "Discourse to Young Ladies," sermon of January 22, 1857 (Washington: Cornelius Wendell, 1857).

39 *"infidels"*: Concise History of Woman Suffrage, vol. 1, 543.

"While the feminine propagandists": Ibid., 608.

"medium-sized and lady-like": Notable American Women.

Women's Loyal National League . . . "There can be no permanent peace": Wagner, She Who Holds, 7.

conspired to cut off all funding . . . to form the National Woman Suffrage: Ibid., 8.

40 *Susan B. Anthony was arrested*: Ida Husted Harper, The Life and Work of Susan B. Anthony: A Story of the Evolution of the Status of Women, vol. I (Indianapolis and Kansas City: the Bowen-Merrill Co., 1898).

"small-brained, pale-faced": Wagner, She Who Holds, 13.

Mrs. Gage clutched a three-foot-long scroll: Ibid., 18.

41 *Amos Bronson Alcott*: Cornell Sun, November 15, 16, 17, 1880.

42 *"one of the most conspicuous advocates"*: Cornell Sun, February 25, 1881.

striking appearance . . . "tall and queenly": National Tribune, 1887, FAYETTE.

"No rebellion has been of like": MJG, Woman, Church and State.

"Her discourse was well received": Cornell Sun, February 28, 1881.

43 *"Maud's mother, lectured here"*: Boulton letters, February 27, 1881.

"Rev. Bridgman (Baptist) preached": Boulton letters, October 3, 1879.

a chapter of Kappa Alpha Theta: Ibid.

the toastmaster: Cornell Sun, March 7, 1881.

the Bal Masque: Cornell Sun, January 24, 1881.

4. Heart of a Tin Man

46   *"I soon grew to love her"*: LFB, *WWOZ*, 70.

    the Thanksgiving weekend . . . invitation from Josie: Boulton letters, December 1, 1881.

    "The doctors killed Garfield": "Guiteau Gets Angry," *New York Times*, December 6, 1881.

47   *other spiritual movements that sprouted*: Conable, *Women at Cornell*, 30.

    the "Burned-over District": Ibid., 29.

    "dreadfully wicked" . . . The raps indicated: Boulton letters, October 31, 1881.

49   *Plank Road . . . being dismantled*: www.northsyracuse.org/history/.

    the steam-powered woodchopper: Robert Henry, "Plank Road Perhaps Gave Birth to the Yellow Brick Road," November 22, 2000, ONONDAGA.

    "I was born the son of a woodman": LFB, *WWOZ*, 70.

50   *"You see . . . in this country"*: LFB, *Ozma of Oz*, 258.

    took Maud by the arm, and escorted her over: Baum and MacFall, *To Please*, 43.

    "Frank Baum . . . I want you to know Maud Gage": Ibid.

51   *"The Evening Song"*: Cornell University Glee Club, www.gleeclub.com/experience/cornellsongs.php.

52   *"very handsome and attractive"*: MGB letter to Jack Snow, June 21, 1943, SYRACUSE.

    "call" to her home: Flynn, "Historical Evolution of Dating."

    "argumentative" . . . "detect and register": *Weekly Recorder*, July 1, 1880, FAYETTE.

    man hater: Wagner, *She Who Holds*, 33.

    the winter term . . . was to begin: CORNELL.

    the pale yellow: FAYETTE; author tour of Gage House, October 2006.

53   *first home . . . indoor plumbing*: FAYETTE.

    Escaped slaves on their way . . . holed up in a crawlspace: *Notable American Women*.

    the National Citizen and Ballot Box . . . "revolutionize the country": Wagner, *She Who Holds*, 31–32.

    Anthony had carved her initials: Author tour of Gage House, GAGE.

    front parlor . . . lit by oil lamp: Self-Guided Tour, Gage Parlor, Gallery N: DAKOTA.

    reserved for reading, writing: 1887 photograph of MJG by LFB.

54   *Henry Gage, was largely immobilized from typhus*: Obituary of Henry Gage, FAYETTE.

    "woman of force": Ramona B. Bowden (grand-niece of MJG), "The Creation of Oz —A Private Glimpse," DeWitt (NY) *News-Times*, July 3, 1975, D4, SYRACUSE.

    "one of those fortunate few": "Letter from Mrs. Gage," *Syracuse Daily Standard*, November 16, 1871, GAGE.

55   *"Preceding Causes"*: *Concise History of Woman Suffrage*, 51.

56   *"I thought I had beaten the Wicked Witch"*: LFB, *WWOZ*, 71.

57   *She was known as Inana*: Karen Armstrong, *A History of God* (New York: Knopf, 1993), 5.

    giant log cabins . . . the Sky Woman descends: Victoria Sherrow, *The Iroquois Indians* (Philadelphia: Chelsea House Publishers, 1992).

    Matilda wrote a series of articles: Sally Roesch Wagner, *Sisters in Spirit: Haudenosaunee (Iroquois) Influence on Early American Feminists* (Summertown, TN: Native Voices, 2001), 28.

    "the division of power between the sexes": Ibid, 48.

58 *"The women and Mother Earth are one"*: Ibid, 59.
   precisely the opposite: Ibid, 30–31.
   "England protects its hunting dogs": Ibid, 19.

5. Roadblock

60 *"before them a great ditch"*: LFB, *WWOZ*, 91.
   running for two nights: SYRACUSE.
   reserved seats for The Maid of Arran: Ibid.
   "The rain has laid the dust": Ibid.
   "beautiful stage settings": Ibid.
   also included Frank's aunt: Ibid.
61 *"Mr. Baum has shown talent"*: Ibid.
   the triple doors: Photograph of Grand Opera House, Oz-Stravaganza display in Chittenango, NY, May 2007.
   home from college to attend: Letter from MGB to Jack Snow, June 21, 1943, SYRACUSE.
   Matilda Gage must have come: MJG letter, HARVARD.
62 *who visits the island of Arran*: Typescript of *The Maid of Arran*, YALE.
   "Put me in that beautiful picture?": Ibid.
63 *signed up for an extensive tour*: SYRACUSE.
   "decided dramatic powers": Ibid.
   "liked the Maid very much": MJG letter, HARVARD.
64 *"A more perfectly mounted"*: SYRACUSE.
   "a bright sparkling drama" . . . *"pleased every one"*: Ibid.
   for an entire week beginning June 24: Ibid.
   "rather heavy for the part of Shiela": Ibid.
65 *a professional tour manager*: Ibid.
   picked his younger brother: Ibid.
   concluded negotiations: Ibid.
66 *Frank proposed right in the front parlor*: Baum and MacFall, *To Please*, 44.
   "I will not have my daughter": Ibid.
   "All right mother": Ibid.
   let out a piercing laugh: Ibid.
67 *"dogma that has wrecked true religion"*: MJG, *Woman, Church and State*, 484.
   "historical rejection of the Mother Goddess": Joseph Campbell with Bill Moyers, *The Power of Myth* (New York: Doubleday, 1988), 48, based on 1987 PBS television interviews, also on audio CD (Highbridge Audio, 2001).
   a member of the Fayetteville Baptist Church: FAYETTE.
   drop out of Cornell: CORNELL.
68 *stint of ten days in Toronto*: "Route for the Maid of Arran, 1882 and 1883," SYRACUSE.
   Powers' Opera House: Ibid.
   October 9 through 15 at the Academy: Ibid.
   "did big business in Chicago": Ibid.
   told Maud he was adding that city: MGB letter to TCG, November 26, 1882.
69 *no breaks in the schedule*: SYRACUSE.
   The wedding of L. Frank Baum: Ibid.
   In attendance were: ABERDEEN.

"Maud Gage is to be married tomorrow": Boulton letters, November 8, 1882.
the open staircase: Sue Bolton research document on Gage House, FAYETTE.
his silk top hat: Gita Dorothy Morena, *The Wisdom of Oz* (Berkeley, CA: Frog Ltd., 2001), 181.
"The promises of the bride": FAYETTE.

70   *honeymoon in Saratoga Springs*: Baum and MacFall, *To Please*, 45.
Thanksgiving holiday: SYRACUSE.
more than a thousand miles away: Ibid.
wearing his fancier costume: Photograph in Hearn, ed., *Annotated Wizard*, xix.
"I like the life very much": MGB letter to TCG, November 26 and December 5, 1882, ABERDEEN.

71   *"in the direction of his dreams"*: Henry David Thoreau, *Walden* (New York: Crowell & Co., 1910), 427.
"I don't like the trains": MGB letter to TCG, November 26 and December 5, 1882, ABERDEEN.
performances in Atchison, Topeka, and Ottawa: SYRACUSE.
extremely low rainfall . . . six degrees below zero: Prof. F. H. Snow, *Meteorological Summary of the Year 1882* (Lawrence: University of Kansas, Kansas Academy of Science, 1883), 81.
"The law is openly violated": *New York Times*, February 19, 1882.

72   *"I don't think much of Kansas"*: MGB letter to TCG, November 26 and December 5, 1882, ABERDEEN.
back to St. Louis: SYRACUSE.
Tour manager John Moak quit: Ibid.
"E. E. Brown, former manager": Ibid.
New Year's Day in Columbus: Ibid.
just before a fire burned that theater: Ibid.
finally returning to Syracuse: Ibid.

73   *"our popular young townsman"*: Ibid.
Frank printed up hundreds of copies: Ibid.
"a Great Success at Wieting": Ibid.
star actor Frank Aiken quit: Ibid.
close its season March 8: Ibid.

74   *"The audience was not large*: Ibid.
broke into flames: Ibid.
Frank's tour reached a dead end: Ibid.
Benjamin William Baum, had returned: Ibid.
a new mixture of castor oil and petroleum: Author interview with Charles F. Mowry, president of Baum's Castorine Company, Inc., Rome, NY, July 2008.
form a family partnership: Company history document, CASTORINE.
deeding the property to his mother: Ferarra, *Family*.
8 Shonnard Street: SYRACUSE.

75   *set up shop on East Water Street*: CASTORINE.
a rectangular, quart-size can: SYRACUSE.
accident during a performance in Richburg: Ibid.
"one thing in the world I am afraid of": LFB, *WWOZ*, 47.
The fire destroyed everything: SYRACUSE.
Maud gave birth: Ibid.

76   *"seemingly unending rounds"*: Swami Adiswarananda (spiritual leader of the Rama-

krishna-Vivekananda Center of New York), *The Four Yogas: A Guide to the Spiritual Paths of Action, Devotion, Meditation and Knowledge* (Woodstock, VT: Skylight Paths, 2006), Introduction.

"What shall we do?": LFB, *WWOZ*, 91.

"The most powerful religious symbol is the circle": Carl G. Jung, *The Portable Jung*, ed. Joseph Campbell (New York: Viking Penguin, 1971).

"When we pitch camp": Campbell, *Power of Myth*, 214–17.

"motherhood was represented by a sphere": MJG, *Woman, Church and State*, 47.

77   *Plato said that the soul is a circle*: Campbell, *Power of Myth*, 175.

6. The Mythic Oilcan

82   *"[My joints] are rusted so badly"*: LFB, *WWOZ*, 65.

"Restlessness and discontent": www.famousquotes.com.

"America thunders past": Andrew Carnegie, *Triumphant Democracy* (New York: Scribners, 1886), 1.

"We live in an age of progress": LFB, *The Emerald City of Oz* (Chicago: Reilly & Britton, 1910; repr. New York: HarperCollins, 1993), 98.

83   *Professor von Baum . . . smoking a pipe, and wearing a jacket and tie*: Photographs, SYRACUSE.

new double storefront, at 28/30 James Street: SYRACUSE.

"so smooth it makes horses laugh": Article, SYRACUSE.

"The Only Perfect Oil" . . . "all grades": SYRACUSE.

"makes the wheels spin": 1893 advertisement, CASTORINE.

84   *"Oil my neck, first" . . . "you have certainly saved my life"*: LFB, *WWOZ*, 65.

85   *"We are using your Castorine"*: Fact sheet and testimonials, Vanderbilt testimonial dated February 11, 1884, CASTORINE.

relocating to 28 Slocum: SYRACUSE.

blazing sunsets . . . blue Krakatoa moon: See Simon Winchester, *Krakatoa: The Day the World Exploded, August 27, 1883* (New York: HarperCollins, 2003) for descriptions of the worldwide optical effects in the two years after the Indonesian island was obliterated.

"There's something inside you": Campbell, *Power of Myth*, 285.

86   *forced to liquidate . . . turned to scrap paper . . . mortgage more and more*: Ferrara, *Family*, 63, 67–69.

One of Mr. Rockefeller's key tactics: Chernow, *Titan*, 136.

87   *a "gigantic combination"*: Ibid., 138.

John Archbold agitated a series of angry protests: Ibid., 139.

Benjamin's firm became associated with John Archbold: SYRACUSE.

"tried to break the grip of Standard Oil": Baum and MacFall, *To Please*, 18.

Archbold won this first round . . . the "most gigantic and daring conspiracy": Chernow, *Titan*, 142.

"to buy when blood is running": www.brainyquote.com.

install his former enemy as one of the top executives: Chernow, *Titan*, 165.

"I advise you to take the stock": Ibid., 144.

88   *"aimed to kill competitive capitalism"*: Ibid., 148.

"barrels of it floated down the creeks and rivers": Ibid., 101.

"crooked river" . . . "river that catches fire": http://en.wikipedia.org/wiki/Cuyahoga_River.

"half the country wanted to lynch": Chernow, Titan, 300.

89   "I am Oz, the Great and Terrible": LFB, WWOZ, 149.

alopecia, or the total loss of hair: Chernow, Titan, 192, 408.

"bald, wizened man" . . . "old, puffy, stooped" . . . "I see you don't know me" . . . "devastating effect on his image . . . hairless ogre": Ibid., 408–9.

"a little old man, with a bald head": LFB, WWOZ, 215.

90   "It's nonsense for a man to complain" . . . "by watching him at the breakfast table": LFB, Aberdeen Saturday Pioneer, February 15, 1890, ABERDEEN.

"the affair of the Bismarcks": Baum and MacFall, To Please, 50.

"You are not to bring food . . . But I also cannot accept wasting food" . . . threw the rest of the doughnuts into the trash: Ibid.

91   Aunt Em serves to her farm hands: The Wizard of Oz (MGM).

"technical consultant" to MGM: Internet Movie Data Base (www.imdb.com).

"unpredictable temper": Baum and MacFall, To Please, 48.

throw the family's cat . . . dangled him outside: Robert Stanton Baum, Baum Bugle, Spring 1970, 17.

92   "listen to the demands of his own spiritual and heart life": Campbell, Power of Myth, 181; full quote on audio CD.

typhus flared up again: Obituary of Henry Gage, FAYETTE.

The dinner was set for Sunday, July 20: Copy of menu, ABERDEEN.

"HOTEL LA FEMME" . . . "La Contents de la Soupdish": Ibid.

7. Witch-hunting

94   "In the civilized countries": LFB, WWOZ, 28.

Henry Gage passed away: Obituary of Henry Gage, FAYETTE.

grieving over their loss: Ibid.

95   "looked stern and solemn": LFB, WWOZ, 15.

"Susan B. Anthony Amendment": Harper, Life and Work.

research consensus puts the witch murders: http://en.wikipedia.org/wiki/Witch_trials_in_Early_Modern_Europe.

"As soon as a system of religion was adopted": MJG, Woman, Church and State, 231.

96   "a woman who had deliberately sold herself to the evil one": Ibid., 225.

mix up brews of knapweed: Seon Manley and Lewis Gogo, eds., Sisters in Sorcery: Two Centuries of Witchcraft Stories by the Gentle Sex (New York: William Morrow, 1976).

seized by church leaders and presented to judges: MJG, Woman, Church and State, 235.

"Women must think for themselves": New York Times, December 9, 1893.

97   In 1577 the French Parliament . . . "burned four hundred women": MJG, Woman, Church and State, 232.

"Trials for witchcraft filled the coffers": Ibid., 247.

"To deny the possibility": Blackstone's Commentaries of the Laws of England, first published in four volumes (1765–67), 390.

two hundred descendants of Mrs. Rebecca Nurse . . . "She was hung by the neck": MJG, Woman, Church and State, 273.

98   "I have not killed anything" . . . "There are her two feet, still sticking out": LFB, WWOZ, 26.

"But I cannot!" . . . "There is now but one Wicked Witch": Ibid., 151.

99   "The political and commercial morals": www.twainquotes.com.

"find little but damaged reputation": Henry Adams, *The Education of Henry Adams: An Autobiography* (Cambridge, MA: Riverside Press, 1918), 294.

Both parties refused to add a women's suffrage plank: David McCullough, *Mornings on Horseback: The Story of an Extraordinary Family, a Vanished Way of Life, and the Unique Child Who Became Theodore Roosevelt* (New York: Simon & Schuster, 1981), 309.

"When men begin to fear the power of women . . . recognized as aggressive": Wagner, *She Who Holds*, 24.

100   *the Women's Christian Temperance Union . . . "quite attached"*: Harper, *Life and Work*, vol. II, 537.

"one absorbing purpose": Anna Gordon, *The Beautiful Life of Frances Willard* (Chicago: Women's Temperance Publishing Association, 1898), 114–15.

"the Christian craft": Harper, *Life and Work*, vol. II, 538.

funding from none other than John D. Rockefeller: Chernow, *Titan*, 187.

"the religious right" . . . "the most dangerous person": Wagner, *Woman, Church and State*, Introduction, and *She Who Holds*, 46.

"it will be political expediency": Harper, *Life and Work*, vol. II, chapter 33.

"Stand by the Republican Party": Ibid.

she threw her support behind: Ibid.

101   *held some gatherings at her home . . . chosen to be placed on the Equal Rights Party ticket*: Wagner, *She Who Holds*, 28.

St. John received almost 150,000 votes: http://en.wikipedia.org/wiki/Prohibition_Party.

the Equal Rights Party received 4,711 votes: Jill Norgren, *Belva Lockwood: The Woman Who Would Be President* (New York: NYU Press, 2007), 141.

"I've always been a Republican": LFB as Edith Van Dyne, *Aunt Jane's Nieces at Work* (Chicago: Reilly & Britton, 1909), 50.

102   *even uttered the words woman*: The Avalon Project at Yale Law School, www.yale.edu/lawweb/avalon/presiden/inaug/inaug.htm.

Reverend Byron Sunderland: Sunderland, *Discourse*.

chaplain of the United States Senate . . . tap Sunderland to perform the ceremony: http://en.wikipedia.org/wiki/Byron_Sunderland.

annual convention of the New York State Woman's Suffrage Association: "Mrs. Blake Alleges That Man Is a Helpless Animal," *New York Times*, February 14, 1885.

"In the case of bees": Ibid.

103   *the triumvirate had signed a contract*: Wagner, *She Who Holds*, 20.

"Susan B. Anthony does not write": Ibid.

"I have not the faculty" . . . "biggest swamp I ever" . . . "obliged to rush over to Fayetteville": Harper, *Life and Work*, vol. II.

104   *forced to take out a mortgage*: Wagner, *She Who Holds*, 21.

Anthony would be in charge of the joint account . . . accused Anthony . . . to purchase all rights . . . all copyrights to these seminal works were transferred: Ibid.

105   *"The Statue of Liberty is a gigantic lie!" . . . "the greatest sarcasm of the nineteenth century"*: Ibid., 28.

Theosophy had been founded by Helena Petrovna Blavatsky: Sylvia Cranston, *H.P.B.: The Extraordinary Life and Influence of Helena Blavatsky, Founder of the Modern Theosophical Movement* (New York: Tarcher/Doubleday, 1993).

"modern magic" . . . threefold quest . . . "Mother of the New Age" . . . "the most living person alive": Ibid., Introduction.

forced at the age of seventeen . . . a mysterious man in London . . . called him Master M: Ibid., 37.

106   *"in America that the transformation will take place"* . . . *"mission and karma"* . . . *"cycles of spirituality"*: Ibid., 48.

they were all mahatmas . . . "one of the grandest figures" . . . translating sutras . . . "not big enough" . . . "the only land of true freedom": Ibid., 83.

107   *two-volume opus:* Helena Petrovna Blavatsky, *Isis Unveiled,* 2 vols. (1877; repr. Wheaton, IL, and Madras, India: Quest Books, 1994).

"The demand for it is quite remarkable": Cranston, H.P.B., 160.

In March of 1885 Matilda attended a conference . . . accepted fellowship in the society: MJG letters, HARVARD.

"crown blessing": Ibid.

"what is called 'death' by people is not death": Ibid.

108   *Edison filled out a membership form, accepting fellowship:* Neil Baldwin, *Edison: Inventing the Century* (Chicago: University of Chicago Press, 1995), 93–94.

"Edison and I got to talking": Cranston, H.P.B., 183.

"a spiritualistic charlatan" . . . "a consummate imposter": Ibid., Introduction.

"Massachusetts Woman Driven Insane by Theosophy": Chicago Tribune, July 12, 1886.

109   *Dr. Elliott Coues . . . caused a stir . . . "Today his dress is careless" . . . "project his spirit from his body"*: Chicago Tribune, May 14, 1886.

"silver cord": See Helena Petrovna Blavatsky, *The Secret Doctrine: The Synthesis of Science, Religion, and Philosophy* (Chicago: Theosophical Books, 1897) vol. III, 545; also see Helena Petrovna Blavatsky and Henry Olcott, *Hypnotism, Mesmerism, and Reincarnation* (Kessinger Publishing Rare Reprints, 2007), 101.

"Or ever the silver cord be loosed": Eccles. 12:6–7 (King James Version).

"The silver shoes are yours": LFB, WWOZ, 29.

the color of these silver shoes was altered: Aljean Harmetz, *The Making of The Wizard of Oz* (New York: Hyperion, 1998).

Dr. W. P. Phelon would oversee the indoctrination of Frank and Maud: LFB letter from Phelon, 1892, HARVARD.

110   *"This is the same genuine, magic, authentic crystal"*: The Wizard of Oz (MGM).

8. Frontier of Hope and Fear

112   *"The north and south winds"*: LFB, WWOZ, 16.

his horse became frightened and bolted . . . couldn't control the reins . . . collided with a hitching post . . . dragged by the rampaging: SYRACUSE.

"A Startled Horse Dashes": Ibid.

"The Proprietor of Rose Lawn Farm Badly Hurt": Syracuse Herald, October 19, 1885, SYRACUSE.

113   *"probably fatally injured"*: "Accident to a Merchant," New York Times, October 20, 1885.

Benjamin W. Baum was dead: SYRACUSE.

"I see no future in it" . . . "an opportunity to be somebody" . . . "struggling mass of humanity": LFB letter to TCG, July 30, 1888, ABERDEEN.

114   *given birth to their second son:* SYRACUSE.

a serious case of peritonitis: Ibid.

43 Holland Street: Ibid.

115 *sending his brother-in-law some words of wisdom . . . "but I have so much on hand" . . .*
"what can a girl do?": LFB letter to TCG, May 4, 1886, ABERDEEN.
"You can now awaken . . . forgetting the ills of life": Ibid.

116 *These were Huck's kind of activities*: Mark Twain, *The Adventures of Huckleberry Finn* (New York: Charles L. Webster & Co., 1884).
"I have the 'Western Fever'": LFB letter to TCG, May 4, 1886.
sickly childhoods, successful fathers, and family tragedy: McCullough, *Mornings on Horseback*.
twenty thousand desolate acres . . . "vigorous open air existence" . . . "the Real West" *. . . "very proud of my first bear"*: Theodore Roosevelt, *Hunting Trips of a Ranchman* (New York: G. P. Putnam's Sons, 1885).

117 *the stage version of* The Wizard of Oz: Mark Evan Swartz, *Oz Before the Rainbow* (Baltimore: Johns Hopkins University Press, 2002), 47, 54.
our "Manifest Destiny": Originally coined by John O'Sullivan, writing in the *New York Morning News*; see Hampton Sides, *Blood and Thunder: An Epic of the American West* (New York: Doubleday, 2006), 45.
blizzards of 1886–87: McCullough, *Mornings on Horseback*, 344–45.
out to Aberdeen in 1881 . . . since 1884 the couple had been homesteading: AB-ERDEEN.
the preemption rules of the Homestead Act: Self-Guided Tour, Rails across the Prairie, Gallery D, DAKOTA.

118 *"deathly cold" . . . "franticly lonely"*: Diary, 1882–1901, Julia Gage Carpenter Papers, University of North Dakota.
a live black twister, captured in Howard, Dakota Territory: see photo, p. 111.
a ferocious one hit Watertown: "A Tornado in Dakota," *New York Times*, April 10, 1887.
whirling into Grand Forks: "A Tornado in Dakota: Dwellings, Stores, Churches Blown Down," *New York Times*, July 23, 1884.
racing into Dell Rapids: "A Tornado in Dakota: Five Persons Killed, Several Injured, and Buildings Wrecked," *New York Times*, June 18, 1887.
"This is awful country": Diary, 1882–1901.

119 *"the house went off its foundation"*: Helen Leslie Gage, "The Dakota Cyclone," *Syracuse Weekly Express*, June 29, 1887, as quoted by Hearn, ed., *Annotated Wizard*, 23.
"one of those great whirlwinds arose" . . . "now came a sharp": LFB, WWOZ, 16.
"It's a twister!": The Wizard of Oz (MGM).
"I feel dreadfully": MGB letter to Helen Leslie Gage, quote in paper by Don Artz, town historian, "On the Road to Oz: Frank Baum's Dakota," 1996, ABER-DEEN.
death of Benjamin Ward Baum: SYRACUSE.

120 *sold off the grand Rose Lawn*: ONONDAGA.
Cynthia lived with her son: Ferrara, *Family*.
In his father's will: Ibid.
"some way to make money": MJG letter to TCG, quoted in Artz, "Road to Oz."
living full-time with Matilda: *DeWitt Times* article, SYRACUSE.
to capture and develop dozens of images of Fayetteville: Ibid.
by her painting easel: LFB photo of MJG at her desk painting (p. 242) is one of his photos from 1887.

Clark sent his mother a detailed map: Artz, "Road to Oz."

121 *seven lines of three great railroads*: Gallery D, DAKOTA.
a telephone system: Galley G, J. L. W. Zietlow Exhibit, DAKOTA.
"Invest in Aberdeen": Artz, "Road to Oz."
with $300 she had set aside: Ibid.
"The firm should be Gage, Beard & Beard": Letter from MJG to TCG, November 28, 1881, quoted in Artz, "Road to Oz."
"the Beard Block" . . . investing in sizable acreage: Ibid.
hosted a small dinner party: SYRACUSE.

122 *skimming cash . . . clerk shot himself in the head . . . discover the dead man*: Baum's Castorine history, CASTORINE.
to a pair of brothers named Stoddard . . . do fine without Frank: Ibid.

123 *the same shoes that T.R. wore*: ERIE.
the largest land grant in U.S. history: Northwest Power & Conservation Council, www.nwcouncil.org/history/Railroads.asp.

124 *"Keep it mum" . . . "I am on a business trip"*: LFB letter to TCG, June 8, 1888, ABERDEEN.
homeland of those who spoke the Siouan . . . By 1700 the Sioux had crossed . . . the animal gives its spirit: Guy E. Gibbon, *The Sioux: The Dakota and Lakota Nations* (Oxford: Blackwell, 2003).

125 *The holdouts were either shot*: Ibid.
posting scalped heads on poles: Marrin, *Sitting Bull*.
"And that country, where the Winkies live": LFB, WWOZ, 30.

126 *the Battle of Little Bighorn*: Marrin, *Sitting Bull*, 82.
"Can you imagine": Campbell, *Power of Myth*; full quote on audio CD.

127 *"the greatest Medicine Man of his time" . . . "a fiery rage still burned" . . . "obtaining vengeance"*: LFB, *Aberdeen Saturday Pioneer*, December 20, 1890.
"stirring of the mythic imagination": Campbell, *Power of Myth*, audio CD, program 3.

9. The Story Store

129 *"The American people love to be humbugged"*: Philip B. Kunhardt Jr., Philip B. Kunhardt III, and Peter W. Kunhardt, *P. T. Barnum: America's Greatest Showman* (New York: Knopf, 1995).
"Exactly so!": LFB, WWOZ, 216.
Frank arrived by train in Aberdeen: LFB letter to TCG, June 8, 1888.
piles of lumber when the Milwaukee railroad first stopped: Artz, "Road to Oz."
The buffalo . . . had already been slaughtered: George Hickman, "The History of Brown County," ABERDEEN.
"Free land was receding at railroad speed:" Hamlin Garland, *A Son of the Middle Border* (New York: P. F. Collier & Son, 1914), 244, 246.

130 *fewer western cowboy types*: Artz, "Road to Oz."
a large U.S. land office . . . Kennard Hotel . . . streets were unpaved: Ibid.
four restaurants: Ibid.
"town in the frog pond": Ibid.
the founder of the Dakota Central Telephone: Gallery G, DAKOTA.
"Aberdeen is destined to be a good city": LFB letter to TCG, July 3, 1888.
said to support thirty-eight bushels: Scrapbook of TCG, 1882 newspaper clipping, ABERDEEN.

131   *a dozen handsome churches*: ABERDEEN.
      Beard, Gage & Beard: Nancy T. Koupal, ed., *Baum's Road to Oz* (Pierre: South Dakota State Historical Society Press, 2000).
      at his brother-in-law's new house: Artz, "Road to Oz."

132   *They owned a two-story building*: Koupal, ed., *Baum's Road.*
      the storefront featured large display windows: Photograph, ABERDEEN.
      "there is an opportunity to be somebody" . . . *"to throw my fortunes in with the town"*: LFB letter to TCG, July 3, 1888, ABERDEEN.
      "I've got an idea into my head" . . . *"missing from Aberdeen is a 'Bazaar'"* . . . *"Is the town big enough"*: Ibid.

133   *"to render such goods popular"*: Ibid.
      grand opening of Baum's Bazaar . . . *arrived at the depot in Aberdeen*: Ibid.

134   *at 211 Ninth Avenue*: Ibid.
      "a new Poetry Grinder": Aberdeen *Daily News* ad, ABERDEEN.

135   *About a thousand customers*: Koupal, ed., *Baum's Road.*
      "has the push and enterprise": Aberdeen *Daily News*, ABERDEEN.
      First month's revenues were $531 . . . *start new clubs*: Koupal, ed., *Baum's Road.*

136   *"Peruse, Ponder, Purchase"*: ABERDEEN.
      kids would come to buy penny candy: Baum and MacFall, *To Please*, 62.

137   *the Cardiff Giant, a story that he once spoofed*: Rose Lawn *Home Journal*, August 1, 1871, SYRACUSE.
      Two workmen were digging a well . . . *a giant petrified man*: Andrew D. White, *Autobiography of Andrew Dickson White* (New York: Century Co., 1917). See chapter LVI, "The Cardiff Giant—A Chapter in the History of Human Folly—1869–1870."
      "shipped a man of monstrous size": LFB, Rose Lawn *Home Journal*, August 1, 1871, SYRACUSE.
      erected an enormous tent: White, *Autobiography.*
      "The interest in the Stone Giant . . . *increases"*: Syracuse *Standard*, October 21, 1869, ONONDAGA.

138   *proclaimed that it was a fraud* . . . *admitted that he had commissioned* . . . *P. T. Barnum offered to buy the giant*: White, *Autobiography.*
      "there's a sucker born every minute": http://en.wikipedia.org/wiki/Cardiff_Giant.

139   *"ought to be ashamed of yourself"* . . . *"it was the only thing I could do"*: LFB, WWOZ, 220.
      Professor Coe arrived one day in Clinton Square . . . *an enormous crowd forming around the giant balloon*: September 1871, photo at ERIE.
      "I went up in a balloon . . . *I couldn't come down again* . . . *a strange and beautiful country"*: LFB, WWOZ, 221.

140   *gave a speech on "social purity"*: Report of the International Council of Women.
      "fail to recognize the femininity of the divine": Ibid.
      arrived in Aberdeen in time for Thanksgiving: MJG letters, HARVARD.

141   *the Path* . . . *named after one of the Tibetan sutras*: Cranston, H.P.B., 86.
      "the day when humanity shall awake . . . *"they're never satisfied"* . . . *she lapsed into a coma* . . . *Mahatma M materialize clearly in the Astral light*: Ibid., 99.

142   *branches could be found in two hundred cities*: Ibid., 197.
      they even hosted séances: Koupal, ed., *Baum's Road*, 67–68.
      "you'd be a damn fool if you didn't write": Koupal, ed., *Baum's Road*, 10–12; Baum and MacFall, *To Please*, 87.

143 *"to examine and criticize his magnificent collection of articles"*: Baum's Bazaar "Holiday Opening" advertisement, December 1, 1888, SYRACUSE.
crowd of twelve hundred patrons: ABERDEEN.
"A glorious Easter is about to dawn . . . a beautiful potted plant": Aberdeen Daily News ad, April 19, 1889, ABERDEEN.

144 *against the wishes of his mother*: Baum and MacFall, *To Please*, 85.
a new organization . . . stock in the Aberdeen Base Ball Association . . . outfield fence: Michael Patrick Hearn, "The Wizard Behind the Plate," in Koupal, ed., *Baum's Road*, chapter 1.
adopted National League rules . . . fine cigars as a bonus . . . "howled itself hoarse": Ibid.

145 *"Aberdeen Forgets How to Play Ball . . . "No one feels an error more keenly" . . . "grand display of fireworks"*: Ibid.

146 *"your private myth, your dream"*: Campbell, *Power of Myth*, 48.
a sweltering heat . . . "has most likely gone up the flume" . . . "Just contradict the rumor" . . . "the best game ever played" . . . "replenished the association's treasury" . . . "the base ball scalps" . . . "a clean sweep" . . . brandishing their brooms: Hearn, "Wizard Behind the Plate."

148 *payroll due through October 5 . . . the ball club had lost $1,000 . . . "someone else will have to do the work" . . . the lumber hauled away*: Ibid.

149 *larger house, at 512 South Kline Street . . . Maud delivered their third son*: ABERDEEN.
"too impractical for a frontier town" . . . "let his tastes run riot": Ibid.

150 *a deal with Henry Marple . . . borrowing $550 for ninety days . . . "a temporary embarrassment"*: Ibid.
Maud finalized a deal to sell . . . the store reopened as Gage's Bazaar: Ibid.

10. The Brainless and the Heartless

152 *"I don't know anything" . . . "the loss of my heart"*: LFB, WWOZ, 72.
census of a decade earlier: U.S. Census data, www.census.gov.

153 *taking it over from John H. Drake . . . appointed by President Benjamin Harrison . . . low monthly payments*: Baum and MacFall, *To Please*, 63.
on the Excelsior Block: Artz, "Road to Oz."
personally delivered copies: Koupal, ed., *Baum's Road*.
"zealously and energetically" . . . Frank's first page 1: Aberdeen Saturday Pioneer, January 25, 1890, ABERDEEN.
just been admitted into the Union: Statehood became official November 2, 1889.

154 *urging citizens to choose Huron*: Pioneer, April 12 and July 5, 1890.
Susan B. Anthony had arrived and submitted: Harper, *Life and Work*, vol. II.
campaign kicked off in January: Concise History of Woman Suffrage.
the movement's six longest-standing leaders: Harper, *Life and Work*, vol. II.

155 *"The WCTU woman" . . . "to wear only the badge of yellow ribbon"*: Concise History of Woman Suffrage.
the Farmers' Alliance . . . "giving our wives and sisters the ballot" . . . Knights of Labor . . . to "support with all our strength": Ibid.
Anthony toured twelve towns, and she donated a full set of History: Harper, *Life and Work*, vol. II.
"Better to lose me": HARVARD.

"*Saint Susan*": At SBA's seventieth birthday banquet in Washington, DC, on February 15, 1890; Harper, *Life and Work*, vol. II, 665.

156 "*the entire State will be in splendid trim*" . . . "*next November with a whoop!*": Ibid.
"*galvanize all our friends*" . . . *women sent in their jewelry*: Ibid.
keep Matilda Gage staying with the Baums: MJG letters, HARVARD.
"*Under God the People Rule*": *Concise History of Woman Suffrage*.
Frank became secretary: Pioneer, April 1890.
"*our brave, helpful western girls*" . . . "*We are engaged in an equal struggle*": Pioneer, March 15, 1890.
"*The key to the success . . . The 'live and let' live policy . . . Bigotry . . . is so intolerable . . . We must do away with sex prejudice*": Pioneer, February 1, 1890.
"*to stop the attempt to place God . . . a departure from the intentions*": Pioneer, April 5, 1890.

157 "*rights which justice and humanity . . . bears in the household*": Pioneer, March 22, 1890.
Sairy Ann Bilkins . . . constantly dropping her false teeth . . . losing hairpins . . . popping buttons: LFB, *Our Landlady*, ed. Nancy Tystad Koupal (Lincoln: University of Nebraska Press, 1996); columns published in book form.
" '*it beats all how hard the times really is*'": LFB, *Our Landlady*, January 25, 1890.
appalled by a tradition at St. Mark's . . . choose which of the girls they wanted to buy . . . "as if they was so many slaves": LFB, *Our Landlady*, February 1, 1890.

158 *Prohibition into effect starting May 1*: Pioneer, May 3, 1890.
" '*This is terrble times!*'" . . . " '*Try reducin' the molasses with it*'": LFB, *Our Landlady*, March 22, 1890.
" '*I put green goggles on my hosses*'": LFB, *Our Landlady*, May 3, 1890.

159 "*eyes protected by the green spectacles*": LFB, WWOZ, 143.
"*croptious*": LFB, *Our Landlady*, May 3, 1890.
"*Oh, the wet, the elegant wet!*": Pioneer, May 24, 1890.
arrival of a mild cyclone, "*completely demolished*" . . . "*The pig was quite uninjured*": Pioneer, May 24, 1890.
refused to seek shelter . . . "A little thing like a cyclone": Hearn, ed., *Annotated Wizard*, 13.
Baum expanded his newspaper: Statement of Circulation, Pioneer, April 19, 1890, SYRACUSE.

160 "*there is practically no important opposition . . . gaining converts*": Pioneer, April 5 and May 31, 1890.
jubilation that the Republican candidate was elected: Ibid., April 19, 1890.
"*the saloons are all closed . . . sold to drunks and minors and women*": Pioneer, May 3, 1890.
"*Mother was father's exact opposite*": *Chicago Daily News*, interview with Harry Neal Baum, April 17, 1965, "Panorama" section, 3, SYRACUSE.

161 *a misprint of a local wedding announcement . . . "roughish smile" . . . to fight a duel*: Harry Neal Baum interview.
"*to celebrate July 4 in Grand Fashion!*": The official program printed by LFB is preserved in the scrapbook of TCG, ABERDEEN.

162 "*the fool judges*": LFB, *Our Landlady*, July 5, 1890.
cutest baby contest . . . best decorated theme wagon: Pioneer, July 11, 1890.
"*barbaric . . . weird . . . ludicrous*": Helen Leslie Gage letter quoted in LFB, *Our Landlady*, July 5, 1890.

A group of Native Americans dressed . . . "Them injines spiled all o' my enjyment": LFB, *Our Landlady*, July 5, 1890.

163   *"All 6,000 of us celebrated . . . we enjoyed ourselves hugely"*: Pioneer, July 5, 1890.
merge and form the Independent Party . . . activist named Henry Langford Loucks: Robert MacMath, *American Populism: A Social History* (New York: Macmillan, 1995), 137.
based right next door to Gage's Bazaar: LFB, *Our Landlady*, July 26, 1890.

164   *"death blow"*: June 3, 1890, telegram to SBA, Harper, *Life and Work*, vol. II.
"The Independents are not wholly degenerate . . . But we are members of one great family, Republicans": Pioneer, October 18, 1890.
"made a fool of himself": Ibid.
"Hard Times Bemoaned": Pioneer, October 4, 1890.
"must strain every nerve": SBA letter, August 30, 1890, HARVARD.

165   *"a disgrace to their homes . . . suckle the babies"*: Harper, *Life and Work*, vol. II, 687.
"the hardships of this campaign of 1890": Ibid., 322.
nearly sixteen hundred total speeches and rallies: Ibid.
"the Daily Nuthin'" . . . *"no brains is necessary"*: LFB, *Our Landlady*, July 26, 1890.
boosted the circulation: Certificate of Circulation, ABERDEEN.
Ten thousand people came in from out of town . . . official printer: LFB, *Our Landlady*, September 20, 1890.
to promote Anthony's speech: Pioneer, September 20, 1890.

166   *"Things was so mixed up"*: LFB, *Our Landlady*, September 20, 1890.
raised advertising rates . . . "Never before has the paper": Pioneer, August 2, 1890.
Western Investor: Ibid.
"Jim River Valley under thorough irrigation . . . the wonder and admiration": Ibid.
New population figures: Ibid.
produced only eight to ten bushels per acre: Ibid.
"cash only" markdown: Ibid.
the Hard Times Club: Pioneer, October 4, 1890.
"nonsensicalist": LFB, *Our Landlady*, October 11, 1890.
"do suthin'": Ibid., October 4, 1890.

167   *his endorsements and his predictions . . . "under Republican rule" . . . "Abandon all myths"*: Pioneer, November 1, 1890.
"the future of our wives, mothers, sisters and daughters": Ibid.
nearly seventy thousand men across South Dakota . . . Pierre became the new state capital . . . a remarkable trouncing of the Republicans: Pioneer, November 8, 1890.
"evils which have never existed": Ibid.
overwhelmingly against the right of women: Concise History of Woman Suffrage.

168   *"I've had enough of politics"*: LFB, *Our Landlady*, November 8, 1890.
"stand as a lasting reproach": Pioneer, November 8, 1890.
"You may come with me, if you like" . . . "If Oz will not give you any brains" . . ." "Do you suppose Oz could give me a heart?": LFB, WWOZ, 47, 66.

11. Field of Blood

171   *"a great meadow of poppies"*: LFB, WWOZ, 111.
wheat harvest had been an utter disaster . . . "the hollowest and most insincere": Pioneer, November 29, 1890.

"the last straw . . . the partial crop failure . . .two successive dry seasons": *Pioneer*, November 29, 1890.

172 *"appointed a dozen or so ladies"*: Ibid.

"I ought to be thankful . . . turkeys is cheaper nor beefsteak": LFB, *Our Landlady*, November 29, 1890.

"Indian scare": *Pioneer*, November 29, 1890.

173 *insufficient rations . . . cut by 20 percent*: Willis Fletcher Johnson, *The Red Record of the Sioux: Life of Sitting Bull and History of the Indian War of 1890–'91* (Edgewood Publishing Co., 1891; repr. North Scituate, MA: Digital Scanning Inc., 2000).

"Discontent has been growing for six months": Ibid., 388.

widely reported that Sioux warriors: Ibid., 259.

Sioux chiefs arrived at agency headquarters . . . three companies of cavalry: Ibid., 391.

"there will be an uprising soon" . . . *"beat out the brains"*: Ibid., 396.

breaking open front doors, smashing every piece: *Pioneer*, December 5, 1890; ibid., 413.

ranch stories: "It sounds like a ranch story," LFB wrote on December 20, 1890, in the *Pioneer*.

174 *"false and senseless scare"*: *Pioneer*, November 29, 1890.

"not literally true": *Pioneer*, December 20, 1890.

"According to the popular rumor . . . our scalps are still in healthy condition": *Pioneer*, November 29, 1890.

"has accomplished one thing . . . in case the Indians should rise . . . entirely at their mercy . . . should be remedied in some manner: Ibid.

175 *"I have never made war"* . . . *"a white man over me"*: Johnson, *Red Record*, 153, 155.

176 *"tamed the Lion of the West"*: *Collections of the State Historical Society of North Dakota*, vol. 1 (Bismarck, ND: Tribune State Printers, 1906), 280.

" 'the lion in his den' ": John F. Finney (war correspondent for the *Chicago Times*), *War-Path & Bivouac: Or, The Conquest of the Sioux* (Chicago: Donohue & Henneberry, 1890), 359.

"God made me to live on the flesh": Johnson, *Red Record*, 162.

came to witness a surrender: Ibid., 159.

Most of the Lakota there laughed at him . . . pushing him off the reservation: Ibid., 160.

"There came from the forest a terrible roar" . . . *"Don't you dare bite Toto!"* . . . *"I didn't bite him"* . . . *"nothing but a big coward"*: LFB, WWOZ, 81.

177 *to the place of his birth*: Johnson, *Red Record*, 168.

tour came to the Wieting: Photo of marquee from collection of David Moyer, GAGE.

requested that the chief join his Wild West Show . . . quit the tour after one season: Marrin, *Sitting Bull*.

on the verge of mass starvation. They complained loudly: Johnson, *Red Record*, 168–69.

178 *"fight our last fight"*: Ibid.

the Messiah was coming . . . The central mountains would erupt: Ibid., 169–70.

a flock of wakinyan . . . "winged one" . . . these fabled birds: James R. Walker (physician at Pine Ridge from 1896 to 1914), *Lakota Belief and Ritual* (Lincoln and London: University of Nebraska Press, 1980; repr. Winnipeg, MB: Bison Books, 1991), 37.

179 *In a typical Ghost Dance ceremony . . . regain his old standing*: Johnson, *Red Record*, 170–72.

perceived as a war dance . . . "in a state of terror": Ibid., 389.

"ghost dance at its height . . . invests the women with greater importance . . . evidence was gathering": Ibid., 173–74.

180 *"God Almighty did not make me an agency Indian"*: Ibid., 178.
impossible to bring in Sitting Bull alive: Ibid., 179.
government initially sent in Buffalo Bill Cody: Ibid., 404.

181 *"bearded the lion in his whiskers . . . started fer the seat o' war"*: LFB, *Our Landlady*, December 6, 1890.
"Don't hurt us, Miss' Bilkins": Ibid.
"What makes you a coward?" . . . "It's a mystery": LFB, WWOZ, 82.
series of stories on the Ghost Dance . . . two thousand armed, war-painted fighting Indian men . . . "the Indians were on the eve of a bloody outbreak . . . on the east bank of the Missouri": Pioneer, December 13, 1890.

182 *expedition to arrest Sitting Bull . . . set out on the morning of December 14 . . . led by Bull Head*: Johnson, *Red Record*, 183–84.
different accounts of what happened . . . "Sitting Bull was still shouting": Ibid., 185–88.
according to the report filed by Agent McLaughlin: "Story of Sitting Bull's Death," Pioneer, December 20, 1890.

183 *"mind and heart of the American people felt sad and ashamed"*: Johnson, *Red Record*, 189.
"Expect an Attack at Any Moment": Pioneer, December 20, 1890.
"Indians are dancing in the snow" . . . "We need protection and we need it now": Ibid.
"With his fall, the nobility of the Redskin is extinguished . . . Why not annihilation? . . . better they should die": Ibid.

184 *"pale-faces are masters of the earth"*: James Fenimore Cooper, *The Last of the Mohicans* (1826), final page.
"If I were King of the For-r-r-e-s-s-s-s-t": *The Wizard of Oz* (MGM).

185 *"it is a pleasant duty to wish all our readers a Merry Christmas"*: Pioneer, December 20, 1890.
"The success of the Pioneer": Ibid.
"It's Sitting Bull!": Johnson, *Red Record*, 426.

186 *the Seventh Cavalry . . . rode into the Pine Ridge Reservation . . . The troops formed a cordon around the natives . . . ordered the Sioux to lay down their guns*: Ibid., 430–32.

187 *Twenty-five U.S. soldiers were killed*: Ibid.
"this high hill of my old age": John G. Neihardt, *Black Elk Speaks* (1931; repr. Winnipeg, MB: Bison Books, 1999).
the U.S. government had spent a billion dollars: Johnson, *Red Record*, 282.
"our only safety depends upon the total extermination": Pioneer, January 3, 1891.

188 *"might take hint from the Indians"*: Wagner, *Sisters in Spirit*.
"To think of the idjuts leavin' . . . the most fertile country on the yearth": LFB, *Our Landlady*, January 10, 1891.

189 *Hagerty's Savings and Loan, went belly-up*: Pioneer, January 17, 1891.
"We ain't lookin' fer truth": LFB, *Our Landlady*, December 6, 1890.

190 *"odor is so powerful that anyone who breathes it falls asleep . . . forever"*: LFB, WWOZ, 111.
emblem of commemoration: Michael Patrick Hearn in *The Annotated Wizard of Oz* cites mythology in which "scarlet poppies were said to grow from the blood of the slain, for they were often seen on battlefields."

"*Theosophy is not a religion . . . To them God is nature and nature God*": Pioneer, January 25, 1890.

191 "*the Karmic destiny of man*": H. P. Blavatsky, *The Key to Theosophy* (1889; repr. Pasedena: Theosophical University Press, 2002), 135–36.

"*accused of studying the Vedas . . . Spiritualism is a stepping stone*": Pioneer, January 17, 1891.

192 *sell the Pioneer back*: Deal finalized April 4, 1890; Koupal, ed., *Baum's Road*.

"*Hold onto your breath, hold onto your heart*": *The Wizard of Oz* (MGM).

12. The Golden Path

196 "*If this road goes in*": LFB, WWOZ, 58.

newly built Grand Central Station: http://en.wikipedia.org/wiki/Grand_Central_Station_(Chicago).

the 1890 census: U.S. Census data, www.census.gov.

197 "*The news of Charlie's death came*": LFB letter to Helen Leslie Gage, January 17, 1891.

"*there is a Road, steep and thorny*": H. P. Blavatsky, *Collected Writings*, vol. 13 (London: Theosophical Publishing House, 1950–1995), 219.

198 *the news about the coming Columbian Exposition*: Erik Larson, *The Devil in the White City* (New York: Crown, 2003), 94.

"*discouragement*" *and* "*hopelessness*": Ibid., 96.

"*the guiding force of the fair*" . . . "*1893 will be*": Ibid., 98.

199 *At just $20 per week*: Baum and MacFall, *To Please*, 78.

Riding a streetcar down Harrison Street: Ibid., 77.

200 *suggested that Hagerty was a felon . . .* "*with his massive brain*" *. . .* "*What good are your churches, preacher?*": Pioneer, January 24, 1891.

"*the acme of meanness*": Koupal, ed., *Baum's Road*, 102 (quoted from January 27, 1891, Aberdeen Daily News).

201 "*a Fine Dose from the Pupils*" . . . "*Baum conspires against the welfare*": Ibid., 104.

a case of angina pectoris . . . tumor beneath his tongue: Angelica S. Carpenter and J. Shirley, *L. Frank Baum: Royal Historian of Oz* (Minneapolis: Lerner Publications, 2002).

"*Mr. Baum has not been out[side]*": Pioneer, February 28, 1891.

202 *Matilda knew her grandfather, who served as a minuteman*: SYRACUSE.

"*the railroads will be ruined*" . . . "*Everything progresses an' evolutes*": LFB, *Our Landlady*, January 31 and February 8, 1891.

203 *the Women's National Liberal Union*: Wagner, *She Who Holds*, 54.

selling or giving away their furniture . . . Frank headed to Chicago . . . buy some beds: Baum and MacFall, *To Please*, 77.

"*This Is the First of May*" . . . "*Many a proud man . . . there is no place like home*": Chicago Evening Post, May 1, 1891, 1, CHICAGO.

204 "*Mme. Blavatsky Dead*": Chicago Tribune, May 8, 1891, UCHICAGO.

205 "*An Astral Vacation*" . . . "*you will see that Blavatsky will rise . . . She is simply in Samadhi*": Chicago Evening Post, May 8, 1891, 1, CHICAGO. (The spelling of *Samadhi* is corrected here for clarity.)

206 *typhoid was spreading . . . An average of 375 people . . .* "*to frighten people from coming*": New York Times, January 26, 1892.

Theosophical Society . . . burgeoned . . . at 66 Adams Street: *Chicago Tribune*, February 3, 1892, UCHICAGO.

207 *"In America, . . . the theosophic 'boom' is on"*: Ibid.

admitted to the society on September 4, 1892, upon the recommendation of Dr. Phelon and issued permanent diplomas by the global parent organization in India on December 5: THEOSOPHY.

"differences in religious dogma" . . . one must renounce such violence . . . "This is a difficult undertaking": Blavatsky, *Key to Theosophy*.

208 *deploring the mistreatment and abuse of animals*: Ibid.

"the Eternity of the Universe in toto as a boundless plane": Cranston, H.P.B., 350.

"Toto did not really care": LFB, WWOZ, 180.

"Mr. Baum was good to animals": MGB letter to Jack Snow, June 21, 1943, SYRACUSE.

209 *"floors of nearly all Buddhist temples are made of yellow polished stone"*: Cranston, H.P.B., 94.

"the noble chord of universal human brotherhood . . . a golden milestone in Man's pathway": J. Henry Barrows, ed., *The World's Parliament of Religions: An Illustrated and Popular Story of the World's First Parliament of Religions, Held in Chicago in Connection with the Columbian Exposition of 1893* (Chicago: Parliament Publishing Company, Lakeside Press, 1893), THEOSOPHY.

210 *Vivekananda swam out to the biggest rock*: Asim Chaudhuri, *Swami Vivekananda in Chicago: New Findings* (Calcutta: Advaita Ashrama, 2000).

209 *The tale of how such a young man received such a high honor would become a legend . . .*

"With this great power" . . . "I hit upon a plan": Swami Bodhasarananda, *The Story of Vivekananda* (Calcutta: Advaita Ashrama, 1970; repr. Hollywood, CA: Vedanta Press, 2007).

210 *They dubbed him the "Swamiji," selecting him to speak, and then began to raise money for his journey*: Ibid.

211 *"The philosophy of yoga tells us . . . loss of contact with our true Self"*: Adiswarananda, *Four Yogas*.

"the Four Yogas" . . . "the grandest idea in the religion of the Vedanta": Ibid.

the swami boarded a steamship in Bombay: Chaudhuri, *Swami Vivekananda in Chicago*.

13. The Glimmering City

213 *"beautiful houses all built of green marble"*: LFB, WWOZ, 143.

"Something new and curious": Adams, *Education*, 338.

Edison had franchised . . . Paris International Exposition . . . "What has struck me so far": Baldwin, *Edison*.

214 *"out-Eiffel Eiffel" . . . "monstrosity" being proposed*: Larson, *Devil*, 156, 179.

Auditorium Hotel: CHICAGO.

"Few knew he was coming . . . the throng that filled the rotunda parted to let him pass . . . Of medium height is the wizard of Menlo Park . . . A massive head is his": *Chicago Evening Post*, May 11, 1891, 1, CHICAGO.

215 *"an enormous Head, without a body"*: LFB, WWOZ, 149.

"Greatly interested in the world's fair is the wizard . . . to throw upon a canvas a perfect picture": *Evening Post*, May 11, 1891.

216 *"a magic lantern run mad"*: Baldwin, *Edison*, 210.
   Muybridge, who had made the most progress: Ibid., 210–11.
   "smiled by way of reply": *Evening Post*, May 11, 1891.

217 *at Siegel, Cooper & Company*: Carpenter and Shirley, *Baum: Royal Historian*. Michael Patrick Hearn disputes whether Baum actually worked at Siegel, Cooper, & Company and says a different Baum may have been listed in employee records.
   an eight-story downtown department store: *Encyclopedia of Chicago*, www.encyclope dia.chicagohistory.org/pages/2847.html.
   four hundred new buildings . . . four thousand men . . . Four men were killed: Larson, *Devil*, 145.
   Francis Bellamy . . . "I pledge allegiance": Ibid., 181.

218 *"to the great navigator" . . . the largest building ever constructed . . . five thousand yellow chairs . . . "the sense of dizziness"*: Ibid.
   its ceiling collapsed: Ibid., 196–97.
   "I fear that . . . great towering masses of white" . . . "dense, broad, luxuriant green bodies of foliage": Ibid., 196.

219 *Engine 999 rolled away from Syracuse*: CHICSCI.
   a state of "gross incompleteness": Larson, *Devil*, 230.
   the newly constructed elevated trains: CHICAGO.
   line of twenty-three black carriages . . . the unfinished Ferris wheel . . . Chief Sitting Bull's preserved cabin: Larson, *Devil*, 235–36.

220 *"a sudden vision of heaven"*: Ibid., 254.
   the Great Basin . . . the Court of Honor . . . stuccolike covering called staff: Stanley Appelbaum, *The Chicago World's Fair of 1893: A Photographic Record* (New York: Dover Publications, 1980).
   "what a magnificent ruin": Denslow diary as quoted by David Levi Strauss, Reviews, *Artforum*, June 1, 2003. Also see Douglas Green and Michael Patrick Hearn, *W. W. Denslow* (Mount Pleasant, MI: Clark Historical Library, 1976).
   "Gathered here are the forces" . . . promoting harmony": Hubert Howe Bancroft, *The Book of the Fair: An Historical and Descriptive Presentation of the World's Science, Art, and Industry, as Viewed through the Columbian Exposition at Chicago in 1893* (Chicago: Bancroft Company, 1893), WALKER.

221 *President Cleveland stepped up . . . Dynamos whirred*: Ibid.
   "Everyone seemed happy and contented": LFB, WWOZ, 144.
   "Human Achievement in Material Form": Bancroft, *Book of the Fair*.
   largest lump of coal . . . first toilet smithed from silver . . . world's widest wedge of cheese . . . purely of Heinz pickles . . . entirely of prunes: *Expo: The Magic of the White City*, documentary on DVD narrated by Gene Wilder (Pittsburgh: Inecom, 2005).

222 *people purchased colored eyeshades*: Larson, *Devil*.
   "the Emerald City would blind you": LFB, WWOZ, 139.
   "brightest thing on Earth": Appelbaum, *Photographic Record*.
   the Kinetoscope . . . A poll of opinion leaders: Baldwin, *Edison*.
   attendance plunged . . . a nationwide panic was triggered: Larson, *Devil*, 239.

223 *"convulsion of 1893" . . . "falsified history . . . unattainable promises"*: Adams, *Education*, 338.
   the fair's Standard Oil Building: Chernow, *Titan*.
   Andrew Carnegie's credo . . . first major philanthropic project . . . "the two projects appeared to blend": Ibid.

224   "no hair upon his head" . . . "Help me and I will help you": LFB, WWOZ, 150.
      On the eighth of June . . . a major luncheon event . . . to honor a royal guest . . . the
      Queen of the Fair: Chicago Tribune, June 9, 1893.

225   When Frank arrived at the Woman's Building . . . removed his silk top hat . . . "father had
      no difficulty": Harry Neal Baum, Baum Bugle, 1965.
      the two places were in many ways polar opposites: Expo documentary.

226   "the most widely known American": Washington Post, April 8, 1891.

227   the Barnum grave and started digging: "Barnum's Body in Peril," New York Times, May
      29, 1893.
      "Barnum was right . . . age of deception": LFB, Pioneer, February 8, 1890.
      "Doesn't anyone else know you're a humbug?": LFB, WWOZ, 219.

14. The Wizard's Challenge

229   "the Witch is Wicked": LFB, WWOZ, 151.
      brick-lined courts surrounded the central staircase: CHICART.
      "The Significance of the Frontier in American History": Frederick Jackson Turner, The
      Significance of the Frontier in American History (New York: Henry Holt, 1920). The
      talk was given on July 12, 1893.

230   "incongruity" . . . he leased fifteen acres . . . played cards together: Larson, Devil,
      250–51.

231   "inner split in the psyche": Author interview with Gita Dorothy Morena, February
      2008.
      "bring the shadow material out . . . integrate into wholeness": Ibid.

232   "Frank went toward the mind . . . This is what we needed to do": Ibid.
      more than a month at sea, the swami: Chronological Record of Swami Vivekananda
      in the West, 1893–1901, compiled and edited by Terrance Hohner and Carolyn
      Kenny (Amala) of the Vedanta Society of Portland, available at www.vedanta.org.
      Their primary source was Marie Louise Burke's six-volume work, Swami Viveka-
      nanda in the West: New Discoveries (Calcutta: Advaita Ashrama, 1983).
      "Is man a tiny boat in a tempest . . . Is there no escape?": Swami Vivekananda, Selec-
      tions from the Complete Works of Swami Vivekananda (Calcutta: Advaita Ashrama,
      1998), 7.
      On July 25, 1893, the swami's ship: Hohner and Kenny, eds., Swami Chronology.
      "a lordly imposing stride, as if he ruled the universe" . . . invited him to stay: Chaudhuri,
      Swami Vivekananda in Chicago.

233   "they spend money like water . . . One must take at least ten days": Vivekananda letter
      of August 20, 1893, www.vivekananda.net/KnownLetters/1893America.html.
      the roster of speakers had already been completed: Chaudhuri, Swami Vivekananda in
      Chicago.
      "It was reserved for America to proclaim": Vivekananda, Selections from the Swami,
      14.
      Vivekananda wrote to his new friend . . . such a sensation at Harvard: Chaudhuri,
      Swami Vivekananda in Chicago.
      a special recommendation addressed to Reverend Barrows . . . "more learned than all our
      learned professors": Ibid.

234   "more powerful than all the rest of us together": LFB, WWOZ, 28.
      "a radiant being who had descended from a higher sphere": Quote by Sister Christine,
      from the introduction to Vivekananda, Selections from the Swami.

"You are a real mahatma": Vivekananda letter of August 30, 1893, www.viveka nanda.net/KnownLetters/1893America.html.

curled up in an empty boxcar . . . Mary Hale spotted him . . . took him to see John Henry Barrows: Chaudhuri, *Swami Vivekananda in Chicago*.

By August: As an aside, August 25 at the fair was Colored People's Day, and Frederick Douglass gave an address on "The Race Problem in America."

letter describing a mystical Theosophy meeting: MJG letter of August 11, 1893, HARVARD.

Theosophy had been fully included: Barrows, ed., *World's Parliament of Religions*.

235   *"a book with a revolution in it"*: Wagner introduction in MJG, *Woman, Church and State*.

"from the radical woman's standpoint" . . . a "revelation": Ibid.

"I thank you in my soul": FAYETTE.

commemorative statues immortalizing: Appelbaum, *Photographic Record*.

"We will glorify your name!": The Wizard of Oz (MGM).

"They have stabbed me": MJG letter to TCG, July 11, 1893, HARVARD.

236   *"I like an active life . . . to be independent"*: MJG letter, 1895, HARVARD.

"We only get what we deserve": Adiswarananda, *Four Yogas*.

At 10:00 a.m. on the morning of September 11: Chaudhuri, *Swami Vivekananda in Chicago*.

on the stage were sixty-five scholars: Daily Columbian (newspaper of the world's fair), September 12, 1893, CHICAGO.

"Religion, like the white light of Heaven": Barrows, ed., *World's Parliament of Religions*.

237   *"attracted the most notice"*: Daily Columbian, September 12, 1893.

"Sisters and Brothers of America" . . . thunderous applause erupted: See any variety of sources, including *Daily Columbian*; *Chicago Tribune*; Chaudhuri, *Swami Vivekananda in Chicago*; Vivekananda, *Selections from the Swami*.

"The present convention . . . 'All men are struggling through paths' . . . Sectarianism, bigotry": Vivekananda, *Selections from the Swami*.

238   *"exhausted with emotion"*: Photographs of Swami Vivekananda 1886–1901, compiled and researched by members of the Vedanta Society of Northern California (Chennai, India: Sri Ramakrishna Math, 2002).

Vivekananda retired to a small meeting room . . . " 'No. 1—keep out'" . . . "The most striking figure": Ibid.

swami sitting behind a desk: Ibid.

"many paths to realization of the True Self": Adiswarananda, *Four Yogas*.

239   *Jnâna Yoga . . . Bhakti Yoga . . . Karma Yoga . . . Râja Yoga*: Ibid.

"most seekers do not have the patience" . . . "if we only know how to knock": Ibid.

"the Wizard's Challenge": Morena, *Wisdom of Oz*, 122.

"something that looks impossible . . . confronting your shadow": Author interview with Gita Dorothy Morena.

240   *"When Dorothy, who was an orphan"*: LFB, WWOZ, 12.

"I'll get you, my pretty . . . and your little dog, too!": The Wizard of Oz (MGM).

"Karma Yoga is the way to freedom": Adiswarananda, *Four Yogas*, 11.

guest speaker at Hull House: Hohner and Kenny, eds., Swami Chronology.

"Brother, yours is an impossible hope": Vivekananda, *Selections from the Swami*.

241   *a three-year contract with a top lecture agency*: Chaudhuri, *Swami Vivekananda in Chicago*.

"To work, alone, you are entitled, but never its fruit": Bhagavad Gita.
"Come up, O lions . . . stop not 'til the goal is reached": Vivekananda, *Selections from the Swami*.

15. The Witch Is Dead

243   "I have been wicked in my day": LFB, WWOZ, 182.
        crowd of seven hundred thousand: Bancroft, *Book of the Fair*.
        "he felt that it was good; he was proud of it": Adams, *Education*, 340.
        a set of unforgettable images: Appelbaum, *Photographic Record*; also see Bancroft, *Book of the Fair*.

244   assassinated in his home: Larson, *Devil*.
        twenty-seven million admissions . . . a dividend of 10¢: Bancroft, *Book of the Fair*.
        ravaged by a series of fires: Appelbaum, *Photographic Record*.

245   Pitkin & Brooks . . . Iowa, Missouri, and the lower half of Illinois . . . wheeling his china bundles to an empty display room: Baum and MacFall, *To Please*, 80.
        "The Emerald City was soon left far behind": LFB, WWOZ, 166.

246   "My present job is until April 1 . . . have not much to fear now": LFB letter to Cynthia Stanton Baum, January 16, 1894, ABERDEEN.
        "he secured orders for an amazing volume": Harry Stanton Baum, *Baum Bugle*.
        "I want my daddy! . . . I-want-a-daddy-with-legs!": Baum and MacFall, *To Please*, 84.
        cook molasses taffy and pop corn: Ibid., 86.
        "these people were all made of china": LFB, WWOZ, 271.

247   a new public playground: May 5, 1894, from database of local events, Jane Addams Hull House Museum, Chicago.
        Anthony Comstock . . . criminal proceedings against any person who should place it in the school library: "Mrs. Gage's Book: A Statement of Her Side of the Case," *Fayetteville Recorder*, August 23, 1894, 1, FAYETTE.
        "as dangerous to liberty . . . as were the old inquisitors": Ibid.
        arrested for trying to vote: Wagner, *She Who Holds*.
        "the most disfranchised woman" . . . "justice will be done": *New York Times*, December 9, 1893.
        "It is outrageous, it is cruel and wicked": Ibid.

248   "never civilization higher": Wagner, *She Who Holds*, 35.
        the Iroquois League: Sherrow, *Iroquois*.
        "The Indian Men when young are Hunters": See www.franklinpapers.org, "Remarks Concerning the Savages of North America."

249   adopted into the Wolf Clan of the Mohawk Nation and given a special Mohawk name: Wagner, *She Who Holds*, 34.

250   "your illness & head trouble . . . Your real self is well": MJG letter to Leslie Gage, March 27, 1895, HARVARD.
        Hypatia . . . in Alexandria: See http://womenshistory.about.com/od/hypati1/a/hypatia.htm.
        "I am very angry . . . you have small faith in my treatment": MJG letter to Helen Leslie Gage, December 5, 1896, HARVARD.

251   "witch hazel": MJG letter, May 15, 1895, HARVARD.
        "the tale of the Witch of Endor": *New York Times*, September 2, 1894.

"Frank came in and kissed me goodbye": MJG letter, 1897, HARVARD.

a contest announced in the Youth Companion . . . *"No love or religion . . . or political or purely sensational stories . . . bring in a cyclone"*: MJG letter to Helen Leslie Gage, February 11, 1895, HARVARD.

253   *he would write down the ideas . . . on old envelopes and scraps:* Baum and MacFall, *To Please*, 80.

"Record of Failure": Douglas G. Greene, "The Periodical Baum," *Baum Bugle*, Autumn 1975, 3.

254   *"The Heretic"*: "La Reine est Morte," "The Heretic," and many of the other stories and poems from 1895–97 were later included in the self-published book by LFB, *By the Candelabra's Glare* (1898), available as a free PDF download at www.lulu.com/content/1960575.

"Yesterday at the Exposition": *Chicago Times-Herald*, February 2, 1896.

"when the 'honest money' faction, seats McKinley in the chair!": *Chicago Times-Herald*, July 12, 1896.

120 Flournoy Street . . . his heart was too weak: MacFall and Baum, *To Please*, 93.

255   *"for the purpose of self-development . . . to gain spiritual growth"*: MJG letter to Helen Leslie Gage, October 31, 1895, HARVARD.

royalties not in cash but in her choice of other books . . . her property taxes: MJG letters to Helen Leslie Gage, December 20, 1895, and early 1896, HARVARD.

visited from Aberdeen . . . group lesson . . . fife-and-drum corps: Ibid.

256   *"L. F. is home but not in good humor"*: MJG letter to Helen Leslie Gage, May 2, 1896, HARVARD.

he had been making up his own silly explanations: Baum and MacFall, *To Please*, 85–86.

"one generation is linked to another" . . . a Boston woman named Eliza Vertigoose: LFB, *Mother Goose in Prose* (Chicago: Way & Williams, 1897).

257   *introduced at the Chicago Press Club:* Baum and MacFall, *To Please*, 87–88.

Adventures in Phunnyland . . . *rejected:* Ibid.

"a monthly journal of practical window trimming": *Show Window*, ABERDEEN.

Caxton Building: See Ron Gordon and John Paulett, *Printer's Row, Chicago* (Chicago: Arcadia, 2003), 14.

258   *"I have been more worried than usual"*: LFB letter to Mary Louise Brewster, October 3, 1897, ABERDEEN.

Mostly it was her lungs, throat, and stomach: MJG letter to Julia Gage Carpenter, June 9, 1896, HARVARD.

"We all must die": MJG letter, undated, 1897, HARVARD.

"I lived through some of the most important events . . . station on the Underground Railroad": MJG letter to TCG, July 15, 1896, HARVARD.

259   *"the two women may have found some resolution"*: Wagner, *She Who Holds*, 65.

to commemorate the fiftieth anniversary . . . Matilda's final speech: Proceedings of the Thirtieth Annual Convention of the National American Woman Suffrage Association, and *The Celebration of the Fiftieth Anniversary of the First Woman's Rights Convention*, held in Washington, DC, February 13–19, 1898, ed. Rachel Foster Avery (Philadelphia: Ferris Press), HARVARD.

"the divinity of the feminine . . . Look within your own soul for light": MJG letter to Helen Leslie Gage, undated, circa 1897, HARVARD.

"set for the redeeming of the Earth . . . to live on the plane . . . my spirit light and potency": MJG letter, undated, circa 1897, HARVARD.

"Who's Afraid?": See LFB, By the Candelabra's Glare, 88.

260   "I think the matter is near the end": LFB letter to TCG, March 13, 1898, AB-
ERDEEN.
"Harmony with oneself": MJG letter, circa 1897, HARVARD.
"her death was caused by apoplexy": New York Times, March 20, 1898.
"will never be able to go home": LFB letter, March 13, 1898.

16. This One Story

262   "We must go back to Oz": LFB, WWOZ, 193.
last will and testament: Admitted to probate in the county of Onondaga, July 11,
1898; available on www.rootsweb.ancestry.com/~nyononda/COURT/W10P72.
htm.

263   "Suddenly, this one [story] moved right in and took possession": LFB quoted in Potter,
"Man Who Invented," 12.
snowy winter's day . . . they at once demanded a story: John J. Doohan, "Birth of a
Wizard," Kansas City Star, 1963, SYRACUSE.
"I shooed the children away": LFB quoted in Potter, "Man Who Invented."
"Crossing a bare common, in snow puddles, at twilight . . . a transparent eye-ball":
Ralph Waldo Emerson, Nature (1836).

264   "through the doors of perception": William Blake, The Marriage of Heaven and Hell
(1793).
"It was pure inspiration": LFB quoted in Potter, "Man Who Invented."
"I grabbed a piece of paper that was lying there": Ibid.

265   "The house whirled around": LFB, WWOZ, 16.
"couldn't be hired to live here": MGB letter to TCG, December 5, 1882, AB-
ERDEEN.

266   "my good friend and comrade, my wife": LFB, WWOZ, dedication page.
"He was a little black dog": Ibid., 15.
"a plane of existence created by": Charles W. Leadbeater, The Astral Plane: Its Scenery,
Inhabitants and Phenomena (London: Theosophical Publishing, 1895; repr. Glouces-
ter, UK: Dodo Press, 2000).

267   three copies of this "very interesting" work: MJG letter, circa 1896, HARVARD.
"a realm of nature . . . like Greenland": Leadbeater, Astral Plane.
invisible plane of transcendence: Campbell, Power of Myth.
"Only the trained visitor from this life . . . realm of illusion": Leadbeater, Astral Plane.
"It is a long way to the Emerald City . . . paved with yellow brick": LFB, WWOZ, 42.

268   "I cannot understand why" . . . "There is no place like home": Ibid., 55.

269   "the children's book of the year": Chicago Tribune advertisement, December 1897.
two-story Victorian at 68 Humboldt . . . featured: Hearn, ed., Annotated Wizard.
formed the National Association of Window Trimmers . . . "official organ": Show Window, September 10, 1899, SYRACUSE.

270   his financial backer, Way & Williams, went belly-up: Baum and MacFall, To Please.
"the losses have grown unbearably great": Show Window, September 10, 1899.
was introduced to a gruff, pipe-smoking man . . . they'd meet at Frank's house . . . eighth-
floor office in the Fine Arts Building: Baum and MacFall, To Please, 97.

271   "All Passes. Art Alone Endures": Author visit to Fine Arts Building, 2007.

daily classes had been given by none other than Swami: Vivekananda gave classes in the Auditorium Hotel next door for sixteen days in January 1895 (Hohner and Kenny, eds., Swami Chronology) and ten days in the Florence Adams studio of the Fine Arts Building in April 1896 (Chaudhuri, *Swami Vivekananda in Chicago*).

"Old Mother Goose became quite new": LFB, *Father Goose, His Book* (Chicago: George M. Hill, 1899), Introduction.

"His best friends could speak to him" . . . *"My characters won't do what I want"* . . . *"living people":* Daniel P. Mannix, "The Father of the Wizard of Oz," *American Heritage,* December 1964, SYRACUSE.

272   *They named the baby Dorothy . . . at the age of five months, Dorothy died . . . "a perfectly beautiful baby":* Sally Roesch Wagner, "Dorothy Gage and Dorothy Gale," 1996, ABERDEEN.

"good judgment, active minds and independence": Pioneer, February 1890.

273   *eyes stopped at a nearby filing cabinet . . . "The land is called:"* Baum and MacFall, *To Please.*

an interview in 1903: Quote from the *St. Louis Republic,* in Morena, *Wisdom of Oz,* 6.

"No one or anything suggested the word. This is fact": MGB letter to Jack Snow, June 21, 1943, SYRACUSE.

Or perhaps it has something: Oz is also a biblical word, meaning "courage" and "strength" in Hebrew.

274   *"One of my greatest fears was the Witches":* LFB, WWOZ, 222.

"the LAW OF GOOD shall stand": Leadbeater, *Astral Plane,* 70.

"with little bells around the brims" . . . *"free from bondage":* LFB, WWOZ, 22–23.

Münchner Kindl, meaning "Munich child": Theory of the name posed by Brian Atteberry, *The Fantasy Tradition in American Literature* (Bloomington: Indiana University Press, 1980), 89.

275   *"the stereotyped genie, dwarf and fairy":* LFB, WWOZ, Introduction.

"the four nations that inhabit the Land of Oz": LFB, *Dorothy and the Wizard of Oz* (Chicago: Reilly & Britton, 1908).

"The Council with the Munchkins": LFB, WWOZ, 19.

"our Indians are in reality foreign powers": Wagner, *Sisters in Spirit.*

276   *"mineral, vegetable, and animal forms":* Blavatsky, *The Secret Doctrine,* vol. II, 42.

278   *the only living figure:* See LFB, *Tik-Tok of Oz* (Chicago: Reilly & Lee, 1914), 134.

279   *"You are a wicked creature!":* LFB, WWOZ, 181.

"never existed save for the imagination of her persecutors": Wagner, *She Who Holds.*

"what is the fate of great nations": Jung, *Portable Jung,* 65.

280   *"who seemed to be as much surprised"* . . . *"fooled everyone for so long":* LFB, WWOZ, 219.

"the Self is revealed in the mirror of the mind": Adiswarananda, *Four Yogas.*

281   *at the London Balloon Society:* Hohner and Kenny, eds., Swami Chronology, November 5, 1895.

in Geneva in the summer of 1896, . . . Henrietta Muller: Ibid.

"We think symbolically": Photographs of Swami Vivekananda.

special seal . . . designed by the swami himself: See www.belurmath.org.

282   *"face to face . . . utterly rotten and corrupt":* Naugatuck Daily News, May 15, 1899, quoting a Bombay newspaper; clip available at www.vivekananda.net.

"a very good man, but I'm a very bad Wizard": LFB, WWOZ, 223.

17. Home Again

284 *"Your Silver Shoes will carry you"*: LFB, WWOZ, 303.

sheets of white typewriter paper fastened by a clipboard: Harry Neal Baum, *The American Book Collector*, December 1962.

in a big upholstered armchair . . . often folding his legs over one side: Baum and MacFall, *To Please*, 112.

The City of Oz: Hearn, ed., *Annotated Wizard*, xxxvii.

split royalties . . . chip in . . . written by hand: Baum and MacFall, *To Please*.

285 *framed the original pencil stub*: SYRACUSE.

he gave copies to two children and a kindergarten teacher: Hearn, ed., *Annotated Wizard*, xxxix.

a contract with Hill to publish . . . The title kept changing: Ibid.

286 Father Goose: His Book *was the best-selling children's book*: Ibid.

didn't view Father Goose *as a good example of his work*: LFB letter to brother Harry, April 8, 1900.

"Why not call the Winged Monkeys": LFB, WWOZ, 251.

"Glinda is a Good Witch, isn't she?": Ibid., 253.

287 *"What can I do for you, my child?"*: Ibid., 300.

"knock the heels together three times": Ibid., 303.

288 *"I think I'll miss you most of all"*: The Wizard of Oz (MGM).

"From the Land of Oz . . . so glad to be at home again!": LFB, WWOZ, 307.

"In the picture language of mythology": Campbell, *Hero*.

289 *"produces the means for the regeneration"*: Campbell, *Power of Myth*.

290 *"as long as the soul seeks an external God"*: Emerson's Journal, 1836. Reprinted as *Journals of R. W. Emerson*, vol. 4 (Kessinger, 2007), 119.

"the kingdom of God is within you": Luke 17:21.

"The boys are growing wonderfully:" LFB letter to Dr. Henry (Harry) Clay Baum, April 8, 1900, original at George Arents Collection, New York Public Library, copy at SYRACUSE.

"those who never forget their childhood": MGB quoted by Teet Carle, *Syracuse Sunday American*, July 30, 1939, ONONDAGA.

sending his oldest son off to a military academy: LFB letter to Harry Baum, April 8, 1900.

291 *"had a real distinction of style"*: Hearn, ed., *Annotated Wizard*, xli.

"The best thing I have ever written, they tell me . . . until the fiat has gone forth": LFB letter to Harry Baum, April 8, 1900.

292 *"really the very first book made of this story"*: Hearn, ed., *Annotated Wizard*, xl.

"It's a number of totality": Author interview with Gita Dorothy Morena. In 2008, America elected its forty-fourth president.

first five-thousand-copy printing: Hearn, ed., *Annotated Wizard*, xlii.

293 *"The generous reception of the American people"*: LFB, *Show Window*, October 1900, Library of Congress.

"originality of method which is denied by his collaborator": Hearn, ed., *Annotated Wizard*, xliv.

"bright and joyous . . . the country's hope": *New York Times*, September 8, 1900.

insist upon some sort of advance payment . . . $3,432.64: Baum and MacFall, *To Please*.

294 *purchased four Christmas trees*: Harry Neal Baum, *Baum Bugle*, 1965.

give a sparkling emerald ring: Frank actually gave this ring to Maud after the publication of *The Emerald City of Oz*. Gita Dorothy Morena still has the emerald, since reset.

"I am very fond of candy": MGB letter to Jack Snow, June 21, 1943, SYRACUSE.

Rector's . . . centerpiece was a model of the Tin Man: Hearn, ed., *Annotated Wizard*.

"So everything conspires to make me glad": LFB letter to Helen Leslie Gage, January 7, 1901, ABERDEEN.

Epilogue: A Great Awakening

296 *Silver Shoes had fallen off:* LFB, WWOZ, 305.

"Every one loved him, he loved every one": LFB, *The Road to Oz* (Chicago: Reilly & Britton, 1909).

opened in Chicago in the summer of 1902: SYRACUSE.

"Mr. Baum settled back in an easy chair in the sunshine": Interview in *San Diego Union*, 1905.

297 *Hollywood because of its charm:* MGB letter to Jack Snow, June 21, 1943. SYRACUSE.

named a strain of chrysanthemums "Matildas": SYRACUSE.

forming with his eldest son the Oz Film Manufacturing Company: Baum and MacFall, *To Please*.

ill-fated Woggle-Bug *and the disastrous* Fairylogue: Hearn, ed., *Annotated Wizard*.

forced him into bankruptcy in 1911: Ibid.

curious pen names like Floyd Akers and Edith Van Dyne: His other pen names included Captain Hugh Fitzgerald, Laura Bancroft, and Schuyler Stanton. In all he wrote more than sixty books.

298 *"This is our house, Maud":* Baum and MacFall, *To Please*.

for a reported $40,000: Hearn, ed., *Annotated Wizard*.

loved how it all turned out: Fricke et al., *50th Anniversary Pictorial History*.

more people would see The Wizard of Oz *than any other film in motion picture history:* Based on a CBS study in 1983 determining it was the first film to be seen by a billion people; ibid.

Postscripts

300 *" 'Rainbow' has always been my song":* Gerald Clark, *Get Happy: The Life of Judy Garland* (New York: Random House, 2000).

"Denslow got a swelled head": MGB letter to Jack Snow, 1943.

"I have always disliked Denslow's Dorothy": Ibid.

King Denslow of Denslow Island: SYRACUSE.

301 *filing for bankruptcy in 1902:* SYRACUSE.

Bobbs-Merrill . . . Reilly & Britton: SYRACUSE.

"Wouldn't it be funny for me to do housework in Kansas" . . . "my chances with the rest of you": LFB, *The Emerald City of Oz*.

302 *excursion to Europe and Egypt . . . Maud's . . . own book:* MGB, edited and with an introduction by LFB, *In Other Lands than Ours* (self-published in 1907; recently reissued by Shreveport: Pumpernickle Pickle, 2008), download at www.lulu.com/content/2107804.

"Father Goose and wife have not quarreled": ABERDEEN.

assets consisted of only his clothing and an old typewriter: SYRACUSE.

"from ever finding Oz": LFB, *The Emerald City of Oz*, 293.

a suggestion from a child's letter: LFB introduction in *The Patchwork Girl of Oz* (Chicago: Reilly & Britton, 1912).

303 *never went back to reread his prior books*: SYRACUSE.

And so the baby's name was changed to Ozma . . . "Our family is very at ease with the world of spirit": Author interview with Gita Dorothy Morena.

amounting to exactly $1,072.96: SYRACUSE.

"made balm of failure": *Syracuse Journal*, May 11, 1919, SYRACUSE.

304 *amounted to less than $15,000*: SYRACUSE.

granting radio rights to NBC: Fricke et al., *50th Anniversary Pictorial History*.

"an analysis of our fan mail": Ibid.

"I have never met Mr. Disney": MGB letter to Stewart Robb, April 17, 1939, YALE.

Goldwyn ended up reselling the rights: Harmetz, *Making of the Wizard of Oz*.

child superstar Shirley Temple: Ibid.

Ray Bolger was originally cast . . . Negotiations with Bert Lahr: Ibid.

305 *"the royal road to the understanding"*: Sigmund Freud, *The Interpretation of Dreams* (1900).

306 *"it really was no miracle"*: *The Wizard of Oz* (MGM).

the "lemon drops," the easy songs . . . "a song of yearning": Harmetz, *Making of the Wizard of Oz*.

Mayer felt the movie was too long: Ibid.

the number-one song of the twentieth century: See archives.cnn.com/2001/SHOW BIZ/music/03/07/365.songs/.

"going back to Baum": Harmetz, *Making of the Wizard of Oz*.

307 *124 little people to serve as Munchkins*: Ibid.

aluminum-flake makeup made Buddy Ebsen . . . violently ill . . . Hamilton actually caught fire . . . got stuck in a toilet: Jay Scarfone and William Stillman, *The Wizardry of Oz: The Artistry and Magic of the 1939 MGM Classic* (New York: Random House, 1999; revised and expanded 2004).

"If I ever go looking for my heart's desire": *The Wizard of Oz* (MGM).

"I even hated it when I was a kid": Author interview with Gita Dorothy Morena.

308 *Harburg, who called it "tripe"*: Harmetz, *Making of the Wizard of Oz*.

"right here in St. Louis!": *Meet Me In St. Louis* (MGM, 1944).

"The Wizard of Oz is a world's fair in itself" . . . "greatest bestseller of modern fiction": Fricke et al., *50th Anniversary Pictorial History*.

the radio show Ripley's Believe It or Not!: Interview available online at www.hun grytigerpress.com/tigertreats/maud.shtml.

the premiere at Grauman's Chinese Theatre: Fricke et al., *50th Anniversary Pictorial History*.

"Success is complete knowing that you loved it": Ibid.

309 *The film finally turned a profit after the war*: Ibid.

On Saturday, November 3, 1956: Ibid.

"That's when all the fuss began": Ibid.

1967 . . . 1970: Ibid.

more than a billion people: 1988 estimate by CBS, Harmetz, *Making of the Wizard of Oz*, 291.

310   *One of the first things to go was the tribute to L. Frank Baum's:* Ibid.

       banned by schools and public libraries: SYRACUSE.

       "secret arts which we have learned from Nature": LFB, *Glinda of Oz* (Chicago: Reilly & Britton, 1920).

       "Books Not Circulated" . . . *"unwholesome for the children":* Articles from February 13, 1959, SYRACUSE. See Martin Gardner, "The Librarians in Oz," *Saturday Review*, April 11, 1959, COLUMBIA.

       "Lessons drawn from The Wizard of Oz *undermine religious education":* Baum Bugle, Winter 1986, 28. Also see "Supreme Court Justices Refuse to Hear Tennessee Case on Bible and Textbooks," *New York Times*, February 23, 1988.

       "Parable of Populism": Henry Littlefield, "The Wizard of Oz: Parable of Populism," *American Quarterly*, no. 16, 1964.

311   *"no evidence that Baum's story is in any way a Populist allegory":* Hearn letter in *New York Times*, January 10, 1992; Hearn traces the misunderstanding back to an error in Baum and MacFall, *To Please*, 111, where the authors incorrectly state that LFB was a supporter of William Jennings Bryan for president.

       "there is no basis in fact": See David Parker, "The Rise and Fall of the Wonderful Wizard of Oz as a Parable on Populism," *Journal of the Georgia Association of Historians* 15 (1994); available at www.halcyon.com/piglet/Populism.htm.

312   *same man who created America's greatest story for children:* "NPR Morning Edition," August 17, 2006.

       "How is it possible?" . . . *"We're here to say we're sorry"* . . . *"I just wanted to talk to the survivors":* Apology discussed by Hudson and Morena at Wonderful Weekend of Oz panel discussions in 2006 and 2007, Fayetteville Free Library.

       "way bigger than L. Frank Baum" . . . *"An apology . . . is an atonement":* Author interview with Gita Dorothy Morena.

314   "They Made America": *Atlantic*, December, 2006.

315   "Ain't it the truth?": The Cowardly Lion in *The Wizard of Oz* (MGM).

CREDITS

Emerald City cover painting (duplicated on part title pages) by Donald A. Peters, courtesy of Diane Steele and available at dianesteele.com as a limited edition lithograph. *Courtesy of the International Wizard of Oz Club*: map of the Marvelous Land of Oz in prologue; Castorine images in chapter 6. *Courtesy of L. Frank Baum Collection, Alexander Mitchell Public Library, Aberdeen, South Dakota*: Baum portrait in prologue; Baum's Bazaar photo and ad in chapter 9; *Aberdeen Saturday Pioneer* page in chapter 10. *Courtesy L. Frank Baum Papers, Special Collections Research Center, Syracuse University Library*: Emerald City pencil image in prologue; Rose Lawn photo in chapter 1; *Maid of Arran* images in chapters 4 and 5; poppy field poster in chapter 11; Maud and the boys photo in chapter 17; Baum at Coronado photo in epilogue. *Courtesy of the Matilda Joslyn Gage Foundation*: Gage photographs in chapters 3 and 15. *Courtesy of Onondaga Historical Association*: Baum barn image in chapter 1. *Courtesy of Corbis*: the International Council of Women photo in chapter 7. *Courtesy of Bygones.com*: the "first cyclone" image in chapter 8, digital image copyright 2008 Bygones.com. *Courtesy of Chicago History Museum*: Chicago Evening Post page in chapter 12. *Courtesy of Peter E. Hanff*: George M. Hill promotional poster in chapter 16. *Courtesy of the Thomas A. Edison Papers, Rutgers University*: Edison portrait in chapter 14. *Courtesy of the Rockefeller Archive Center*: Rockefeller portrait in chapter 14. *Courtesy of the Museum of the City of New York*: Barnum portrait in chapter 14. *Courtesy of Columbia University's Avery Library*: World's Columbian Exposition image in chapter 13. *Courtesy of Warner Brothers Entertainment, Inc.*: photo of Judy Garland with Maud Gage Baum in postscripts.

INDEX

Page numbers in italics refer to illustrations.

IMPASSABLE

The MARVEL

DEADLY DESERT

OOGABOO
Quick City
Parashuter
CORUMBIA SAMAN-DRA CORABIA
Flathead Mt.
Skeezers
Reera
Hills of Humber
KAPURTA
Desert of Ho-Ta
Stiff R.
Gamex
Kuma Party
PATCH
(Subterranea-U)
Double Up
Zeebo
Mist Valley
Spiders
Ozwoz
GILLIKIN
Jack Pott
Upandup Mt.
Land of Lanterns
Buttonwood
KIMBALOO
Gillikin
River
Forest of Gugu
ma ga
Yellow Lake
WACKA-JAMMY
Hoopers
Somewhere
Backn
Soap Slide Suds
Dangerous Passage
Tidy Town
Laughing Willows
HOTCHINPOTCH
Dwindlebury
(Inland Sea)
Whitherwood Town
Scooters
Tons
Bewilderness
Catty Corners
Blankenburg
Pristinia
Sun Top Mt.
Tune Town
Gozzerland
Dr. Nikidi
Wish Way
Pokes
Candy Giant
Fix City
Twigs
Bordermoor
Kite Is.
Hidden Valley
Equinots
Wyndups
Shadow Mt.
Mombi
Winkie
River
WINKIE
Lake Lily
Herbertha
Taffy & Fudge
Perhaps City
Ice town
Book ville
Flicker's
Serpent Tree
Candles
Marsh land
Loonville
Maybe Mts.
Play City
Witch of the West
Squirrel King
Wish Way
Monday Mt.
Tree of Whutter Wee
Village of Field Mice
Black Forest
Mt. Much
Tin Woodman's Castle
Art Colony Woods
Scarecrow's Tower
Dog Wood
Jack Pumpkinhead
Wise Acres
Lake Quad
E
Ugu
Great Orchard
Merry-Go-Round Mts.
Game Preserve
Rolling Prairie
River
Herku
Thi
COUNTRY
Bear Center
Tottenhots
Flutterbudgets
Scare City
Chimneyville
Ute
Bunbu
Bunny
Winkie Woods Bottles
Up & Down Water fall
Mr. Yoop
Hoppers
Horners
Rigmarok Town
Winkie
River
Trick River
Swing City
Big (Loxo)
Little I.
Bourne
Land of the Barons
Red
N W E S Z
Big Top Mt.
Baffleburg
Lollypop Village
QUADLING
Ruby Imp's Cavern
Carrot Mt.
Truth Pond
South Mt.
Dark Forest
Twinlet Town
Posties
Wicked Witch of the

YIPS

GREAT

S

Based on the
Original Map
drawn by
Professor
H.M.WOGGLEBUG,T.E.

Revised
in accordance with
the
Royal Histories
of
OZ

JAMES E. HAFF
Delineavit